DEADPOOL

SAMURAI

1

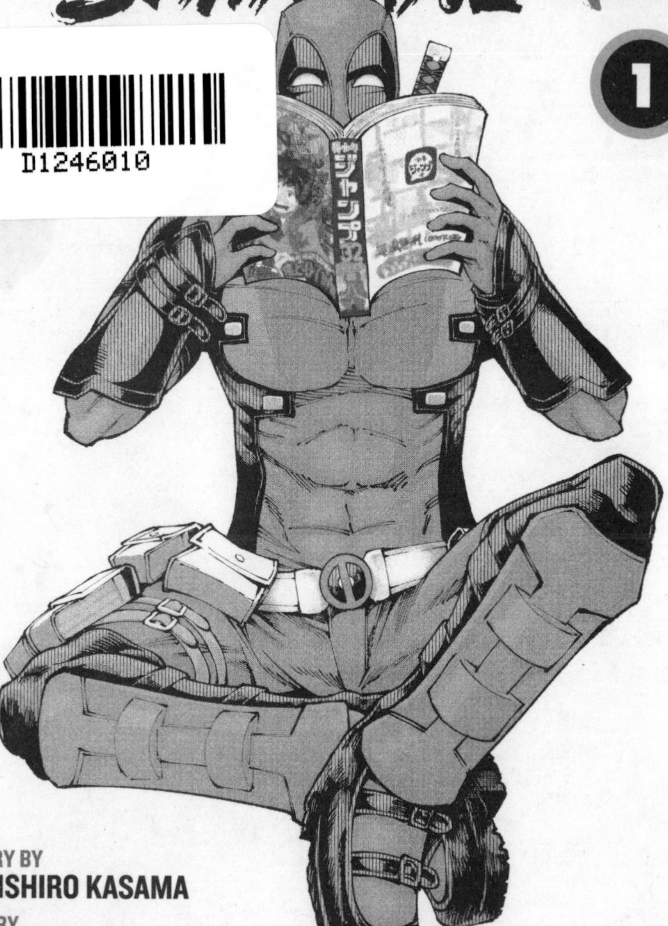

STORY BY
SANSHIRO KASAMA
ART BY
HIKARU UESUGI

DEADPOOL SAMURAI

1

CONTENTS

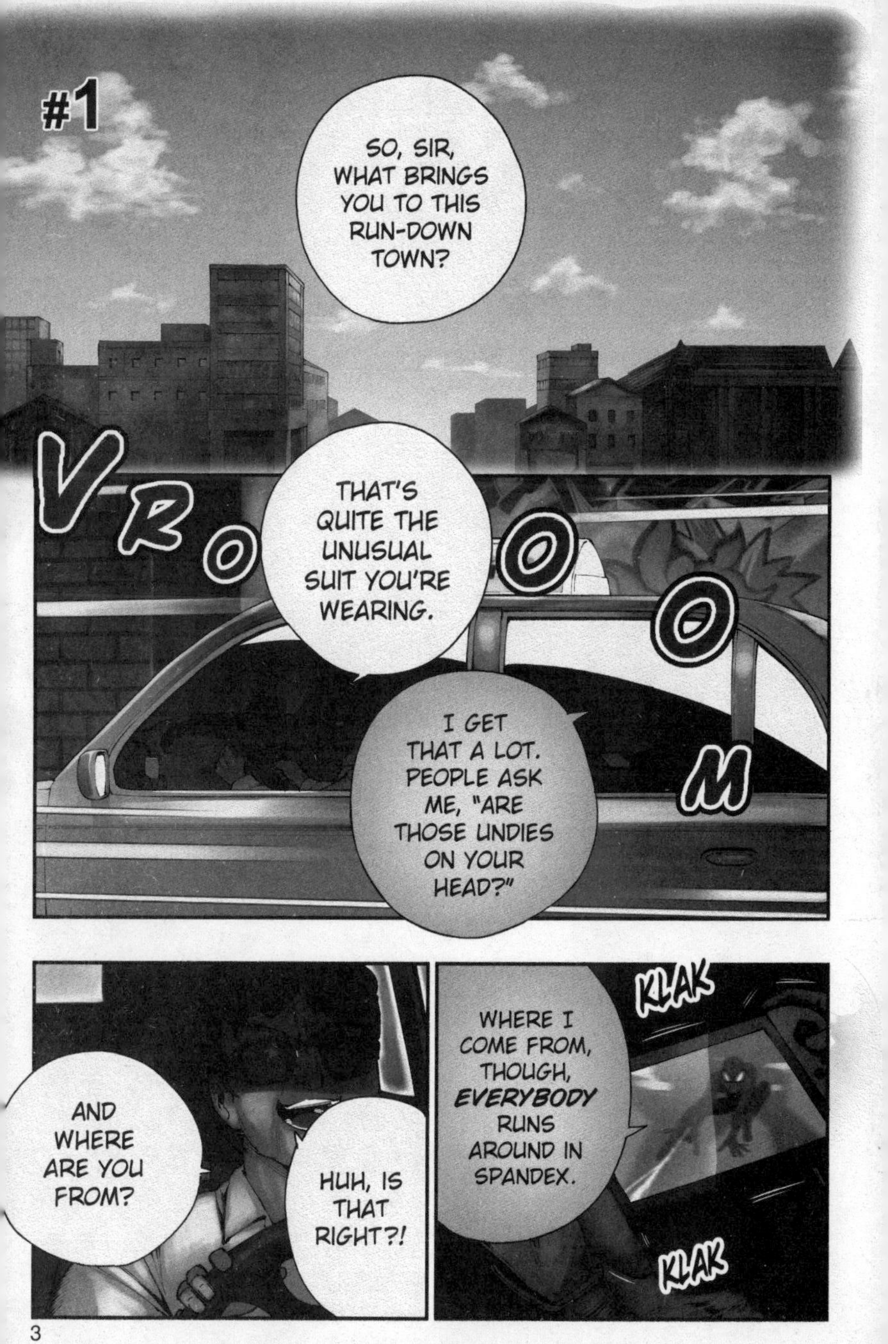
#1
SO, SIR, WHAT BRINGS YOU TO THIS RUN-DOWN TOWN?
VROOOM
THAT'S QUITE THE UNUSUAL SUIT YOU'RE WEARING.
I GET THAT A LOT. PEOPLE ASK ME, "ARE THOSE UNDIES ON YOUR HEAD?"
KLAK
WHERE I COME FROM, THOUGH, *EVERYBODY* RUNS AROUND IN SPANDEX.
KLAK
HUH, IS THAT RIGHT?!
AND WHERE ARE YOU FROM?

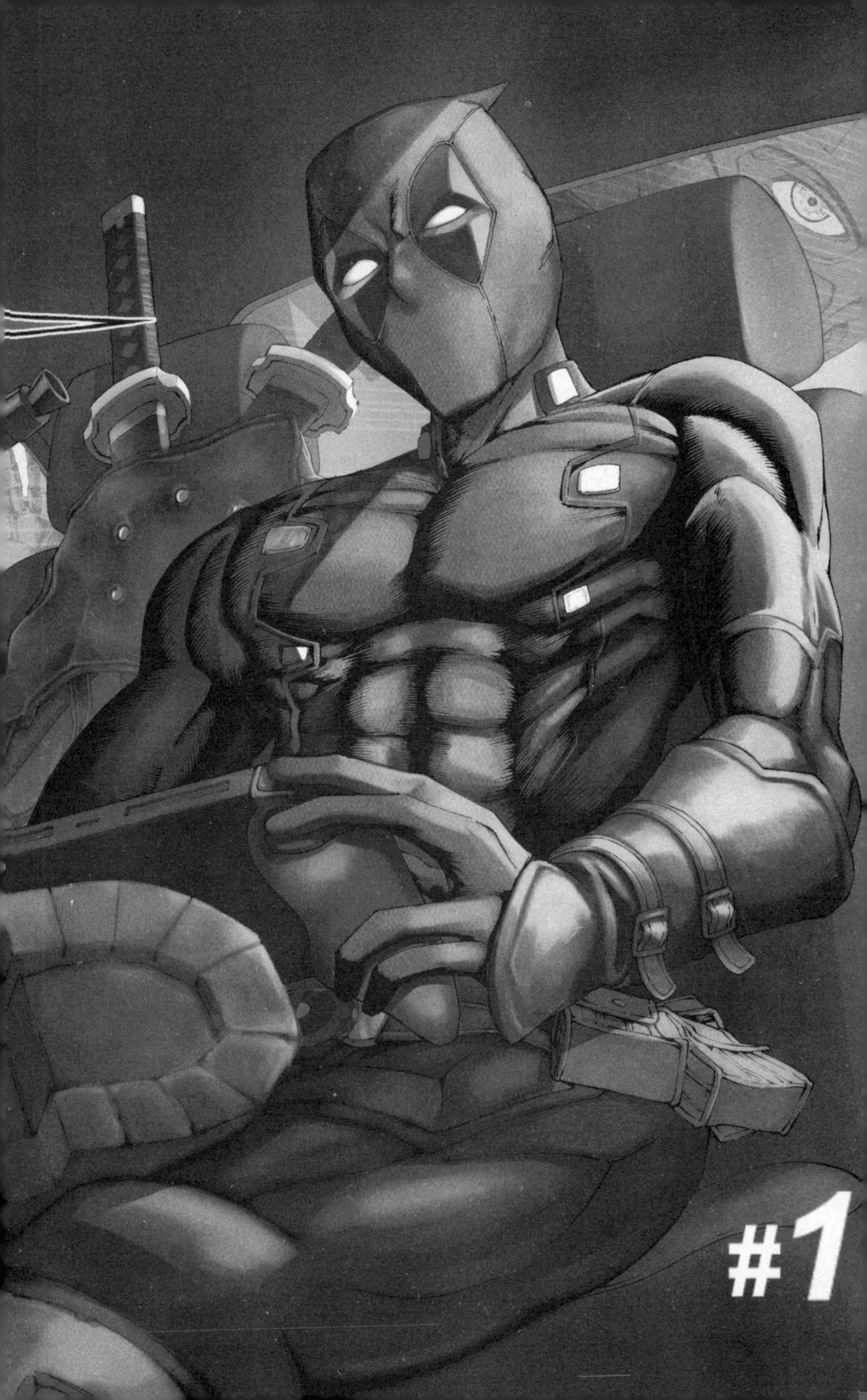
#1

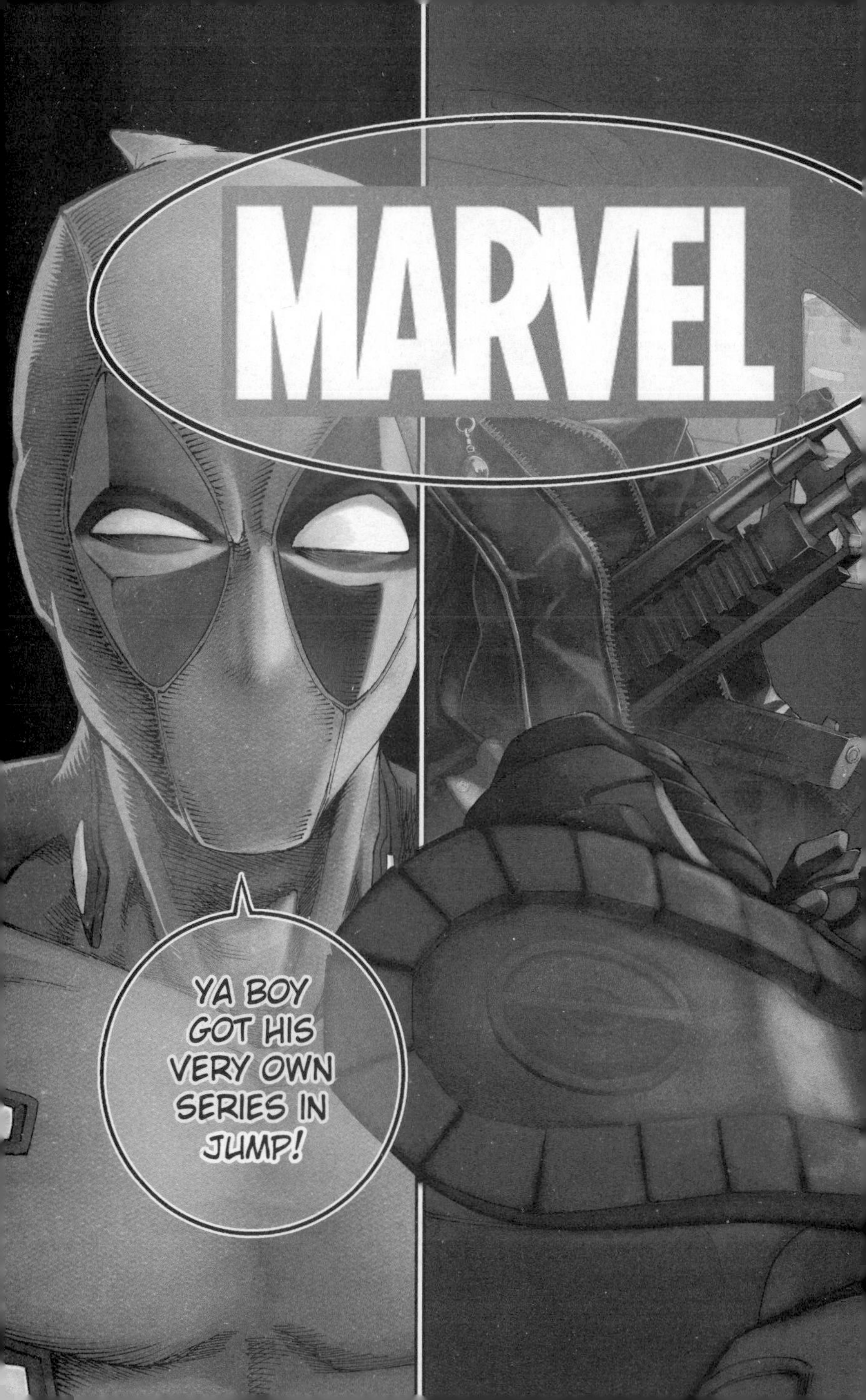
MARVEL
YA BOY GOT HIS VERY OWN SERIES IN JUMP!

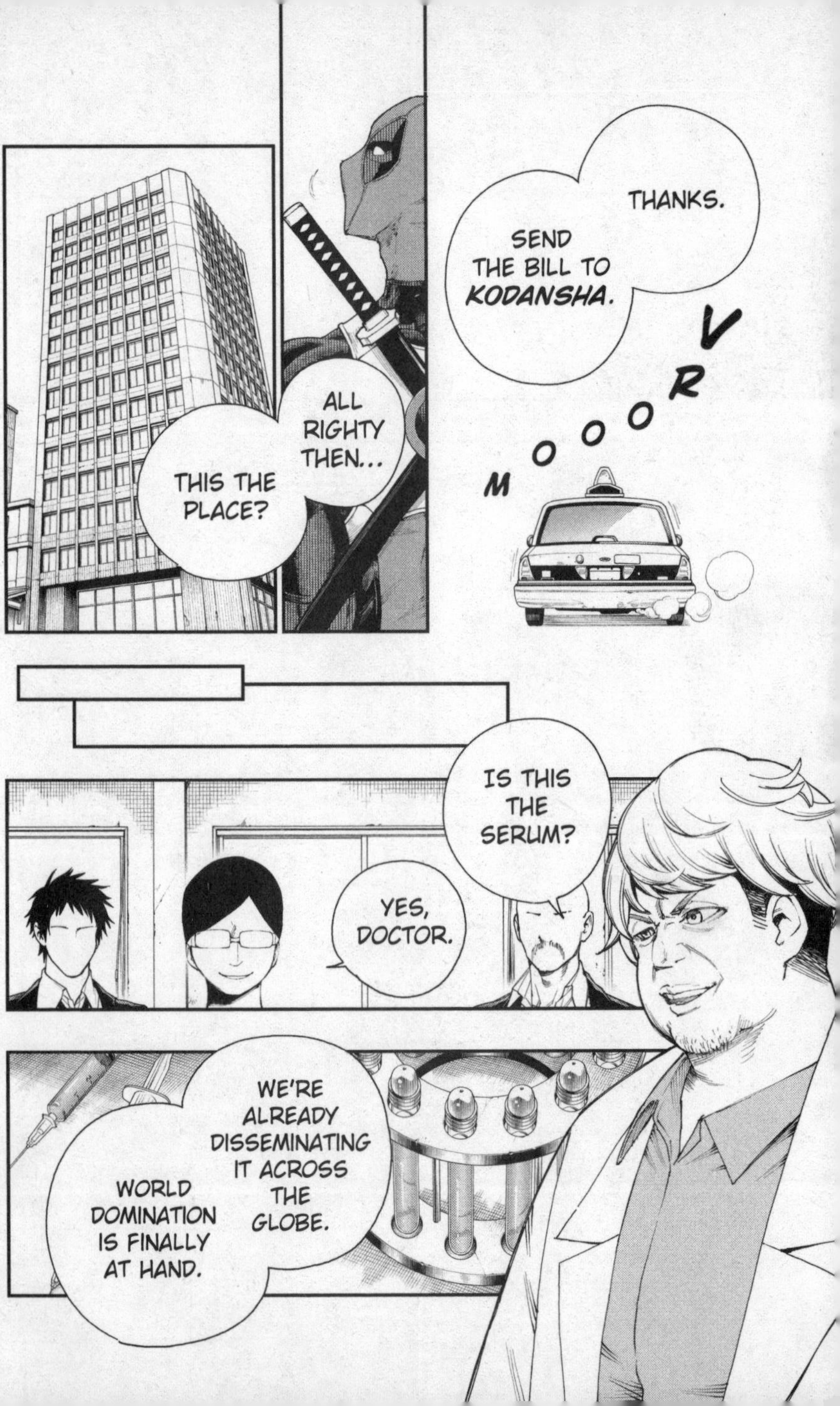

THANKS.
SEND THE BILL TO KODANSHA.
MOOOORV
ALL RIGHTY THEN...
THIS THE PLACE?
IS THIS THE SERUM?
YES, DOCTOR.
WE'RE ALREADY DISSEMINATING IT ACROSS THE GLOBE.
WORLD DOMINATION IS FINALLY AT HAND.

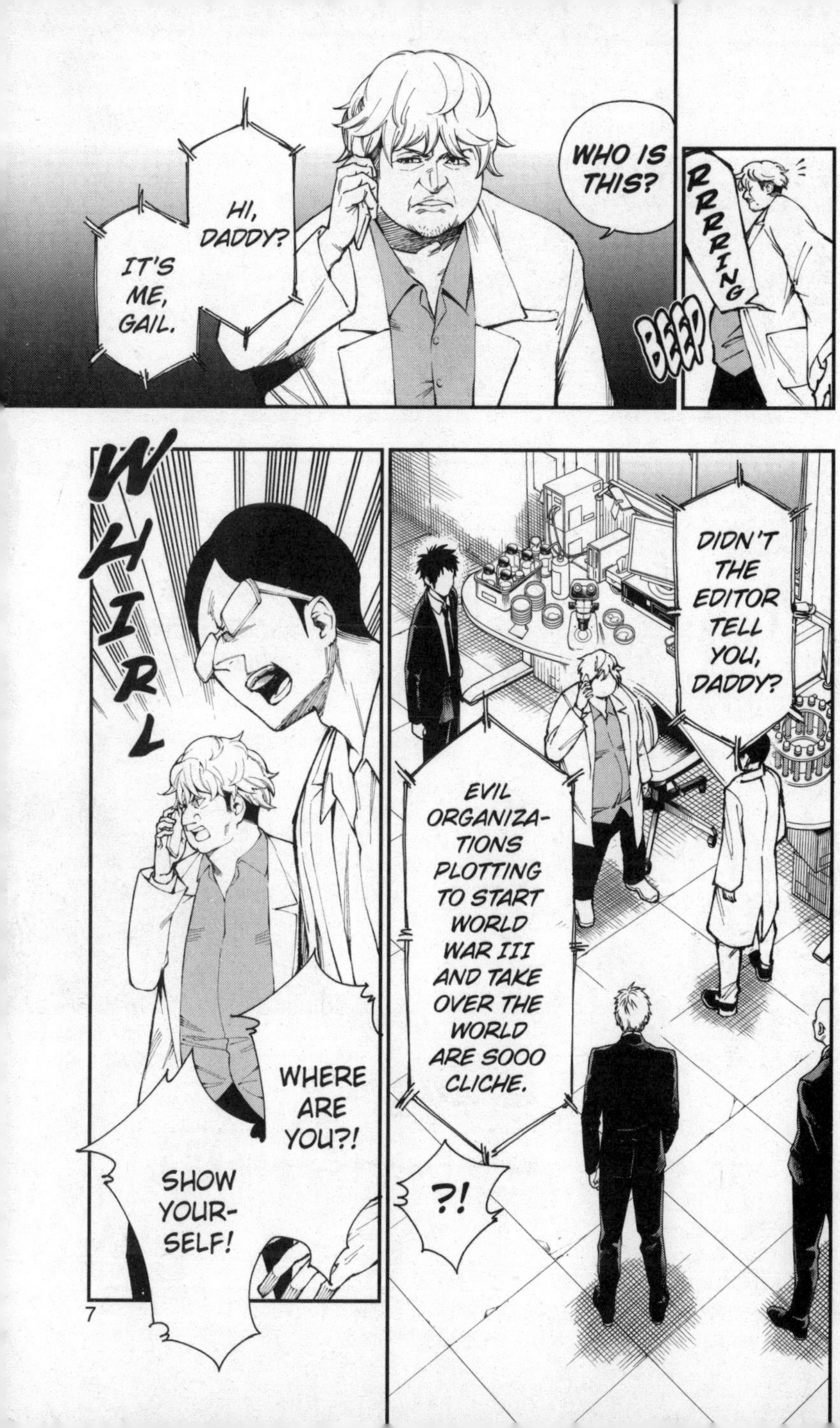
RRRING
BEEP
WHO IS THIS?
HI, DADDY?
IT'S ME, GAIL.
DIDN'T THE EDITOR TELL YOU, DADDY?
EVIL ORGANIZATIONS PLOTTING TO START WORLD WAR III AND TAKE OVER THE WORLD ARE SOOO CLICHE.
?!
WHIRL
WHERE ARE YOU?!
SHOW YOURSELF!

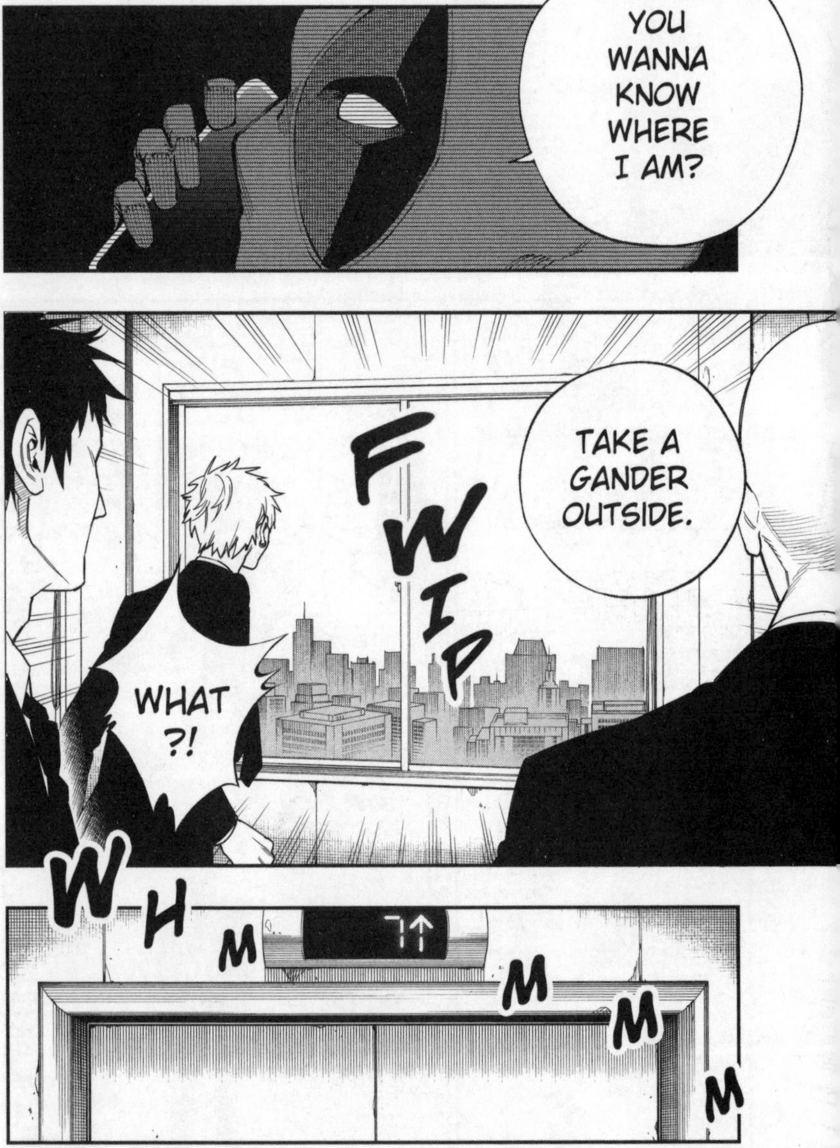
YOU WANNA KNOW WHERE I AM?
TAKE A GANDER OUTSIDE.
FWIP
WHAT?!
WHMMMM

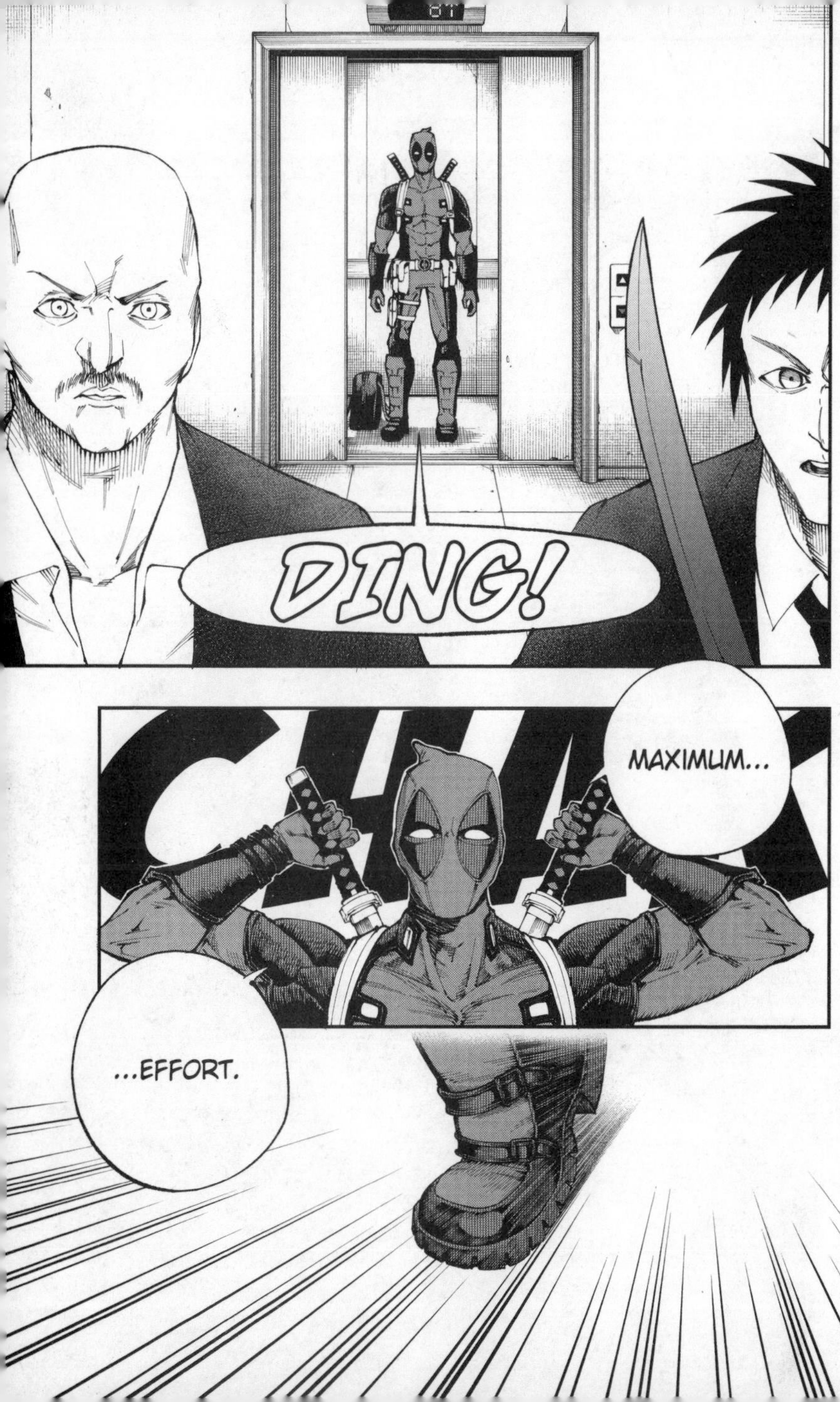
DING!
MAXIMUM...
...EFFORT.

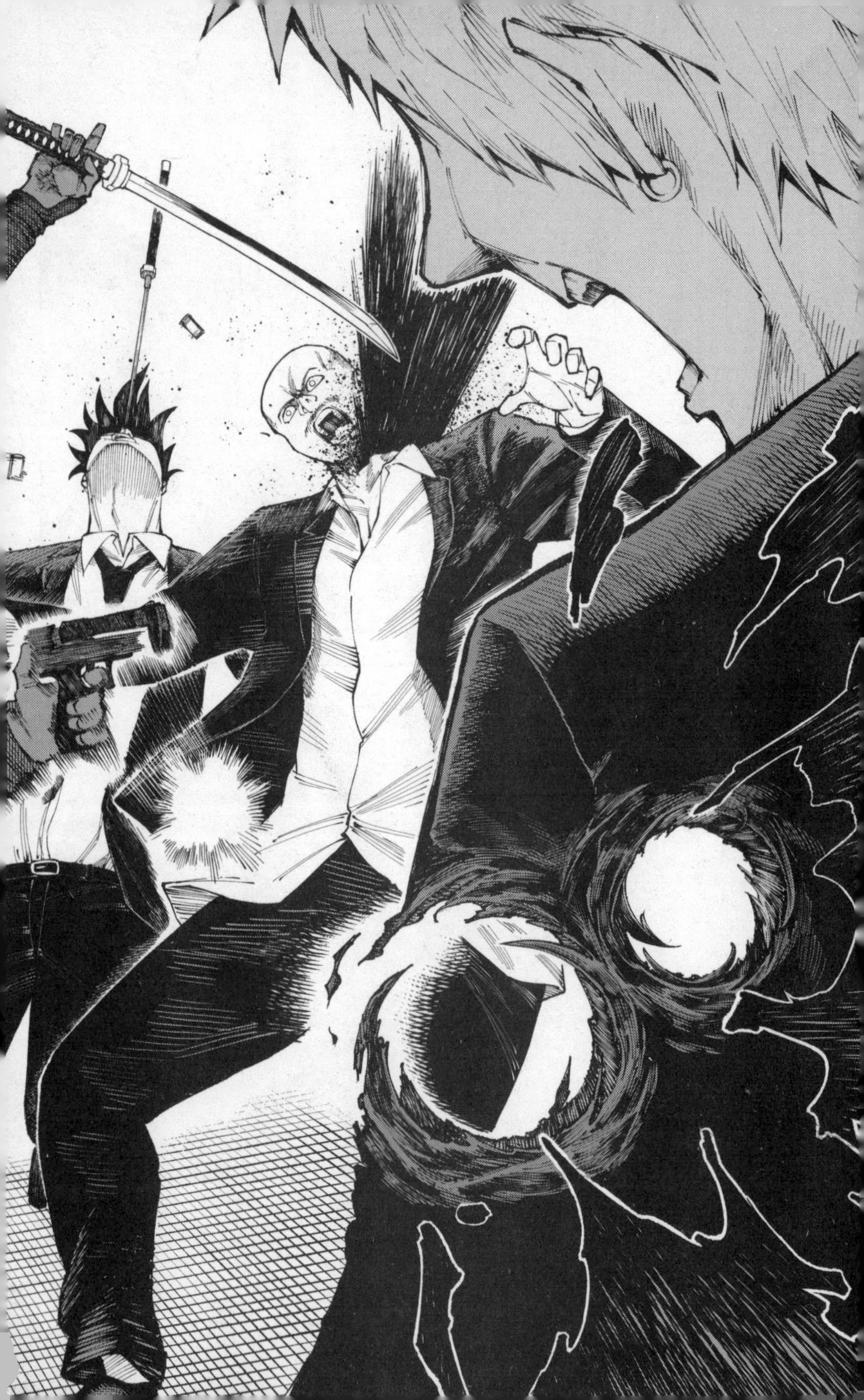

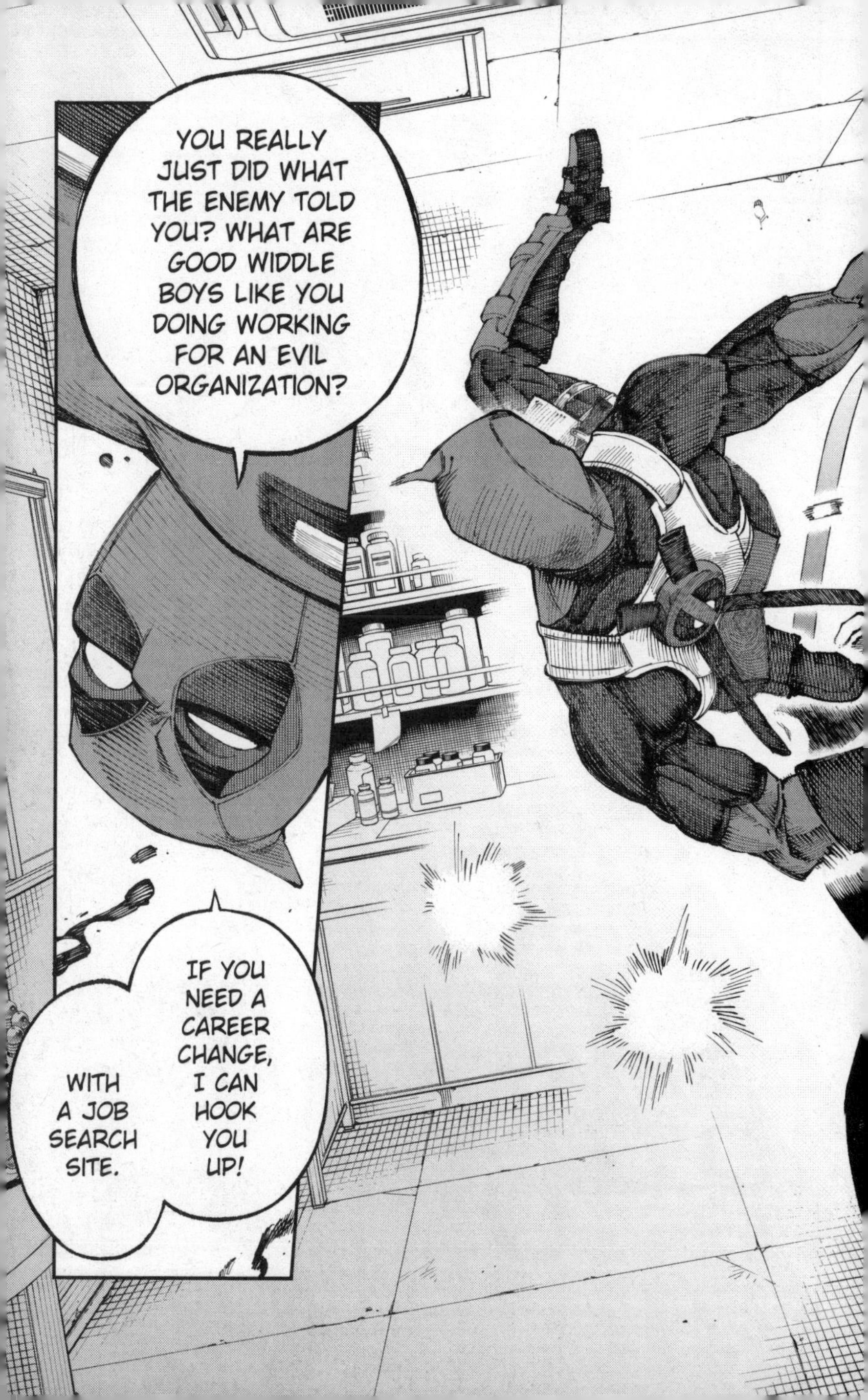
YOU REALLY JUST DID WHAT THE ENEMY TOLD YOU? WHAT ARE GOOD WIDDLE BOYS LIKE YOU DOING WORKING FOR AN EVIL ORGANIZATION?
IF YOU NEED A CAREER CHANGE, I CAN HOOK YOU UP!
WITH A JOB SEARCH SITE.

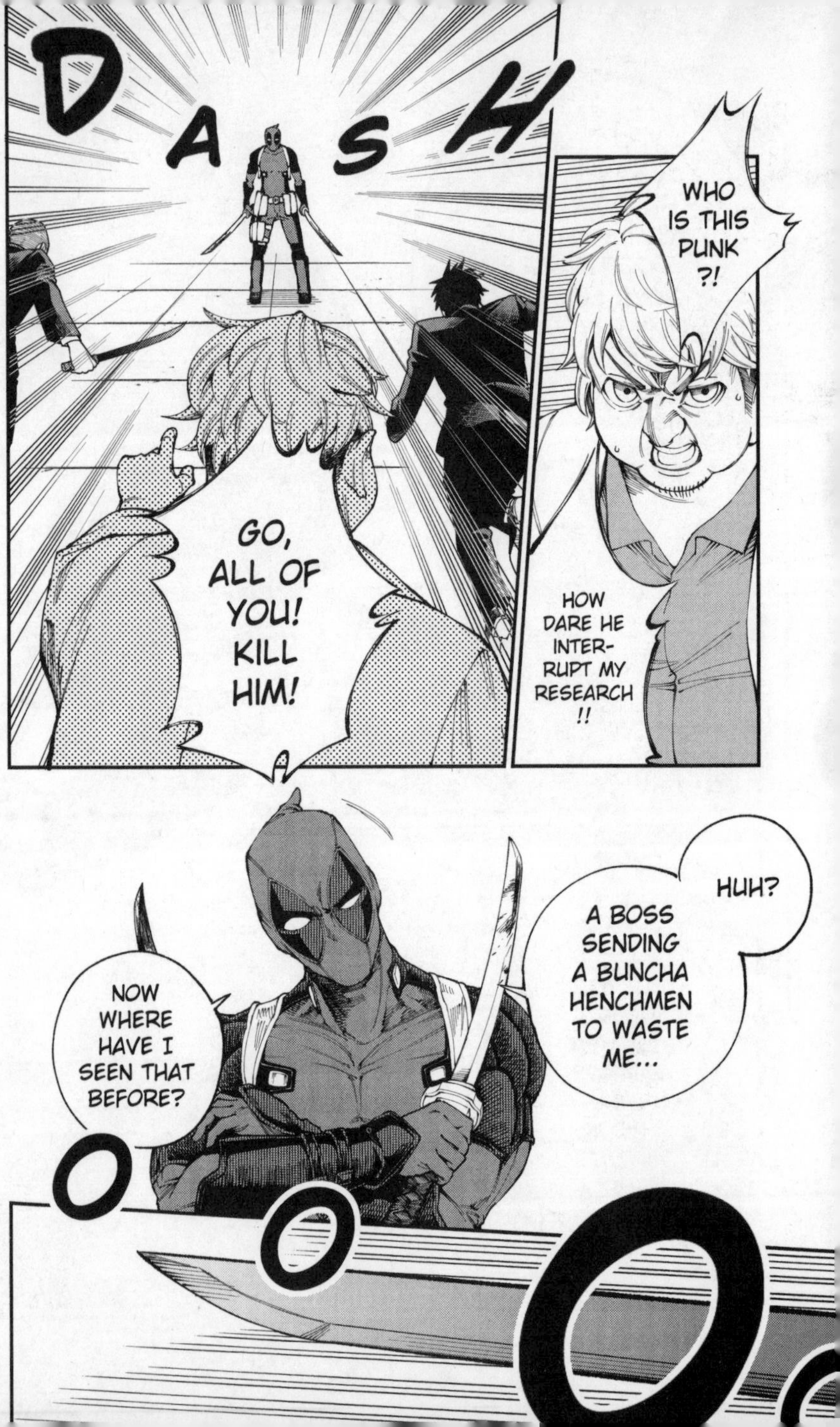
WHO IS THIS PUNK ?!
HOW DARE HE INTER-RUPT MY RESEARCH !!
DASH
GO, ALL OF YOU! KILL HIM!
HUH?
A BOSS SENDING A BUNCHA HENCHMEN TO WASTE ME...
NOW WHERE HAVE I SEEN THAT BEFORE?

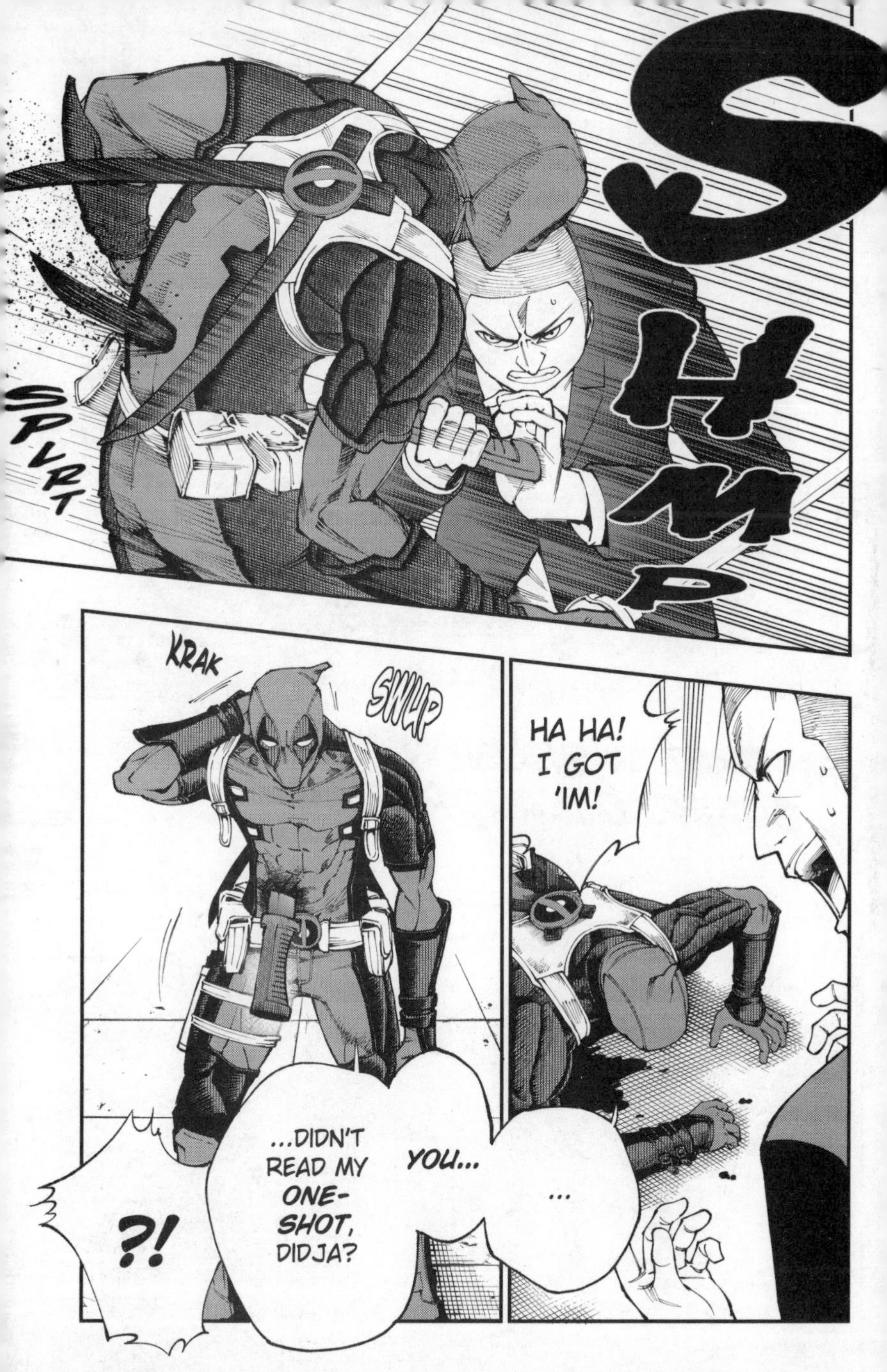
SHMP
SPLRT
HA HA! I GOT 'IM!
KRAK
SWUP
...
YOU...
...DIDN'T READ MY ONE-SHOT, DIDJA?
?!

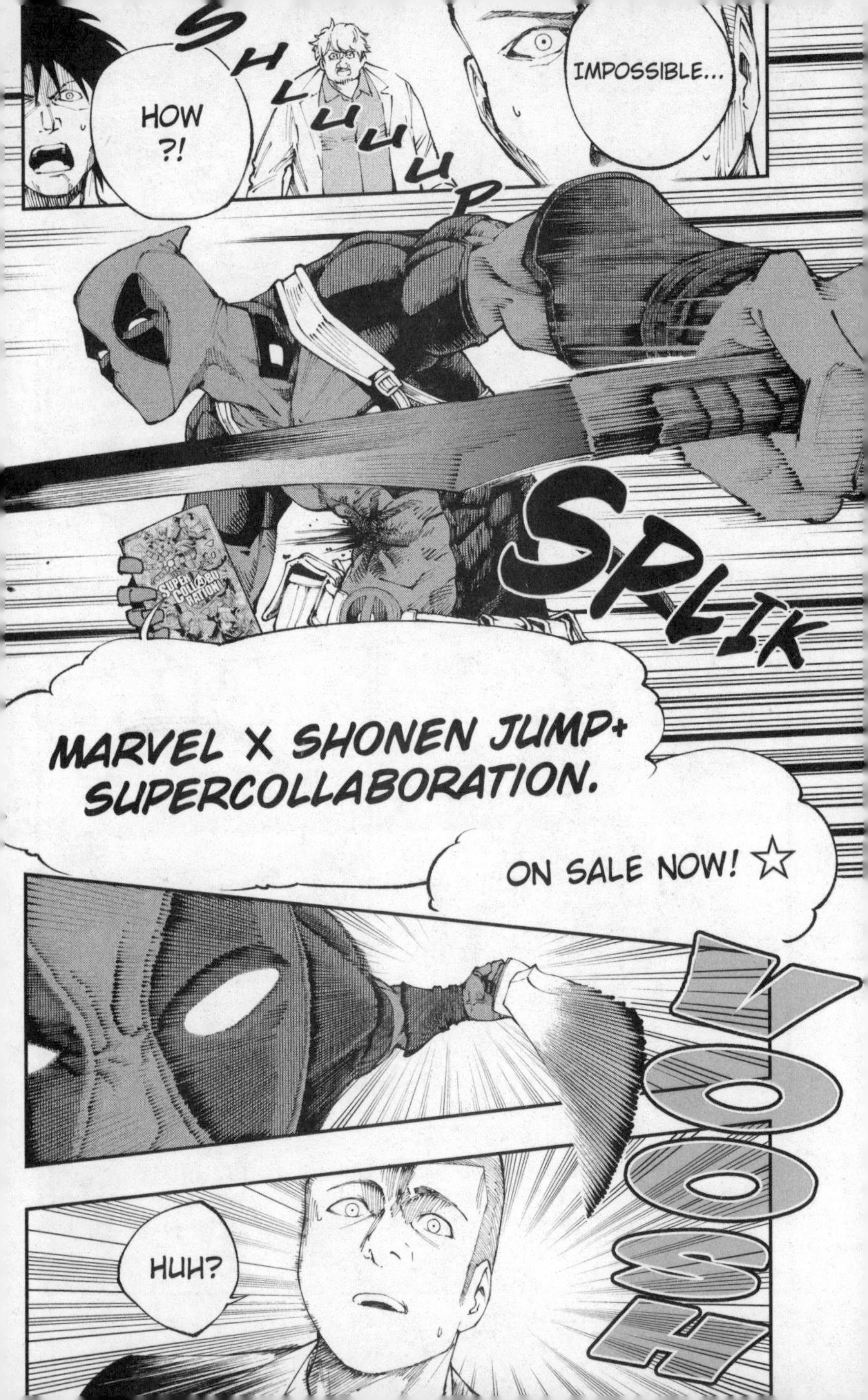
IMPOSSIBLE...
HOW ?!
SHLUUUUP
SPLIK
MARVEL X SHONEN JUMP+ SUPERCOLLABORATION.
ON SALE NOW! ☆
VOOSH
HUH?

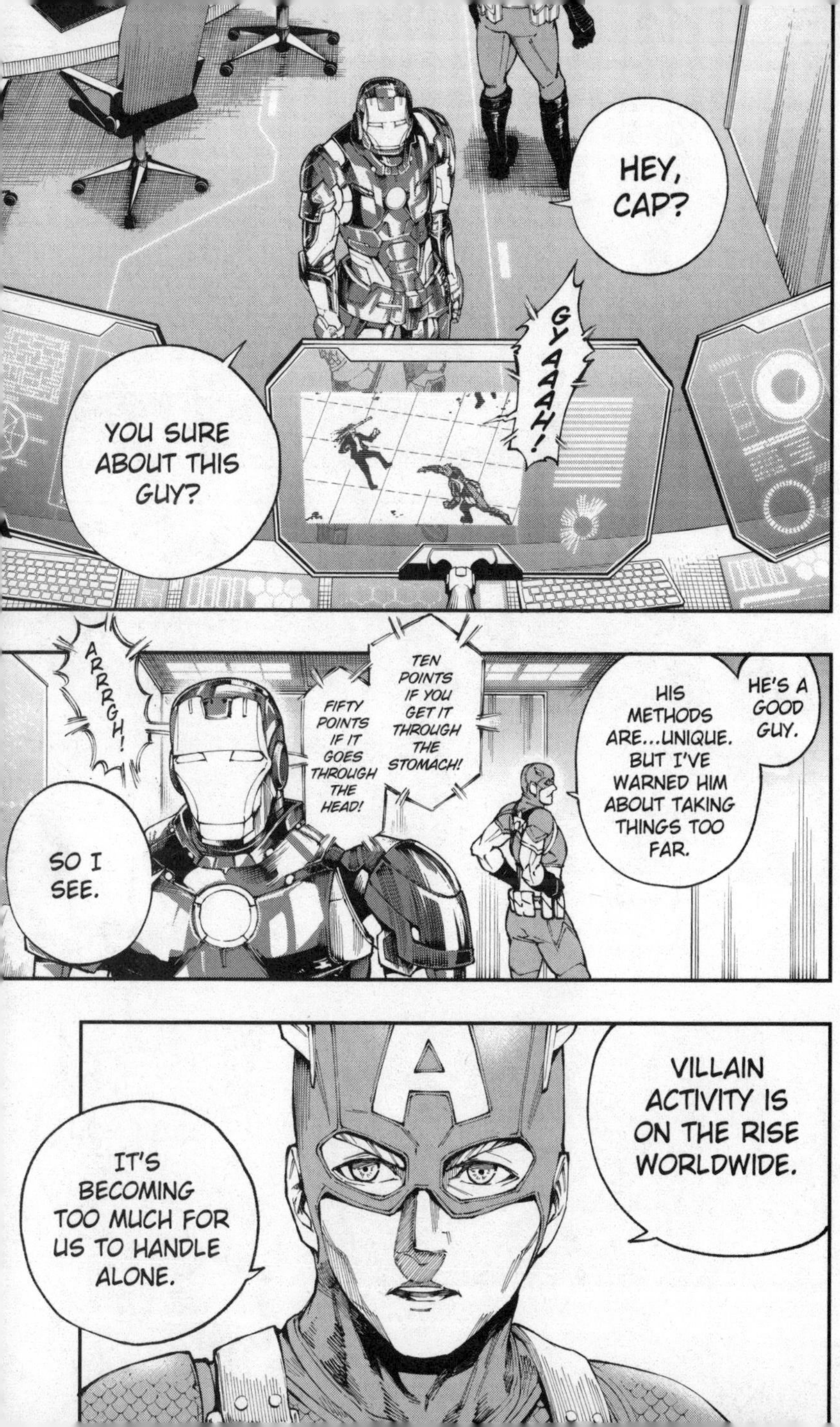
HEY, CAP?
GYAAAAH!
YOU SURE ABOUT THIS GUY?
HE'S A GOOD GUY.
HIS METHODS ARE...UNIQUE. BUT I'VE WARNED HIM ABOUT TAKING THINGS TOO FAR.
TEN POINTS IF YOU GET IT THROUGH THE STOMACH!
FIFTY POINTS IF IT GOES THROUGH THE HEAD!
ARRRGH!
SO I SEE.
VILLAIN ACTIVITY IS ON THE RISE WORLDWIDE.
IT'S BECOMING TOO MUCH FOR US TO HANDLE ALONE.

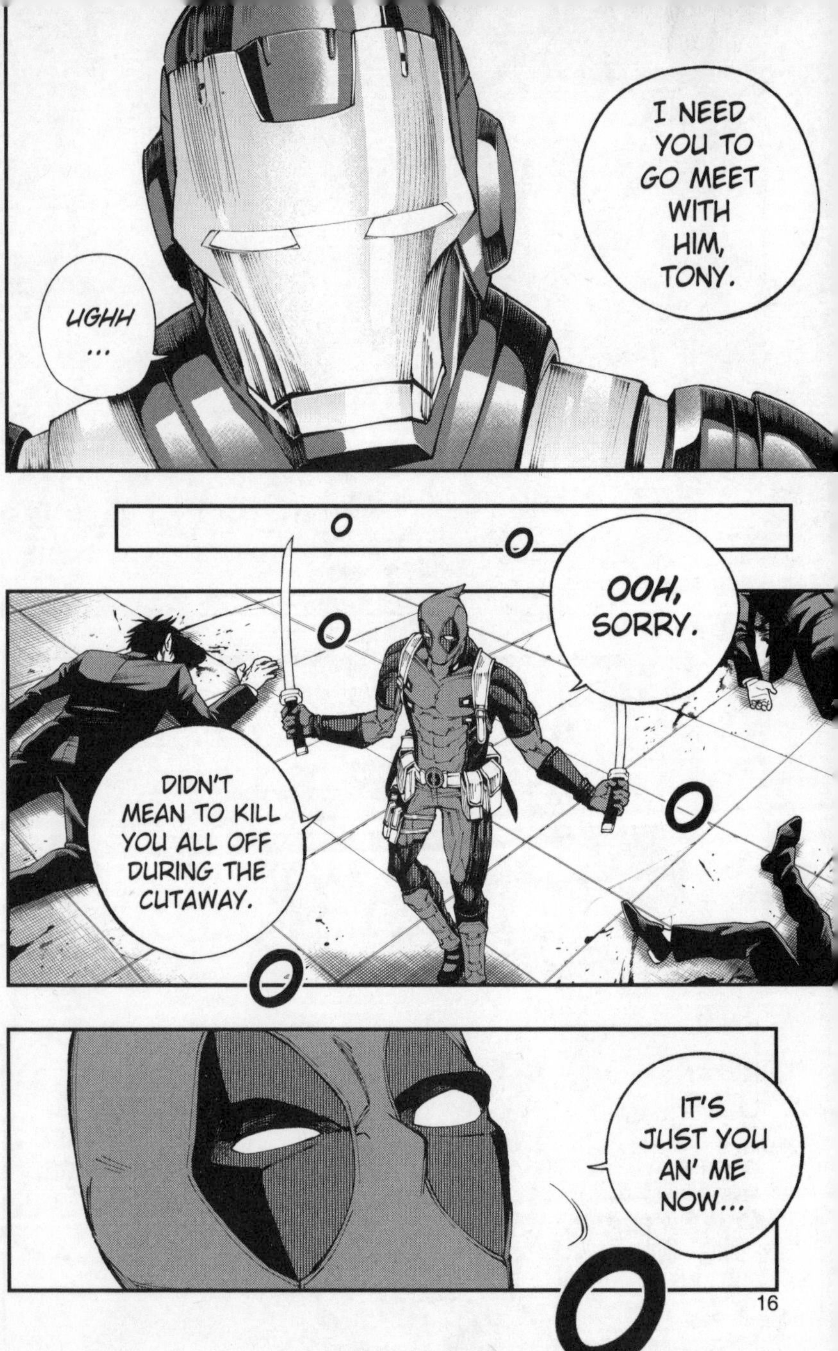
I NEED YOU TO GO MEET WITH HIM, TONY.
UGHH ...
OOH, SORRY.
DIDN'T MEAN TO KILL YOU ALL OFF DURING THE CUTAWAY.
IT'S JUST YOU AN' ME NOW...

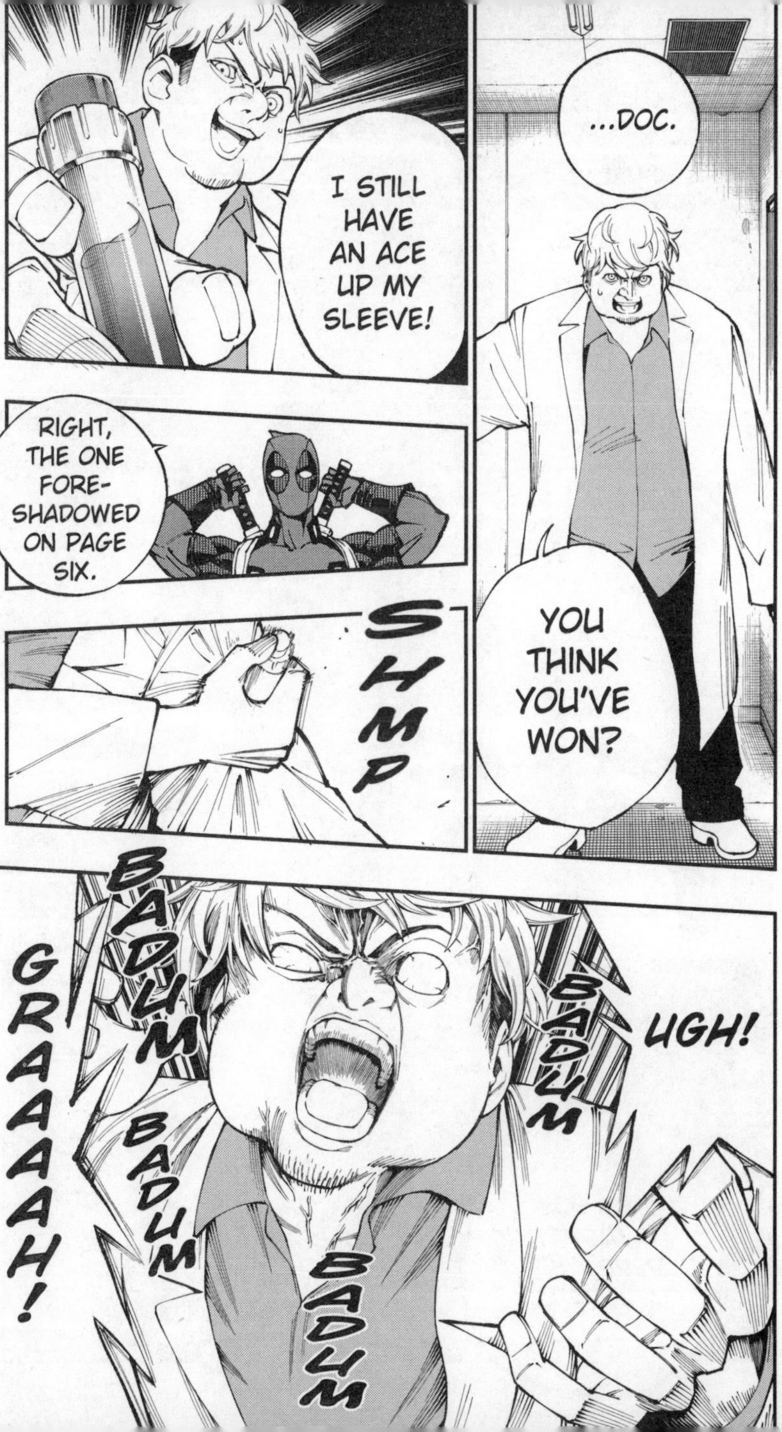
...DOC.
YOU THINK YOU'VE WON?
I STILL HAVE AN ACE UP MY SLEEVE!
RIGHT, THE ONE FORE-SHADOWED ON PAGE SIX.
SHMP
UGH!
BADUM
BADUM
BADUM
BADUM
GRAAAAAH!

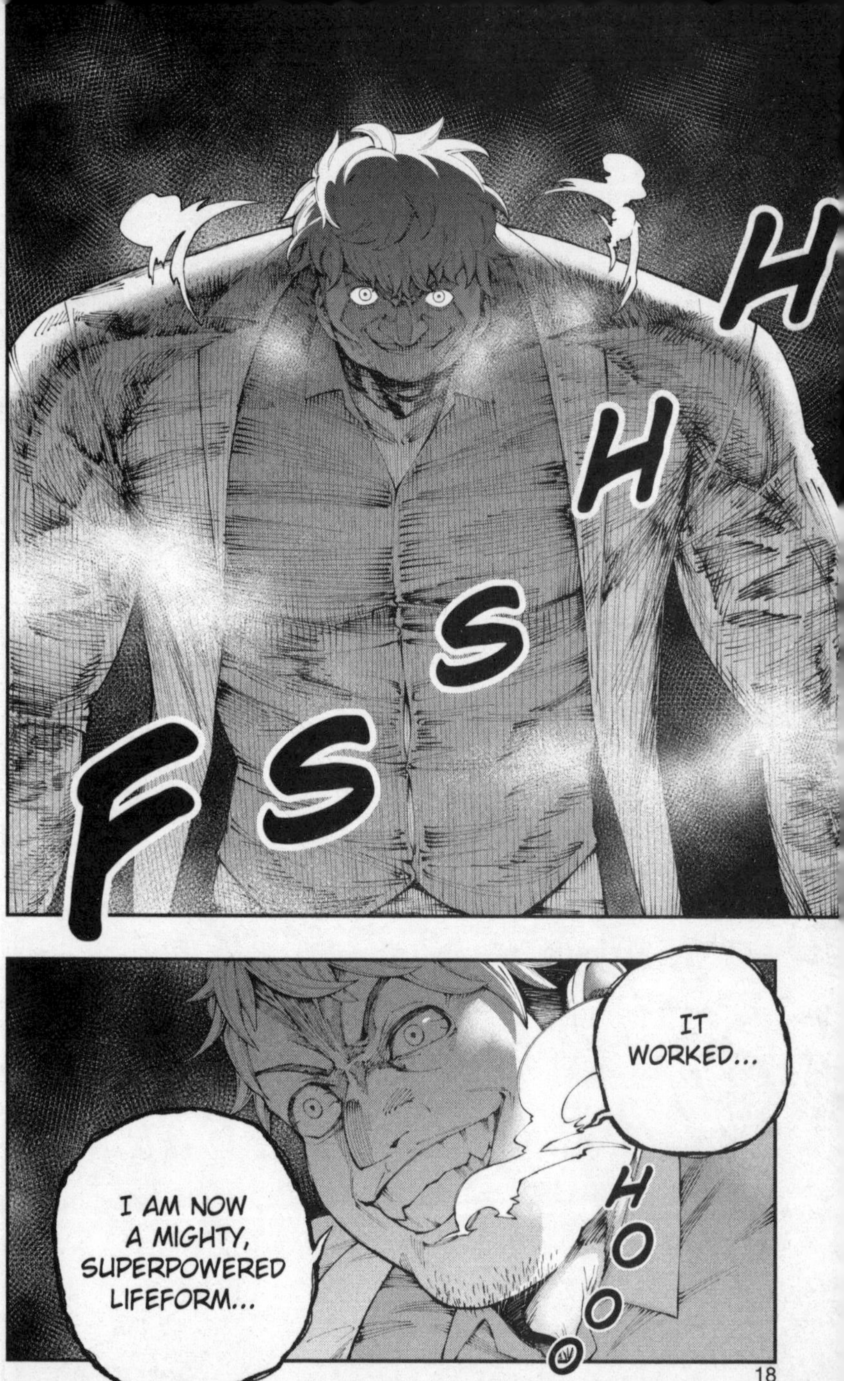
FSSHH
IT WORKED...
HOOOO
I AM NOW A MIGHTY, SUPERPOWERED LIFEFORM...

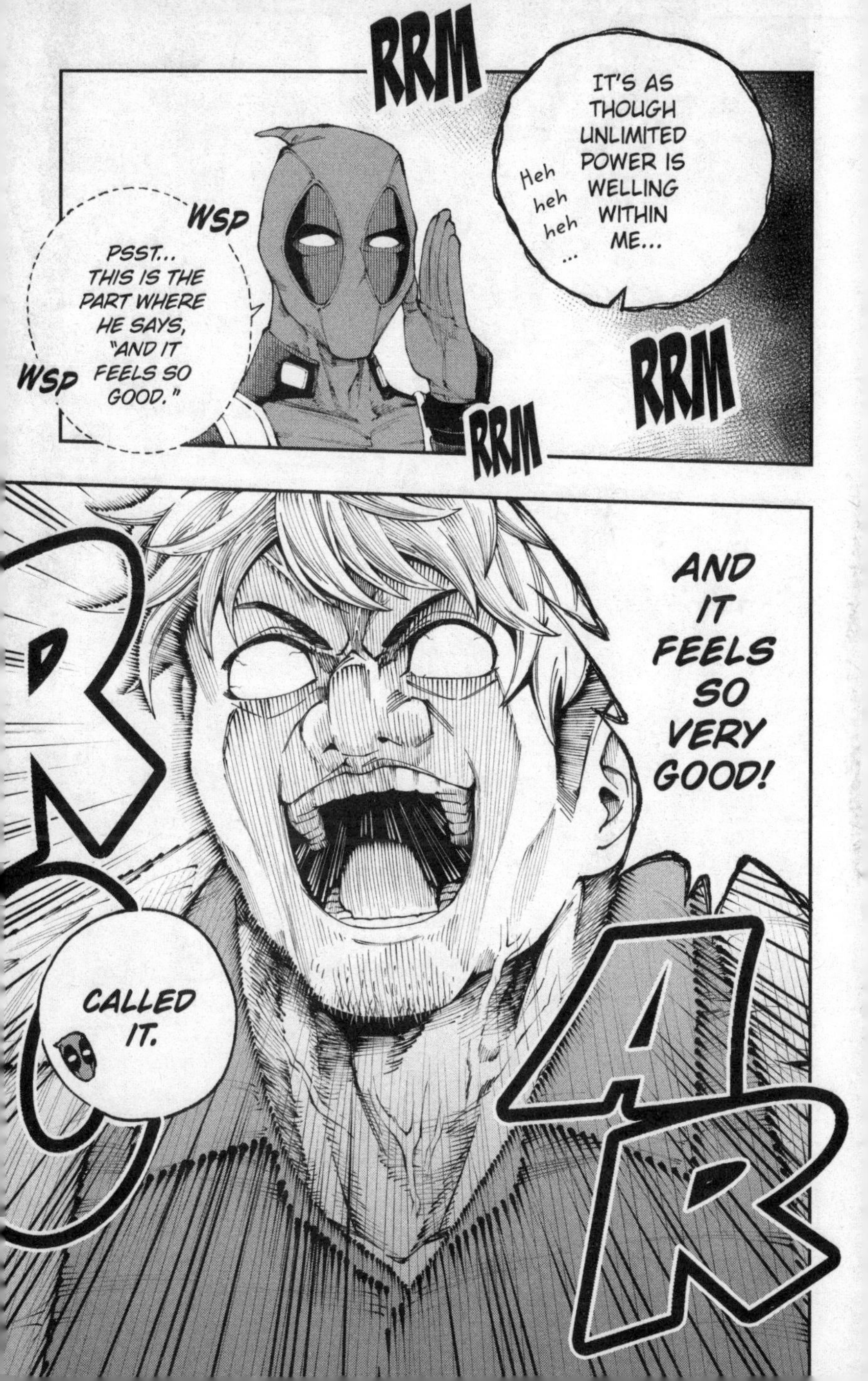
RRM
Heh heh heh...
IT'S AS THOUGH UNLIMITED POWER IS WELLING WITHIN ME...
WSP
PSST... THIS IS THE PART WHERE HE SAYS, "AND IT FEELS SO GOOD."
WSP
RRM
RRM
AND IT FEELS SO VERY GOOD!
ROAR
CALLED IT.

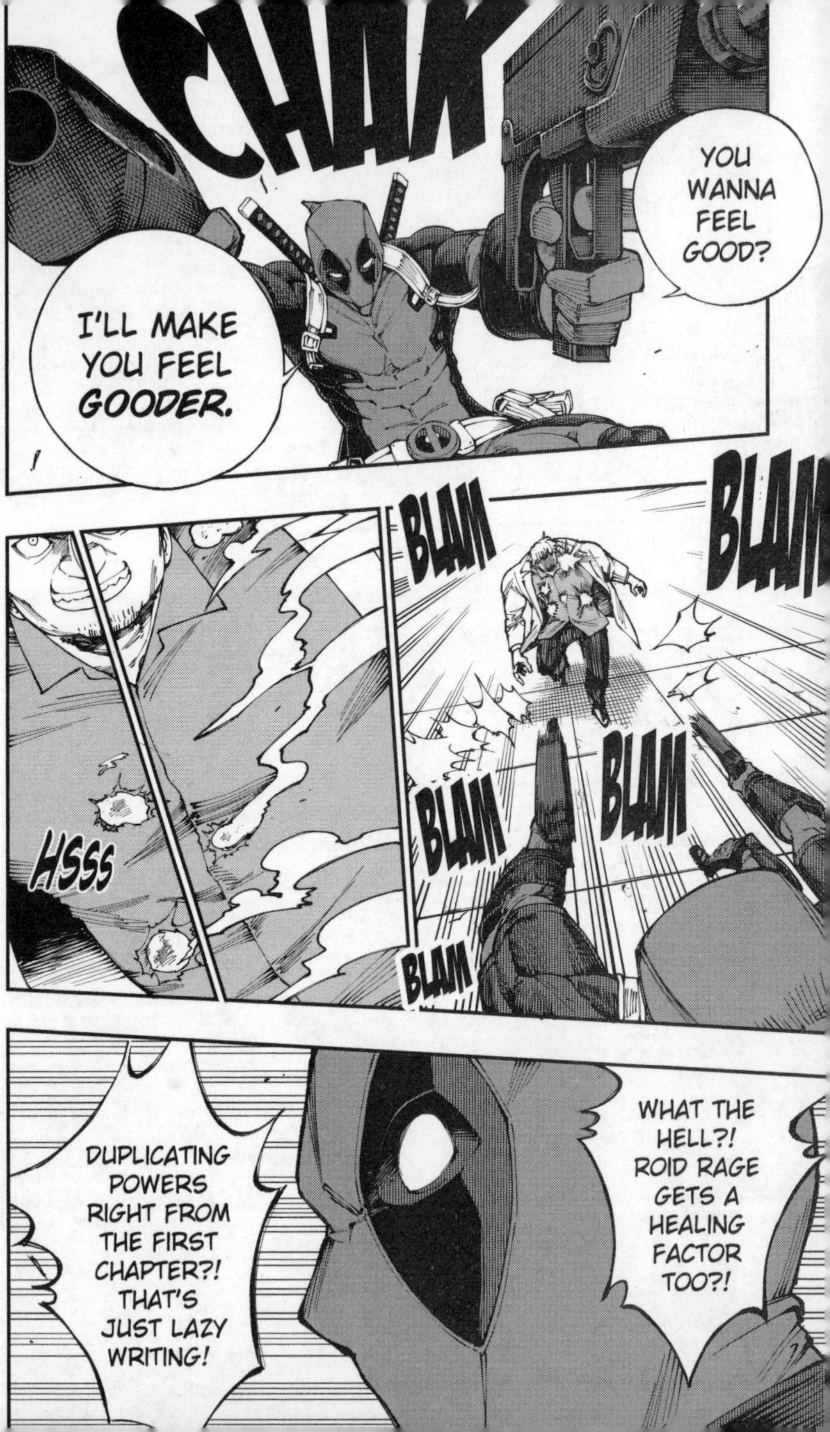
CHAK
YOU WANNA FEEL GOOD?
I'LL MAKE YOU FEEL GOODER.
BLAM
BLAM
BLAM
BLAM
BLAM
HSSS
WHAT THE HELL?! ROID RAGE GETS A HEALING FACTOR TOO?!
DUPLICATING POWERS RIGHT FROM THE FIRST CHAPTER?! THAT'S JUST LAZY WRITING!

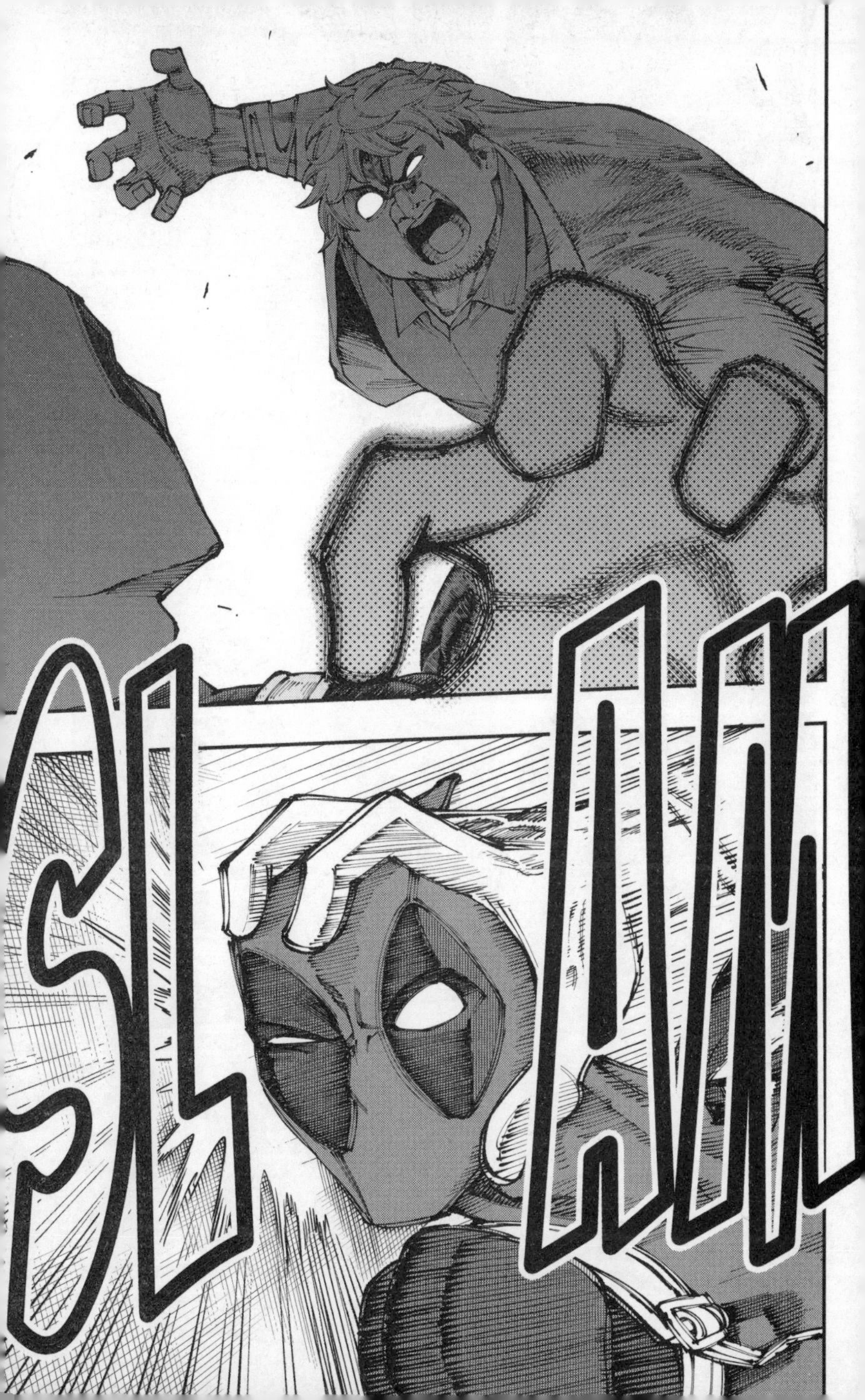
SLAM

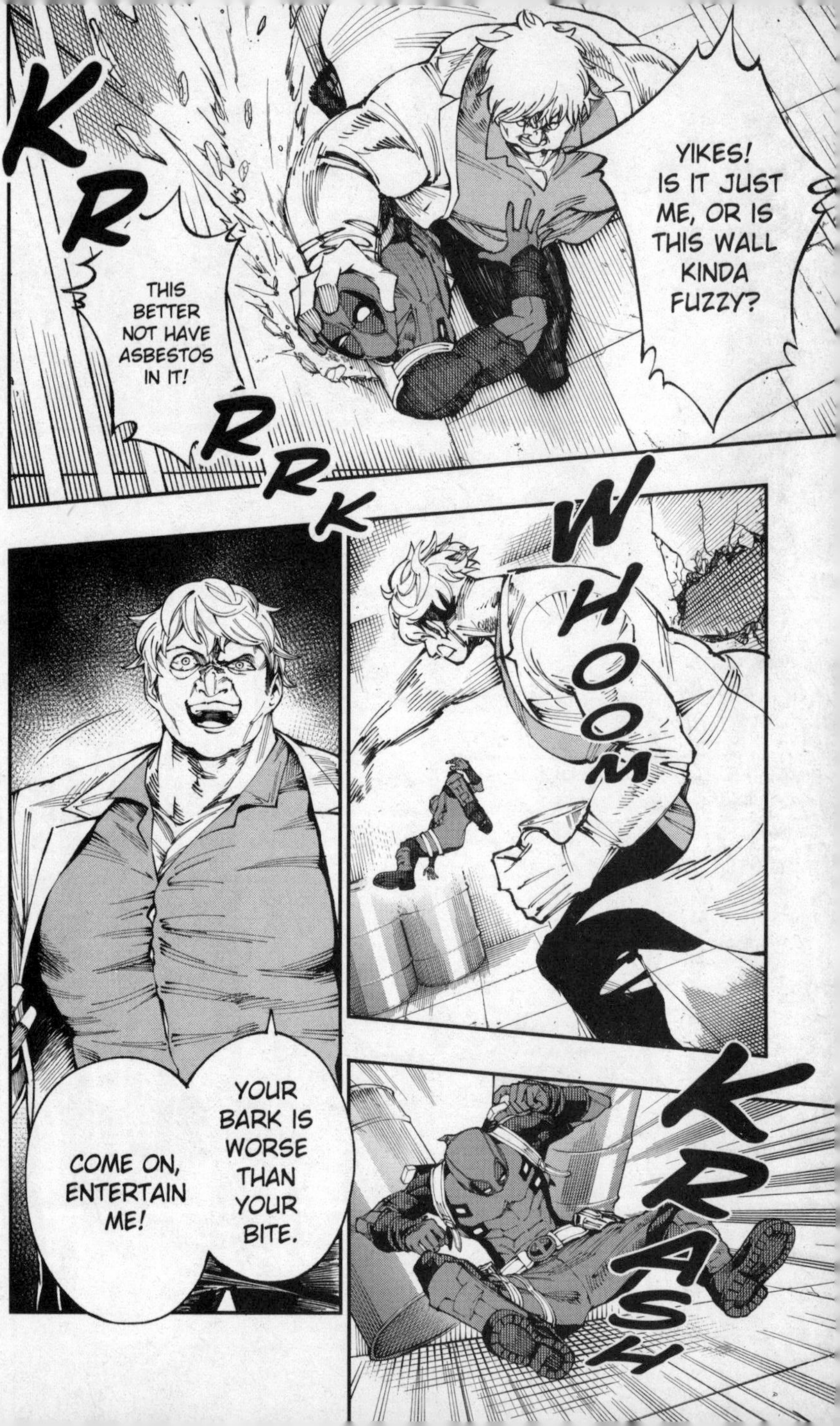
YIKES! IS IT JUST ME, OR IS THIS WALL KINDA FUZZY?
THIS BETTER NOT HAVE ASBESTOS IN IT!
KRRRK
WHOOM
KRASH
YOUR BARK IS WORSE THAN YOUR BITE.
COME ON, ENTERTAIN ME!

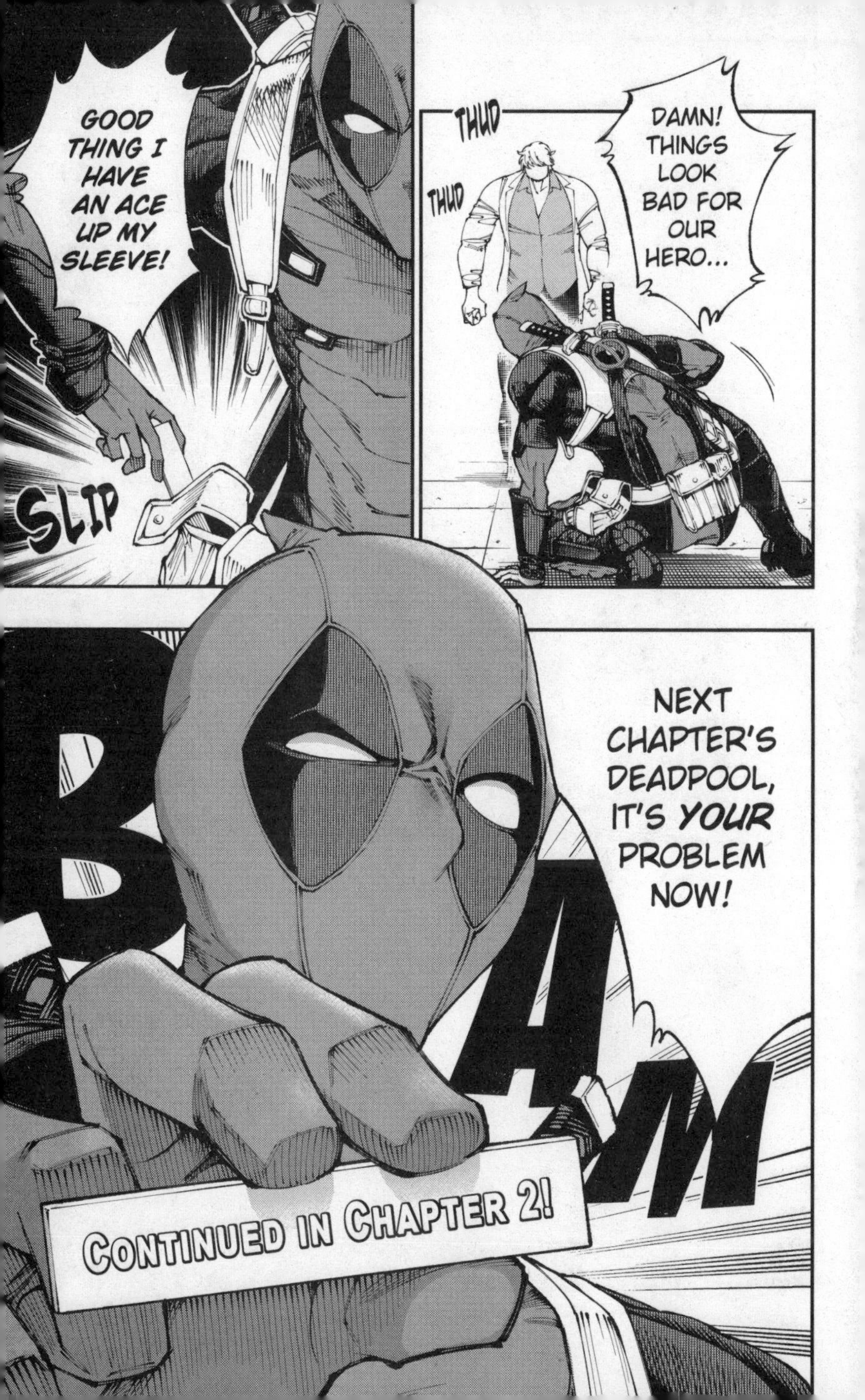
THUD
THUD
DAMN! THINGS LOOK BAD FOR OUR HERO...
GOOD THING I HAVE AN ACE UP MY SLEEVE!
SLIP
NEXT CHAPTER'S DEADPOOL, IT'S *YOUR* PROBLEM NOW!
CONTINUED IN CHAPTER 2!

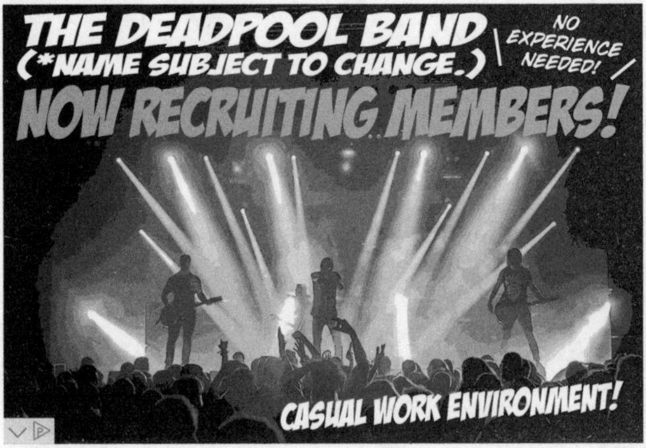
THE DEADPOOL BAND
(*NAME SUBJECT TO CHANGE.)
NO EXPERIENCE NEEDED!
NOW RECRUITING MEMBERS!
CASUAL WORK ENVIRONMENT!

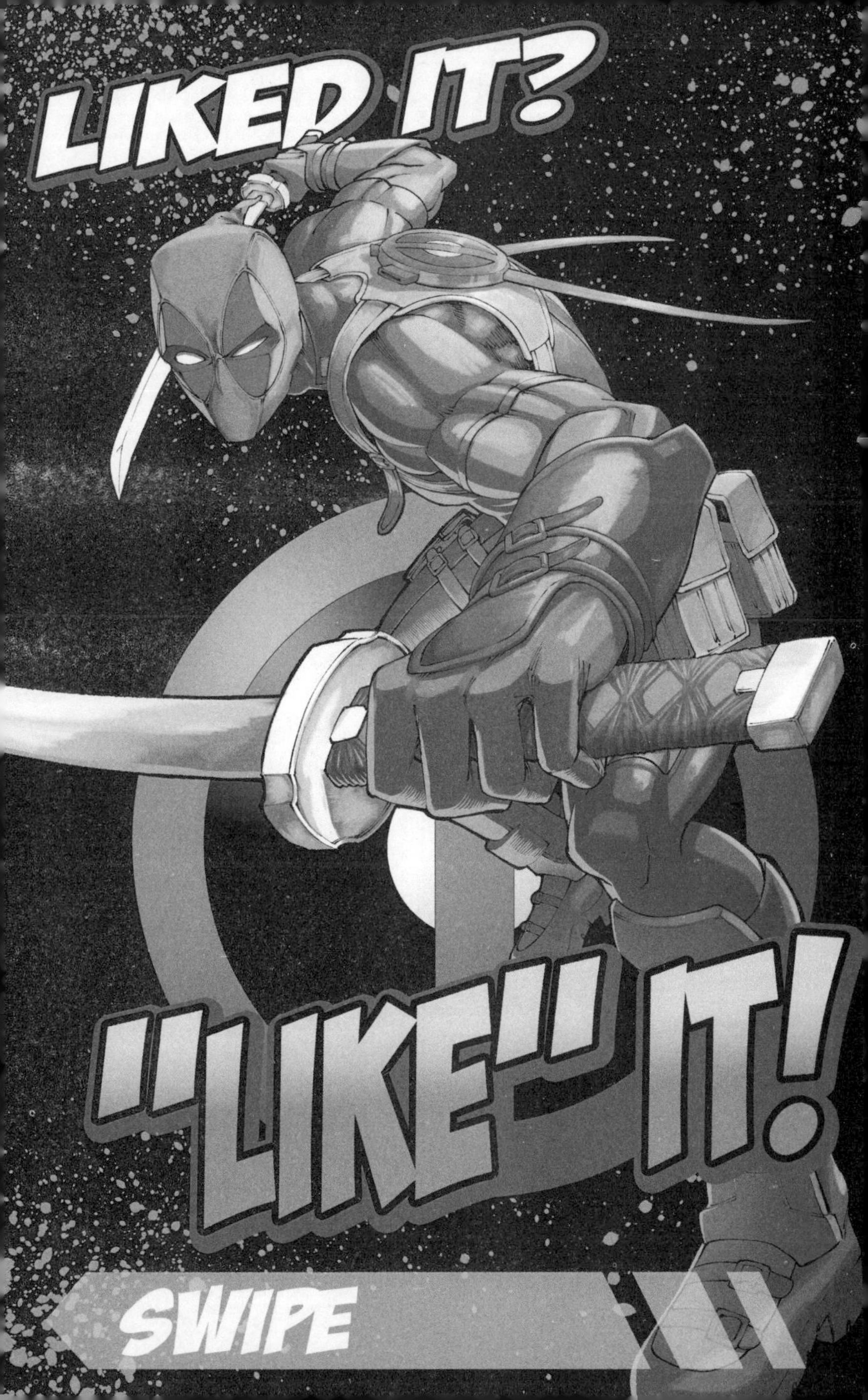
LIKED IT?
"LIKE" IT!
SWIPE

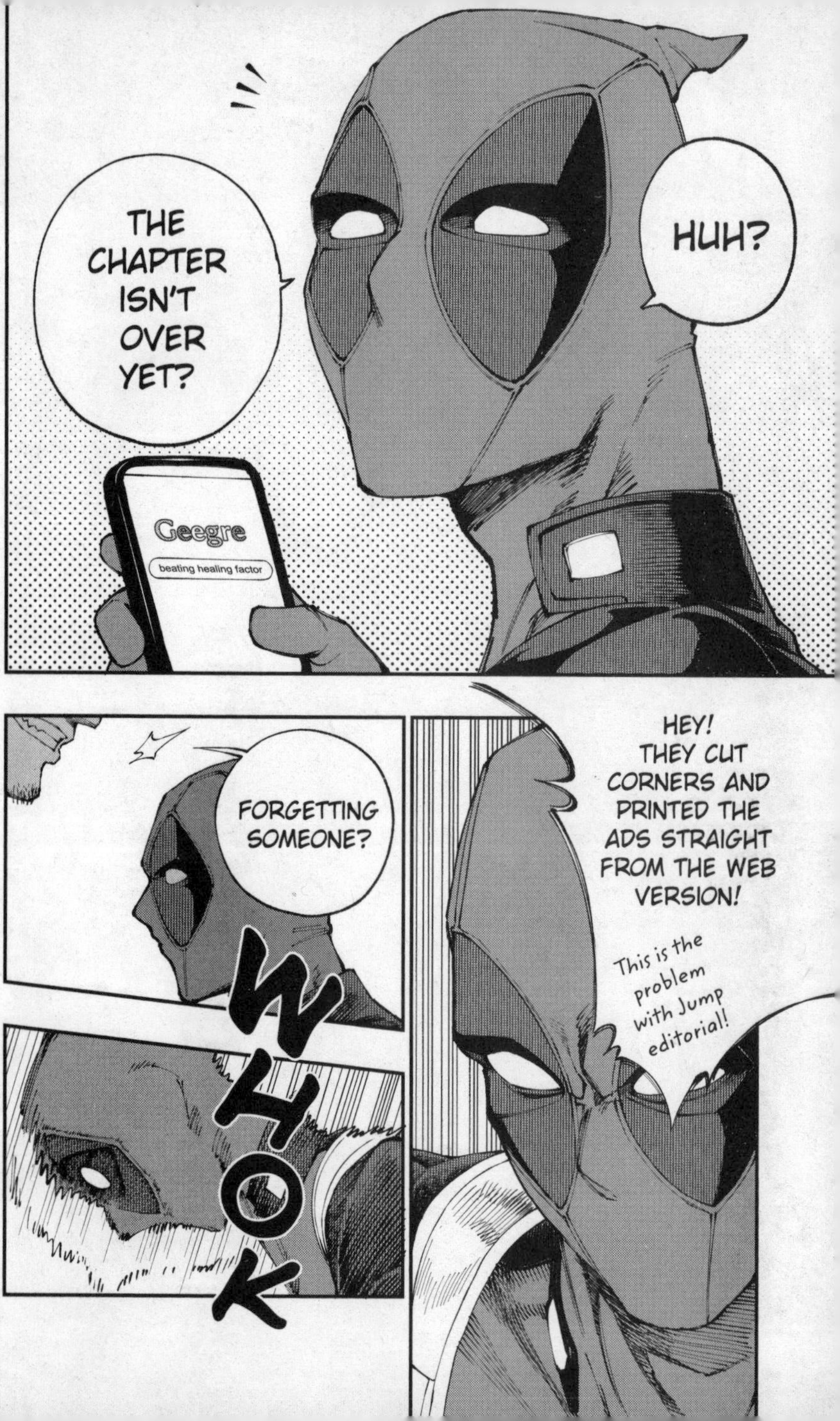
HUH?
THE CHAPTER ISN'T OVER YET?
Geegre
beating healing factor
HEY! THEY CUT CORNERS AND PRINTED THE ADS STRAIGHT FROM THE WEB VERSION!
This is the problem with Jump editorial!
FORGETTING SOMEONE?
WHOK

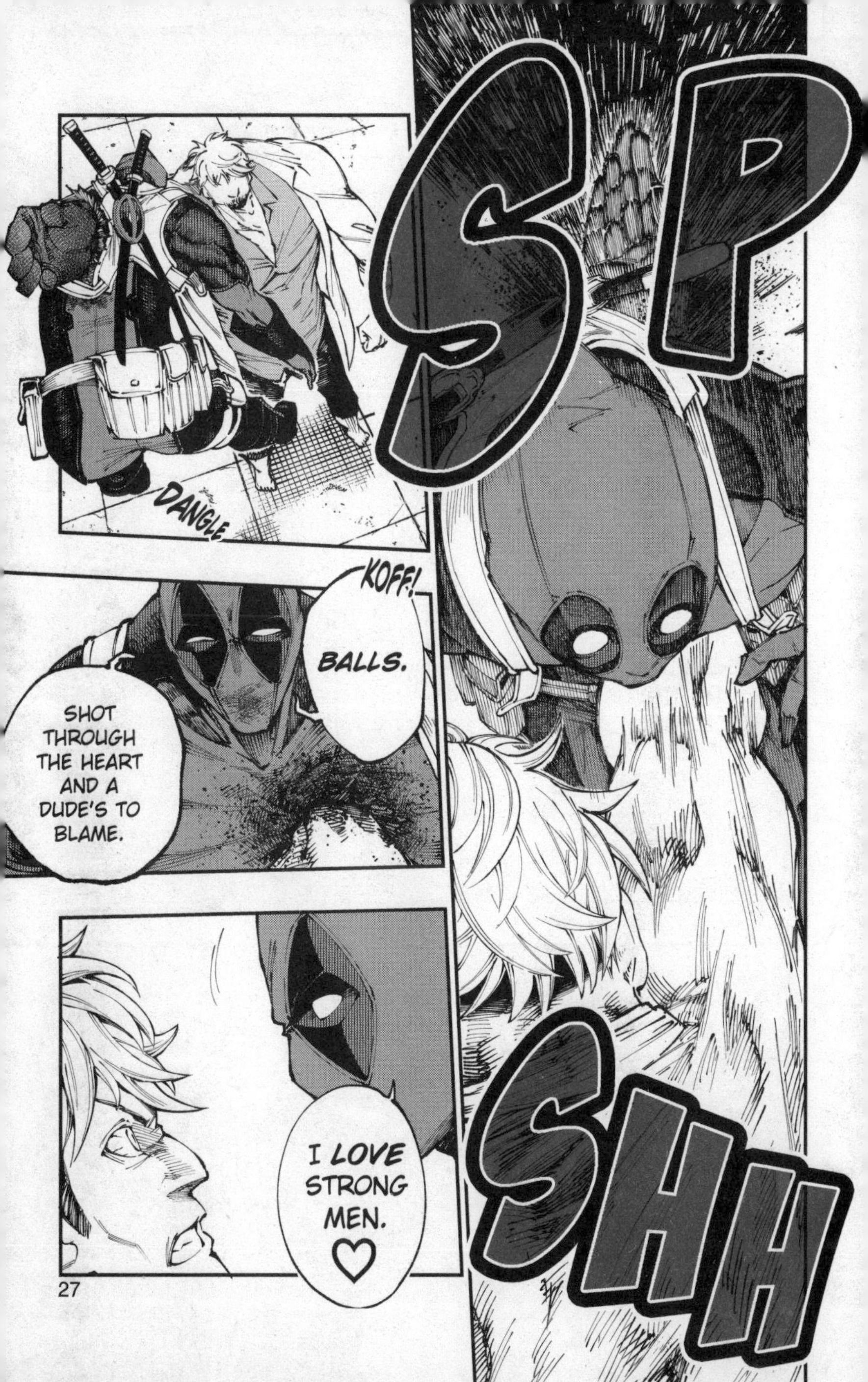
SP
SHH
DANGLE
KOFF!
BALLS.
SHOT THROUGH THE HEART AND A DUDE'S TO BLAME.
I LOVE STRONG MEN. ♡

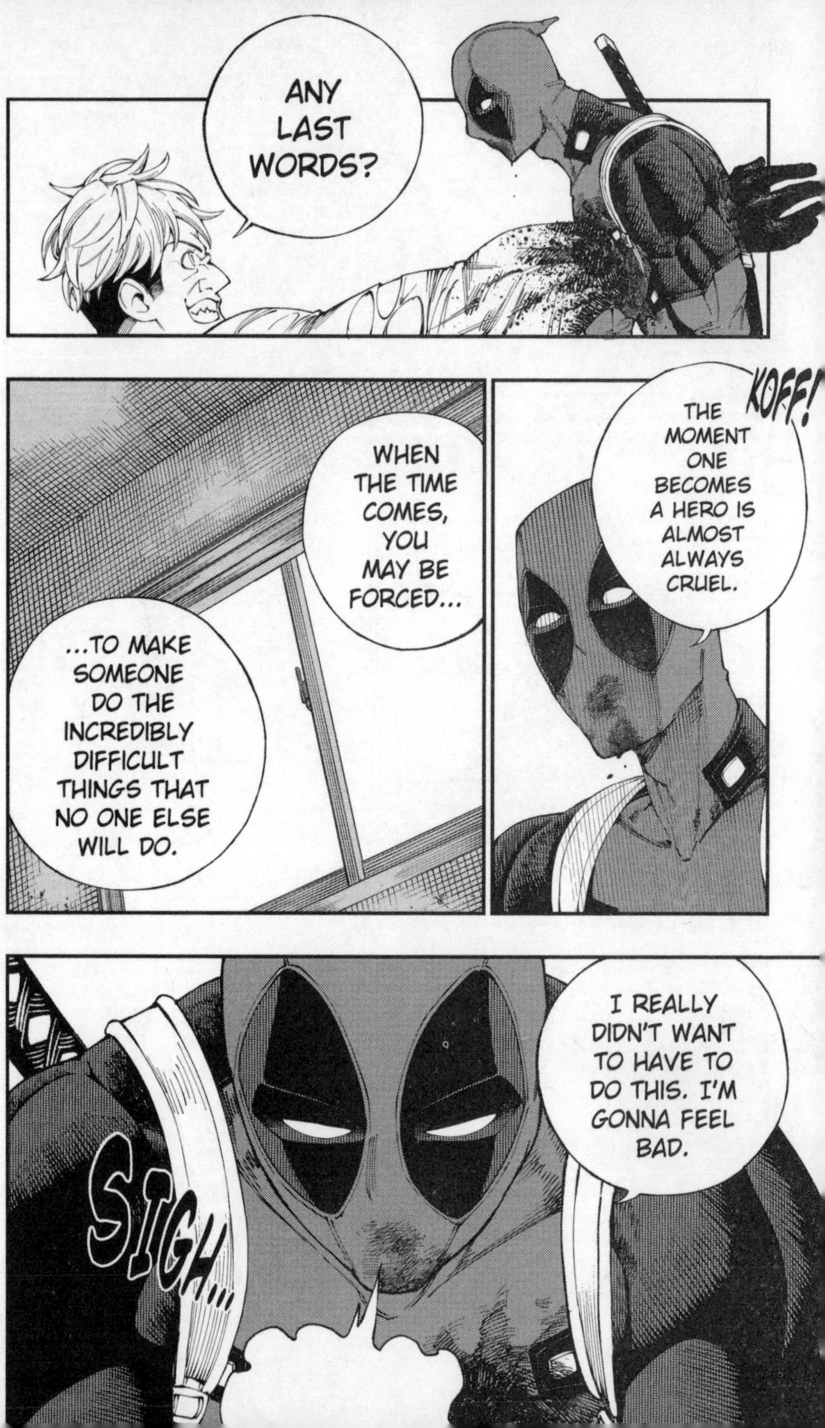

ANY LAST WORDS?
KOFF!
THE MOMENT ONE BECOMES A HERO IS ALMOST ALWAYS CRUEL.
WHEN THE TIME COMES, YOU MAY BE FORCED...
...TO MAKE SOMEONE DO THE INCREDIBLY DIFFICULT THINGS THAT NO ONE ELSE WILL DO.
I REALLY DIDN'T WANT TO HAVE TO DO THIS. I'M GONNA FEEL BAD.
SIGH...

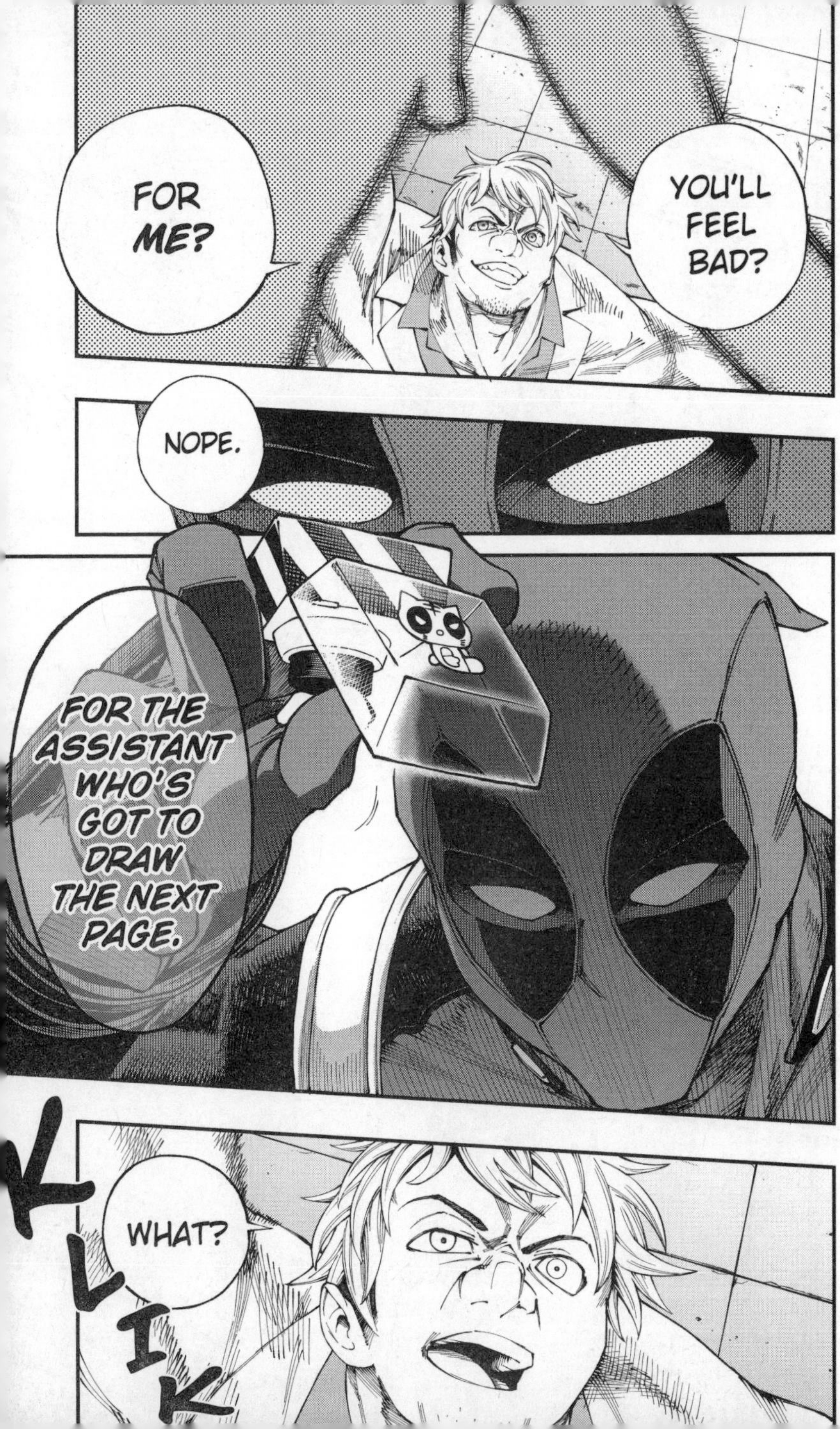
YOU'LL FEEL BAD?
FOR ME?
NOPE.
FOR THE ASSISTANT WHO'S GOT TO DRAW THE NEXT PAGE.
WHAT?
KLLIK

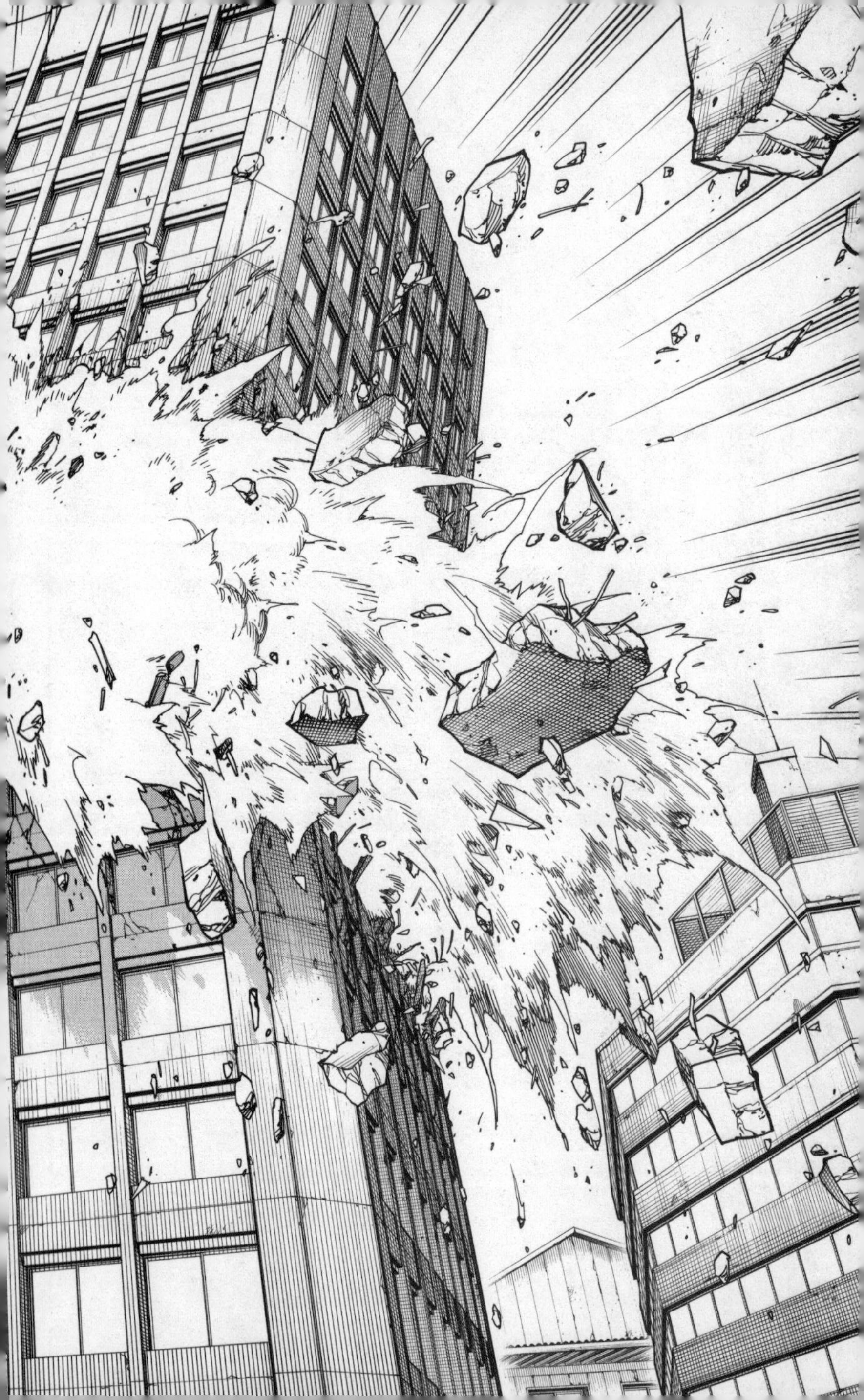

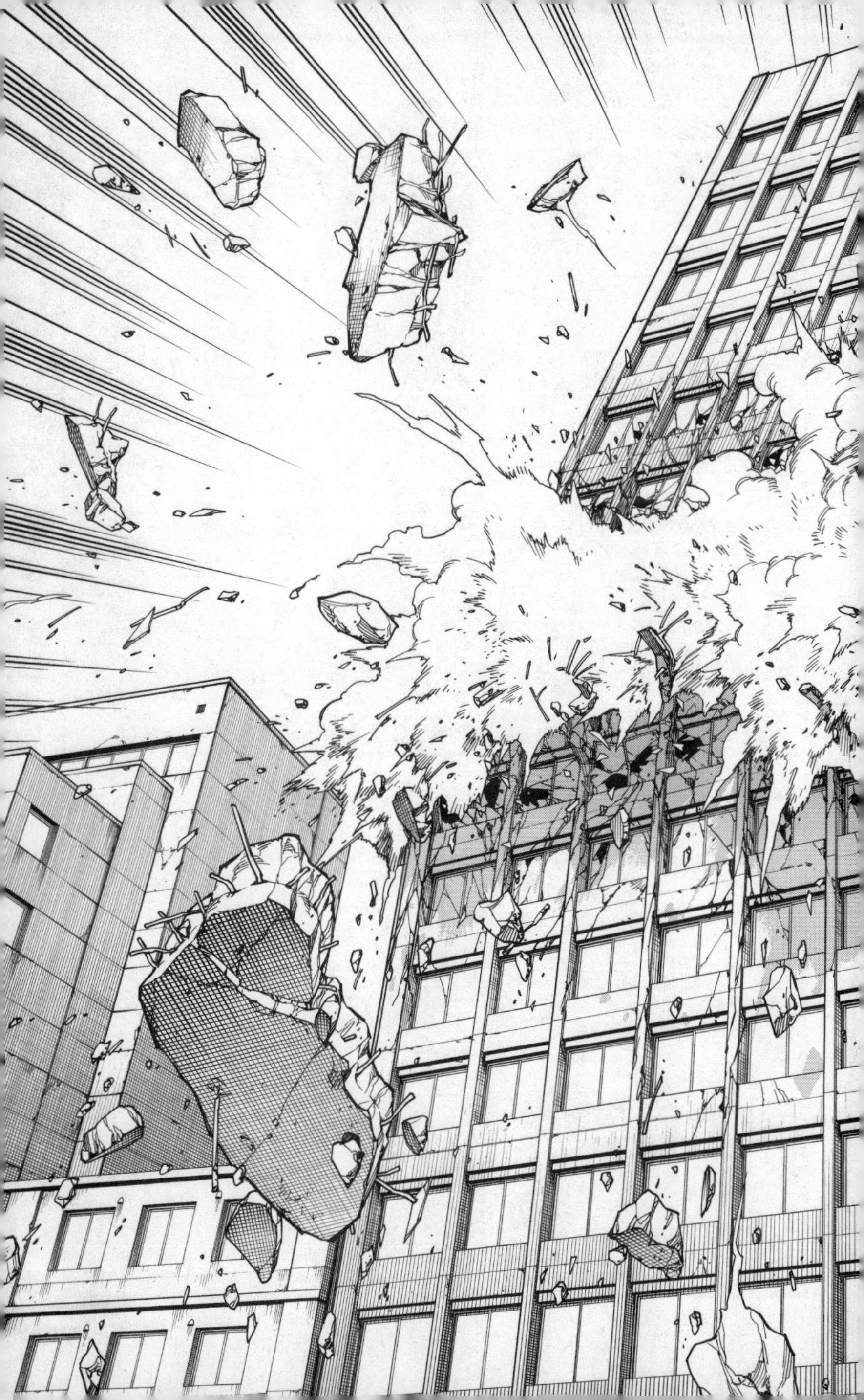

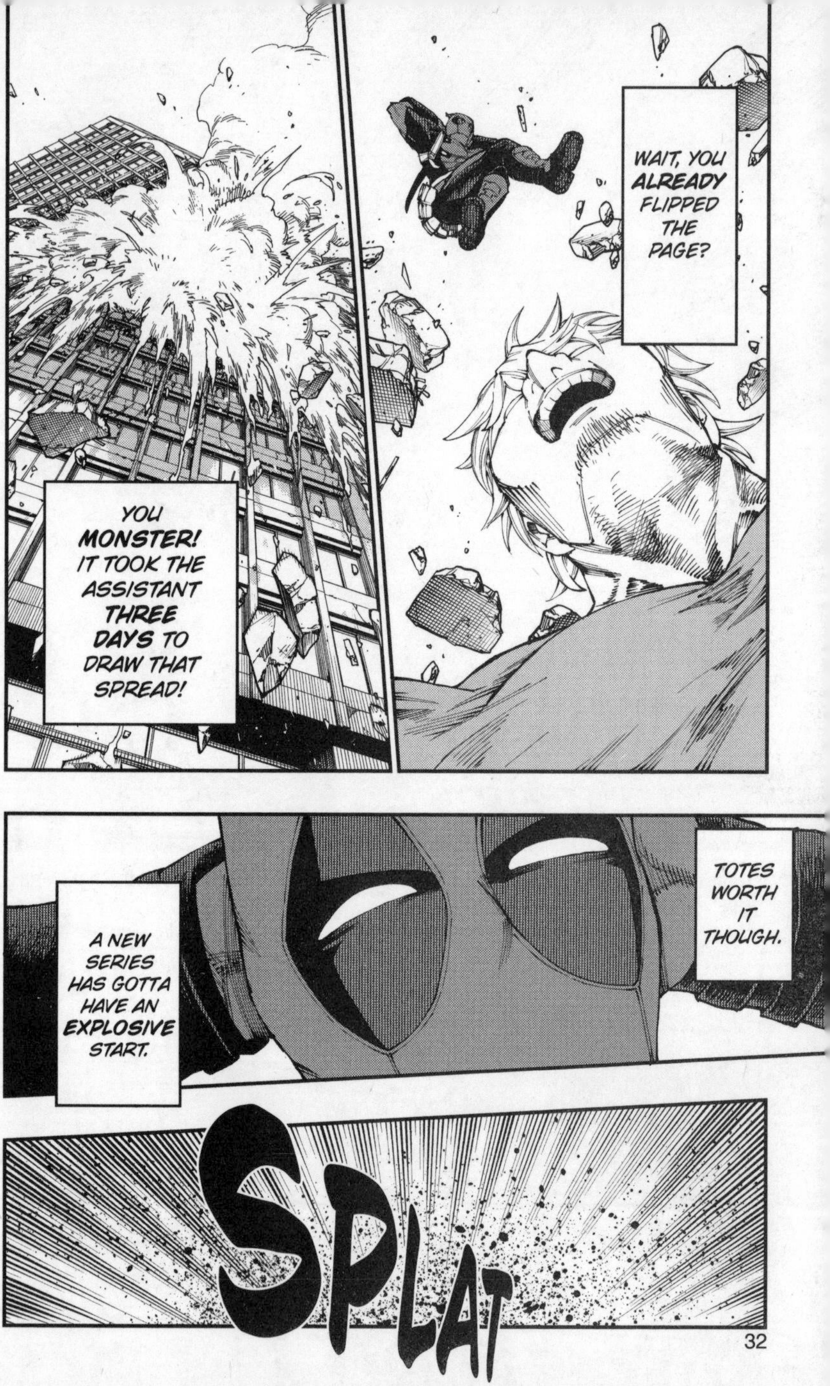
WAIT, YOU ALREADY FLIPPED THE PAGE?
YOU MONSTER! IT TOOK THE ASSISTANT THREE DAYS TO DRAW THAT SPREAD!
TOTES WORTH IT THOUGH.
A NEW SERIES HAS GOTTA HAVE AN EXPLOSIVE START.
SPLAT

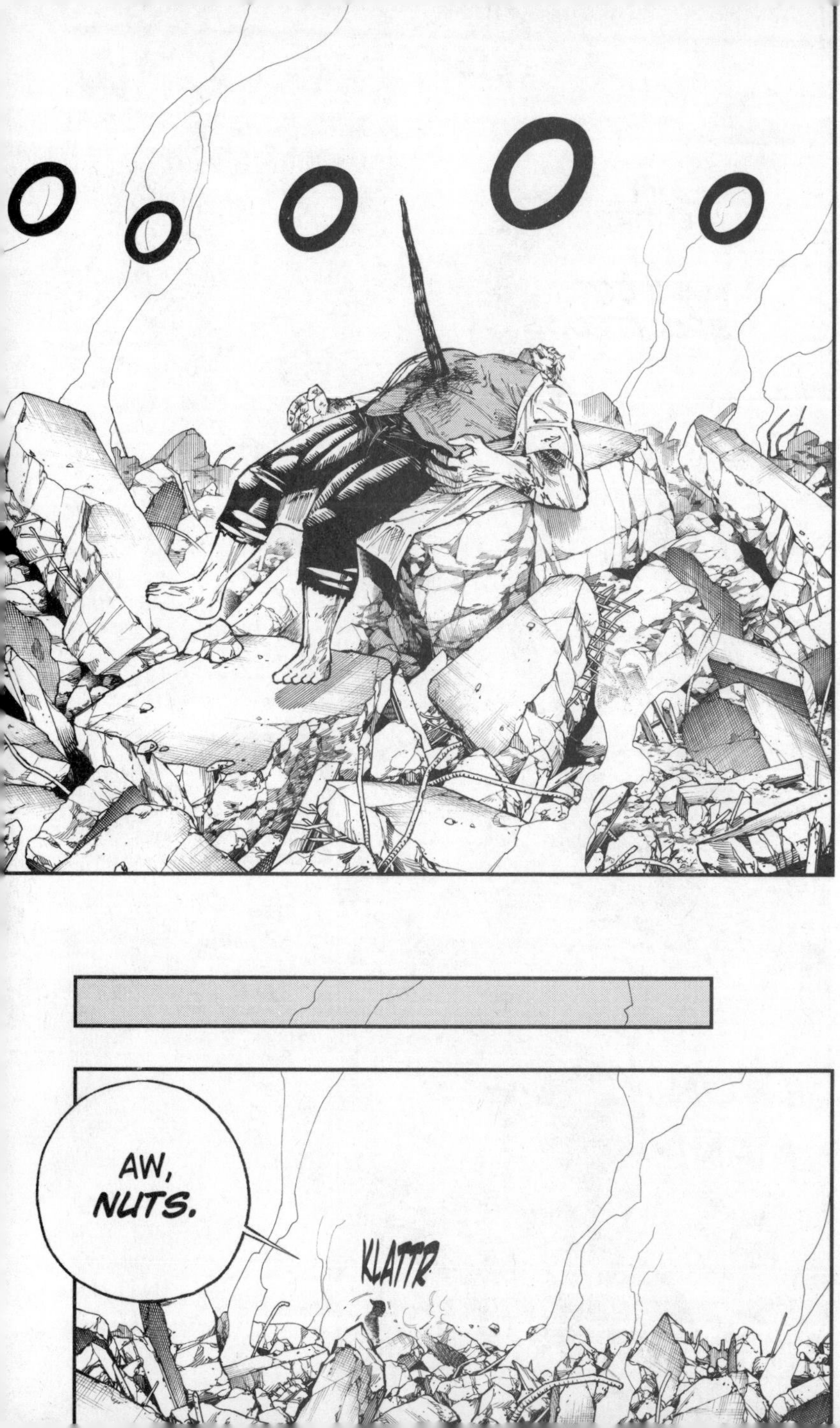
OOOOO
AW, NUTS.
KLATTR

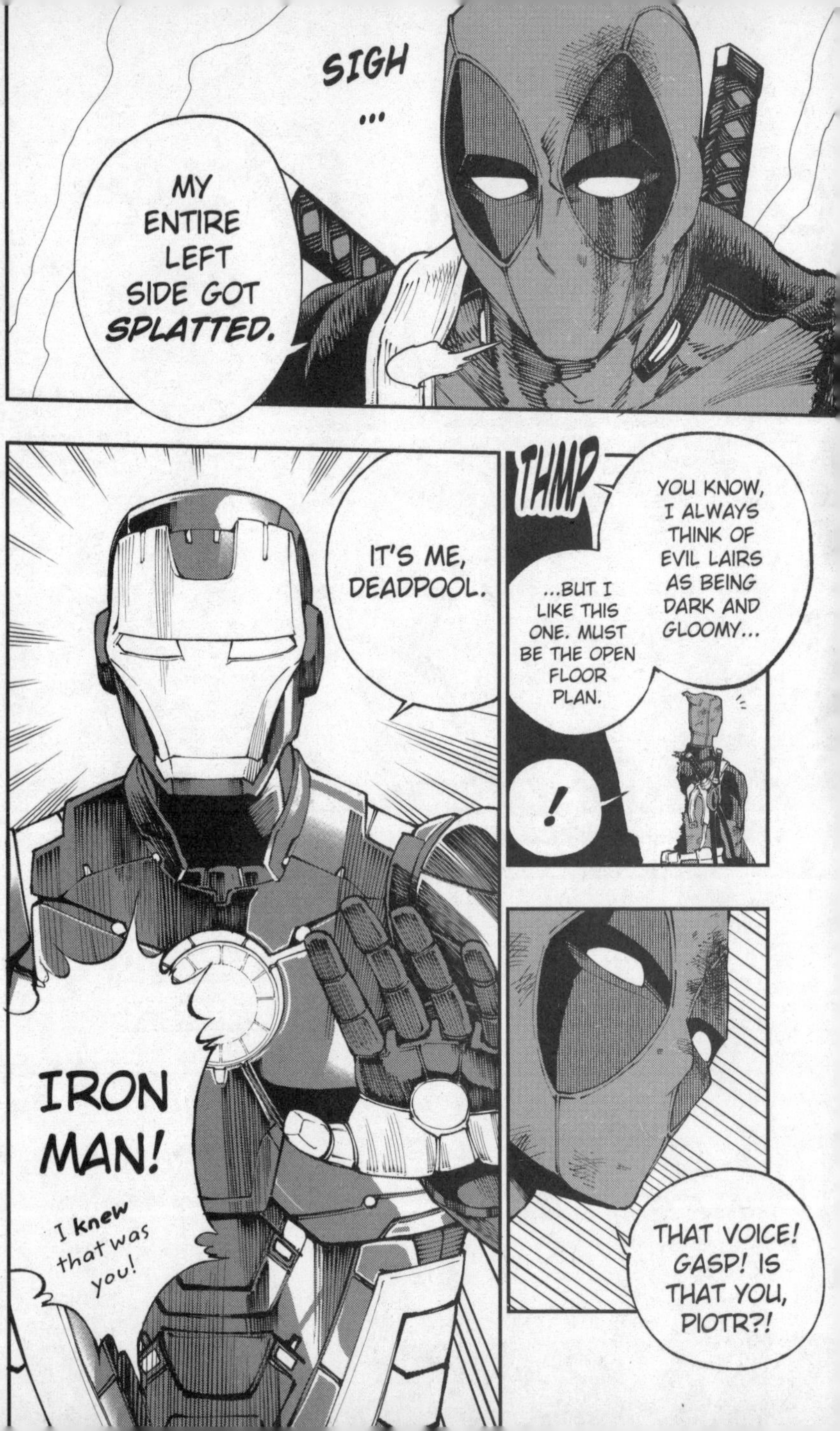
SIGH ...
MY ENTIRE LEFT SIDE GOT SPLATTED.
THMP
YOU KNOW, I ALWAYS THINK OF EVIL LAIRS AS BEING DARK AND GLOOMY...
...BUT I LIKE THIS ONE. MUST BE THE OPEN FLOOR PLAN.
!
THAT VOICE! GASP! IS THAT YOU, PIOTR?!
IT'S ME, DEADPOOL.
IRON MAN!
I knew that was you!

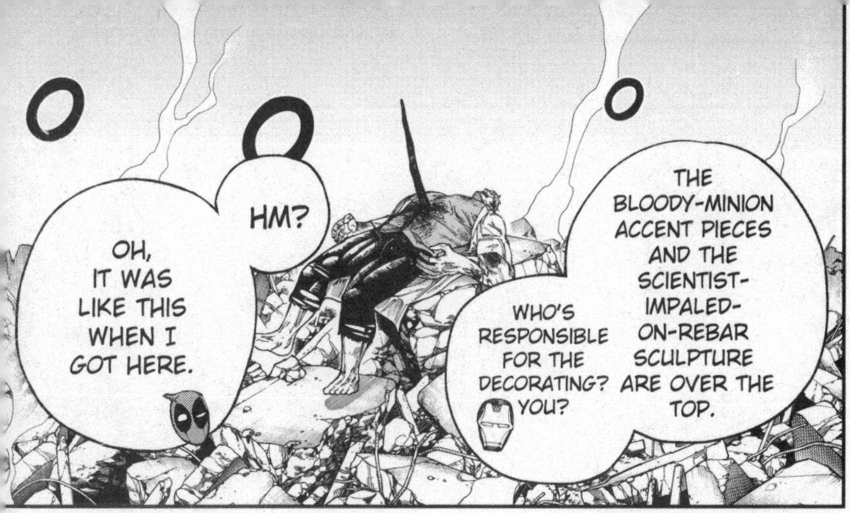
THE BLOODY-MINION ACCENT PIECES AND THE SCIENTIST-IMPALED-ON-REBAR SCULPTURE ARE OVER THE TOP.
WHO'S RESPONSIBLE FOR THE DECORATING? YOU?
HM?
OH, IT WAS LIKE THIS WHEN I GOT HERE.

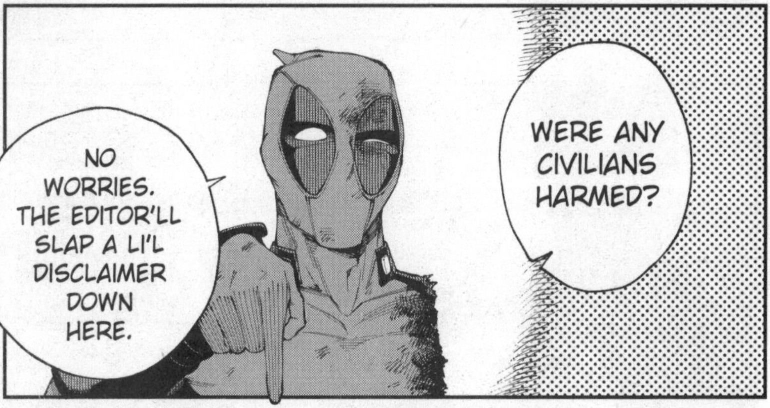
WERE ANY CIVILIANS HARMED?
NO WORRIES. THE EDITOR'LL SLAP A LI'L DISCLAIMER DOWN HERE.

*Editor's note: All explosions supervised by a safety expert.

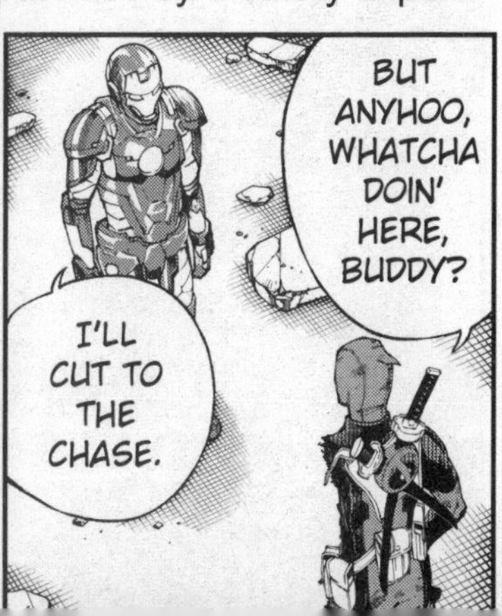
BUT ANYHOO, WHATCHA DOIN' HERE, BUDDY?
I'LL CUT TO THE CHASE.

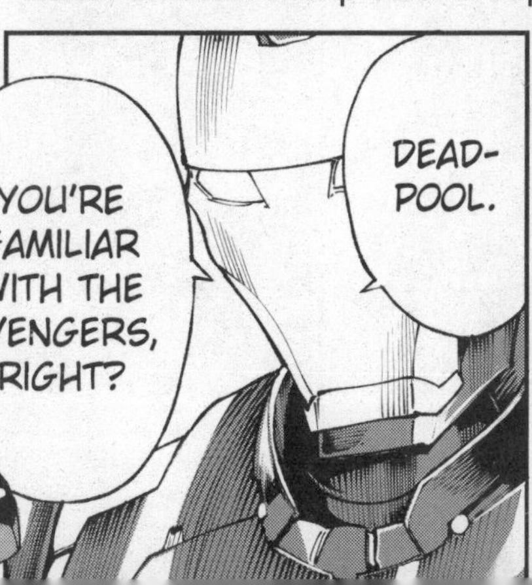
DEAD-POOL.
YOU'RE FAMILIAR WITH THE AVENGERS, RIGHT?

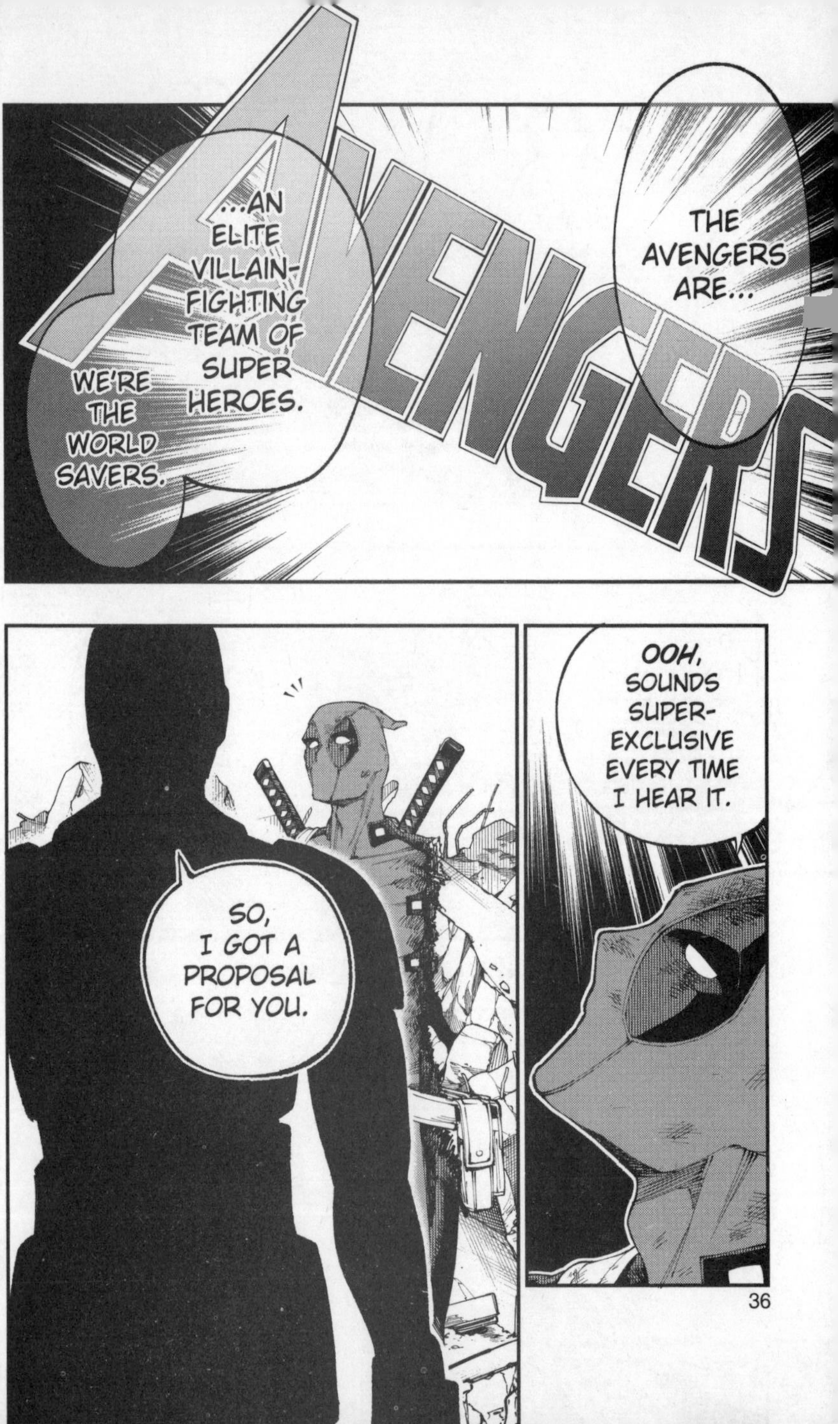
THE AVENGERS ARE...
AVENGERS
...AN ELITE VILLAIN-FIGHTING TEAM OF SUPER HEROES.
WE'RE THE WORLD SAVERS.
OOH, SOUNDS SUPER-EXCLUSIVE EVERY TIME I HEAR IT.
SO, I GOT A PROPOSAL FOR YOU.

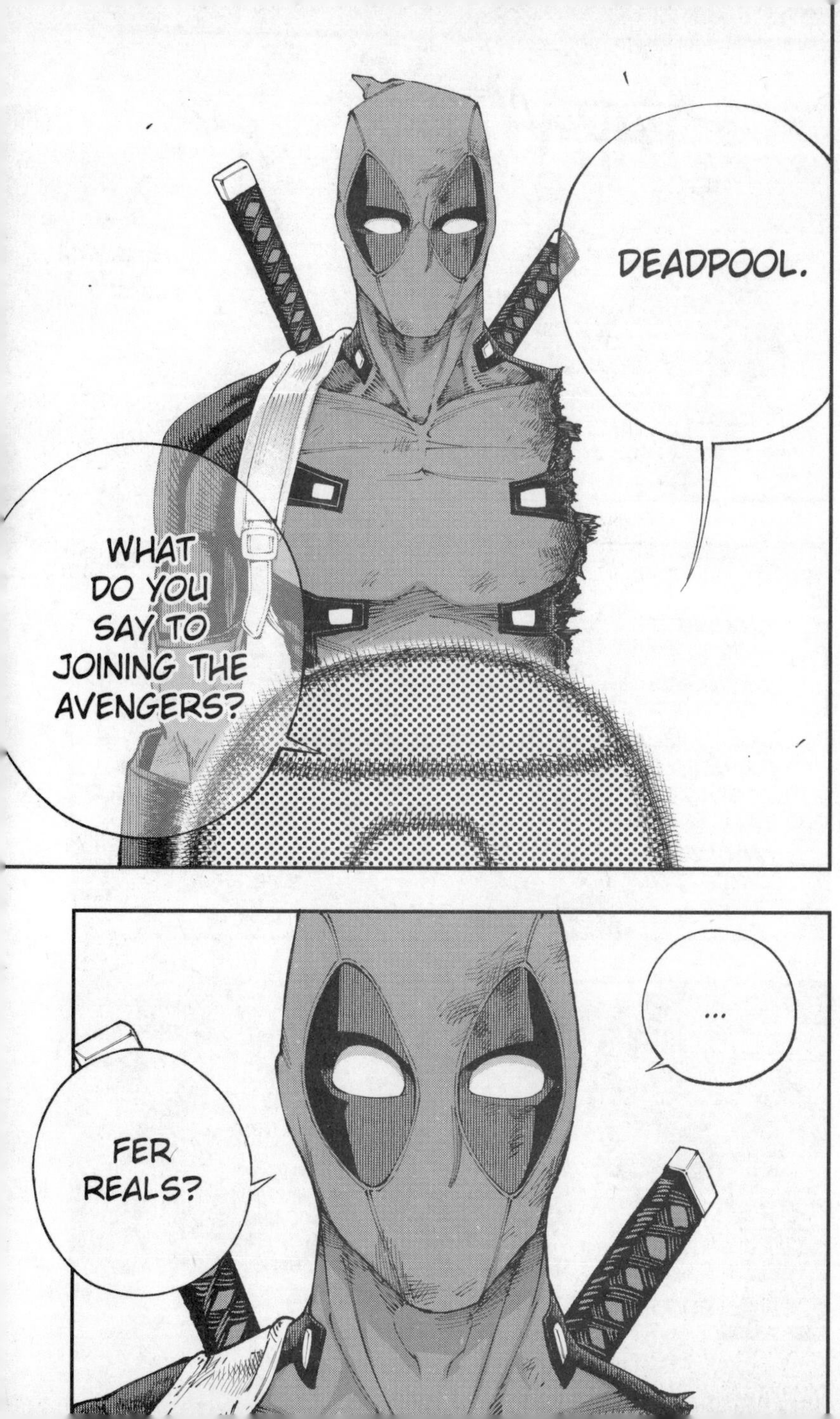
DEADPOOL.
WHAT DO YOU SAY TO JOINING THE AVENGERS?
...
FER REALS?

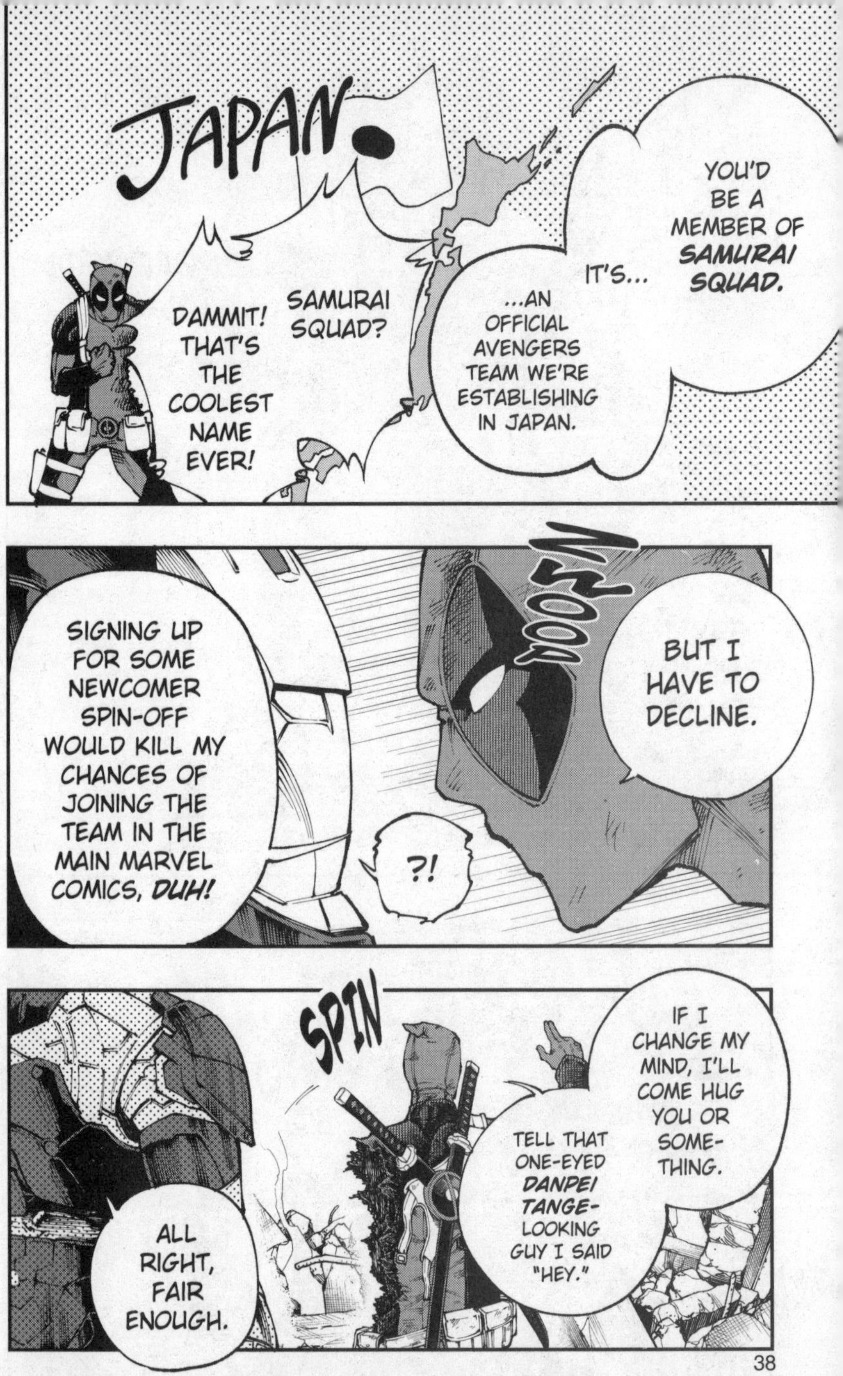
YOU'D BE A MEMBER OF SAMURAI SQUAD.
IT'S...
...AN OFFICIAL AVENGERS TEAM WE'RE ESTABLISHING IN JAPAN.
SAMURAI SQUAD?
DAMMIT! THAT'S THE COOLEST NAME EVER!
JAPAN.
BUT I HAVE TO DECLINE.
?!
SIGNING UP FOR SOME NEWCOMER SPIN-OFF WOULD KILL MY CHANCES OF JOINING THE TEAM IN THE MAIN MARVEL COMICS, DUH!
IF I CHANGE MY MIND, I'LL COME HUG YOU OR SOME-THING.
SPIN
TELL THAT ONE-EYED DANPEI TANGE-LOOKING GUY I SAID "HEY."
ALL RIGHT, FAIR ENOUGH.

HOW MUCH?

THIS MUCH.

THEN I GUESS WE'LL DONATE THE MONEY WE WERE PREPARED TO PAY YOU TO A COMMUNITY COLLEGE.

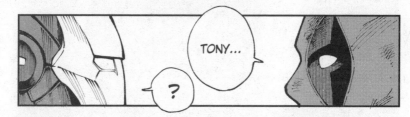

?

TONY...

CLASP

?!

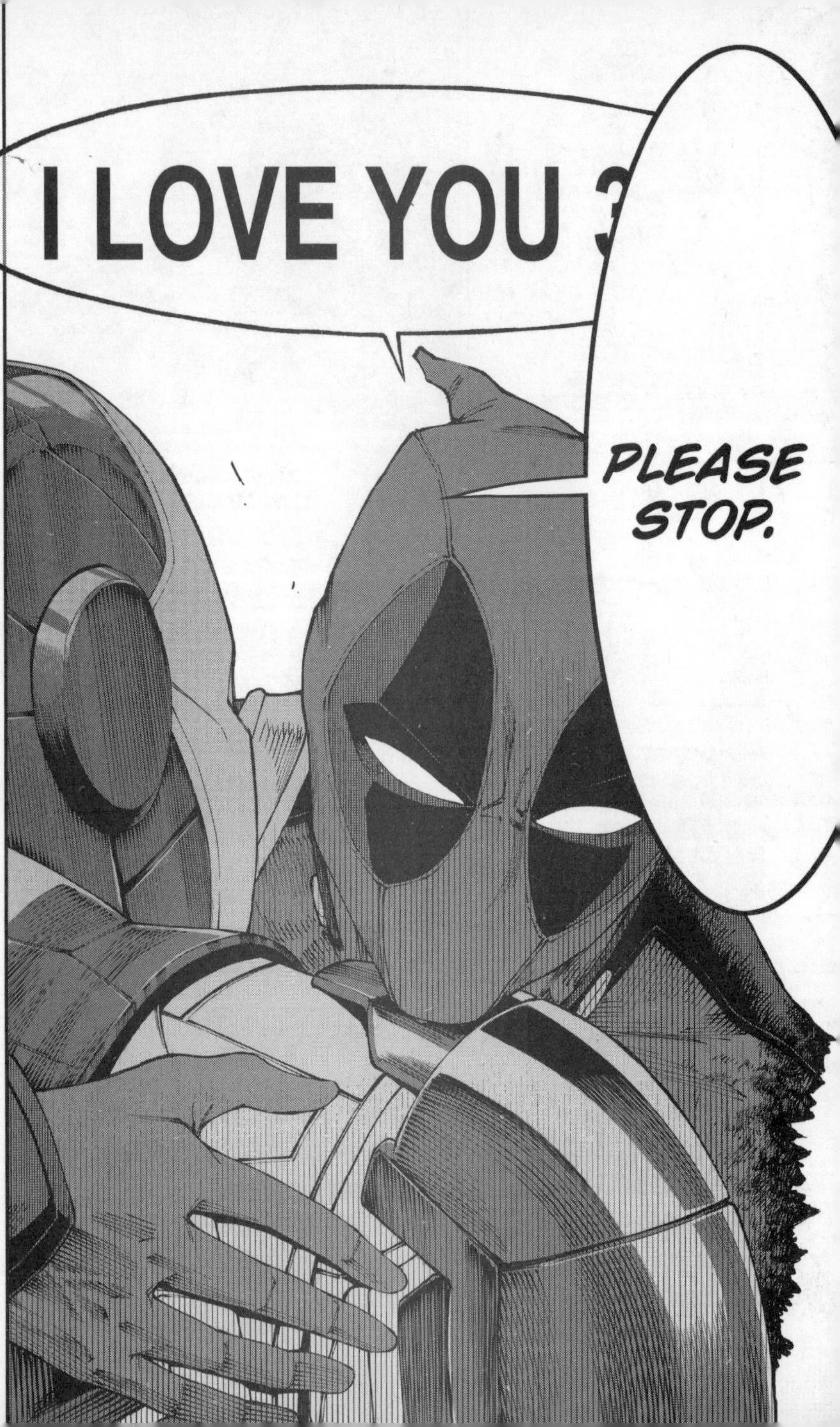

PLEASE STOP.
I LOVE YOU

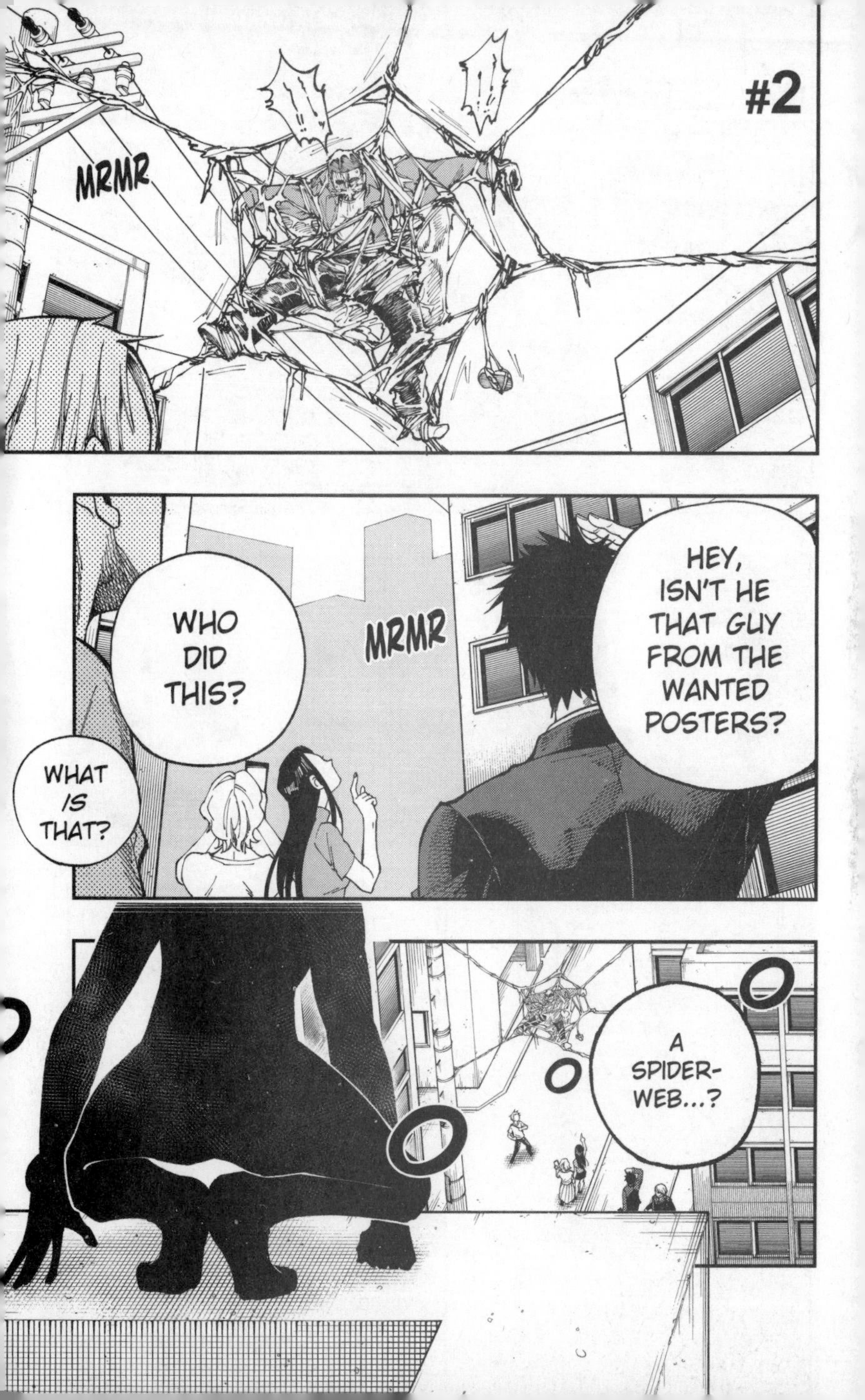
#2
!!
!!
MRMR
HEY, ISN'T HE THAT GUY FROM THE WANTED POSTERS?
MRMR
WHO DID THIS?
WHAT IS THAT?
A SPIDER-WEB...?

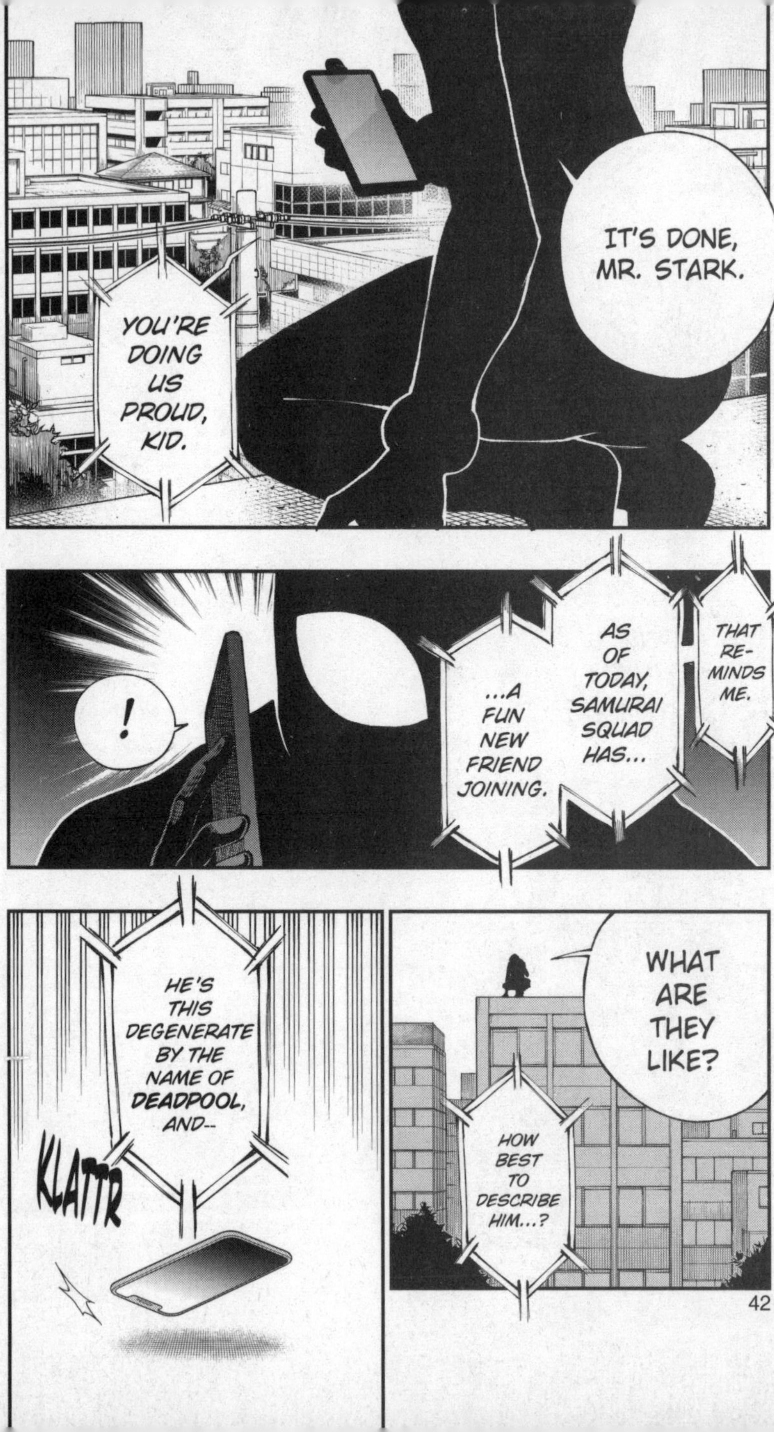
IT'S DONE, MR. STARK.
YOU'RE DOING US PROUD, KID.
THAT RE-MINDS ME.
AS OF TODAY, SAMURAI SQUAD HAS...
...A FUN NEW FRIEND JOINING.
!
WHAT ARE THEY LIKE?
HOW BEST TO DESCRIBE HIM...?
HE'S THIS DEGENERATE BY THE NAME OF DEADPOOL, AND--
KLATTR

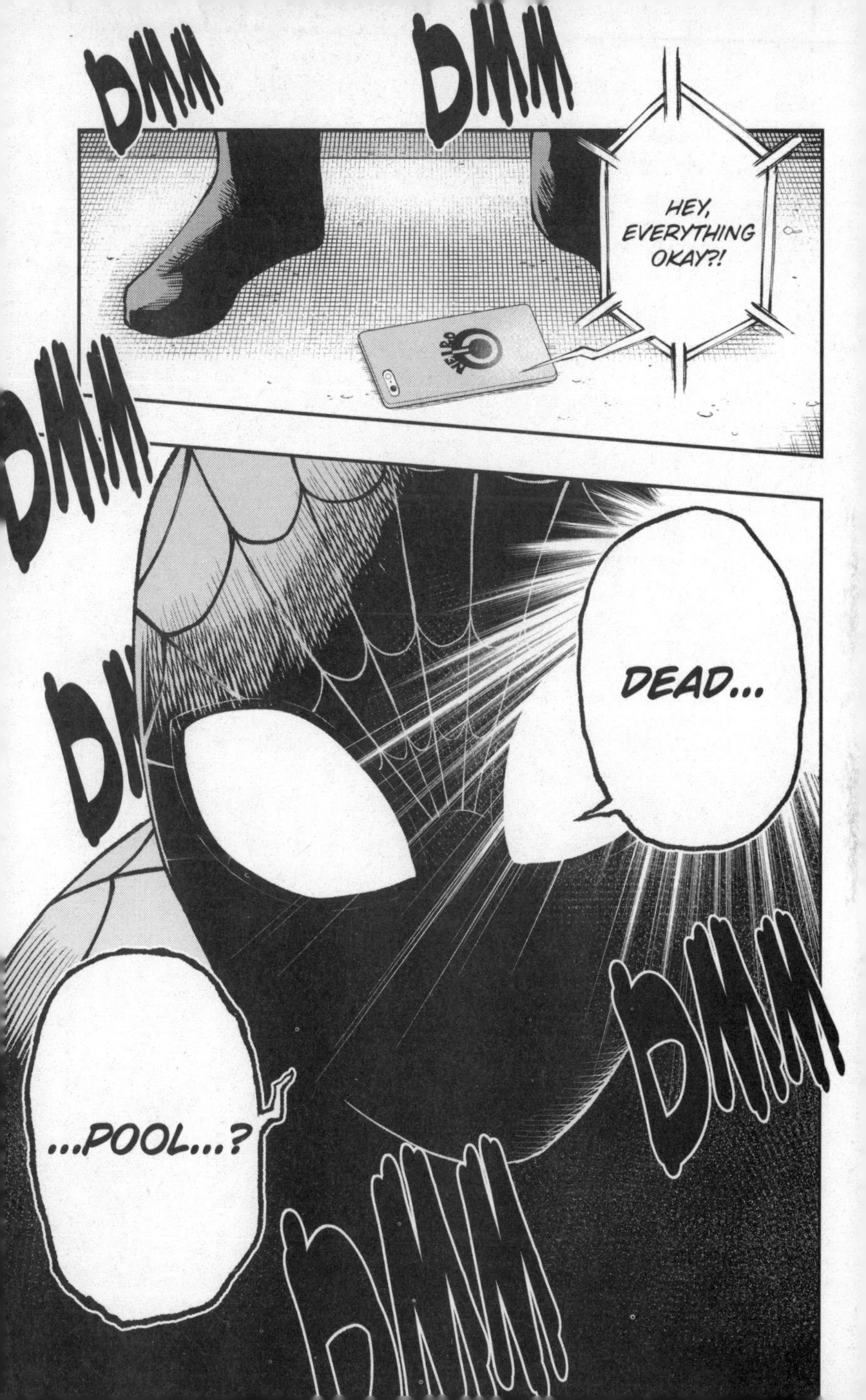
DMM
DMM
HEY, EVERYTHING OKAY?!
DMM
DEAD...
DMM
DMM
...POOL...?
DMM

DEADPOOL SAMURAI

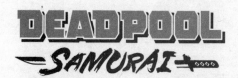

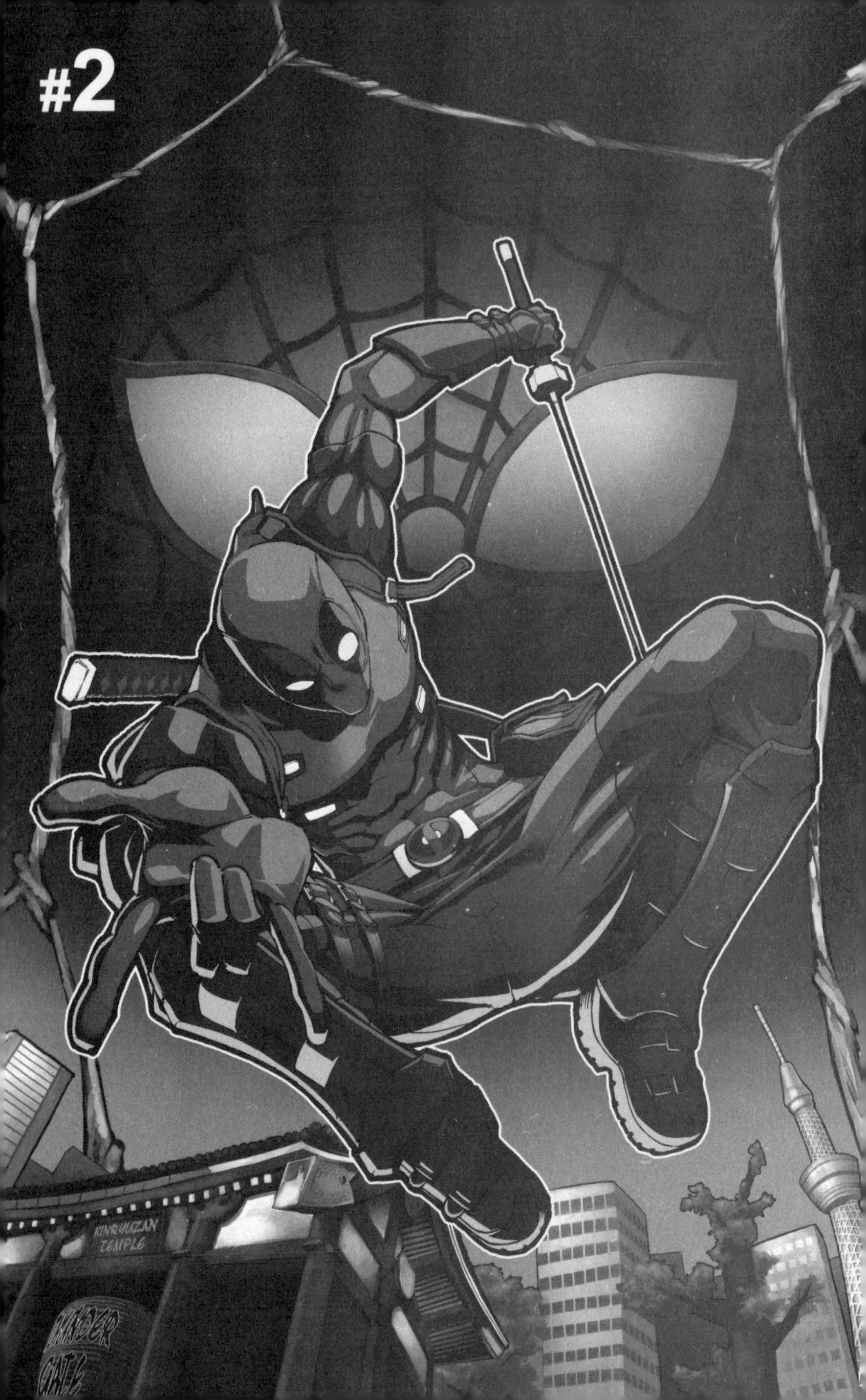
#2
KINRYUZAN
TEMPLE

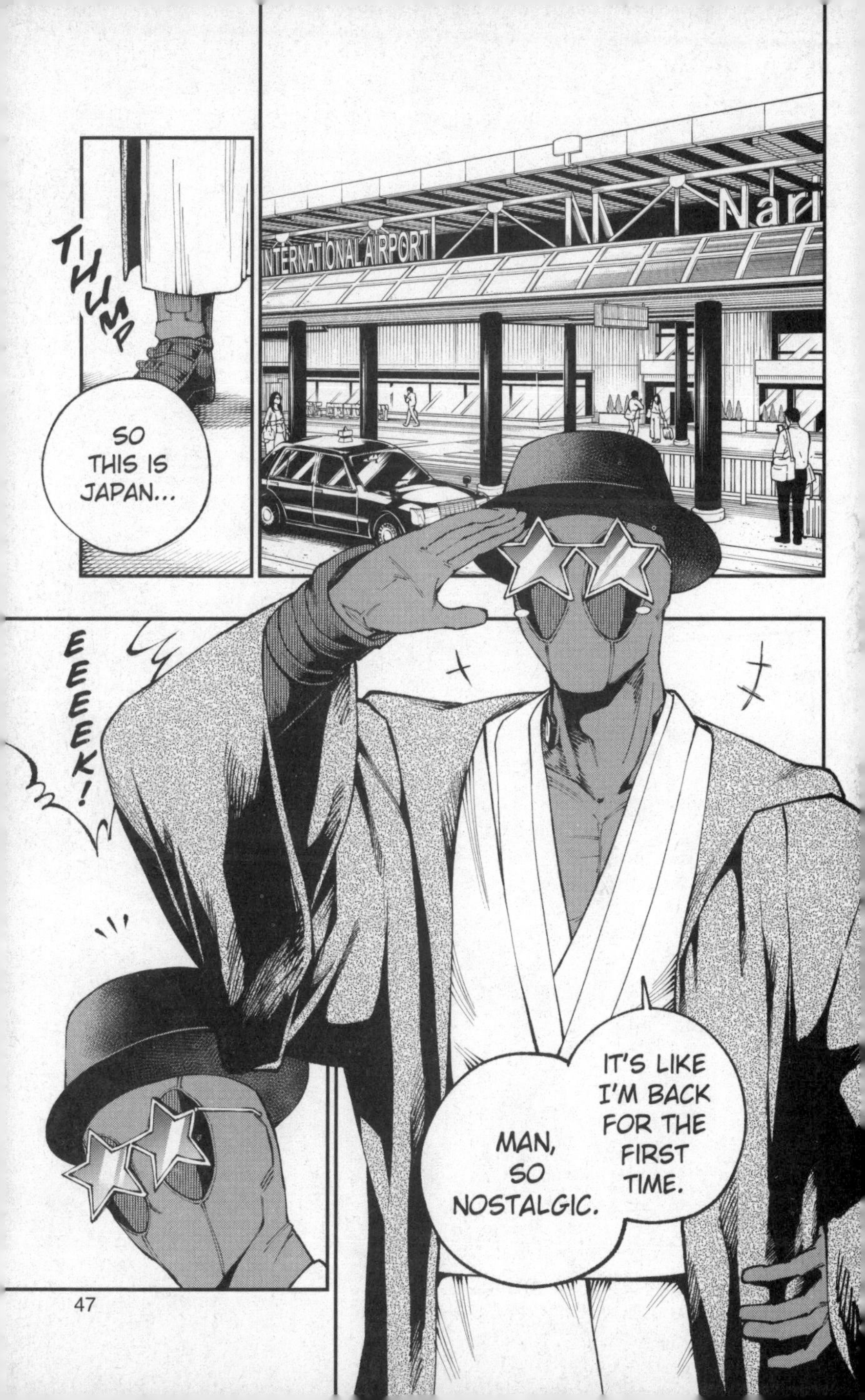
INTERNATIONAL AIRPORT
Nari
THUMP
SO THIS IS JAPAN...
IT'S LIKE I'M BACK FOR THE FIRST TIME.
MAN, SO NOSTALGIC.
EEEEEK!

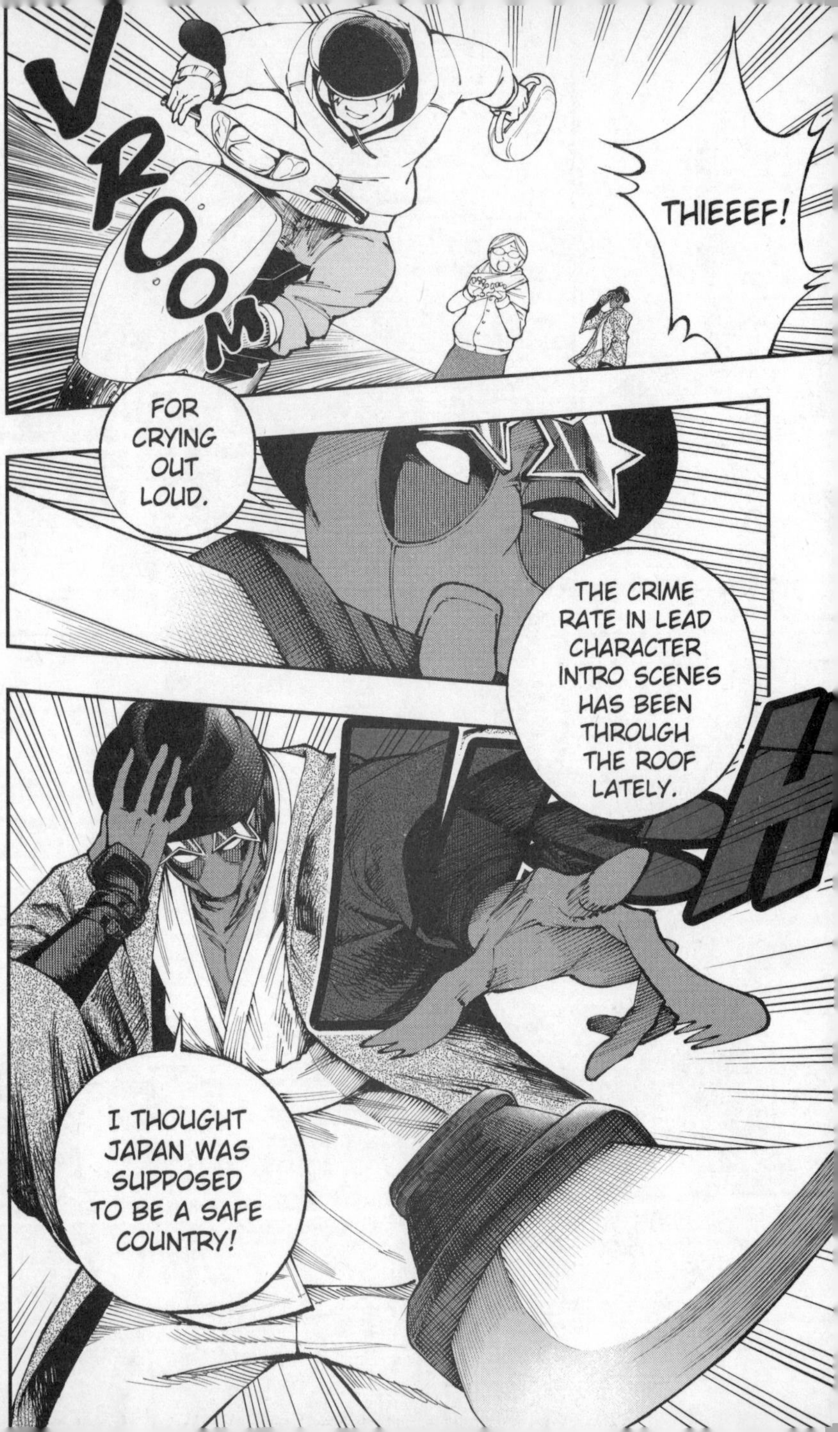
THIEEEF!
VROOM
FOR CRYING OUT LOUD.
THE CRIME RATE IN LEAD CHARACTER INTRO SCENES HAS BEEN THROUGH THE ROOF LATELY.
I THOUGHT JAPAN WAS SUPPOSED TO BE A SAFE COUNTRY!

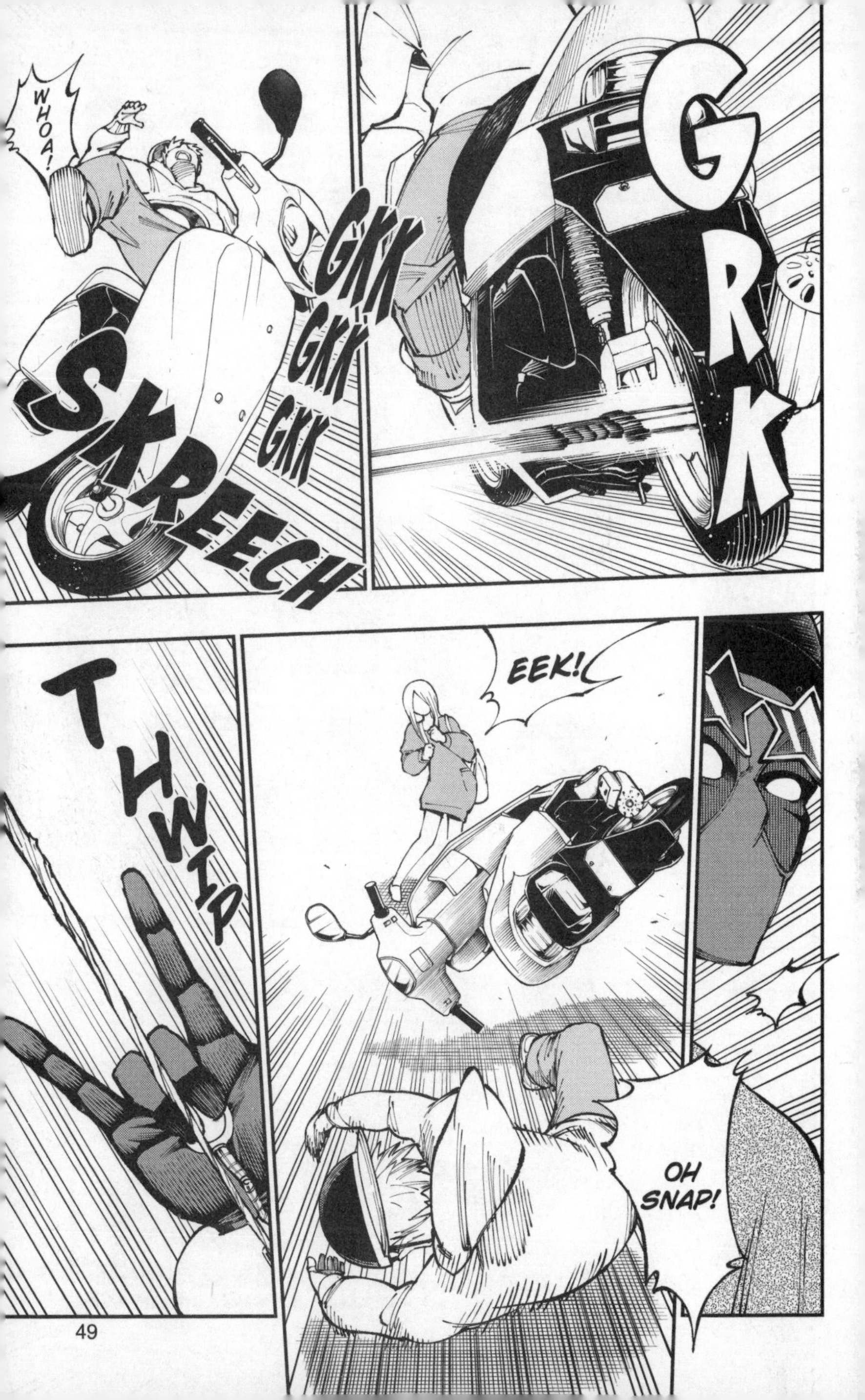
GRK
WHOA!
GKK GKK GKK
SKREECH
EEK!
OH SNAP!
THWIP

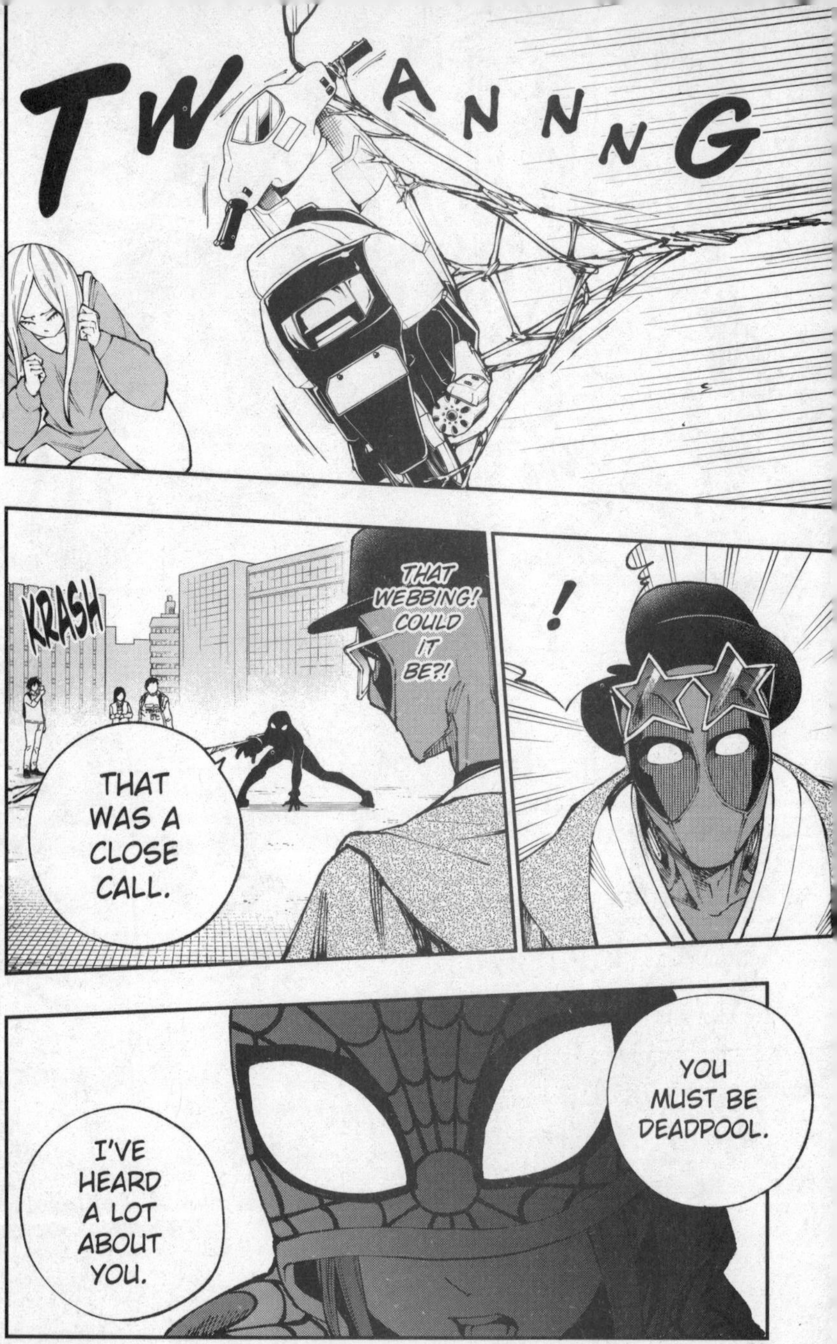
TWANNNG
!
THAT WEBBING! COULD IT BE?!
KRASH
THAT WAS A CLOSE CALL.
YOU MUST BE DEADPOOL.
I'VE HEARD A LOT ABOUT YOU.

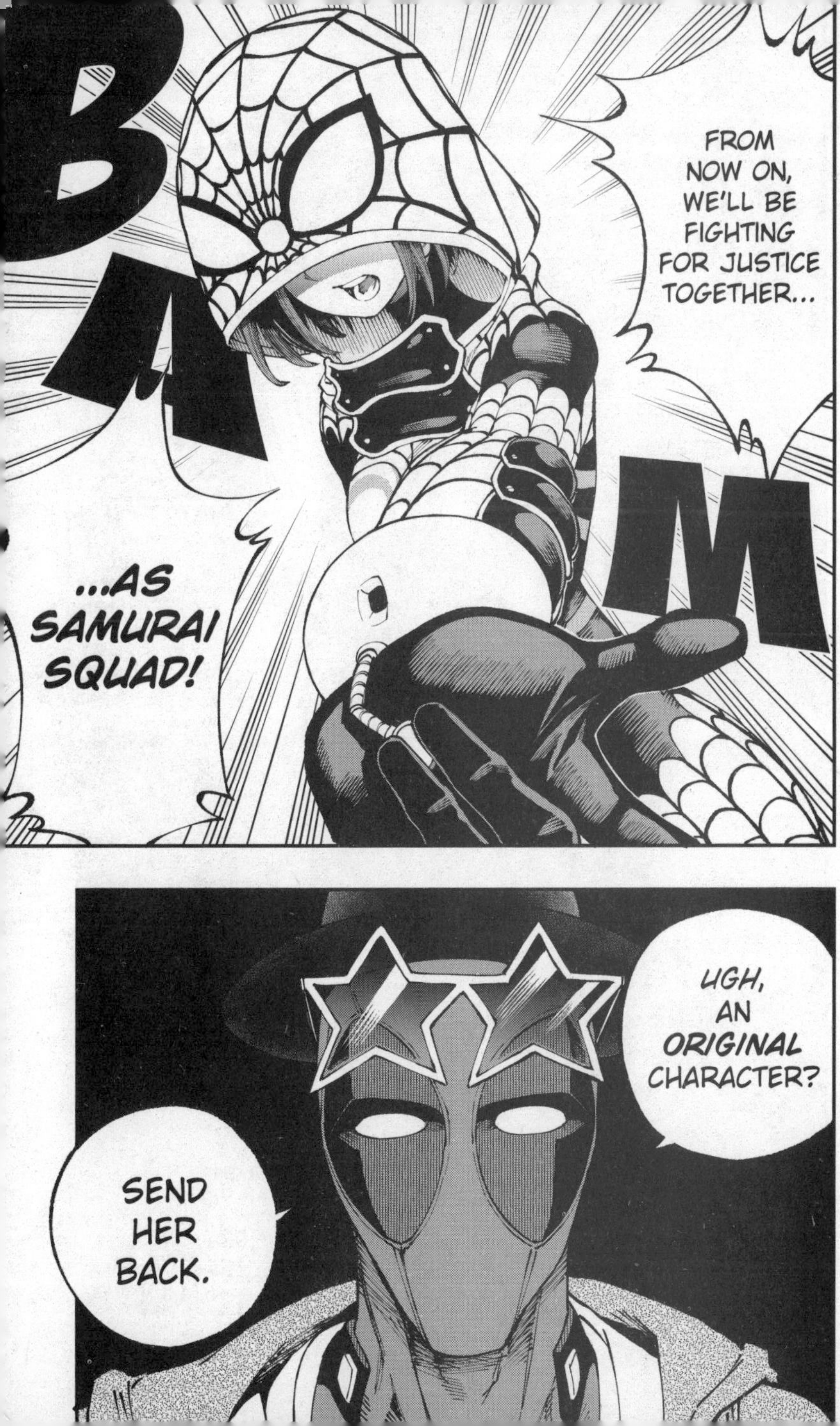
FROM NOW ON, WE'LL BE FIGHTING FOR JUSTICE TOGETHER...
BAM
...AS SAMURAI SQUAD!
UGH, AN ORIGINAL CHARACTER?
SEND HER BACK.

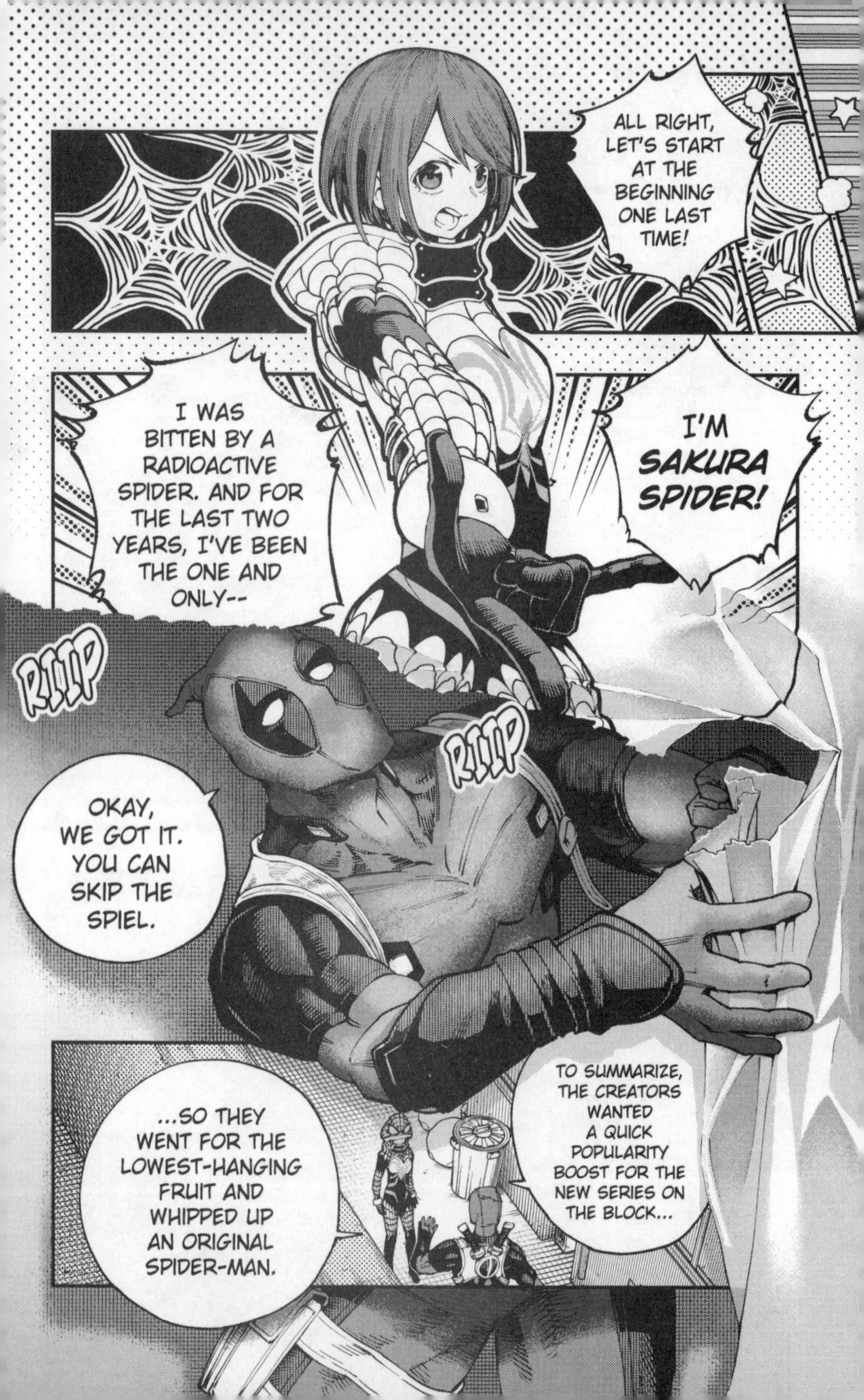
ALL RIGHT, LET'S START AT THE BEGINNING ONE LAST TIME!
I'M SAKURA SPIDER!
I WAS BITTEN BY A RADIOACTIVE SPIDER. AND FOR THE LAST TWO YEARS, I'VE BEEN THE ONE AND ONLY--
RIIIP
RIIIP
OKAY, WE GOT IT. YOU CAN SKIP THE SPIEL.
TO SUMMARIZE, THE CREATORS WANTED A QUICK POPULARITY BOOST FOR THE NEW SERIES ON THE BLOCK...
...SO THEY WENT FOR THE LOWEST-HANGING FRUIT AND WHIPPED UP AN ORIGINAL SPIDER-MAN.

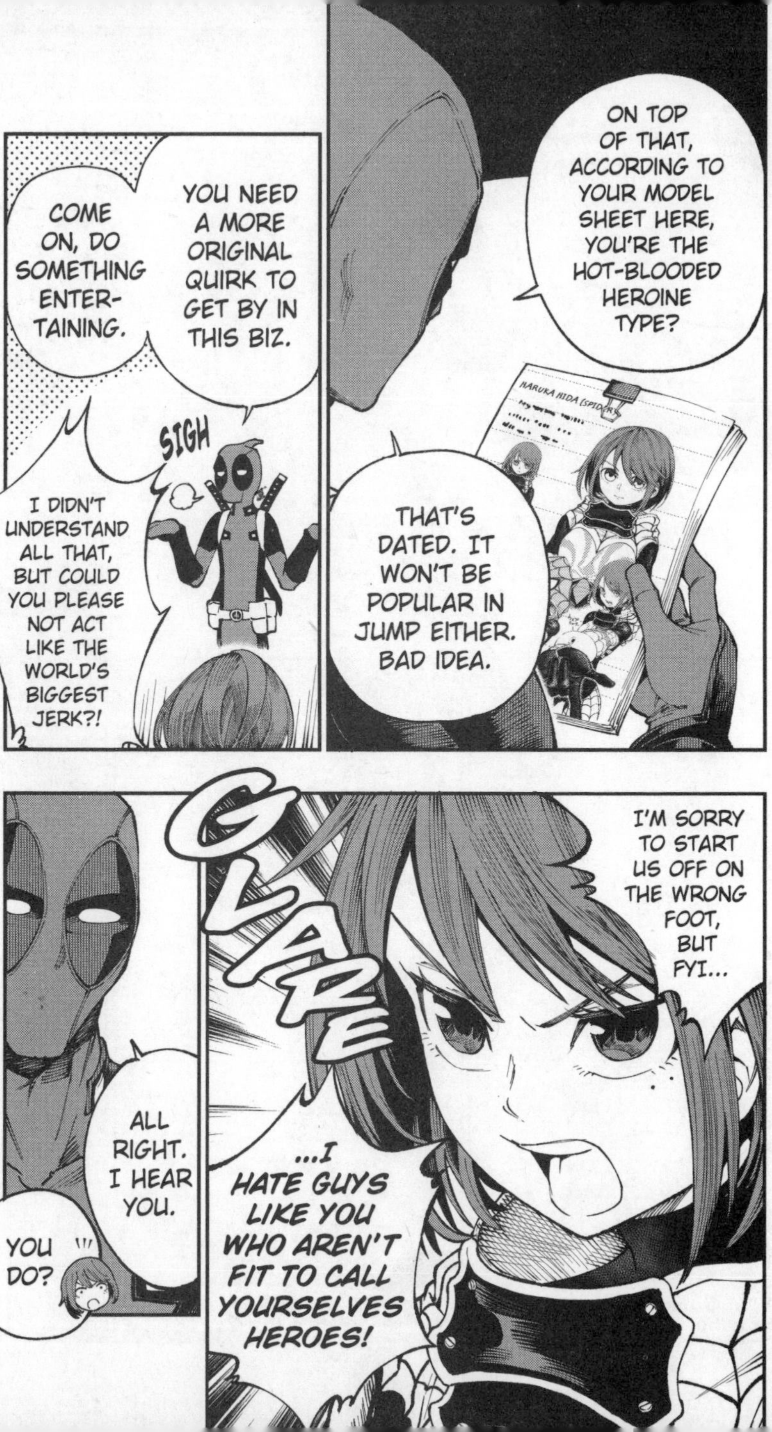
ON TOP OF THAT, ACCORDING TO YOUR MODEL SHEET HERE, YOU'RE THE HOT-BLOODED HEROINE TYPE?
HARUKA HIDA
THAT'S DATED. IT WON'T BE POPULAR IN JUMP EITHER. BAD IDEA.
YOU NEED A MORE ORIGINAL QUIRK TO GET BY IN THIS BIZ.
COME ON, DO SOMETHING ENTER-TAINING.
SIGH
I DIDN'T UNDERSTAND ALL THAT, BUT COULD YOU PLEASE NOT ACT LIKE THE WORLD'S BIGGEST JERK?!
GLARE
I'M SORRY TO START US OFF ON THE WRONG FOOT, BUT FYI...
...I HATE GUYS LIKE YOU WHO AREN'T FIT TO CALL YOURSELVES HEROES!
ALL RIGHT. I HEAR YOU.
YOU DO?

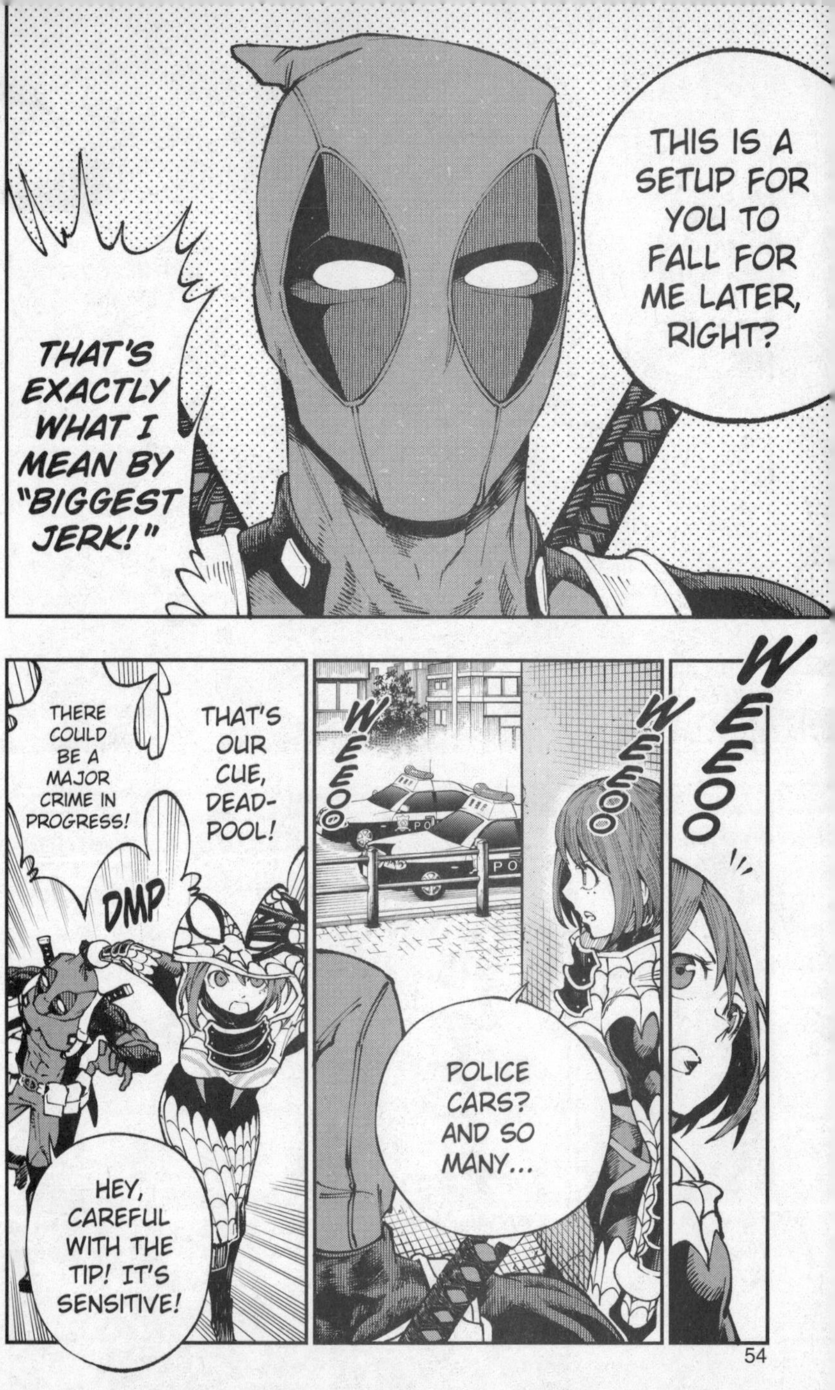
THIS IS A SETUP FOR YOU TO FALL FOR ME LATER, RIGHT?
THAT'S EXACTLY WHAT I MEAN BY "BIGGEST JERK!"
WEEEOO
WEEEOO
WEEEOO
POLICE CARS? AND SO MANY...
THAT'S OUR CUE, DEADPOOL!
THERE COULD BE A MAJOR CRIME IN PROGRESS!
DMP
HEY, CAREFUL WITH THE TIP! IT'S SENSITIVE!

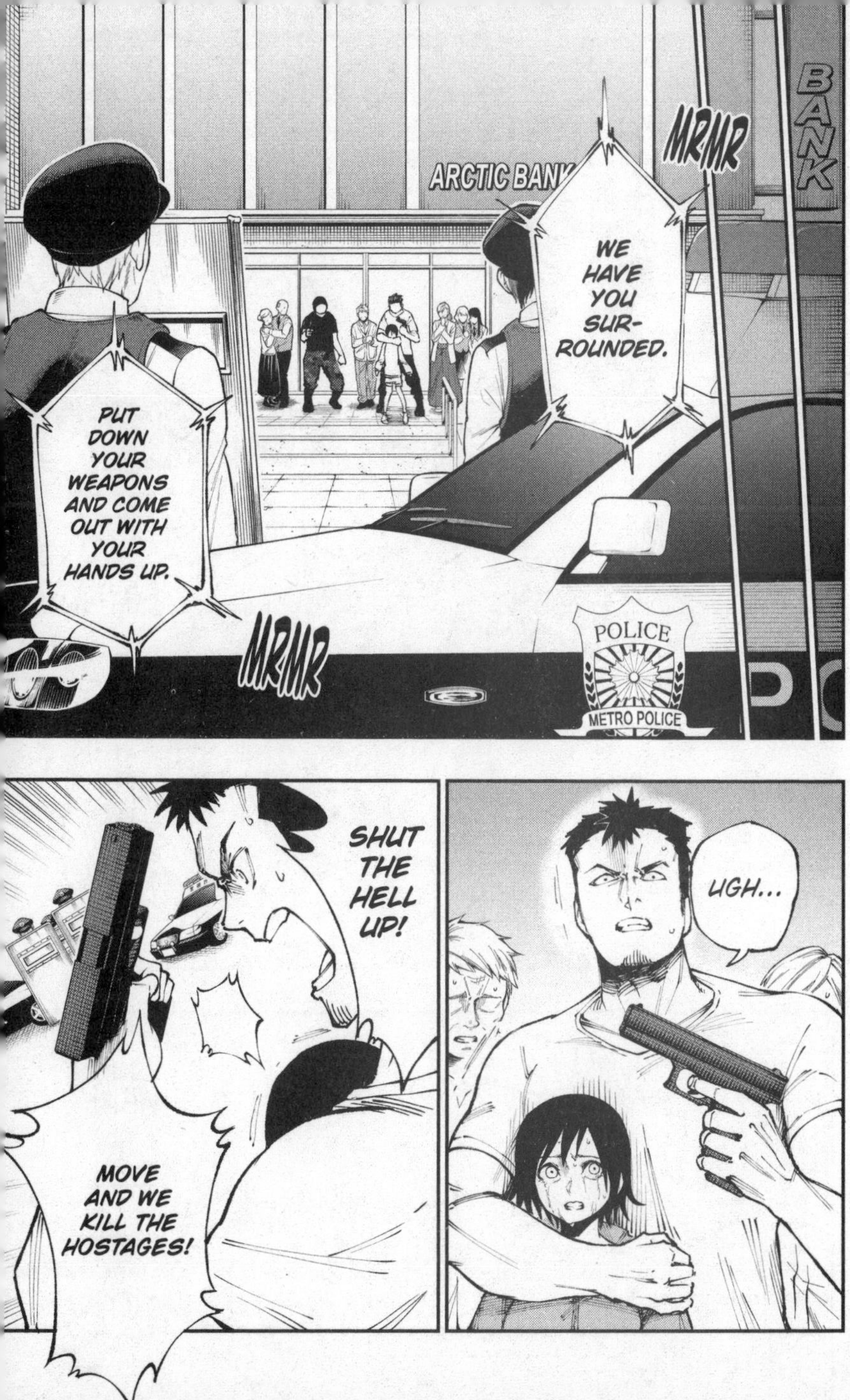
BANK
MRMR
ARCTIC BANK
WE HAVE YOU SUR-ROUNDED.
PUT DOWN YOUR WEAPONS AND COME OUT WITH YOUR HANDS UP.
MRMR
POLICE
METRO POLICE
UGH...
SHUT THE HELL UP!
MOVE AND WE KILL THE HOSTAGES!

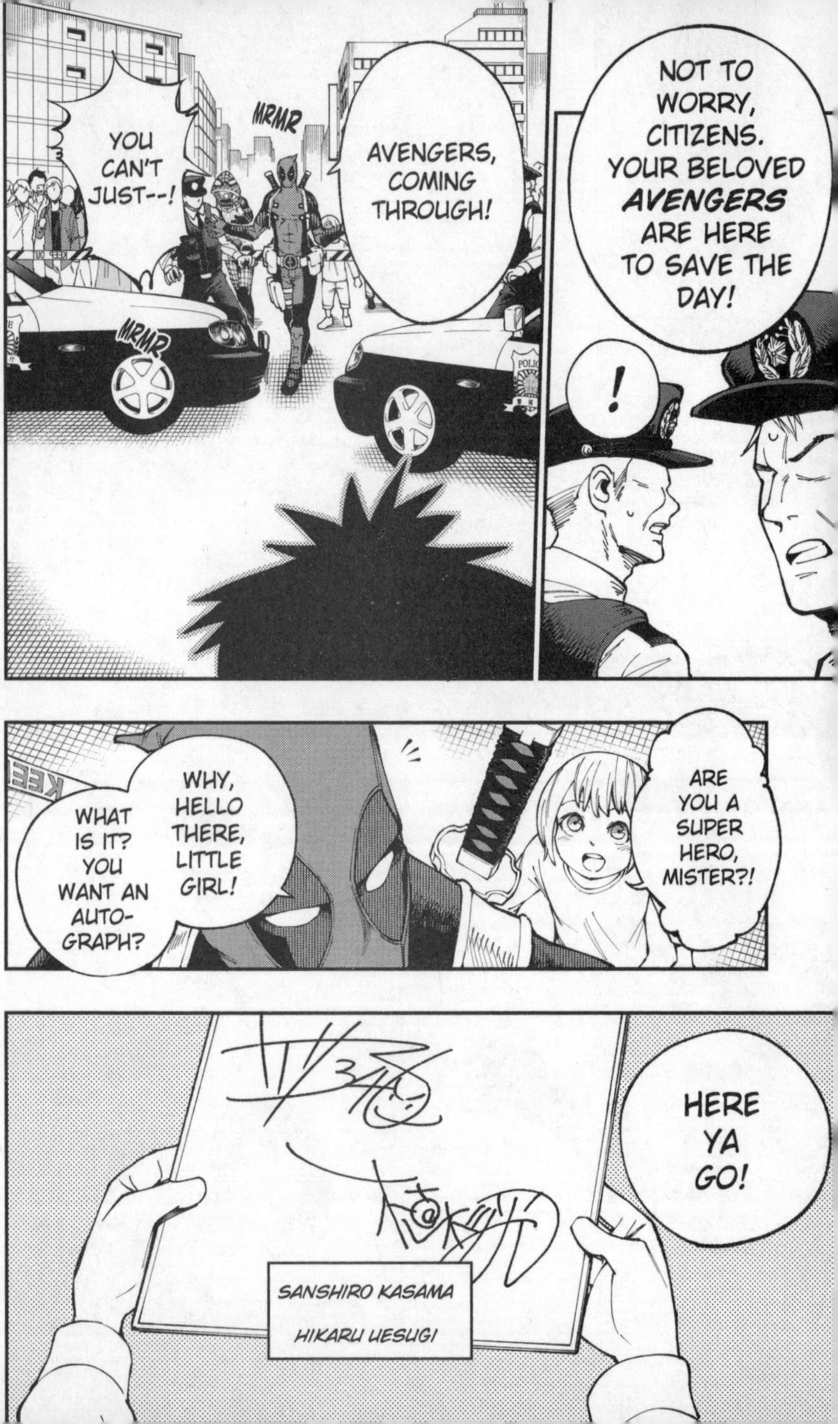
NOT TO WORRY, CITIZENS. YOUR BELOVED AVENGERS ARE HERE TO SAVE THE DAY!
!
AVENGERS, COMING THROUGH!
MRMR
YOU CAN'T JUST--!
MRMR
ARE YOU A SUPER HERO, MISTER?!
WHY, HELLO THERE, LITTLE GIRL!
WHAT IS IT? YOU WANT AN AUTO-GRAPH?
HERE YA GO!
SANSHIRO KASAMA
HIKARU UESUGI

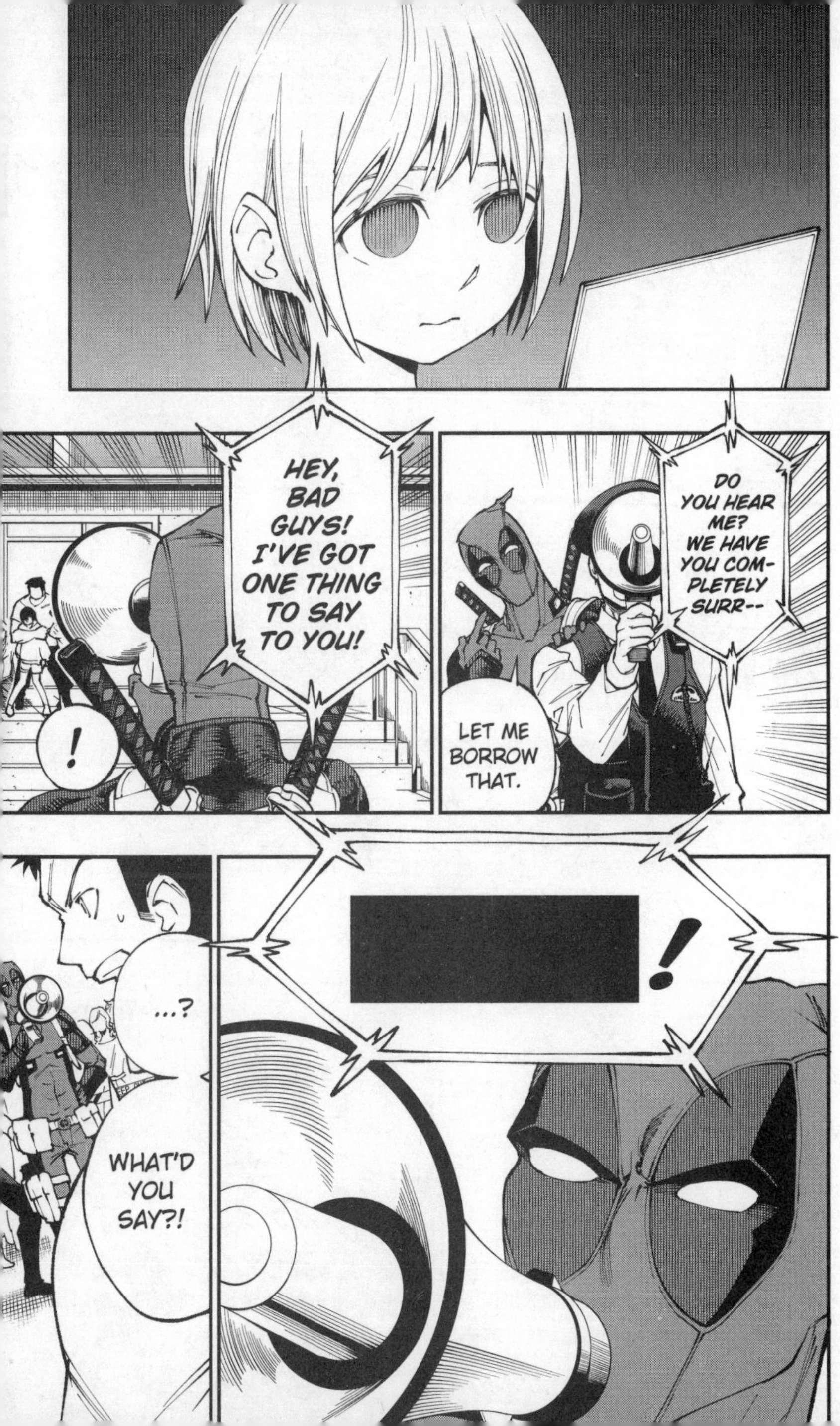
DO YOU HEAR ME? WE HAVE YOU COM-PLETELY SURR--
LET ME BORROW THAT.
HEY, BAD GUYS! I'VE GOT ONE THING TO SAY TO YOU!
!
[redacted] !
...?
WHAT'D YOU SAY?!

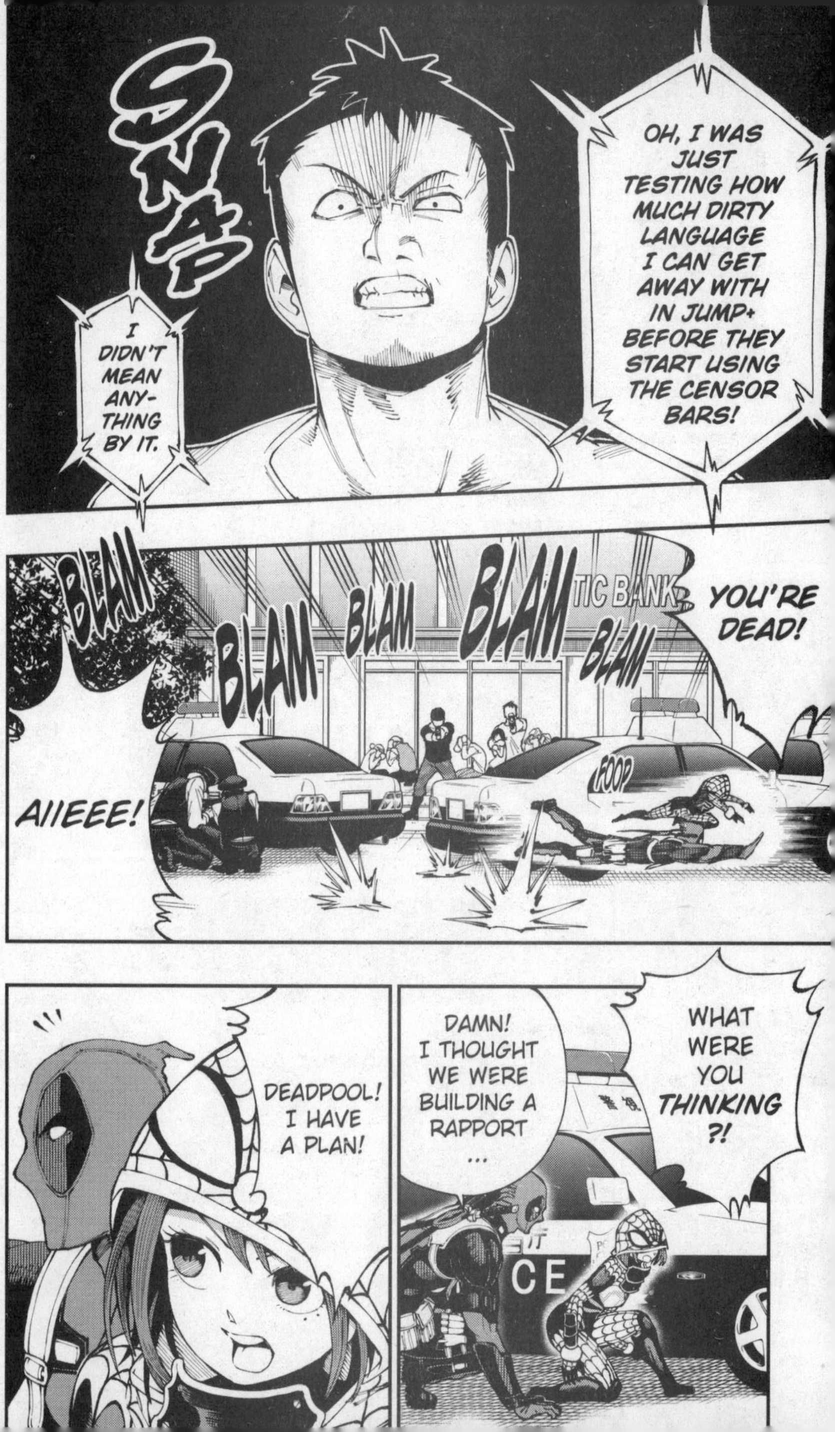
OH, I WAS JUST TESTING HOW MUCH DIRTY LANGUAGE I CAN GET AWAY WITH IN JUMP+ BEFORE THEY START USING THE CENSOR BARS!
SNAP
I DIDN'T MEAN ANY-THING BY IT.
YOU'RE DEAD!
TIC BANK
BLAM
BLAM
BLAM
BLAM
BLAM
BLAM
FOOP
AIIEEE!
WHAT WERE YOU THINKING?!
DAMN! I THOUGHT WE WERE BUILDING A RAPPORT...
CE
DEADPOOL! I HAVE A PLAN!

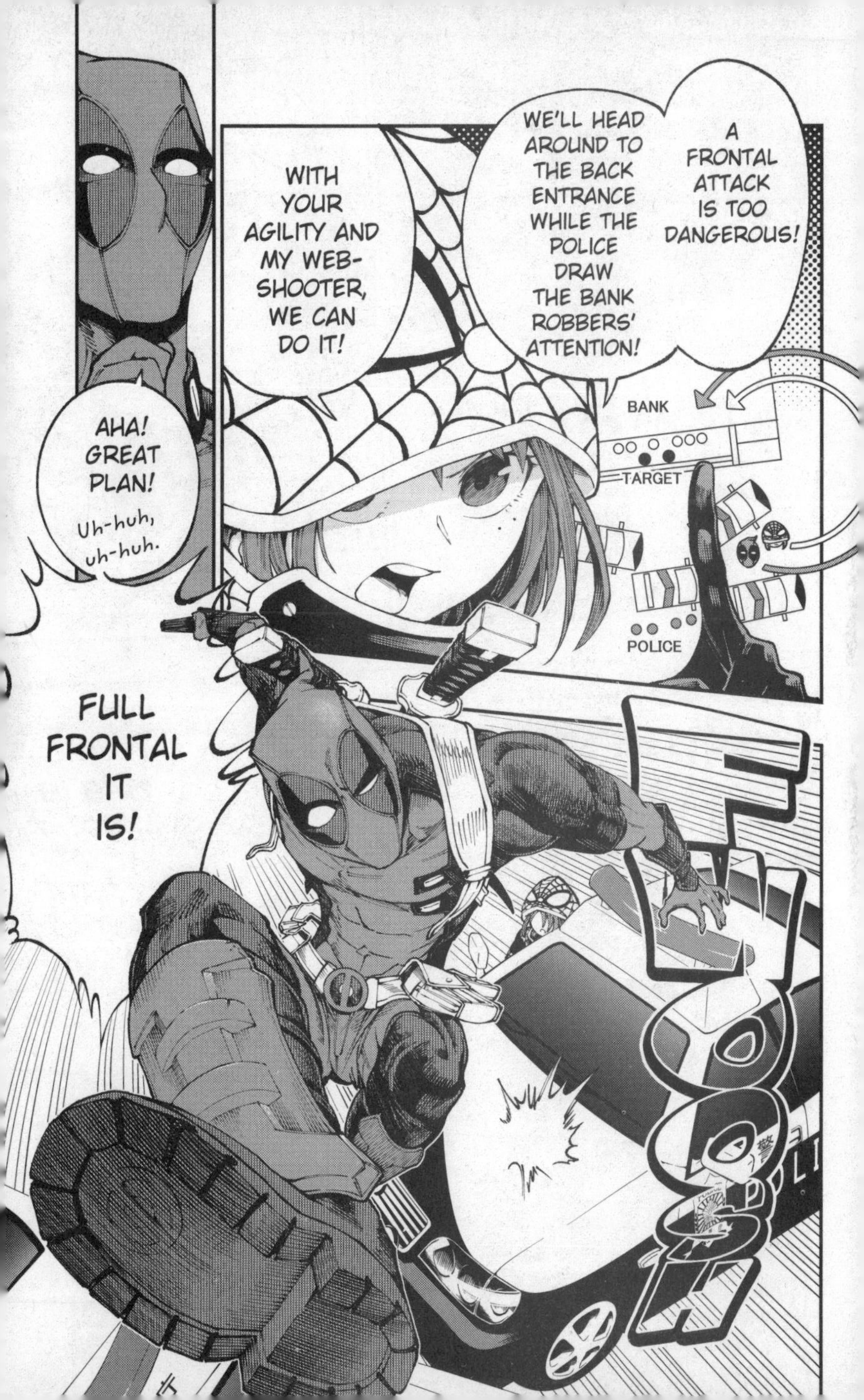
A FRONTAL ATTACK IS TOO DANGEROUS!
WE'LL HEAD AROUND TO THE BACK ENTRANCE WHILE THE POLICE DRAW THE BANK ROBBERS' ATTENTION!
WITH YOUR AGILITY AND MY WEB-SHOOTER, WE CAN DO IT!
BANK
TARGET
POLICE
AHA! GREAT PLAN!
Uh-huh, uh-huh.
FULL FRONTAL IT IS!

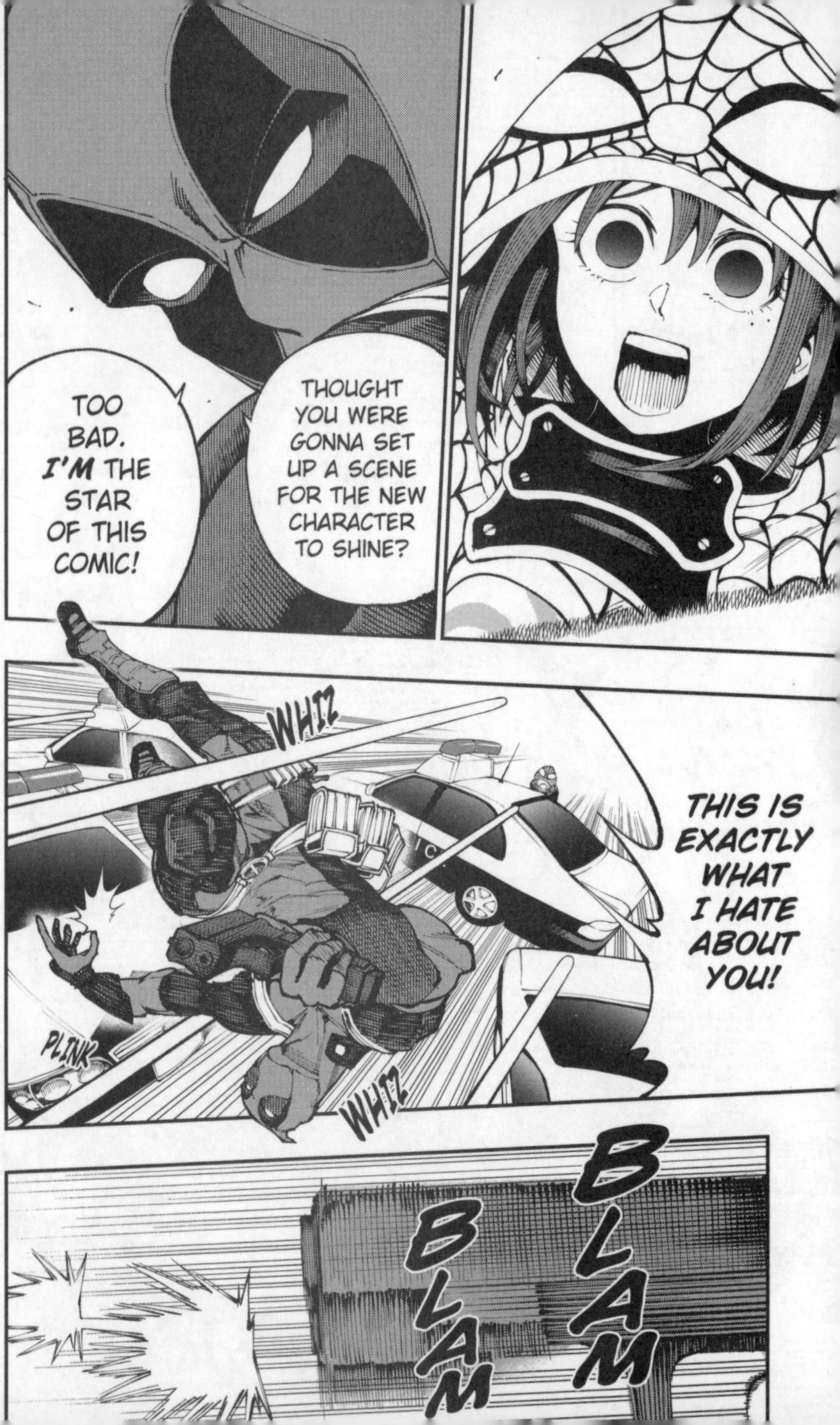
THOUGHT YOU WERE GONNA SET UP A SCENE FOR THE NEW CHARACTER TO SHINE?
TOO BAD. *I'M* THE STAR OF THIS COMIC!
THIS IS EXACTLY WHAT I HATE ABOUT YOU!
WHIZ
PLINK
WHIZ
BLAM
BLAM

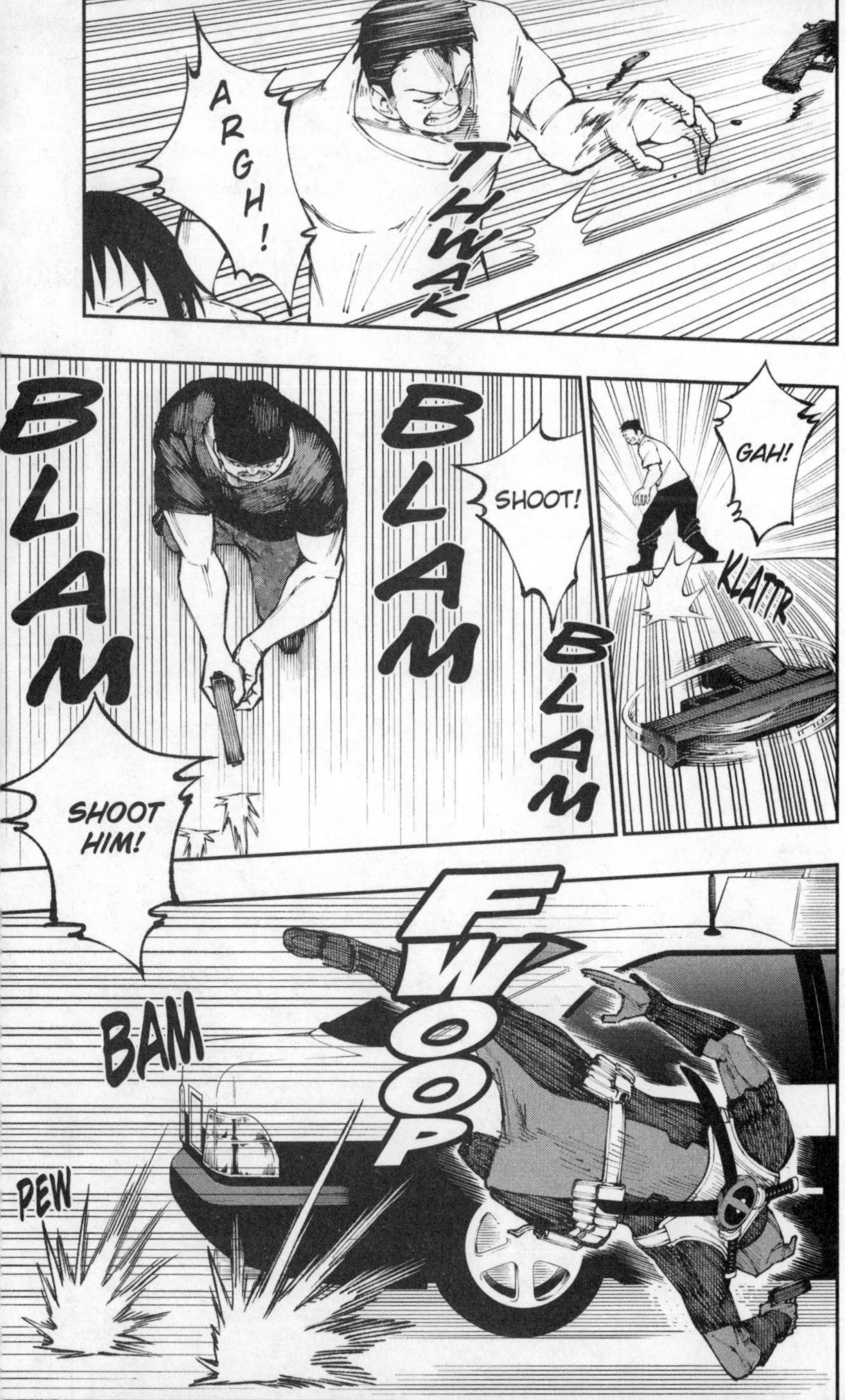
ARGH!
THWAK
GAH!
KLATTR
SHOOT!
BLAM
BLAM
BLAM
SHOOT HIM!
FWOOP
BAM
PEW

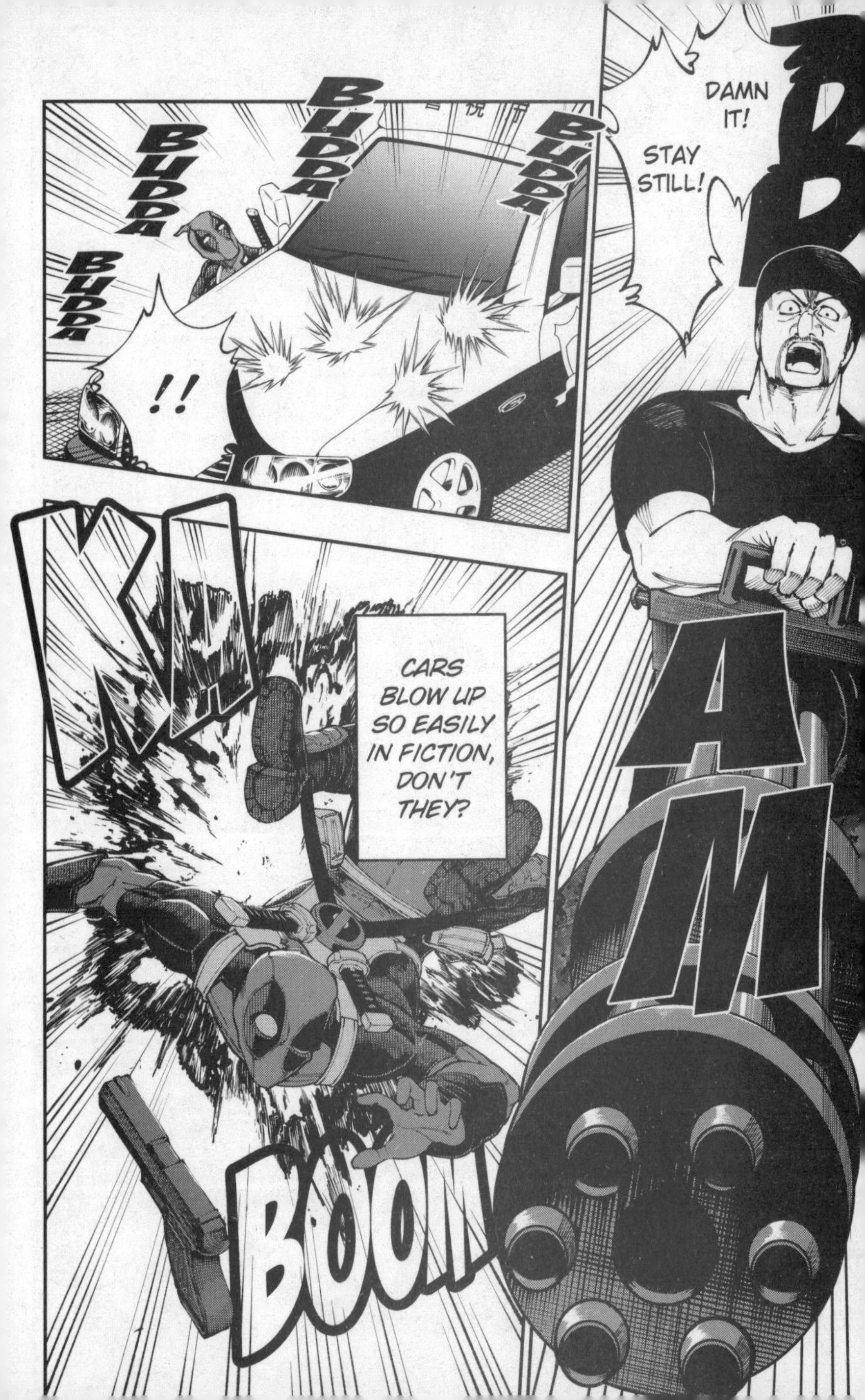
DAMN IT!
STAY STILL!
BUDDA
BUDDA
BUDDA
BUDDA
!!
CARS BLOW UP SO EASILY IN FICTION, DON'T THEY?
BOOM

BUDDA BUDDA BUDDA BUDDA

EAT THIS!

YOU'RE COMPLETELY EXPOSED.

YOU PERVERT! ♡

AH! DEAD-POOL, LOOK OUT!

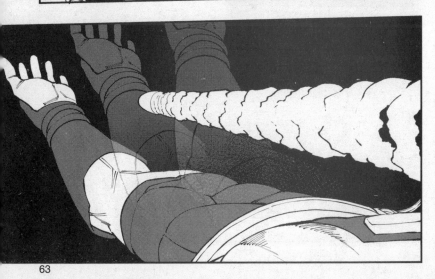

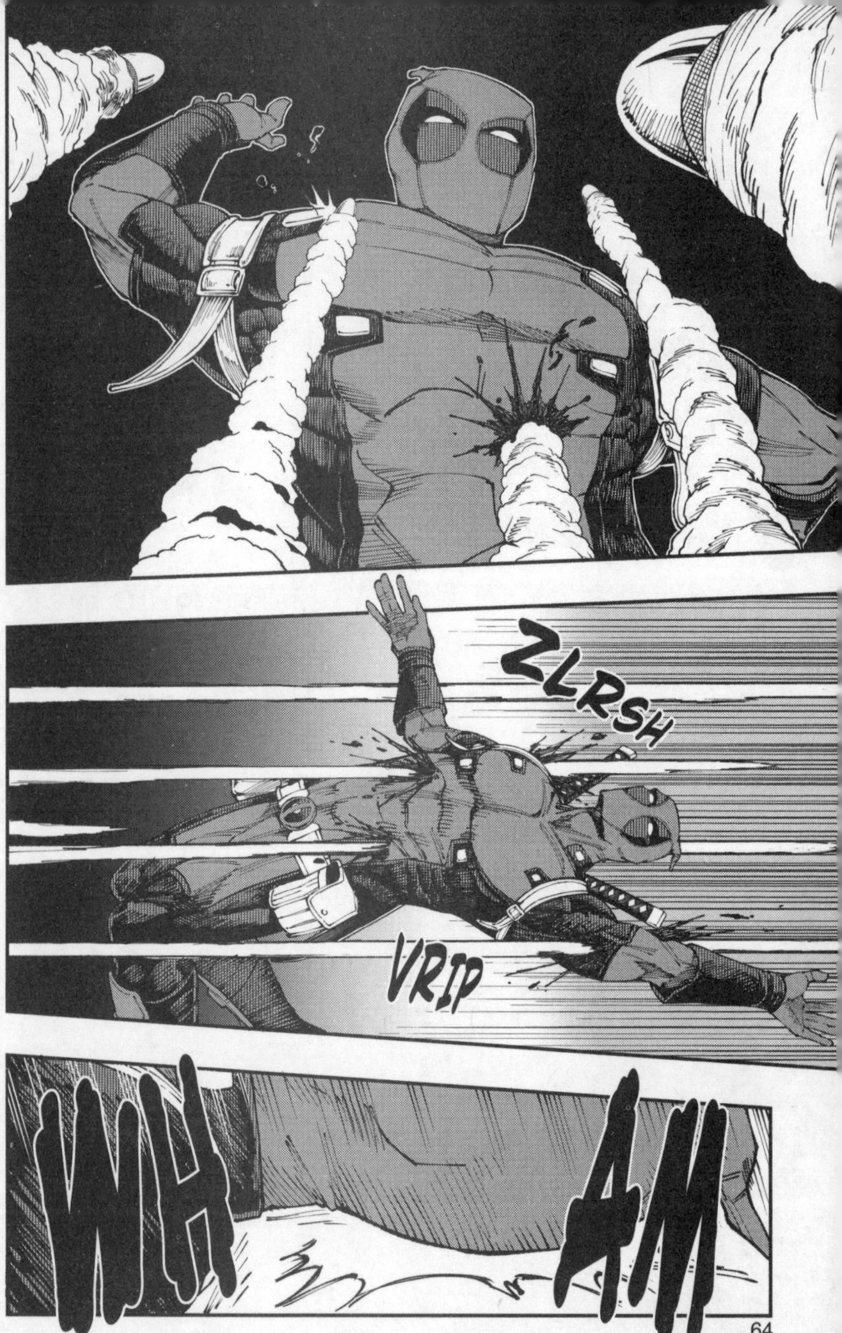
ZLRSH
VRIP
WHAM

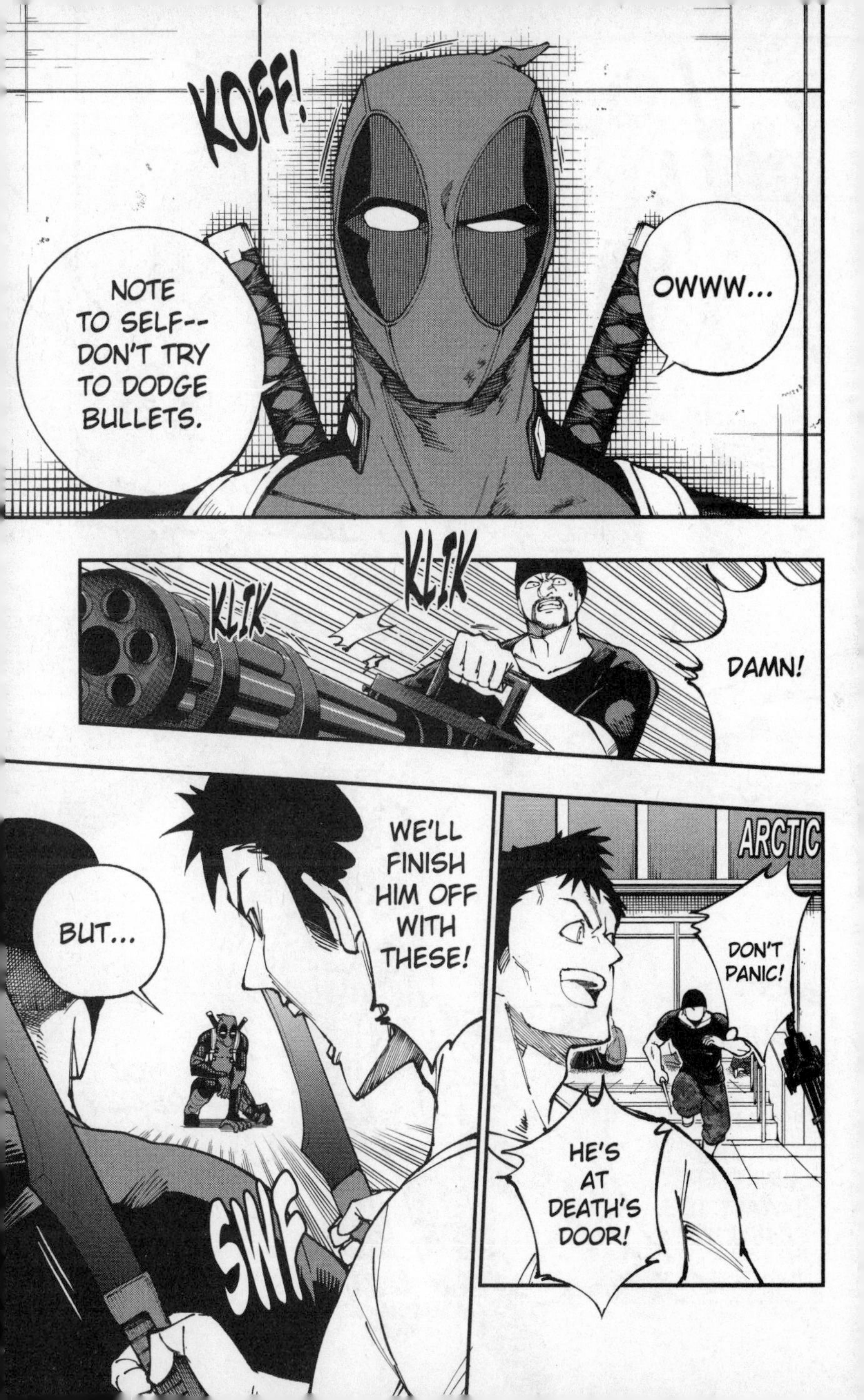
KOFF!
OWWW...
NOTE TO SELF-- DON'T TRY TO DODGE BULLETS.
KLIK
KLIK
DAMN!
ARCTIC
DON'T PANIC!
HE'S AT DEATH'S DOOR!
WE'LL FINISH HIM OFF WITH THESE!
BUT...
SWF

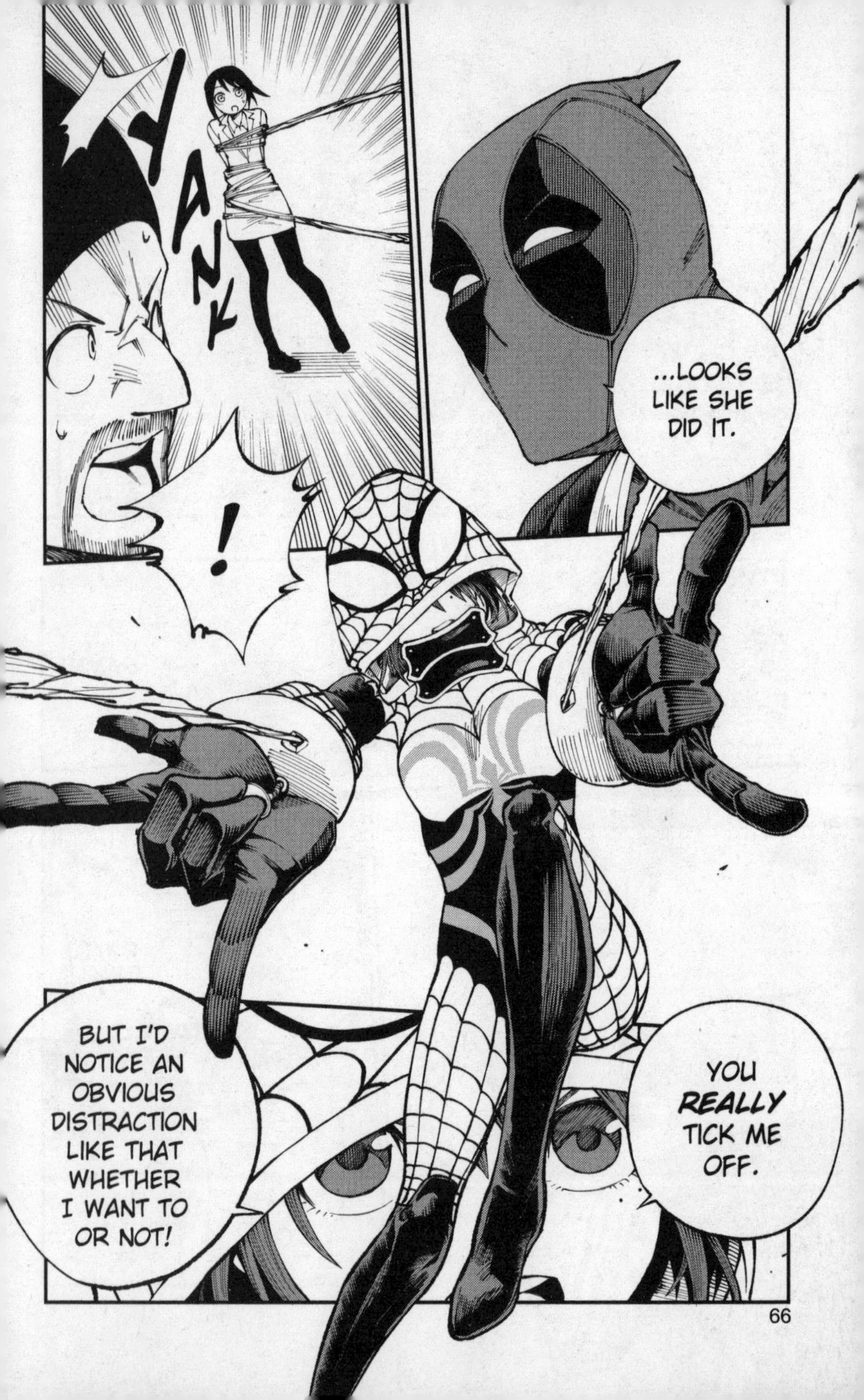
...LOOKS LIKE SHE DID IT.
YANK
!
YOU *REALLY* TICK ME OFF.
BUT I'D NOTICE AN OBVIOUS DISTRACTION LIKE THAT WHETHER I WANT TO OR NOT!

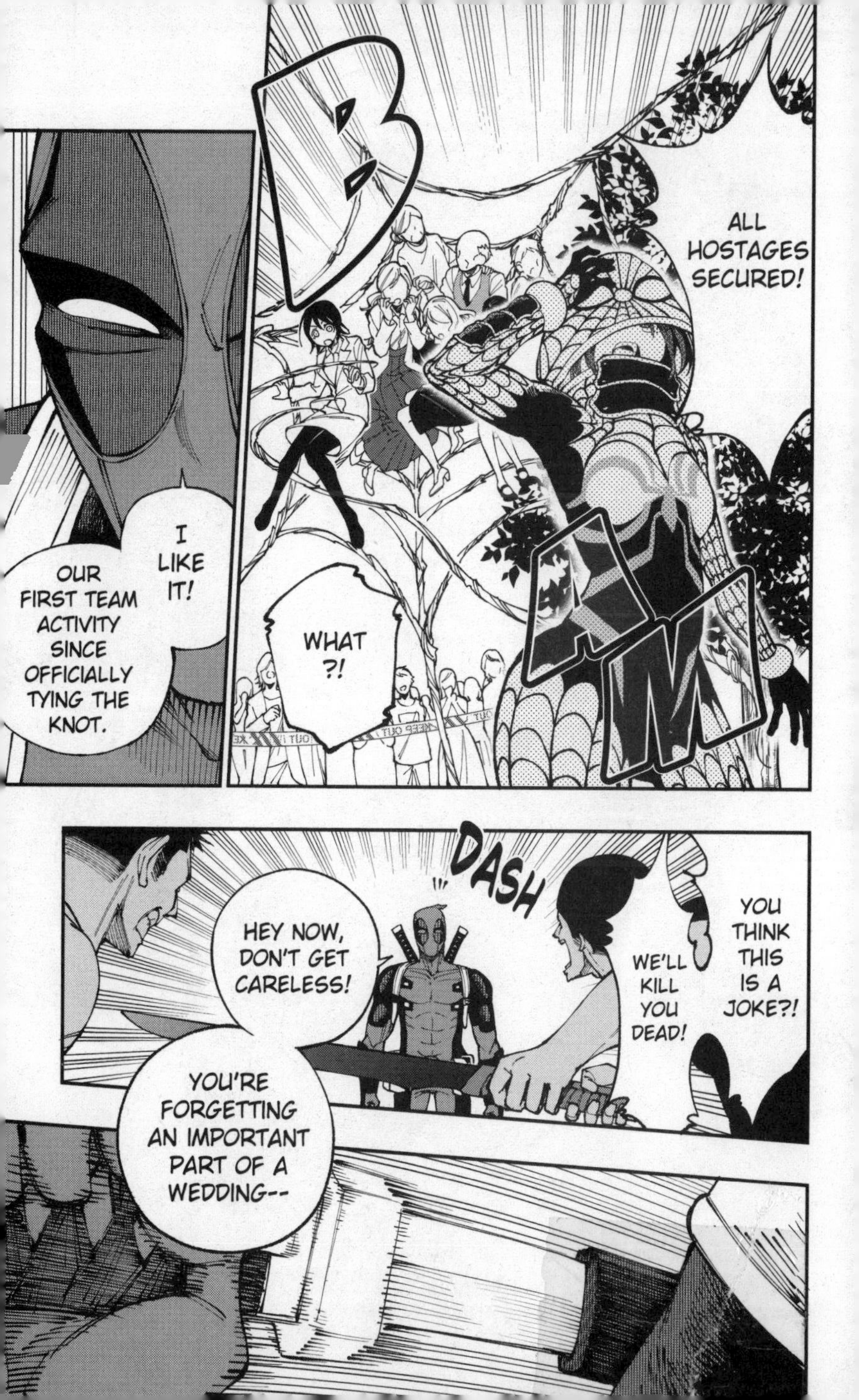

ALL HOSTAGES SECURED!
WHAT?!
I LIKE IT!
OUR FIRST TEAM ACTIVITY SINCE OFFICIALLY TYING THE KNOT.
YOU THINK THIS IS A JOKE?!
WE'LL KILL YOU DEAD!
DASH
HEY NOW, DON'T GET CARELESS!
YOU'RE FORGETTING AN IMPORTANT PART OF A WEDDING--

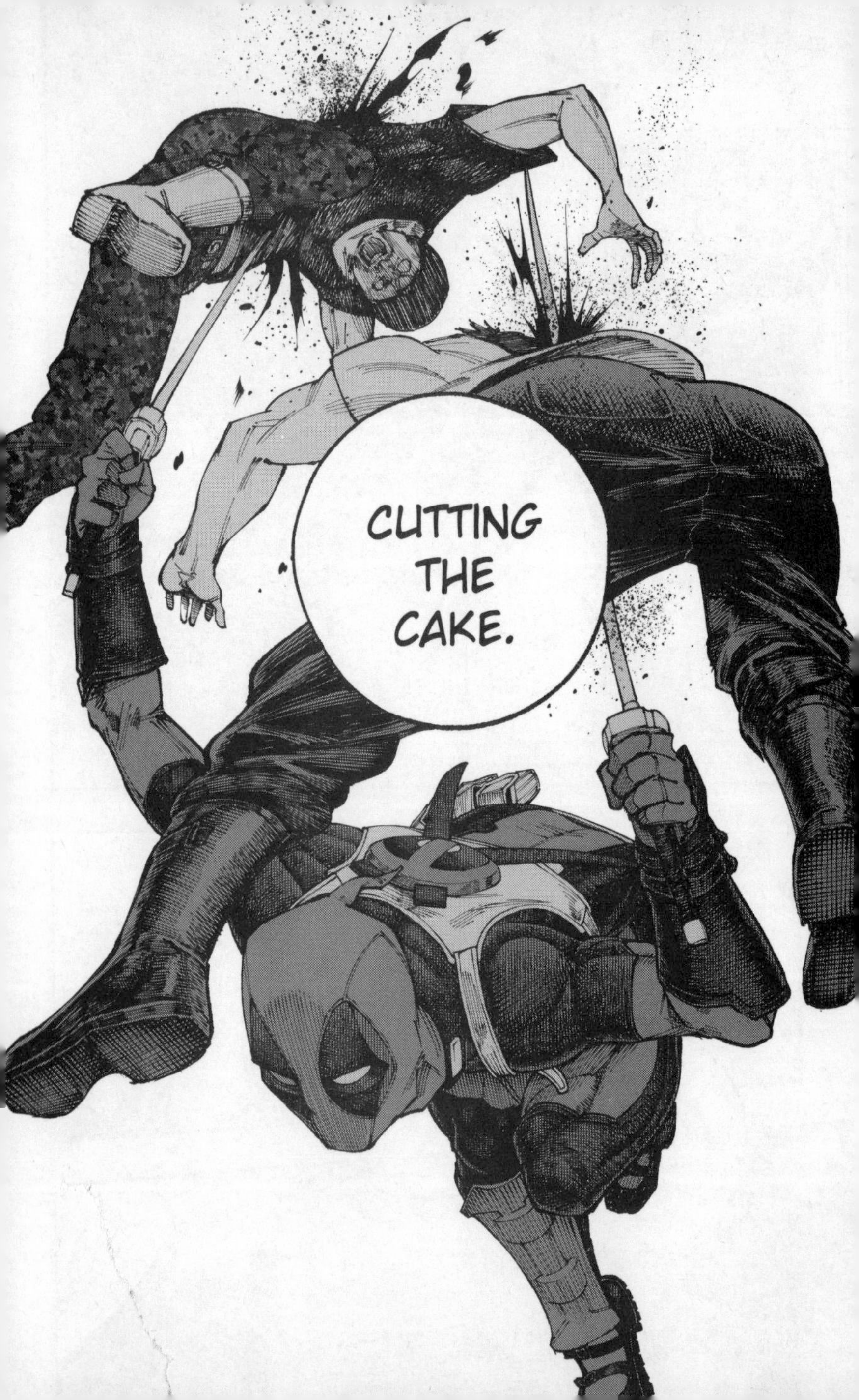
CUTTING THE CAKE.

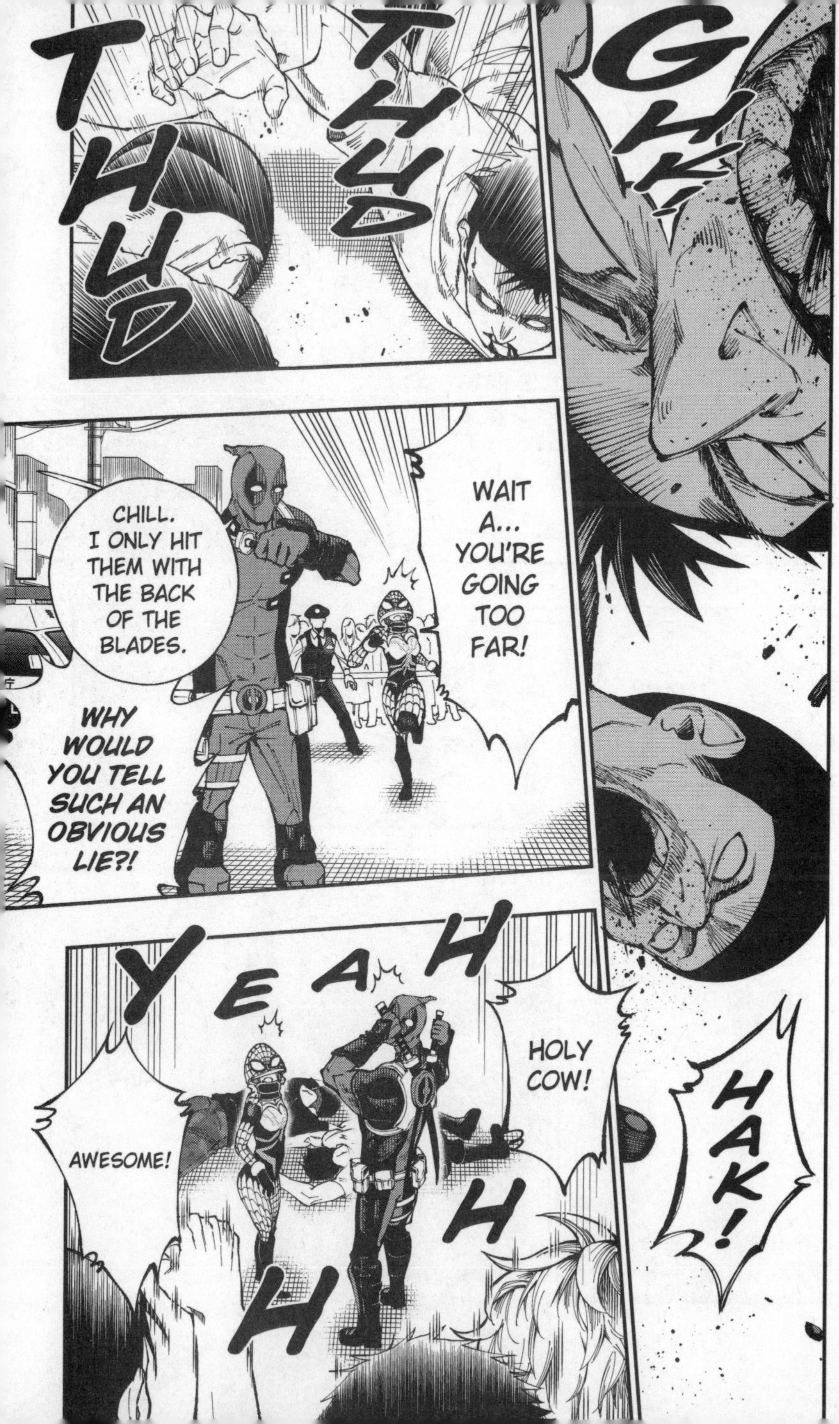
GHK!
THUD
THUD
WAIT A... YOU'RE GOING TOO FAR!
CHILL. I ONLY HIT THEM WITH THE BACK OF THE BLADES.
WHY WOULD YOU TELL SUCH AN OBVIOUS LIE?!
HAK!
YEAHHH
HOLY COW!
AWESOME!

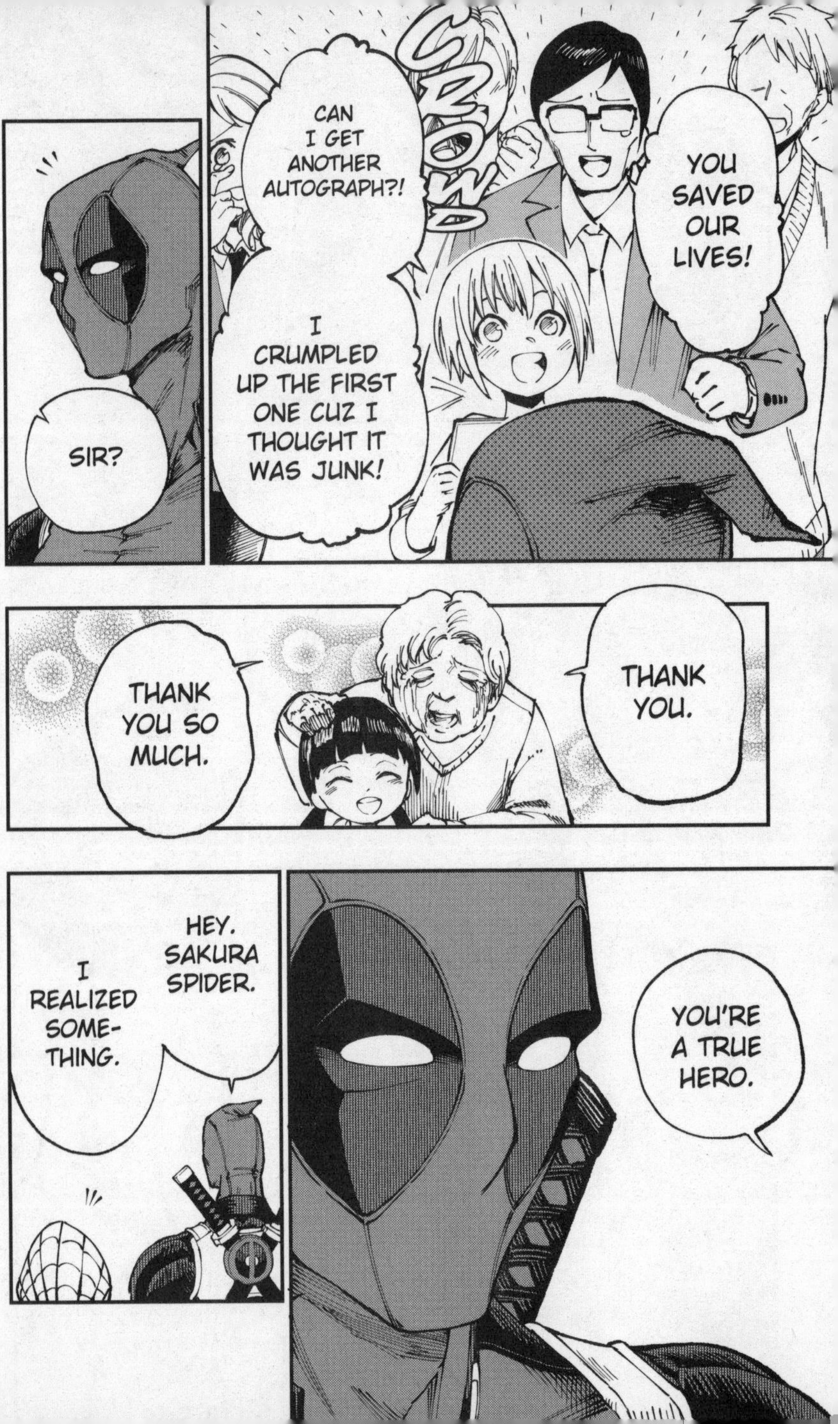
YOU SAVED OUR LIVES!
CROWD
CAN I GET ANOTHER AUTOGRAPH?!
I CRUMPLED UP THE FIRST ONE CUZ I THOUGHT IT WAS JUNK!
SIR?
THANK YOU.
THANK YOU SO MUCH.
YOU'RE A TRUE HERO.
HEY. SAKURA SPIDER.
I REALIZED SOME-THING.

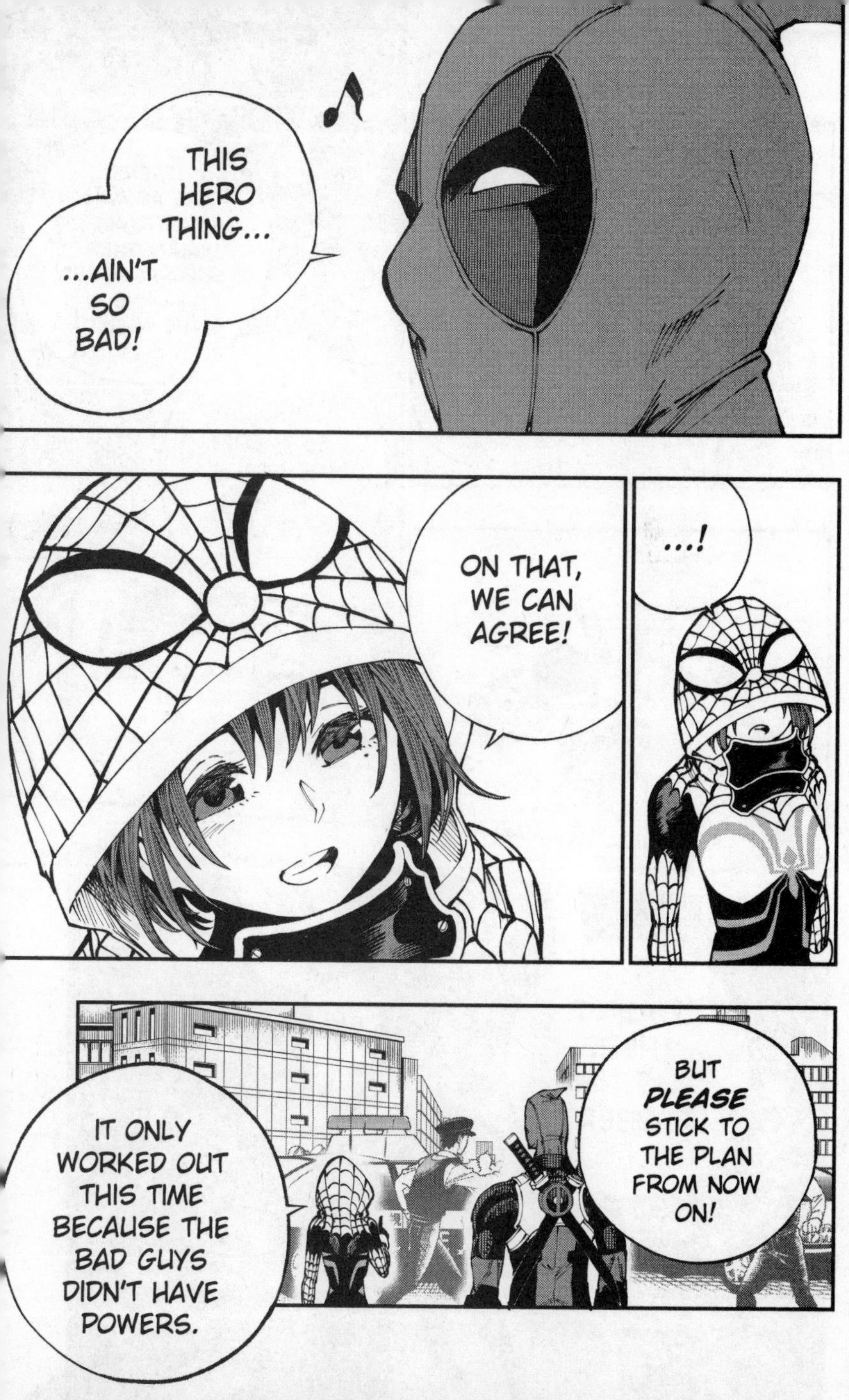

THIS HERO THING...
...AIN'T SO BAD!
...!
ON THAT, WE CAN AGREE!
BUT *PLEASE* STICK TO THE PLAN FROM NOW ON!
IT ONLY WORKED OUT THIS TIME BECAUSE THE BAD GUYS DIDN'T HAVE POWERS.

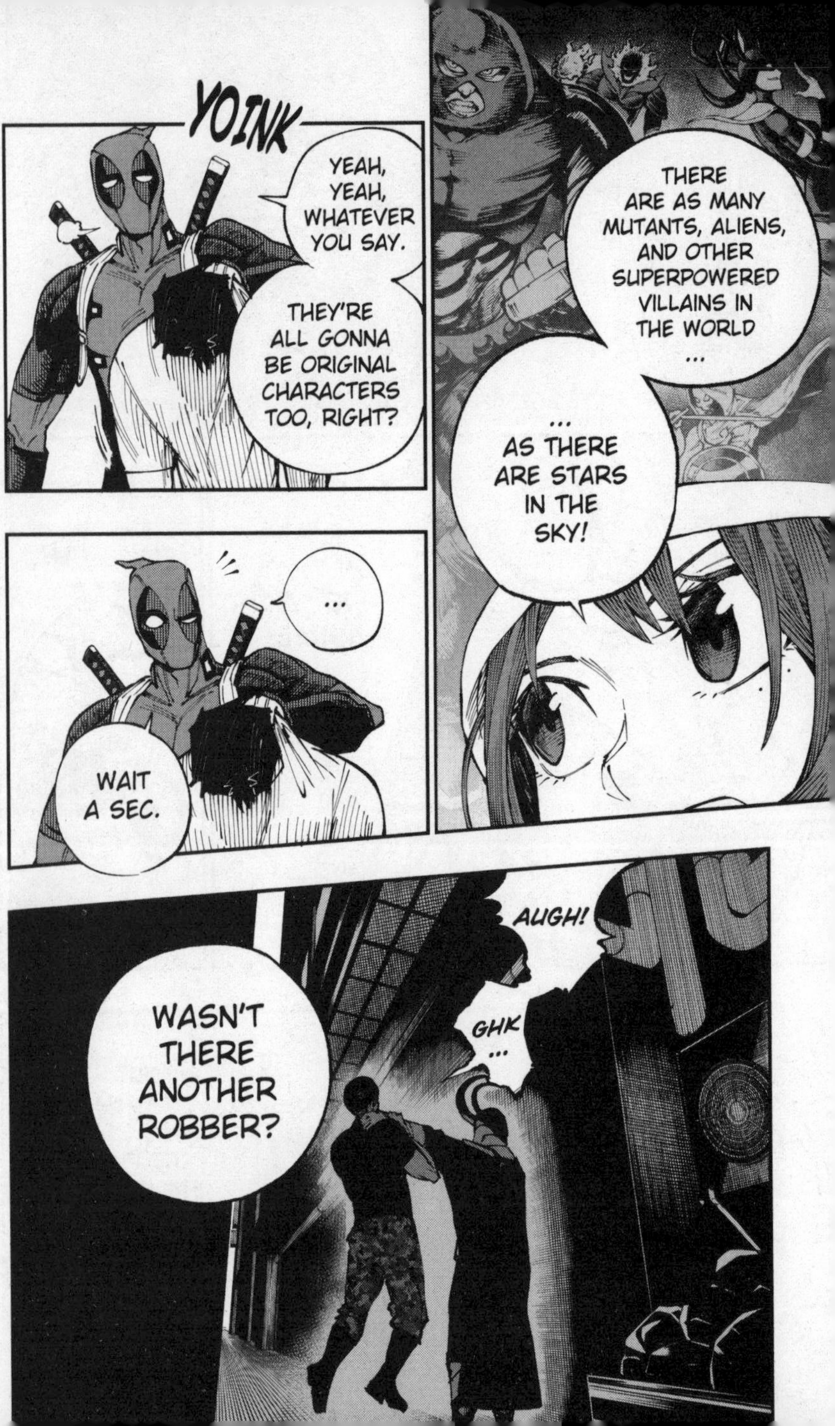
THERE ARE AS MANY MUTANTS, ALIENS, AND OTHER SUPERPOWERED VILLAINS IN THE WORLD ...
... AS THERE ARE STARS IN THE SKY!
YOINK
YEAH, YEAH, WHATEVER YOU SAY.
THEY'RE ALL GONNA BE ORIGINAL CHARACTERS TOO, RIGHT?
...
WAIT A SEC.
AUGH!
GHK ...
WASN'T THERE ANOTHER ROBBER?

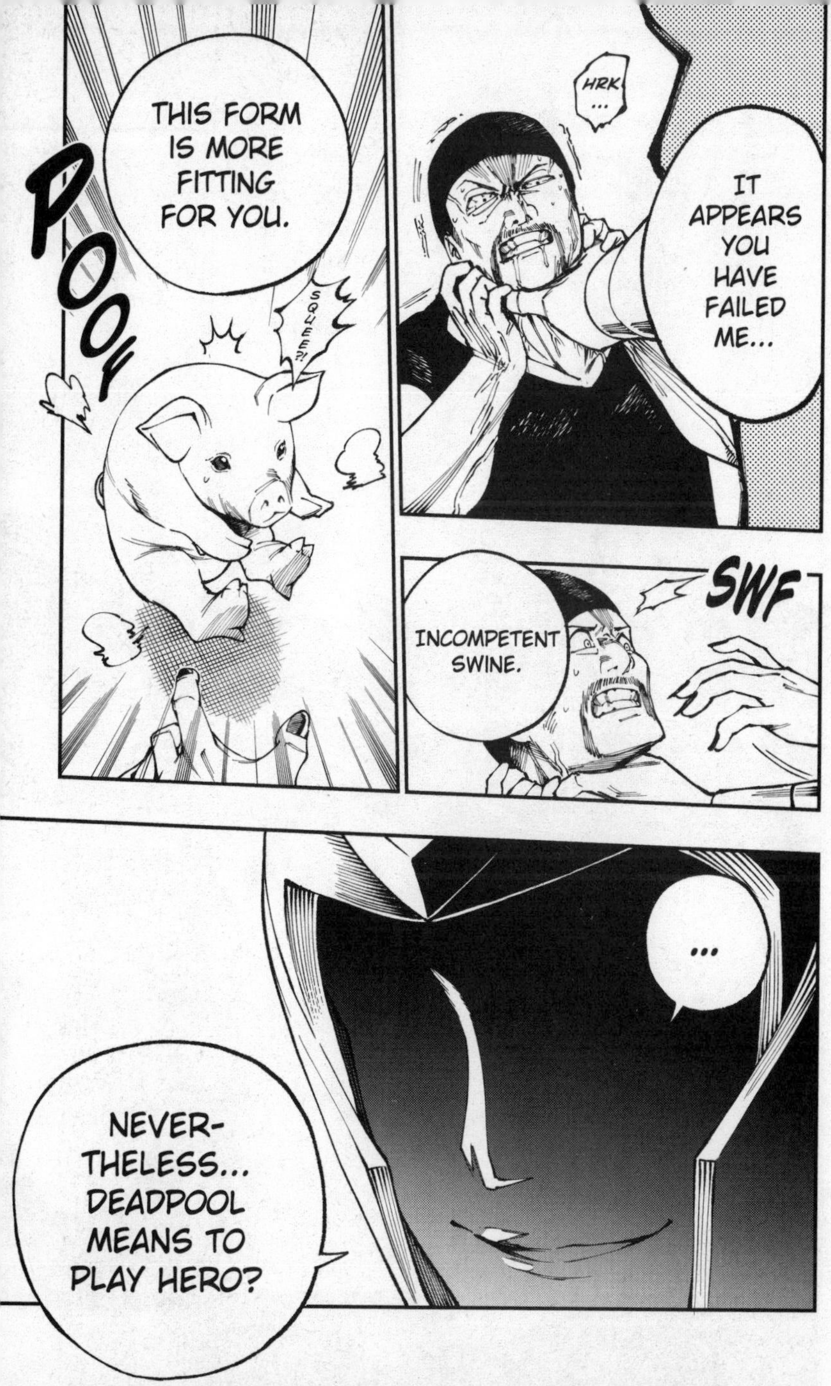
HRK...
IT APPEARS YOU HAVE FAILED ME...
SWF
INCOMPETENT SWINE.
POOF
THIS FORM IS MORE FITTING FOR YOU.
SQUEEE?!
...
NEVER-THELESS... DEADPOOL MEANS TO PLAY HERO?

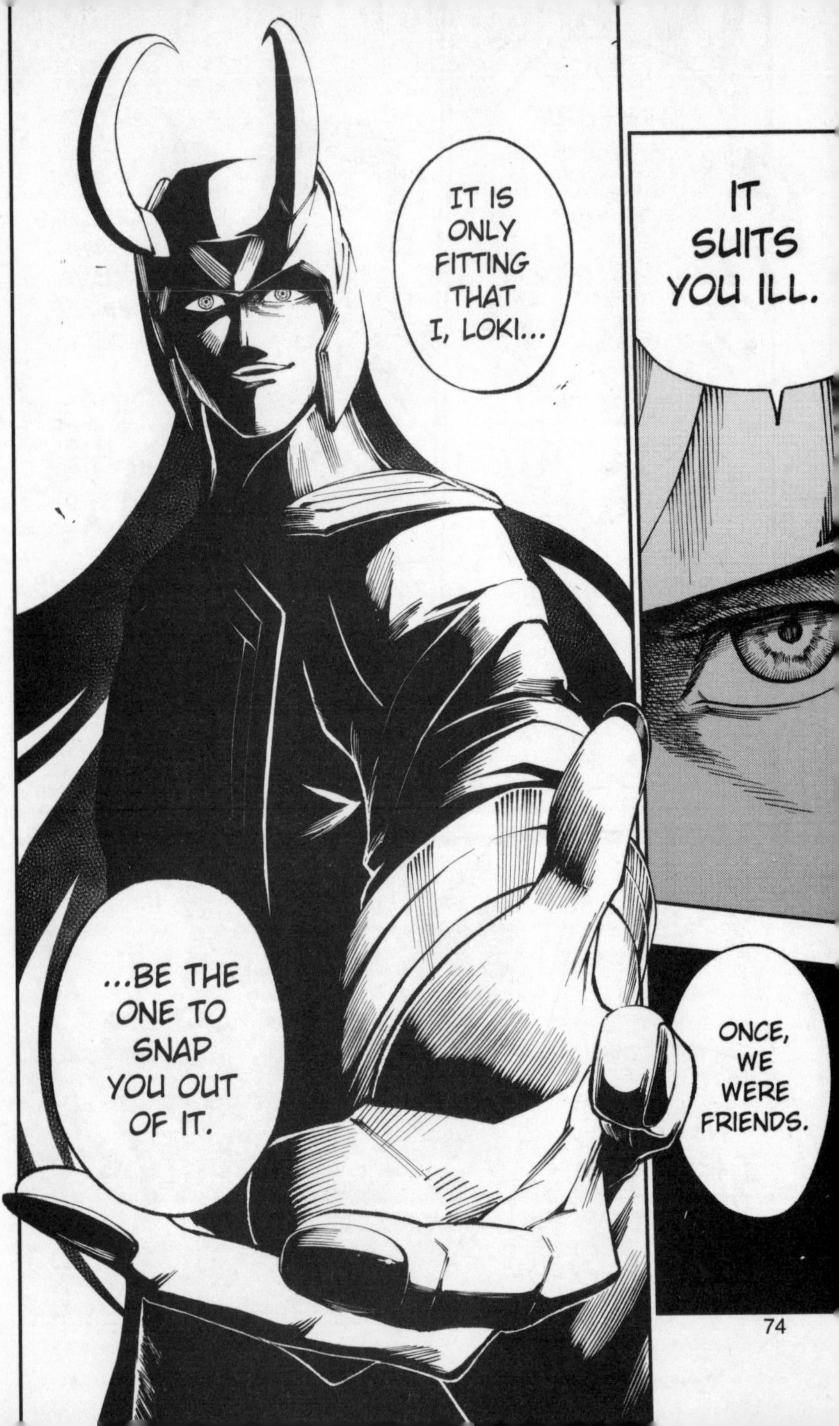
IT SUITS YOU ILL.
ONCE, WE WERE FRIENDS.
IT IS ONLY FITTING THAT I, LOKI...
...BE THE ONE TO SNAP YOU OUT OF IT.

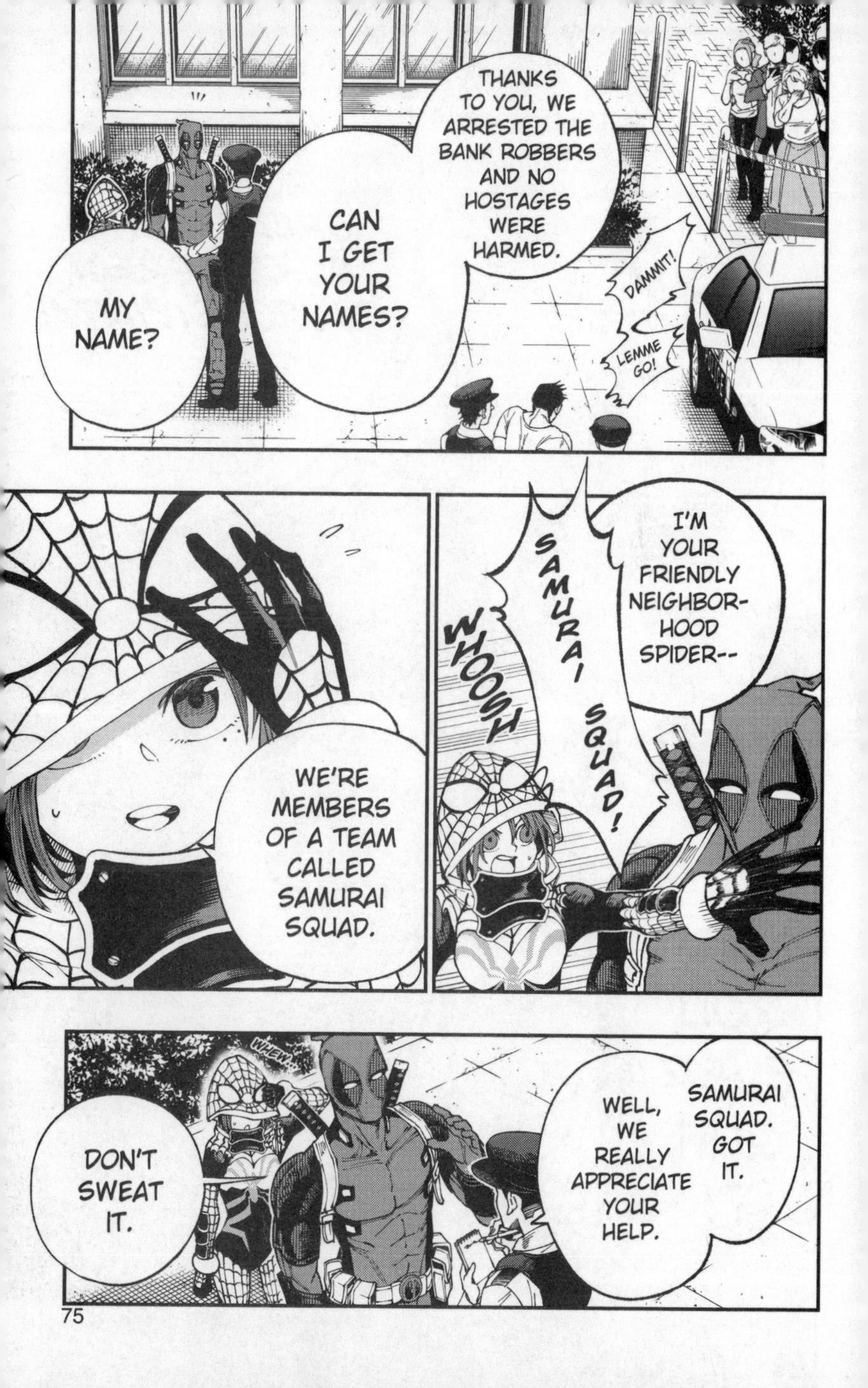
THANKS TO YOU, WE ARRESTED THE BANK ROBBERS AND NO HOSTAGES WERE HARMED.
DAMMIT!
LEMME GO!
CAN I GET YOUR NAMES?
MY NAME?
I'M YOUR FRIENDLY NEIGHBOR-HOOD SPIDER--
SAMURAI SQUAD!
WHOOSH
WE'RE MEMBERS OF A TEAM CALLED SAMURAI SQUAD.
SAMURAI SQUAD. GOT IT.
WELL, WE REALLY APPRECIATE YOUR HELP.
WHEW...
DON'T SWEAT IT.

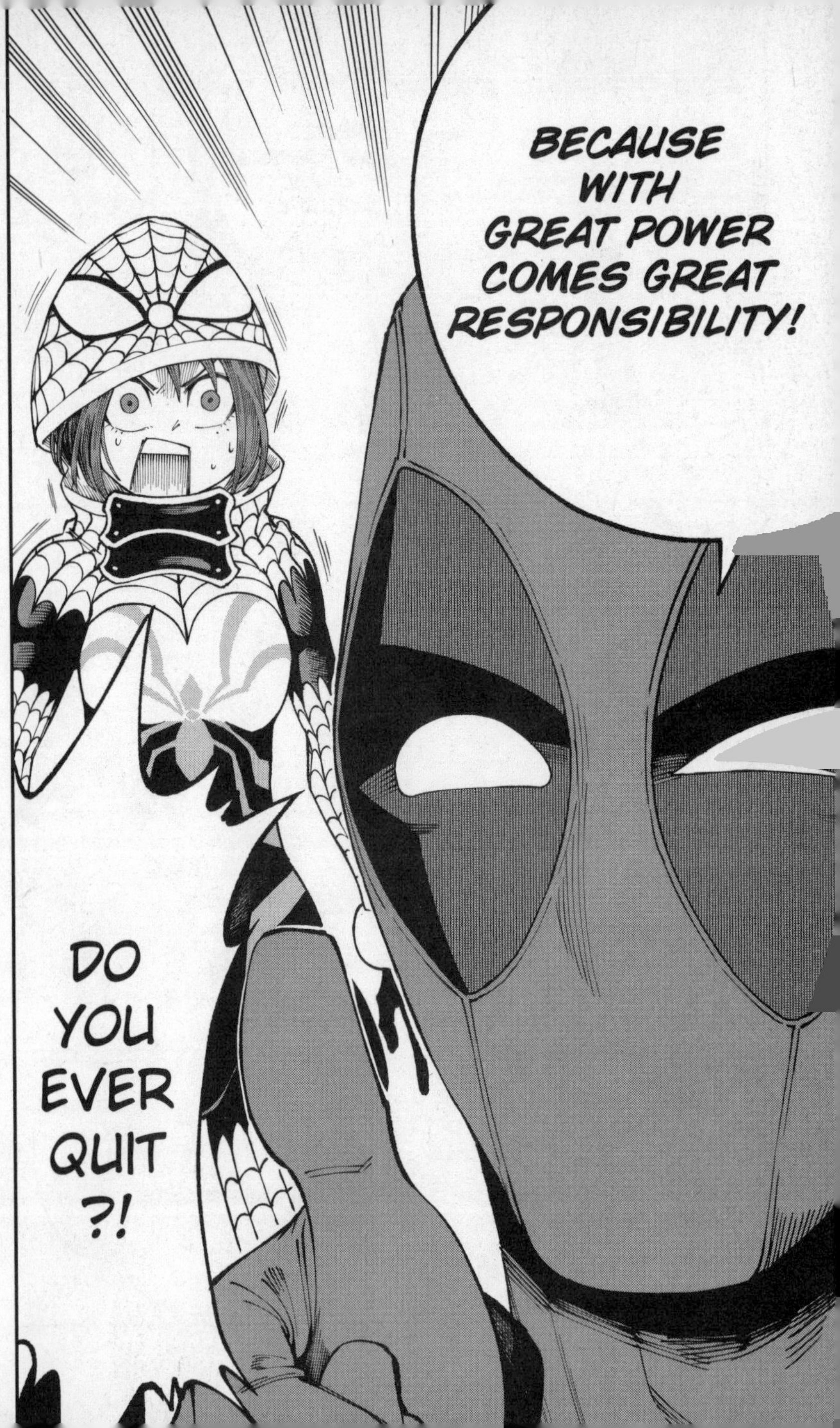
BECAUSE WITH GREAT POWER COMES GREAT RESPONSIBILITY!
DO YOU EVER QUIT ?!

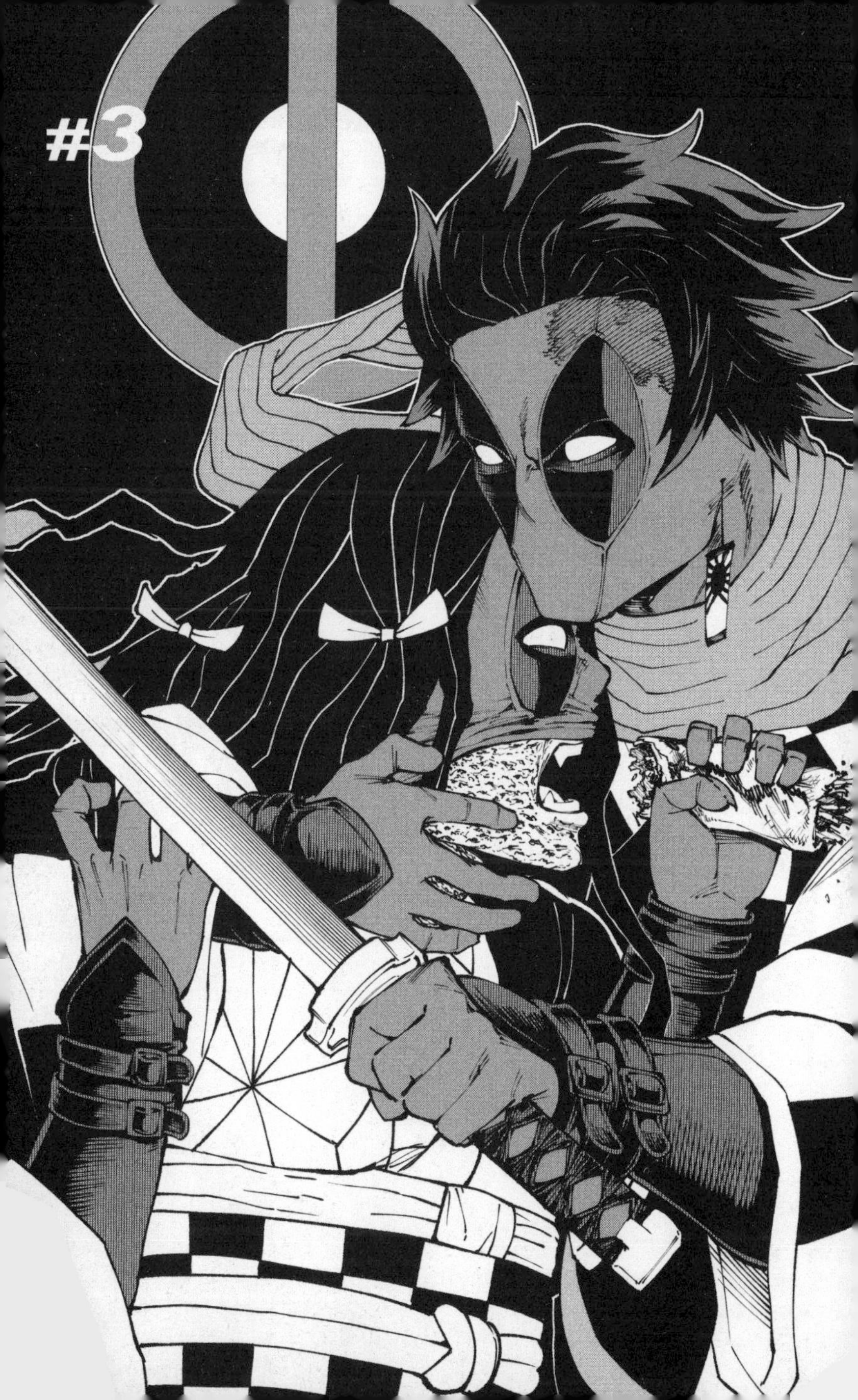
#3

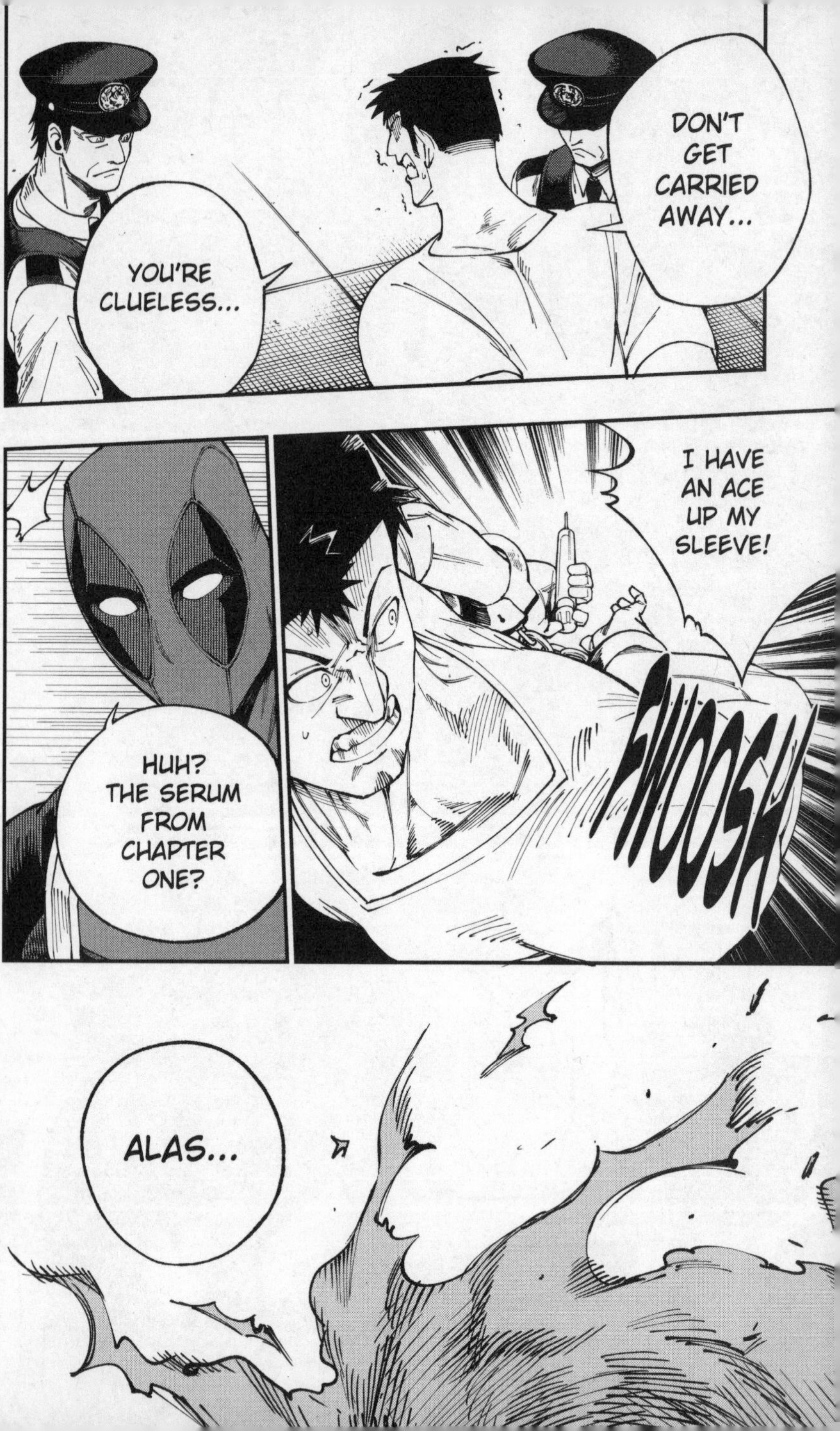
DON'T GET CARRIED AWAY...
YOU'RE CLUELESS...
I HAVE AN ACE UP MY SLEEVE!
FWOOSH
HUH? THE SERUM FROM CHAPTER ONE?
ALAS...

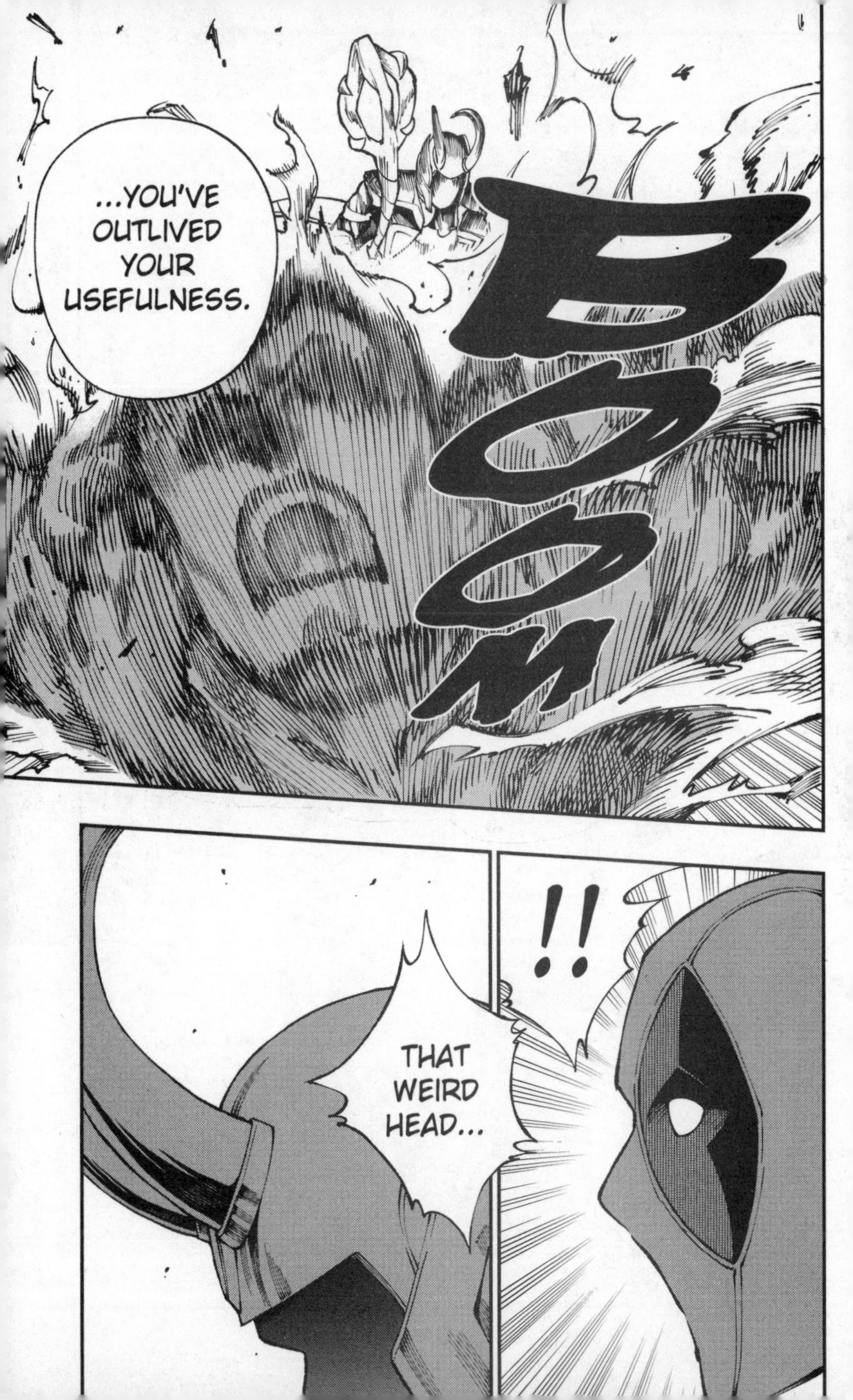
...YOU'VE OUTLIVED YOUR USEFULNESS.
BOOM
!!
THAT WEIRD HEAD...

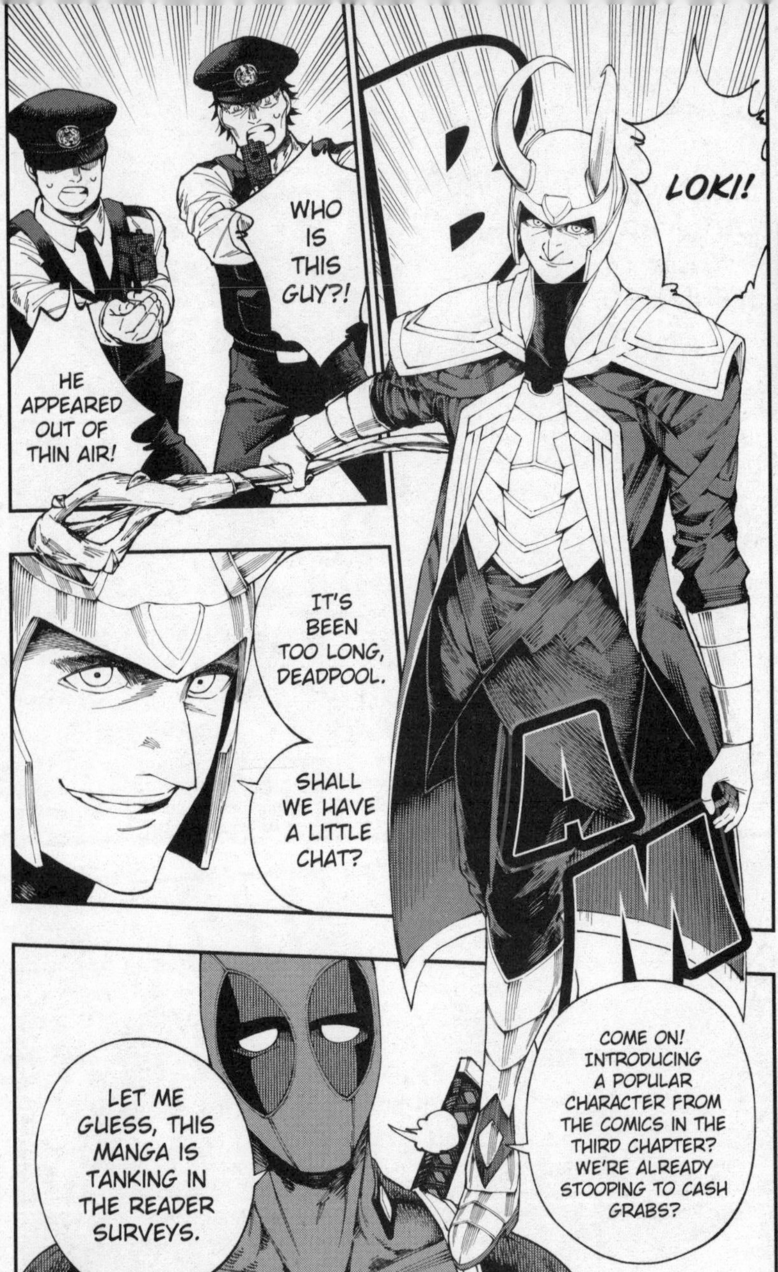
LOKI!
BAM
WHO IS THIS GUY?!
HE APPEARED OUT OF THIN AIR!
IT'S BEEN TOO LONG, DEADPOOL.
SHALL WE HAVE A LITTLE CHAT?
COME ON! INTRODUCING A POPULAR CHARACTER FROM THE COMICS IN THE THIRD CHAPTER? WE'RE ALREADY STOOPING TO CASH GRABS?
LET ME GUESS, THIS MANGA IS TANKING IN THE READER SURVEYS.

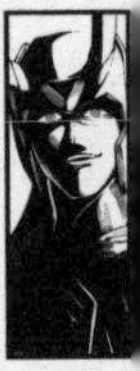

LOKI: ADOPTED BROTHER OF THE MIGHTY THOR AND VILLAIN OUT TO CONQUER EARTH. THE WEIRD THING ABOUT AMERICAN SUPER HERO COMICS IS THAT YOU NEED NOTES LIKE THIS TO UNDERSTAND THEM.

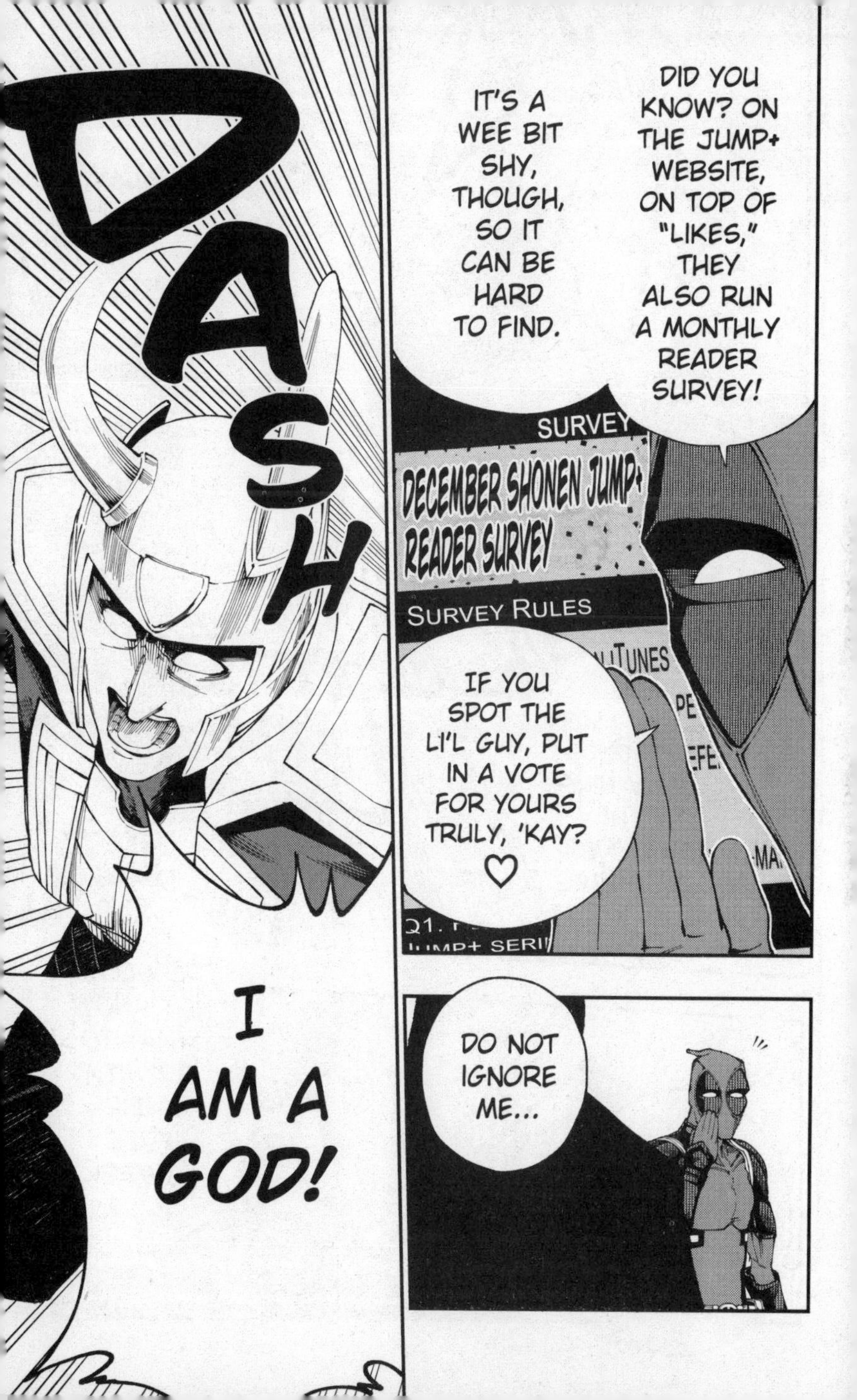
DID YOU KNOW? ON THE JUMP+ WEBSITE, ON TOP OF "LIKES," THEY ALSO RUN A MONTHLY READER SURVEY!
IT'S A WEE BIT SHY, THOUGH, SO IT CAN BE HARD TO FIND.
SURVEY
DECEMBER SHONEN JUMP+ READER SURVEY
SURVEY RULES
IF YOU SPOT THE LI'L GUY, PUT IN A VOTE FOR YOURS TRULY, 'KAY? ♡
DO NOT IGNORE ME...
DASH
I AM A GOD!

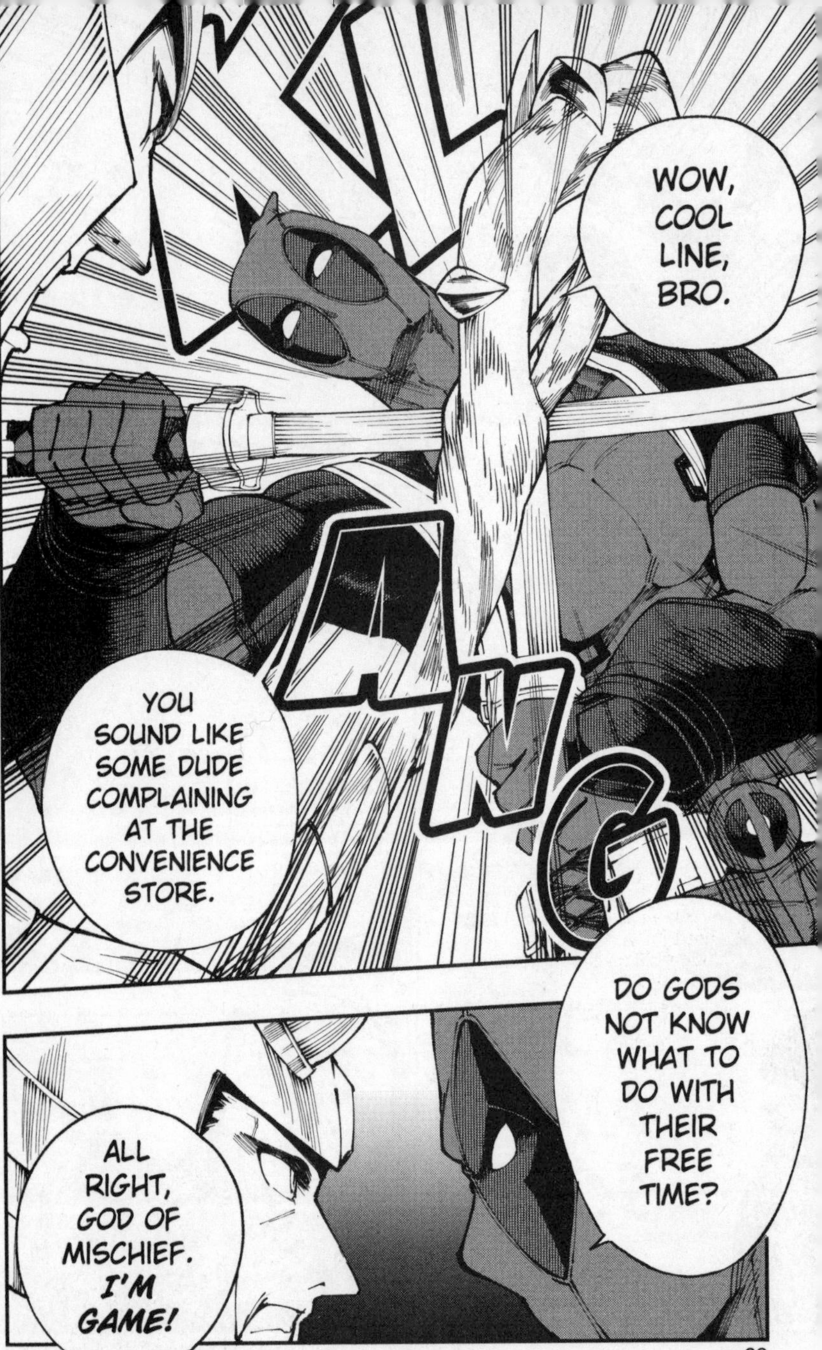
WOW, COOL LINE, BRO.
ANG
YOU SOUND LIKE SOME DUDE COMPLAINING AT THE CONVENIENCE STORE.
DO GODS NOT KNOW WHAT TO DO WITH THEIR FREE TIME?
ALL RIGHT, GOD OF MISCHIEF. *I'M GAME!*

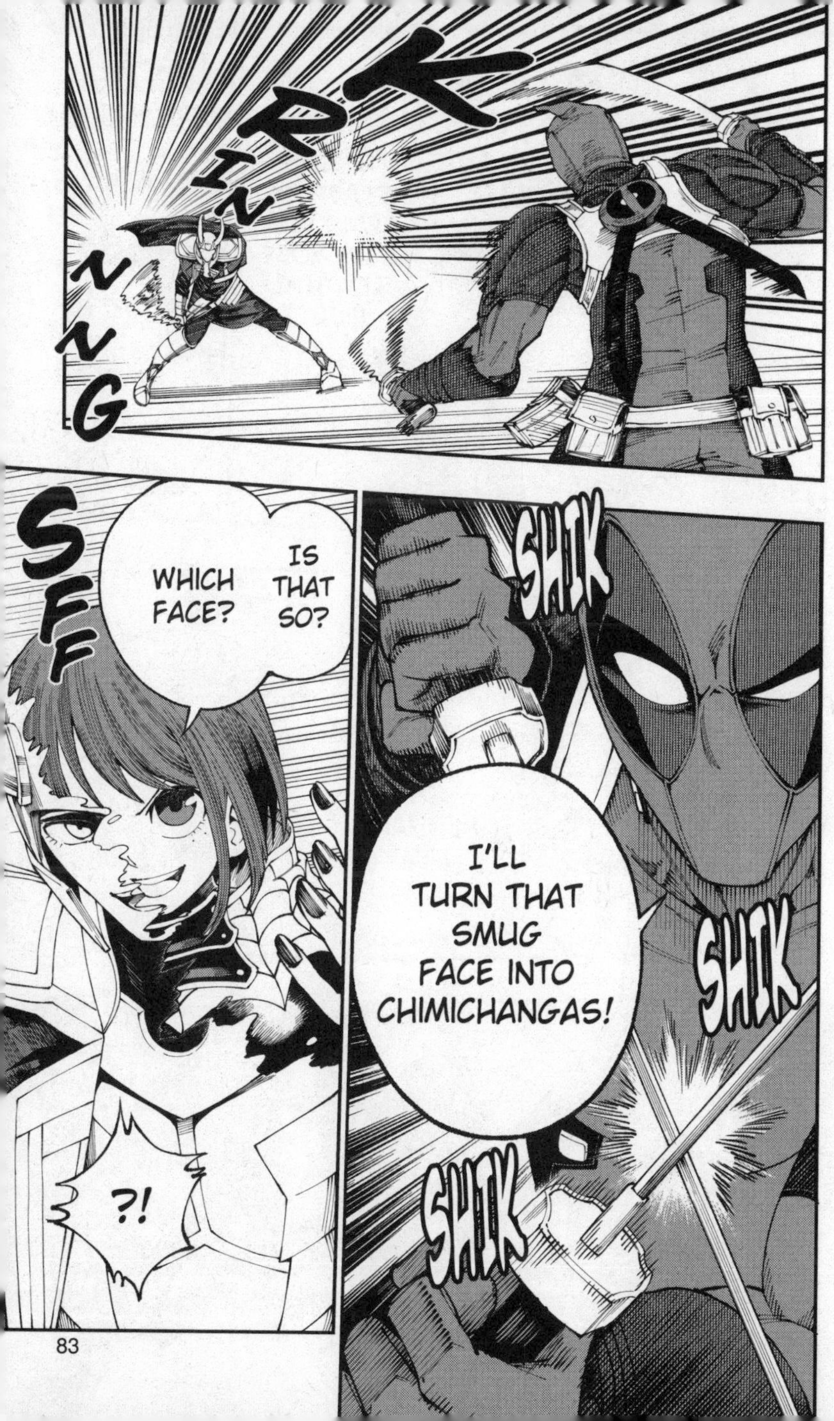
KRINNNG
SHIK
I'LL TURN THAT SMUG FACE INTO CHIMICHANGAS!
SHIK
SHIK
SFF
IS THAT SO?
WHICH FACE?
?!

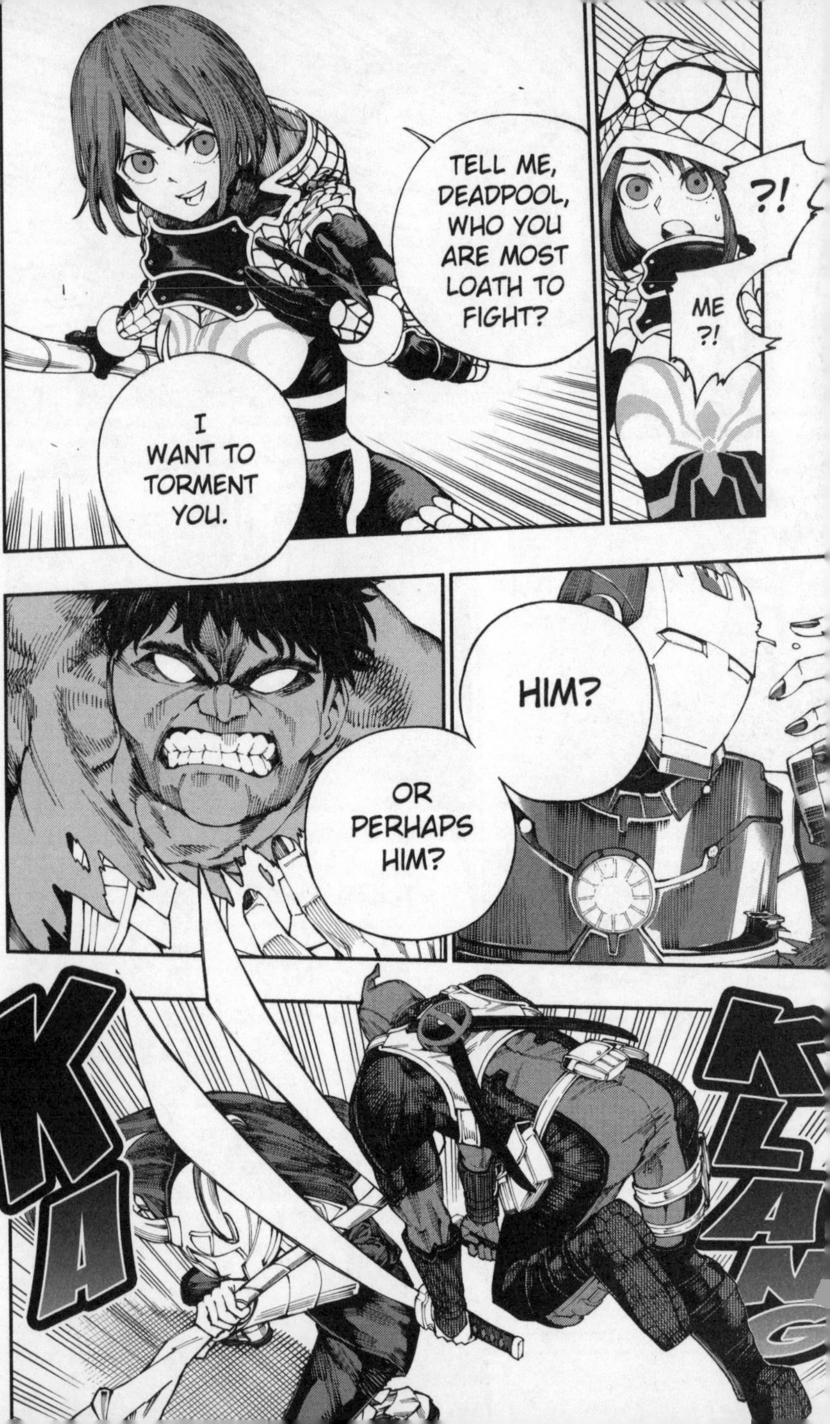
?!
ME ?!
TELL ME, DEADPOOL, WHO YOU ARE MOST LOATH TO FIGHT?
I WANT TO TORMENT YOU.
HIM?
OR PERHAPS HIM?
KLANG
KA

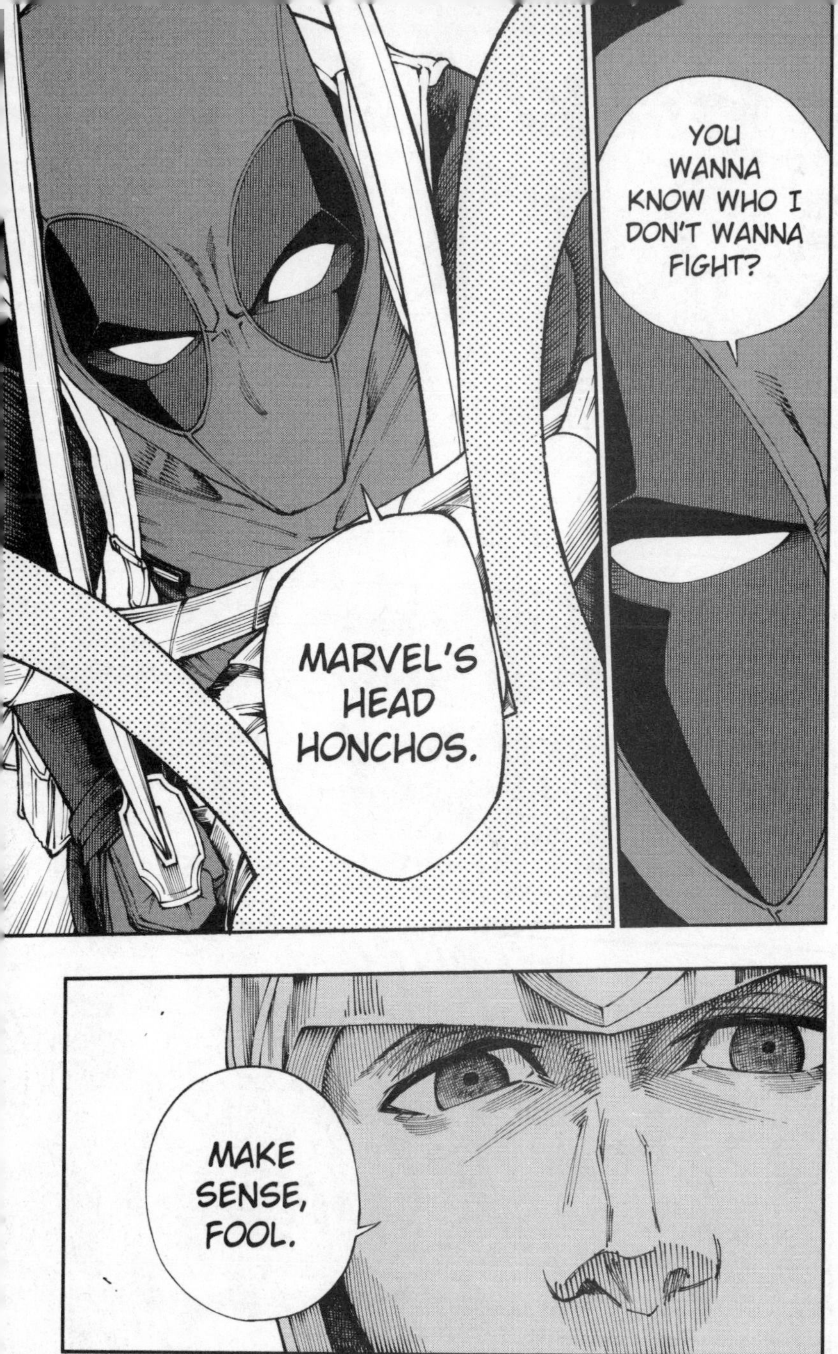
YOU WANNA KNOW WHO I DON'T WANNA FIGHT?
MARVEL'S HEAD HONCHOS.
MAKE SENSE, FOOL.

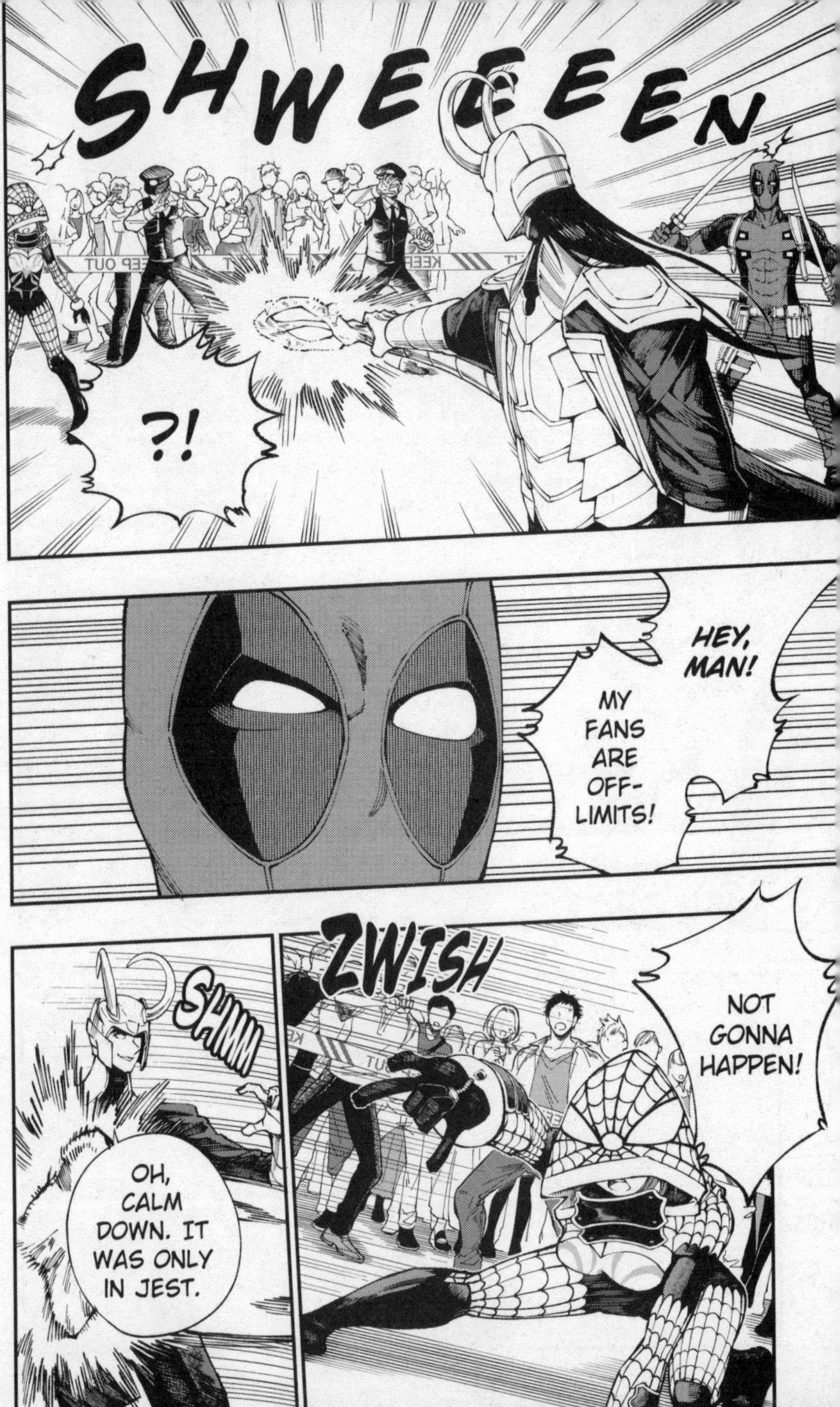
SHWEEEEN
?!
HEY, MAN!
MY FANS ARE OFF-LIMITS!
ZWISH
NOT GONNA HAPPEN!
OH, CALM DOWN. IT WAS ONLY IN JEST.

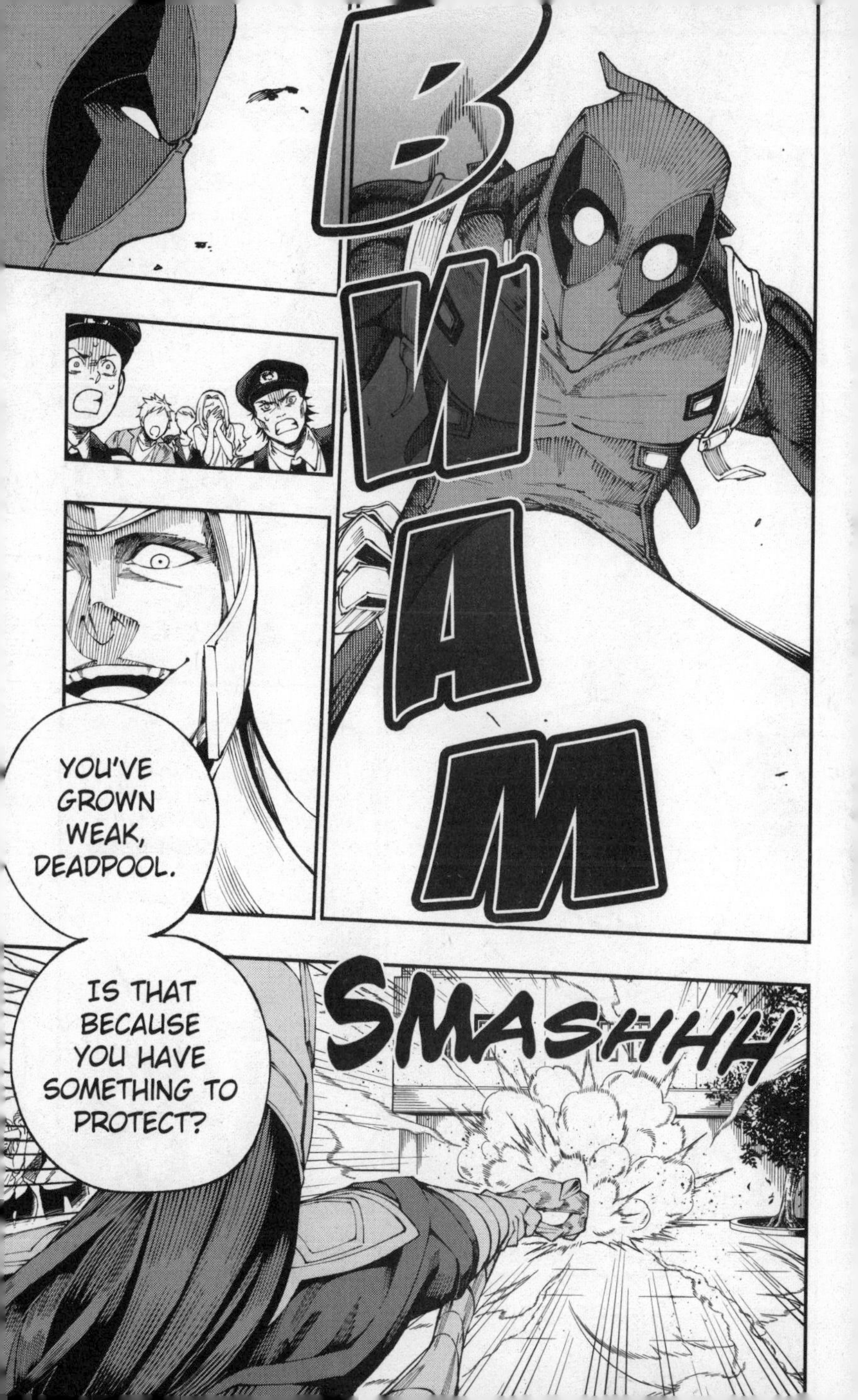
BWAM
YOU'VE GROWN WEAK, DEADPOOL.
SMASHHH
IS THAT BECAUSE YOU HAVE SOMETHING TO PROTECT?

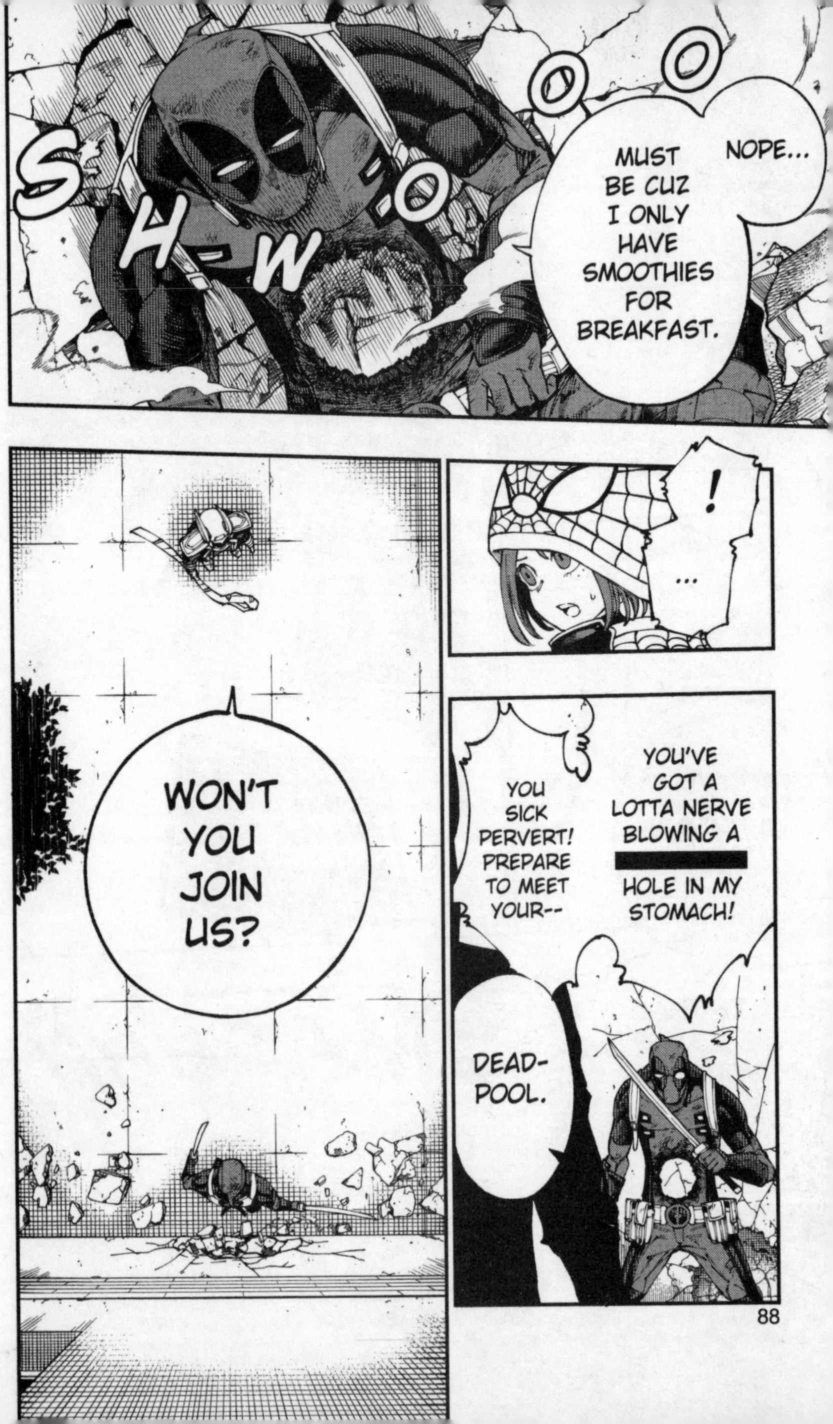
SH-WOOOOO
NOPE... MUST BE CUZ I ONLY HAVE SMOOTHIES FOR BREAKFAST.
!
...
YOU'VE GOT A LOTTA NERVE BLOWING A [redacted] HOLE IN MY STOMACH!
YOU SICK PERVERT! PREPARE TO MEET YOUR--
DEAD-POOL.
WON'T YOU JOIN US?

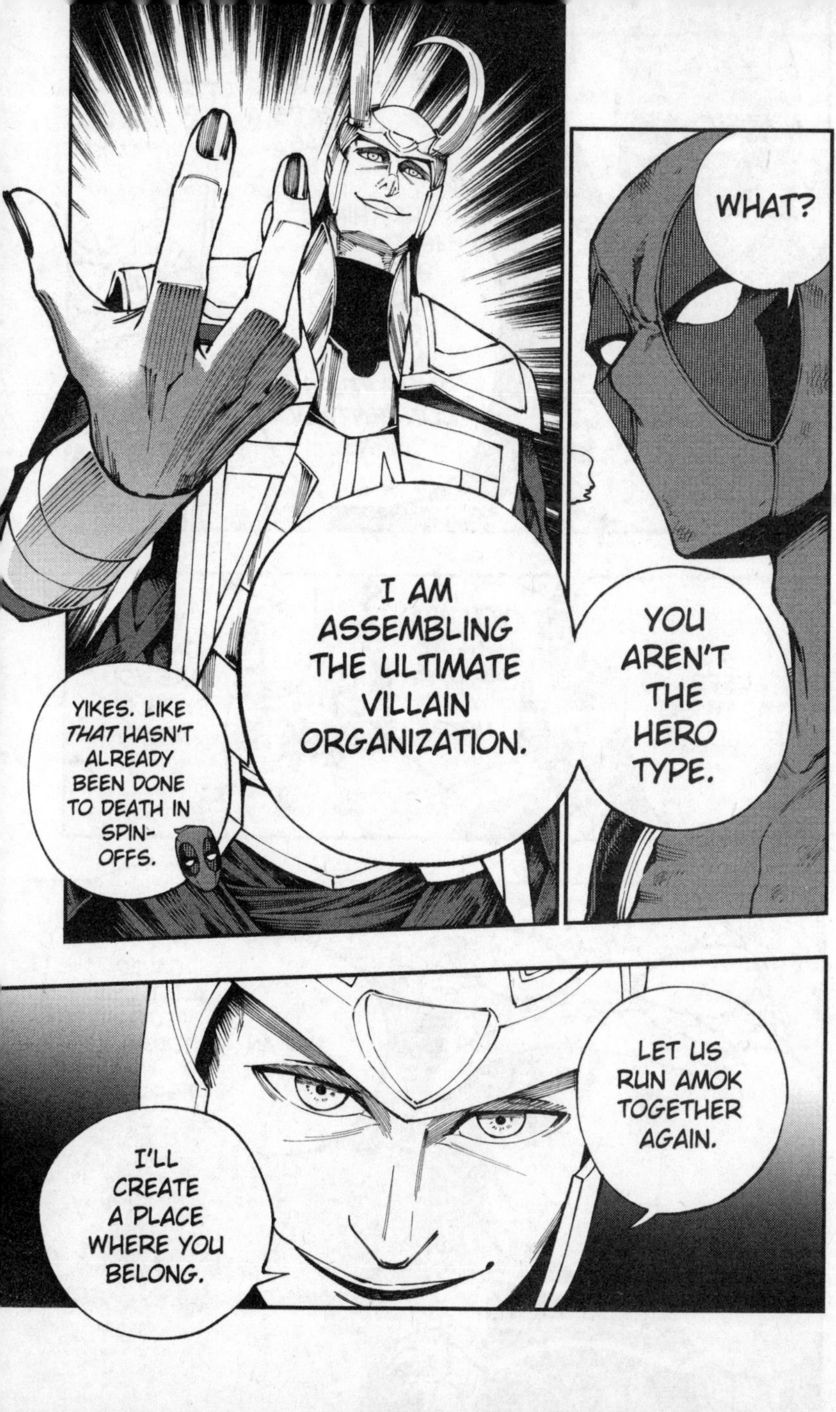
WHAT?
YOU AREN'T THE HERO TYPE.
I AM ASSEMBLING THE ULTIMATE VILLAIN ORGANIZATION.
YIKES. LIKE *THAT* HASN'T ALREADY BEEN DONE TO DEATH IN SPIN-OFFS.
LET US RUN AMOK TOGETHER AGAIN.
I'LL CREATE A PLACE WHERE YOU BELONG.

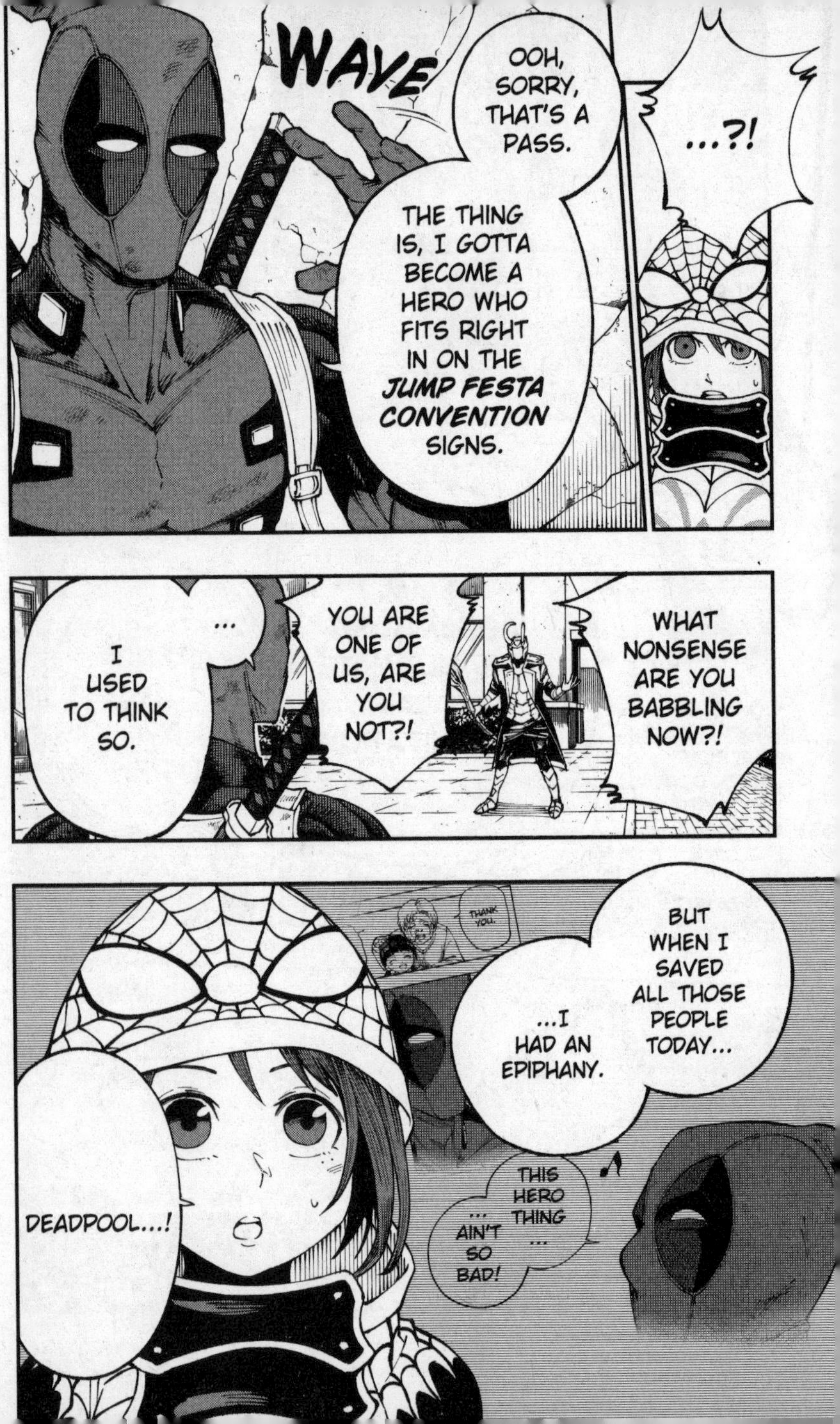
...?!
OOH, SORRY, THAT'S A PASS.
WAVE
THE THING IS, I GOTTA BECOME A HERO WHO FITS RIGHT IN ON THE *JUMP FESTA CONVENTION* SIGNS.
WHAT NONSENSE ARE YOU BABBLING NOW?!
YOU ARE ONE OF US, ARE YOU NOT?!
...
I USED TO THINK SO.
BUT WHEN I SAVED ALL THOSE PEOPLE TODAY...
THANK YOU.
...I HAD AN EPIPHANY.
THIS HERO THING...
...AIN'T SO BAD!
DEADPOOL...!

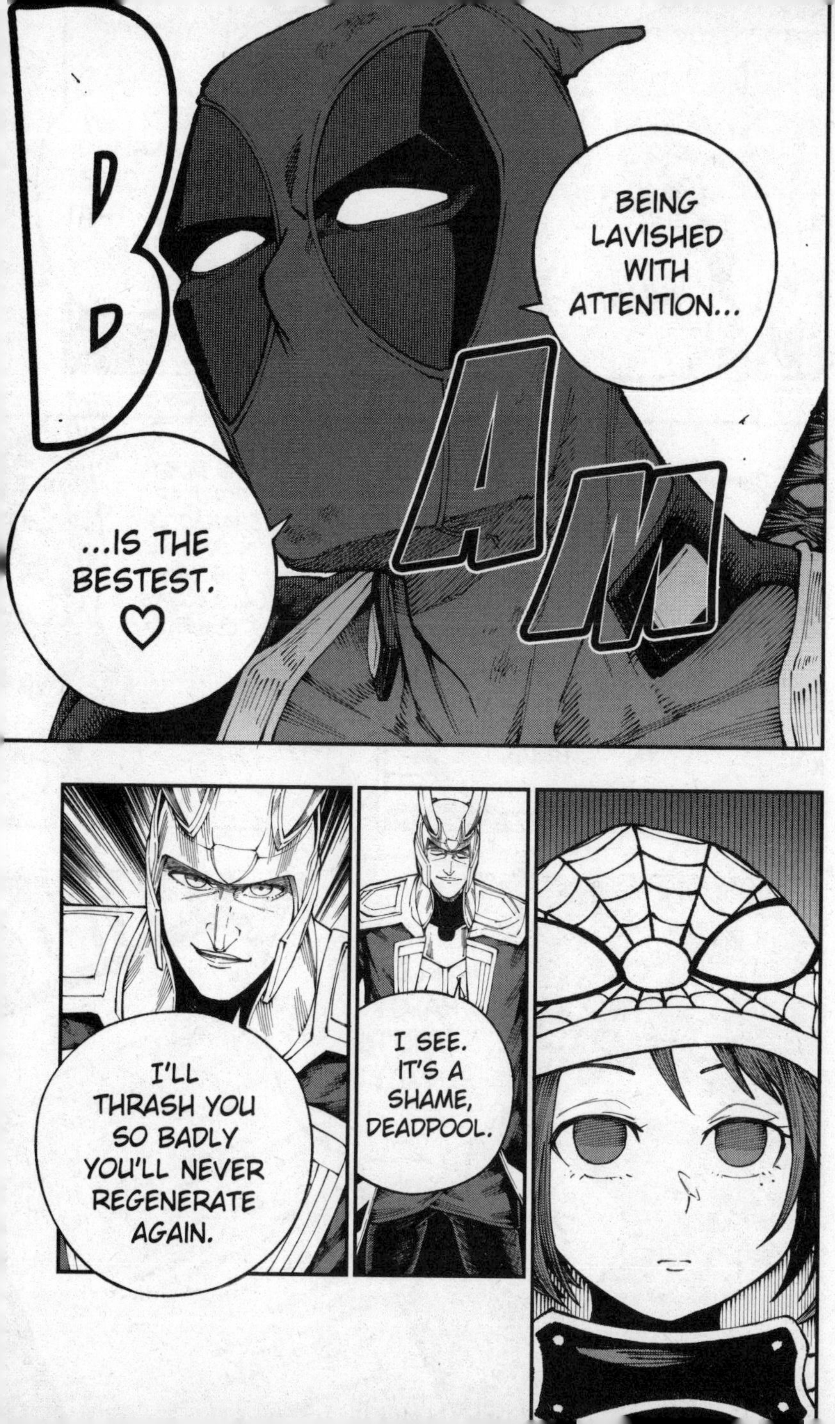
BEING LAVISHED WITH ATTENTION...
BDDAM
...IS THE BESTEST. ♡
I SEE. IT'S A SHAME, DEADPOOL.
I'LL THRASH YOU SO BADLY YOU'LL NEVER REGENERATE AGAIN.

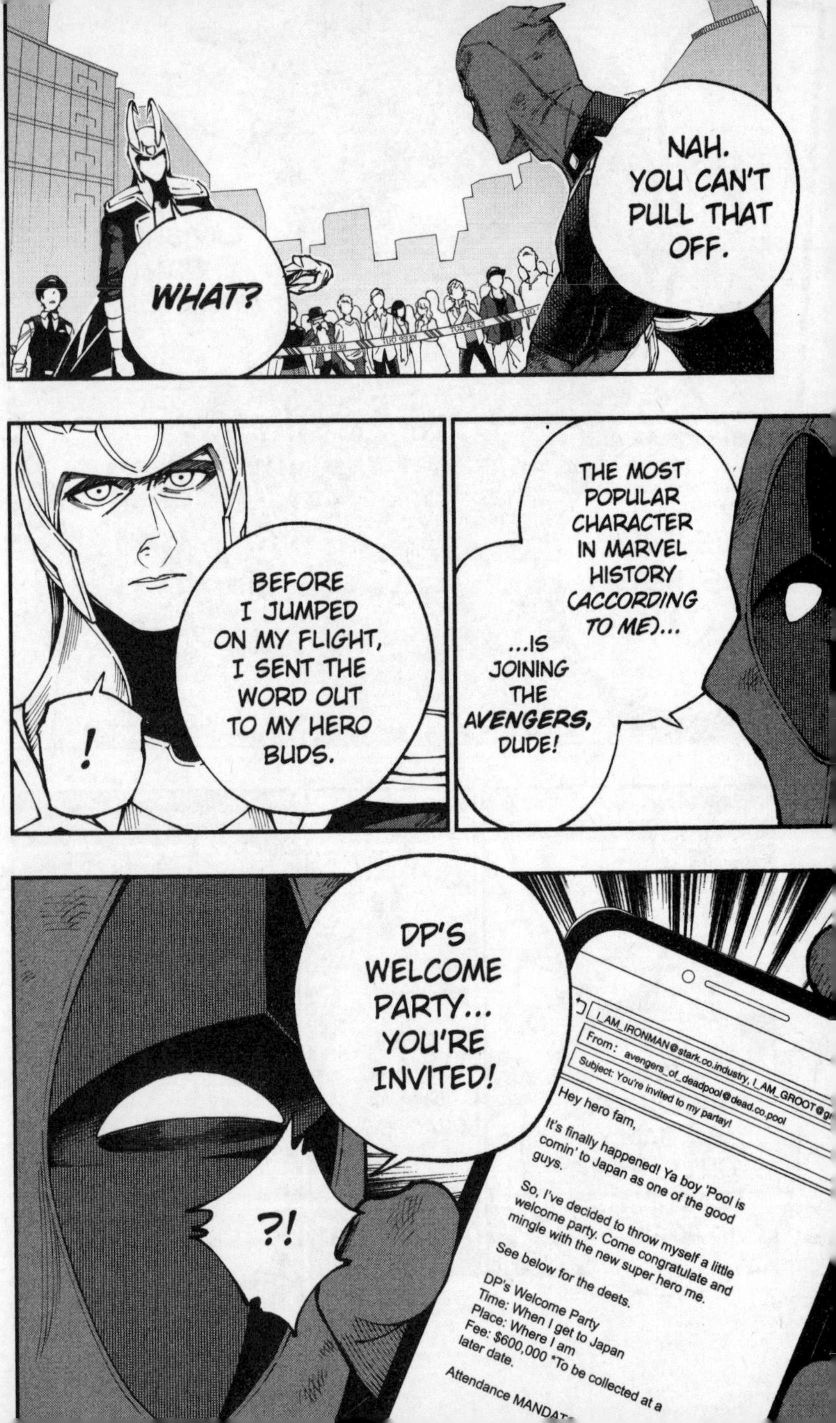
NAH. YOU CAN'T PULL THAT OFF.
WHAT?
THE MOST POPULAR CHARACTER IN MARVEL HISTORY (ACCORDING TO ME)...
...IS JOINING THE AVENGERS, DUDE!
BEFORE I JUMPED ON MY FLIGHT, I SENT THE WORD OUT TO MY HERO BUDS.
!
DP'S WELCOME PARTY... YOU'RE INVITED!
I_AM_IRONMAN@stark.co.industry, I_AM_GROOT@g
From: avengers_of_deadpool@dead.co.pool
Subject: You're invited to my partay!
Hey hero fam,
It's finally happened! Ya boy 'Pool is comin' to Japan as one of the good guys.
So, I've decided to throw myself a little welcome party. Come congratulate and mingle with the new super hero me.
See below for the deets.
DP's Welcome Party
Time: When I get to Japan
Place: Where I am
Fee: $600,000 *To be collected at a later date.
Attendance MANDAT
?!

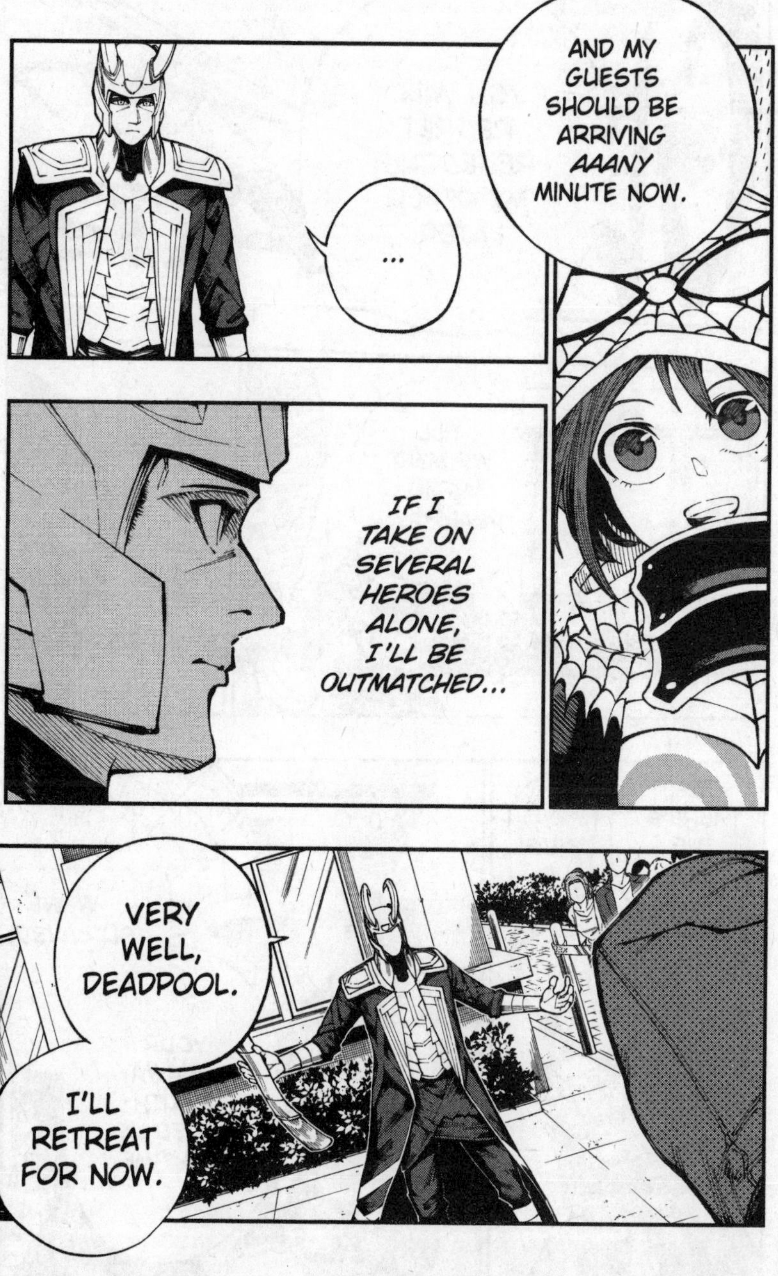
AND MY GUESTS SHOULD BE ARRIVING *AAANY* MINUTE NOW.
...
IF I TAKE ON SEVERAL HEROES ALONE, I'LL BE OUTMATCHED...
VERY WELL, DEADPOOL.
I'LL RETREAT FOR NOW.

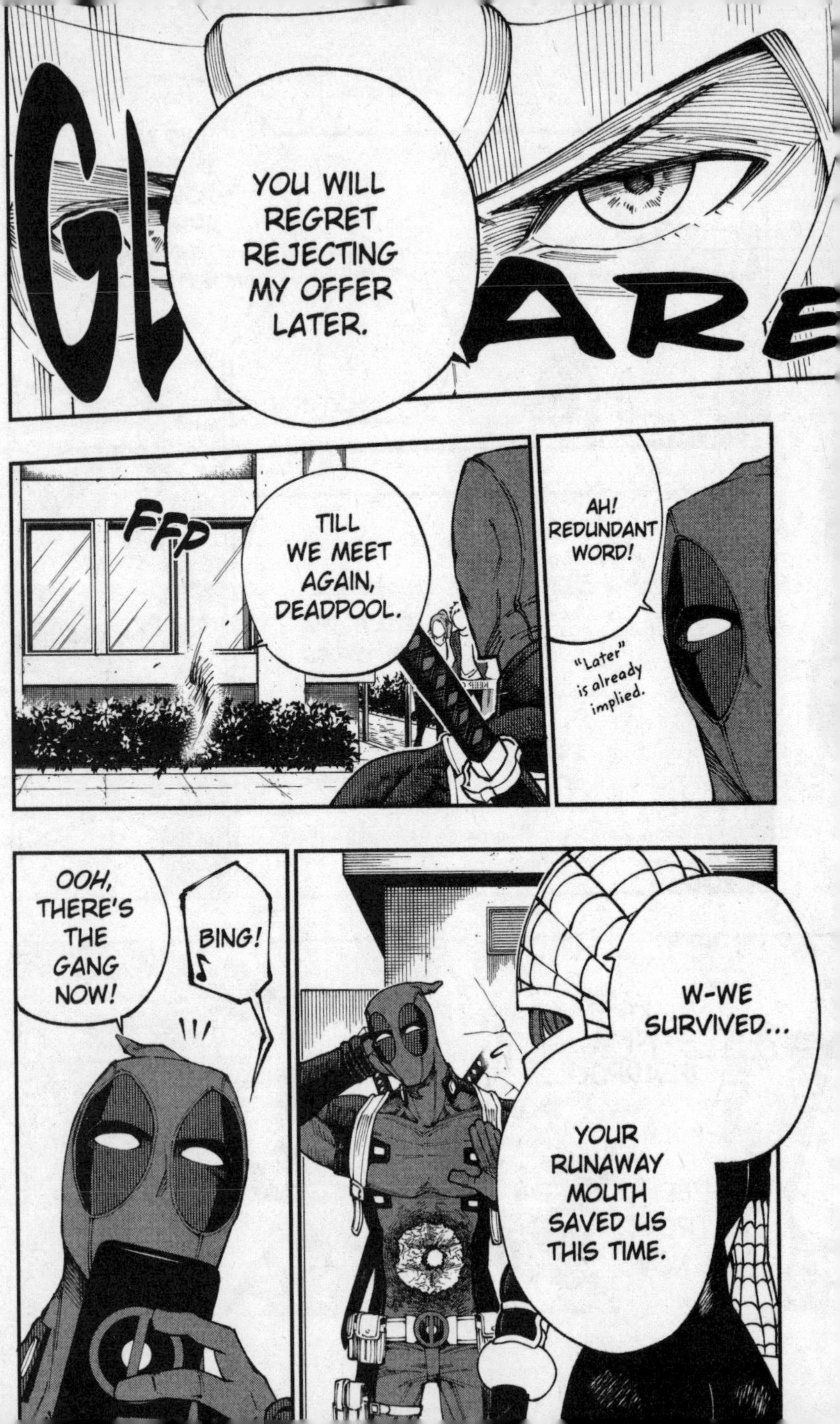
GLARE
YOU WILL REGRET REJECTING MY OFFER LATER.
AH! REDUNDANT WORD!
"Later" is already implied.
FFP
TILL WE MEET AGAIN, DEADPOOL.
W-WE SURVIVED...
YOUR RUNAWAY MOUTH SAVED US THIS TIME.
BING!
OOH, THERE'S THE GANG NOW!

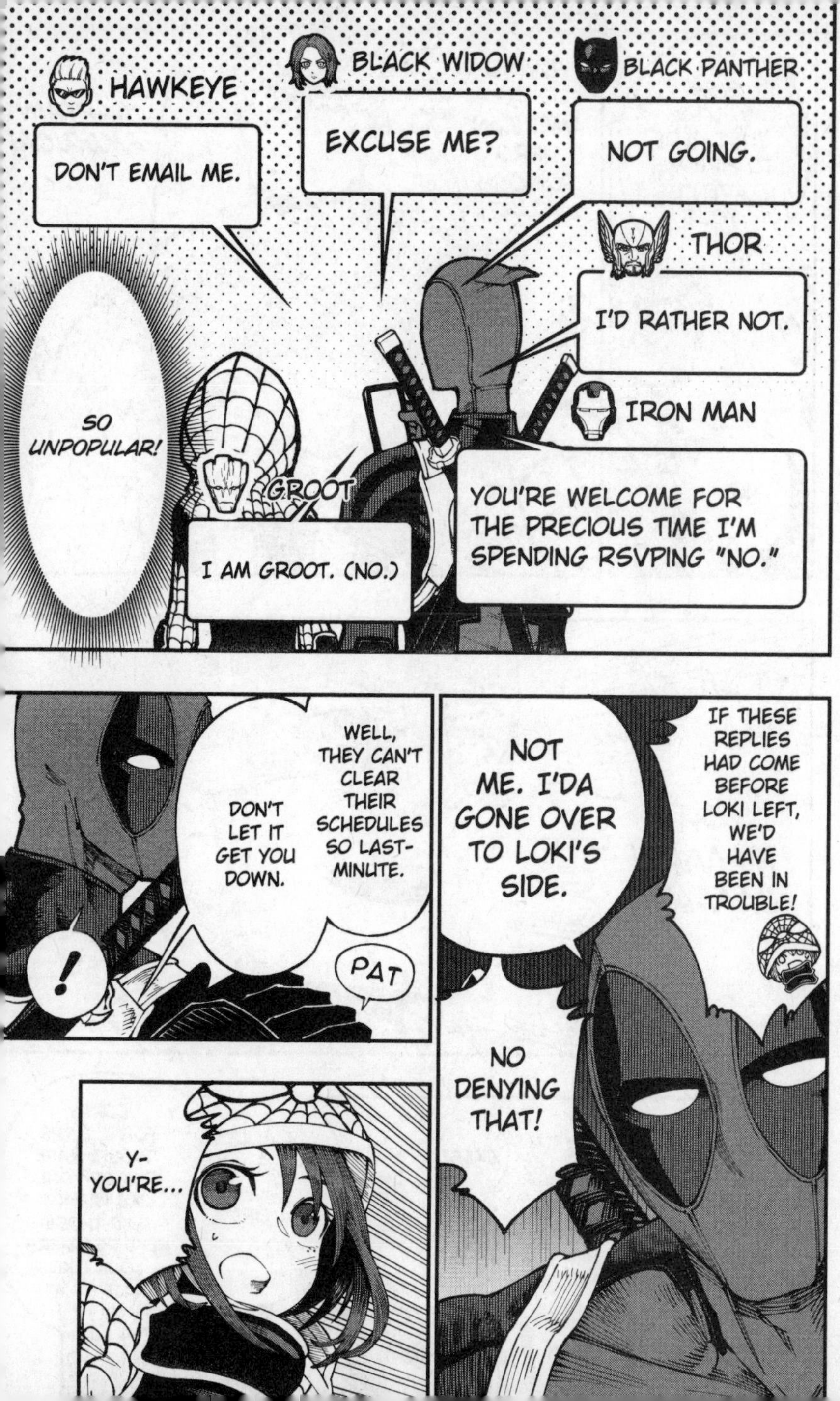
BLACK PANTHER
NOT GOING.
BLACK WIDOW
EXCUSE ME?
HAWKEYE
DON'T EMAIL ME.
THOR
I'D RATHER NOT.
IRON MAN
YOU'RE WELCOME FOR THE PRECIOUS TIME I'M SPENDING RSVPING "NO."
GROOT
I AM GROOT. (NO.)
SO UNPOPULAR!
IF THESE REPLIES HAD COME BEFORE LOKI LEFT, WE'D HAVE BEEN IN TROUBLE!
NOT ME. I'DA GONE OVER TO LOKI'S SIDE.
NO DENYING THAT!
WELL, THEY CAN'T CLEAR THEIR SCHEDULES SO LAST-MINUTE.
DON'T LET IT GET YOU DOWN.
PAT
!
Y-YOU'RE...

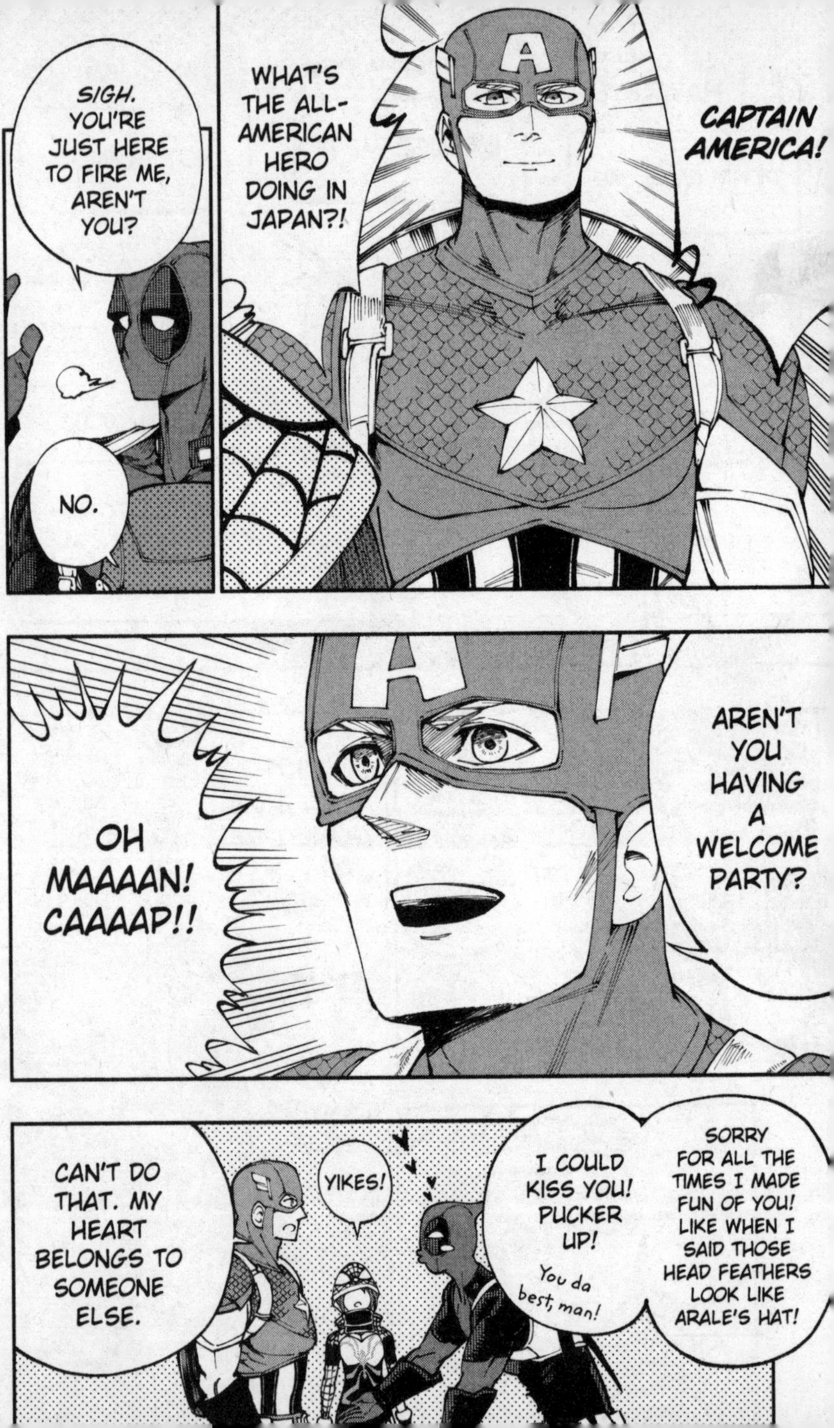
CAPTAIN AMERICA!
WHAT'S THE ALL-AMERICAN HERO DOING IN JAPAN?!
SIGH. YOU'RE JUST HERE TO FIRE ME, AREN'T YOU?
NO.
AREN'T YOU HAVING A WELCOME PARTY?
OH MAAAAN! CAAAAP!!
SORRY FOR ALL THE TIMES I MADE FUN OF YOU! LIKE WHEN I SAID THOSE HEAD FEATHERS LOOK LIKE ARALE'S HAT!
I COULD KISS YOU! PUCKER UP!
You da best, man!
YIKES!
CAN'T DO THAT. MY HEART BELONGS TO SOMEONE ELSE.

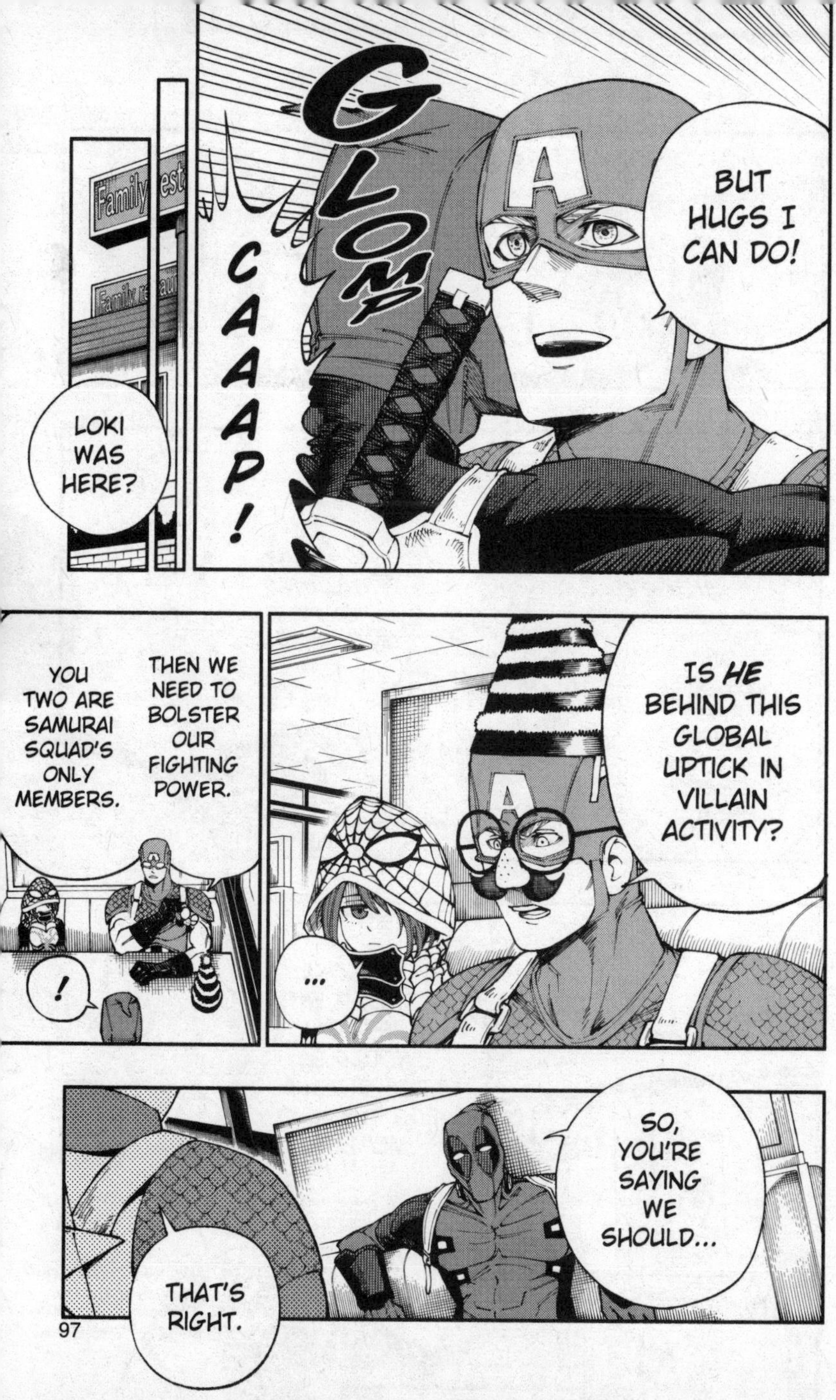
BUT HUGS I CAN DO!
GLOMP
CAAAAP!
LOKI WAS HERE?
IS *HE* BEHIND THIS GLOBAL UPTICK IN VILLAIN ACTIVITY?
...
THEN WE NEED TO BOLSTER OUR FIGHTING POWER.
YOU TWO ARE SAMURAI SQUAD'S ONLY MEMBERS.
!
SO, YOU'RE SAYING WE SHOULD...
THAT'S RIGHT.

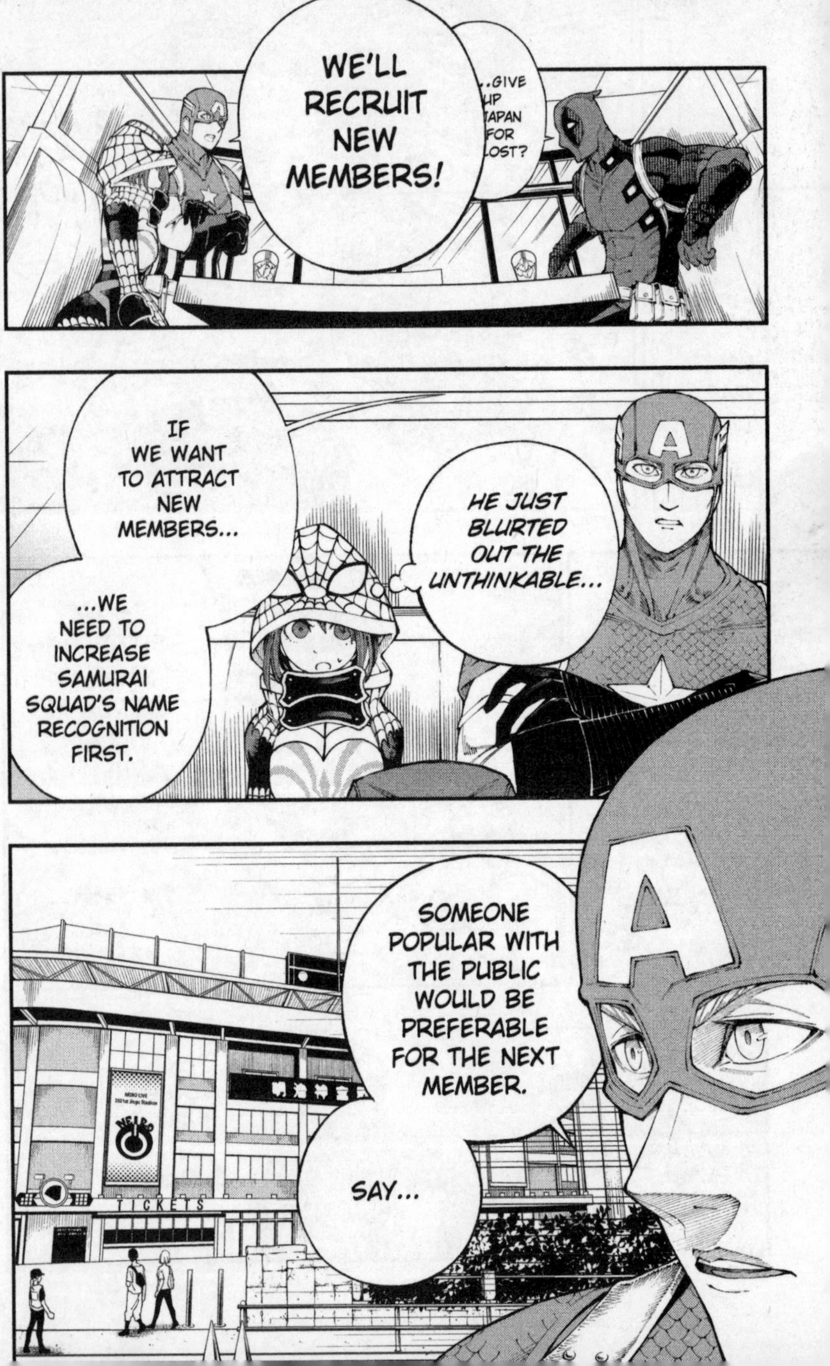
..GIVE UP JAPAN FOR LOST?
WE'LL RECRUIT NEW MEMBERS!
HE JUST BLURTED OUT THE UNTHINKABLE...
IF WE WANT TO ATTRACT NEW MEMBERS...
...WE NEED TO INCREASE SAMURAI SQUAD'S NAME RECOGNITION FIRST.
SOMEONE POPULAR WITH THE PUBLIC WOULD BE PREFERABLE FOR THE NEXT MEMBER.
SAY...
TICKETS

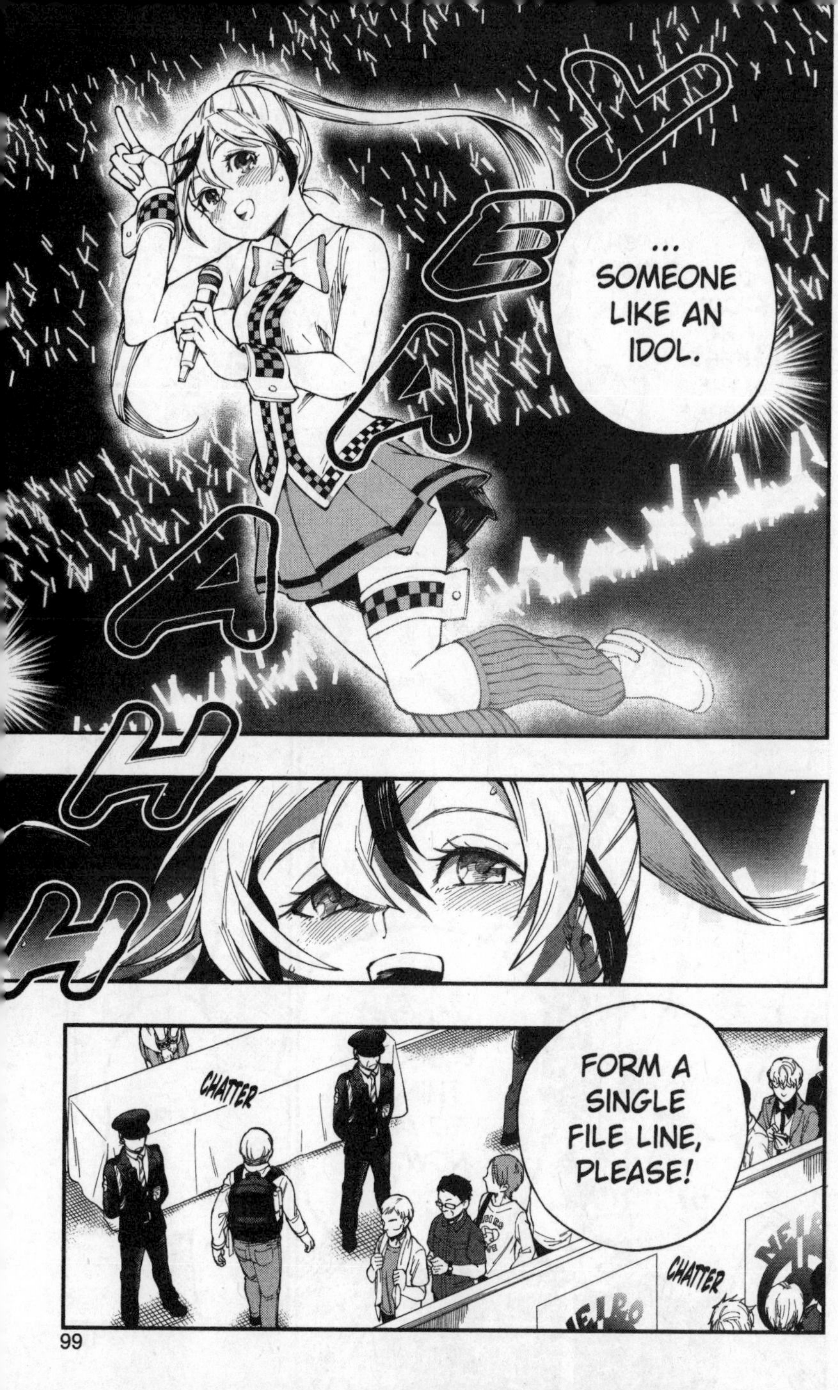
YEAAHH
... SOMEONE LIKE AN IDOL.
FORM A SINGLE FILE LINE, PLEASE!
CHATTER
CHATTER

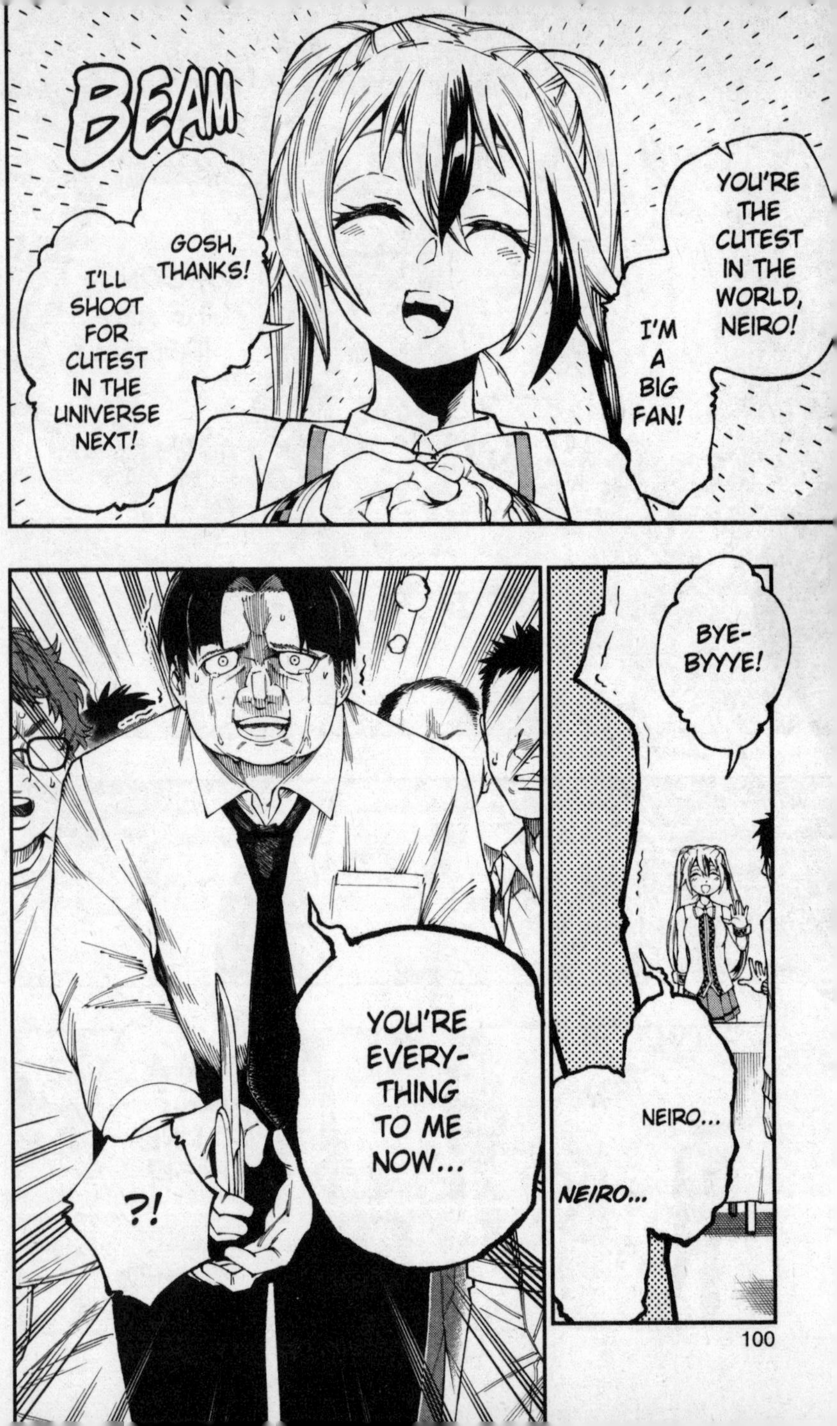
YOU'RE THE CUTEST IN THE WORLD, NEIRO!
I'M A BIG FAN!
GOSH, THANKS!
I'LL SHOOT FOR CUTEST IN THE UNIVERSE NEXT!
BEAM
BYE-BYYYE!
NEIRO...
NEIRO...
YOU'RE EVERY-THING TO ME NOW...
?!

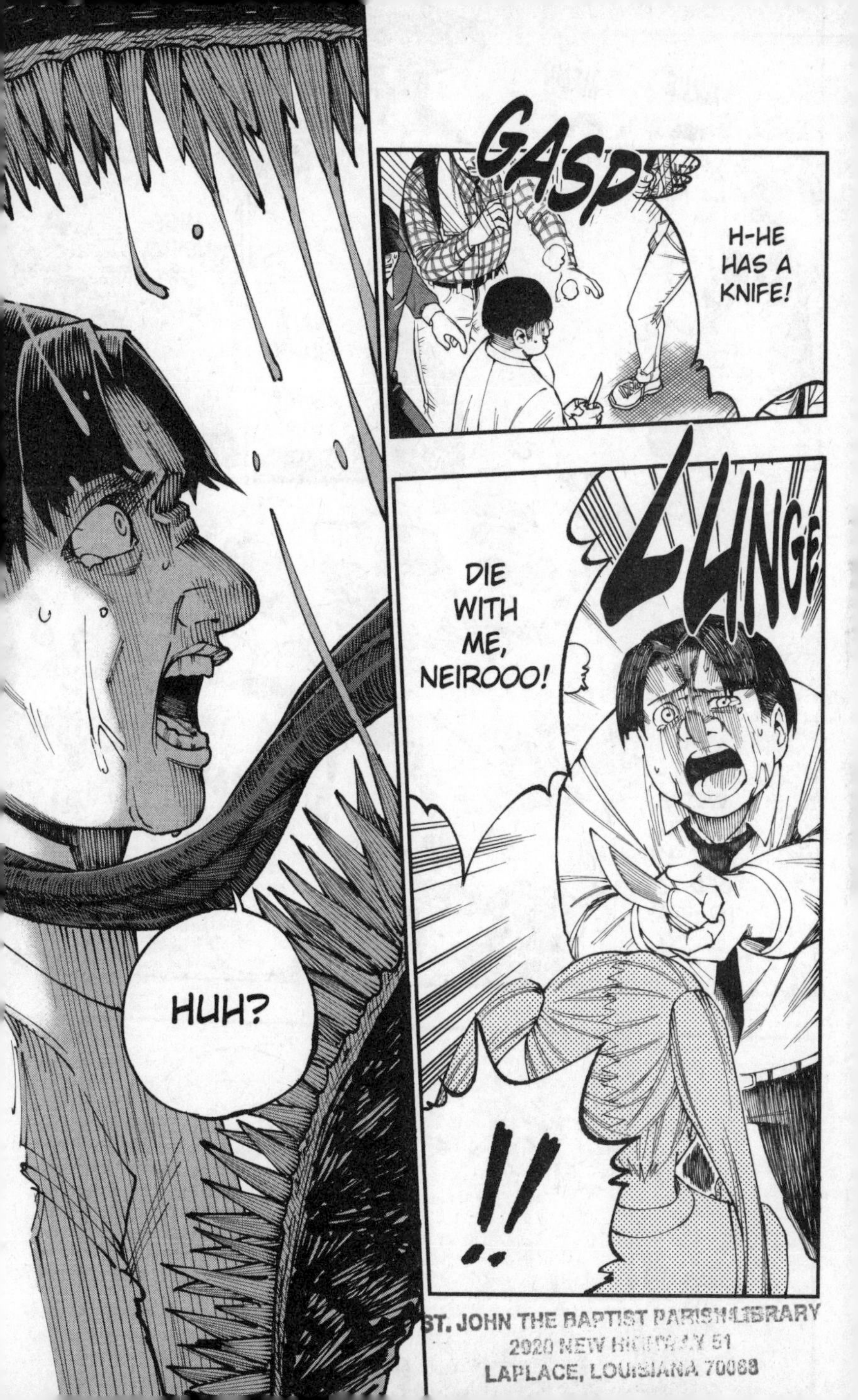
GASP
H-HE HAS A KNIFE!
LUNGE
DIE WITH ME, NEIROOO!
!!
HUH?

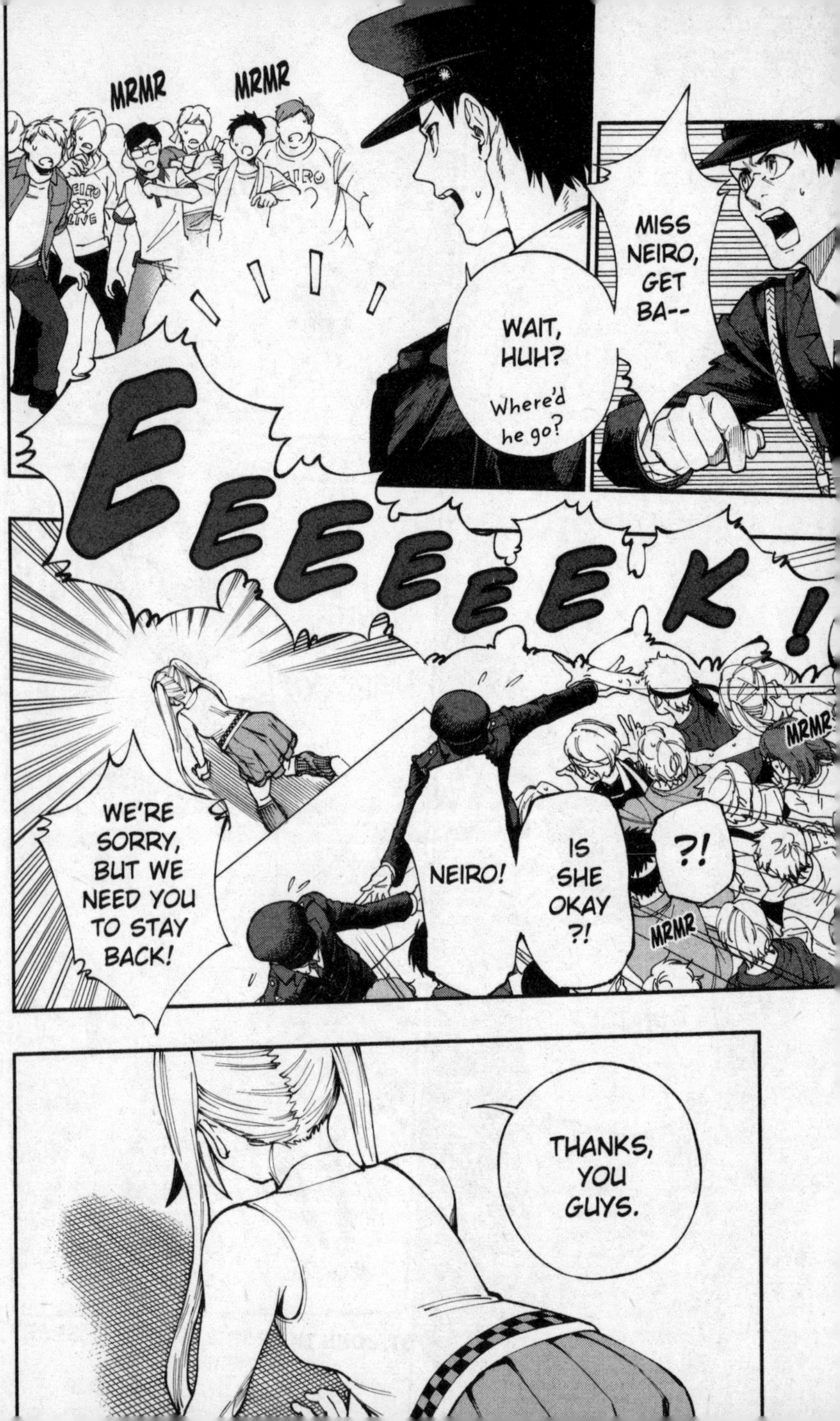
MISS NEIRO, GET BA--
WAIT, HUH?
Where'd he go?
MRMR
MRMR
EEEEEEK!
MRMR
?!
IS SHE OKAY?!
NEIRO!
MRMR
WE'RE SORRY, BUT WE NEED YOU TO STAY BACK!
THANKS, YOU GUYS.

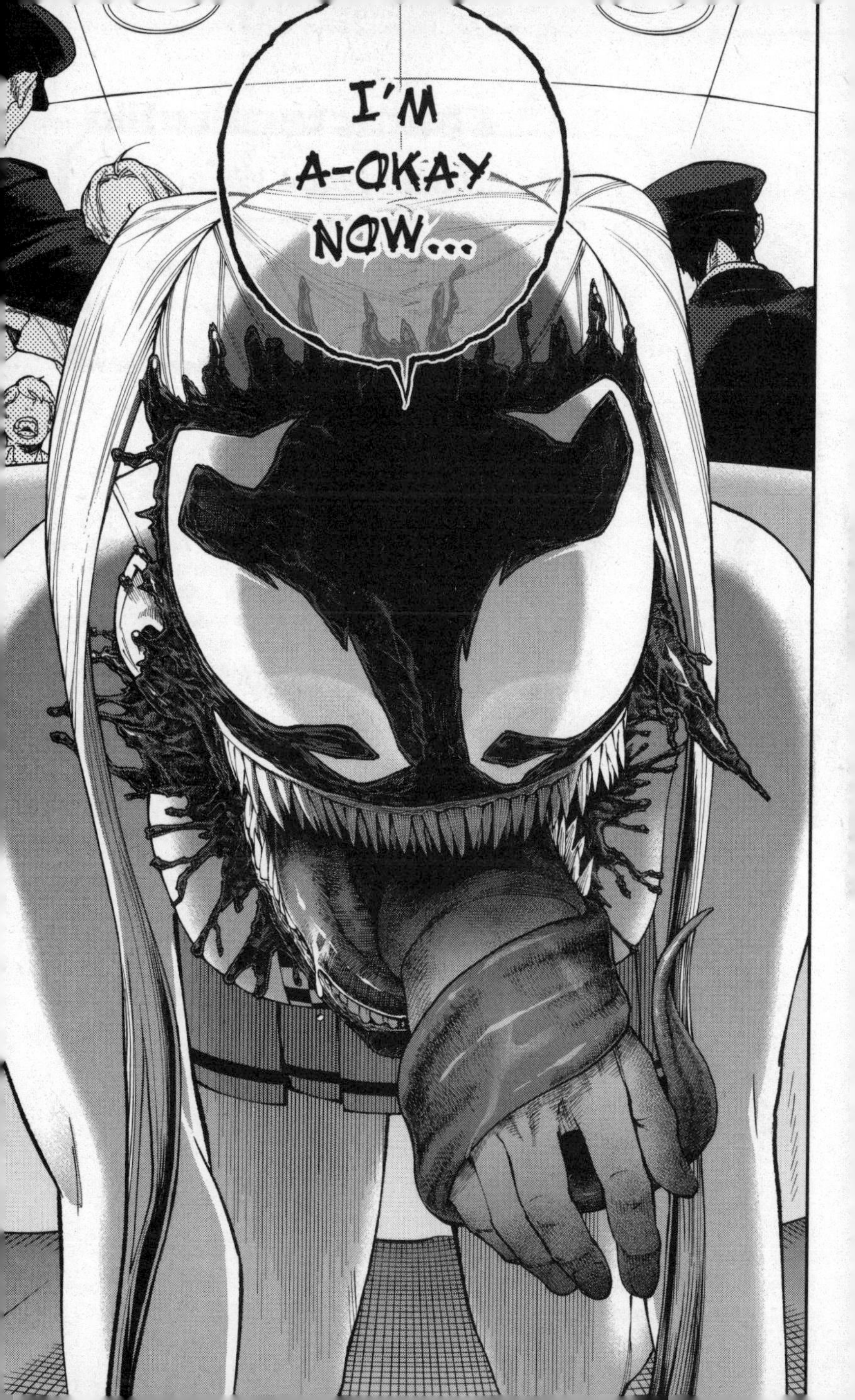
I'M A-OKAY NOW...

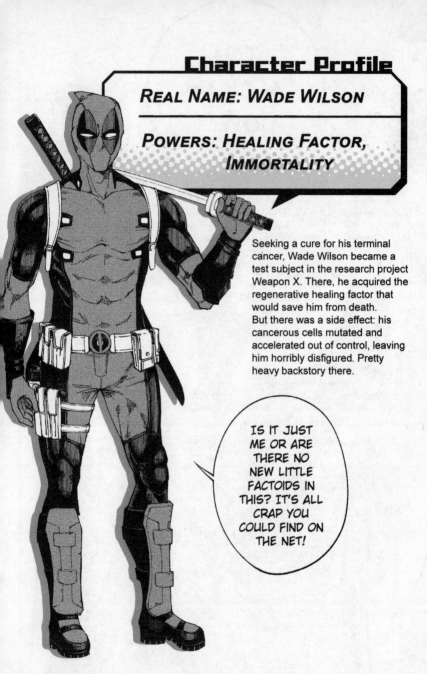

Character Profile

REAL NAME: WADE WILSON

POWERS: HEALING FACTOR, IMMORTALITY

Seeking a cure for his terminal cancer, Wade Wilson became a test subject in the research project Weapon X. There, he acquired the regenerative healing factor that would save him from death. But there was a side effect: his cancerous cells mutated and accelerated out of control, leaving him horribly disfigured. Pretty heavy backstory there.

IS IT JUST ME OR ARE THERE NO NEW LITTLE FACTOIDS IN THIS? IT'S ALL CRAP YOU COULD FIND ON THE NET!

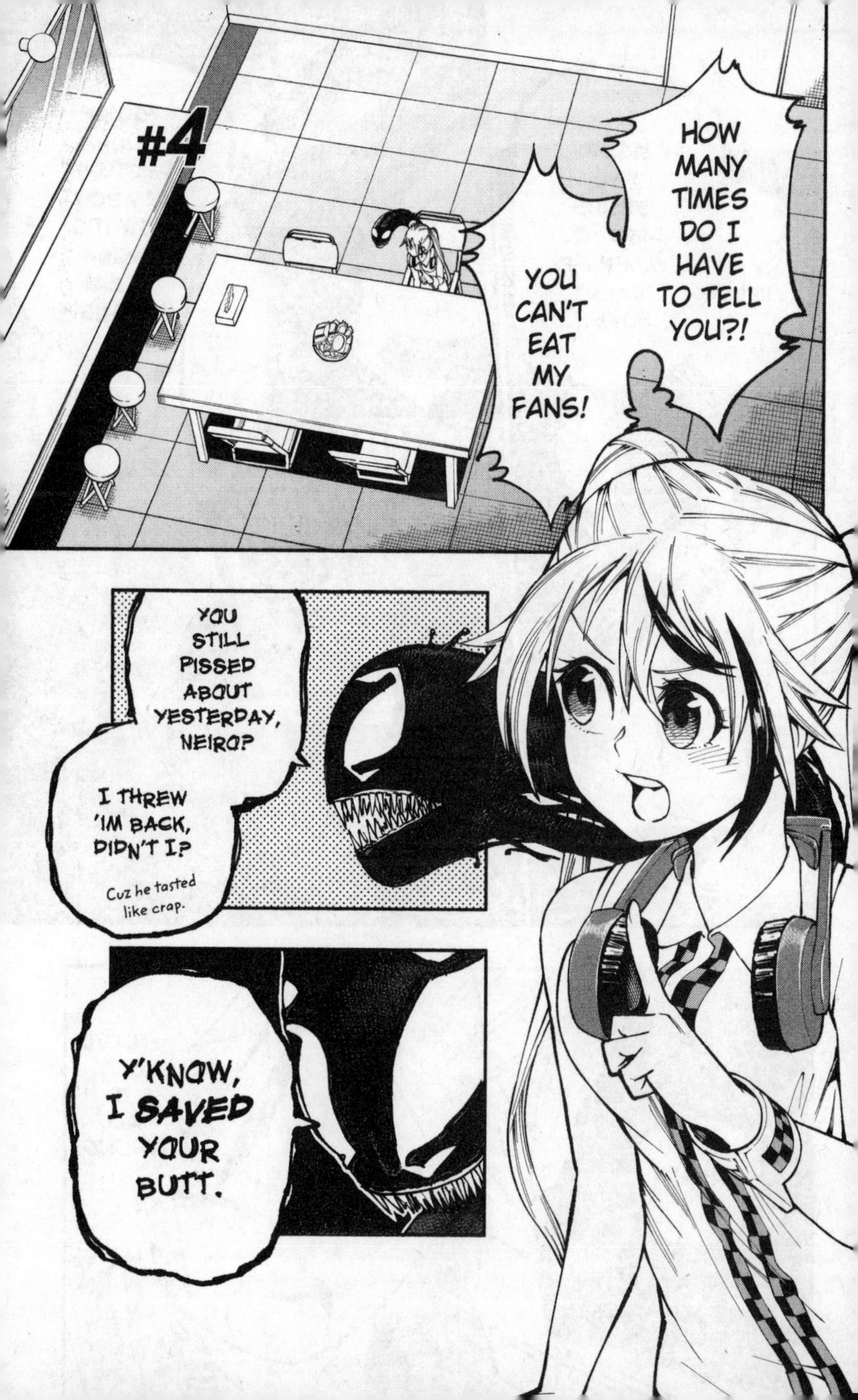
#4
HOW MANY TIMES DO I HAVE TO TELL YOU?!
YOU CAN'T EAT MY FANS!
YOU STILL PISSED ABOUT YESTERDAY, NEIRO?
I THREW 'IM BACK, DIDN'T I?
Cuz he tasted like crap.
Y'KNOW, I SAVED YOUR BUTT.

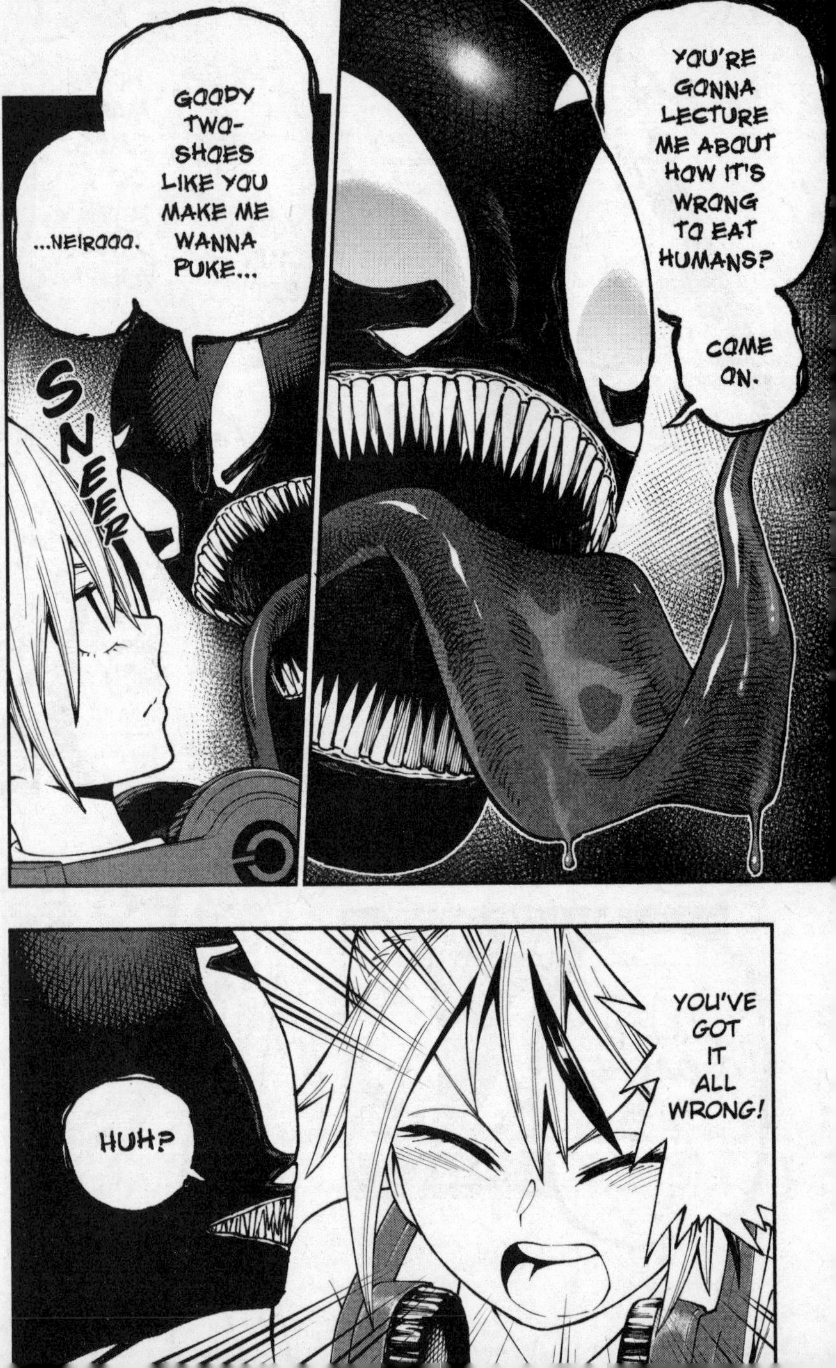
YOU'RE GONNA LECTURE ME ABOUT HOW IT'S WRONG TO EAT HUMANS?
COME ON.
...NEIROOO.
GOODY TWO-SHOES LIKE YOU MAKE ME WANNA PUKE...
SNEER
YOU'VE GOT IT ALL WRONG!
HUH?

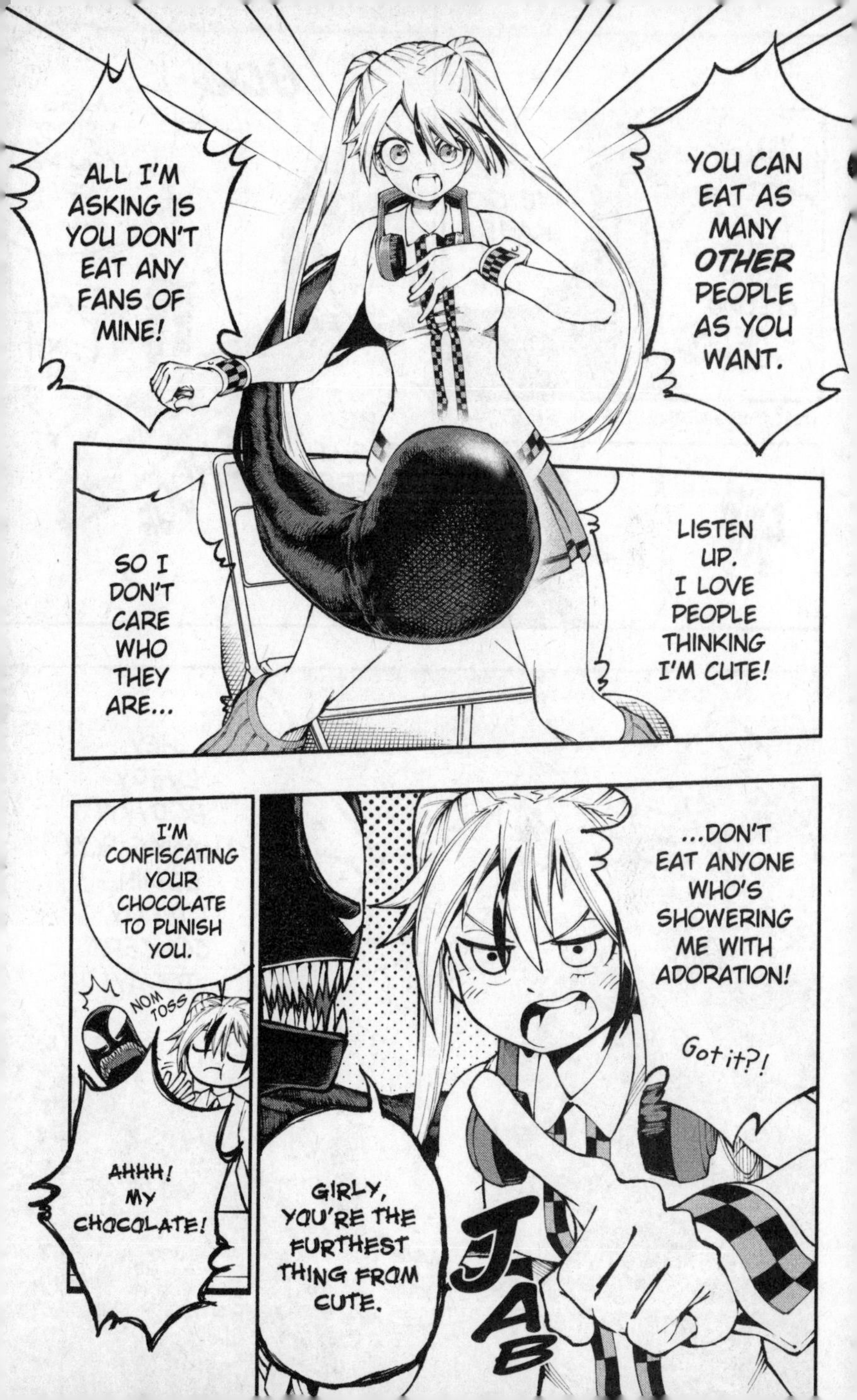
YOU CAN EAT AS MANY *OTHER* PEOPLE AS YOU WANT.
ALL I'M ASKING IS YOU DON'T EAT ANY FANS OF MINE!
LISTEN UP. I LOVE PEOPLE THINKING I'M CUTE!
SO I DON'T CARE WHO THEY ARE...
...DON'T EAT ANYONE WHO'S SHOWERING ME WITH ADORATION!
Got it?!
GIRLY, YOU'RE THE FURTHEST THING FROM CUTE.
JAB
I'M CONFISCATING YOUR CHOCOLATE TO PUNISH YOU.
NOM
TOSS
AHHH! MY CHOCOLATE!

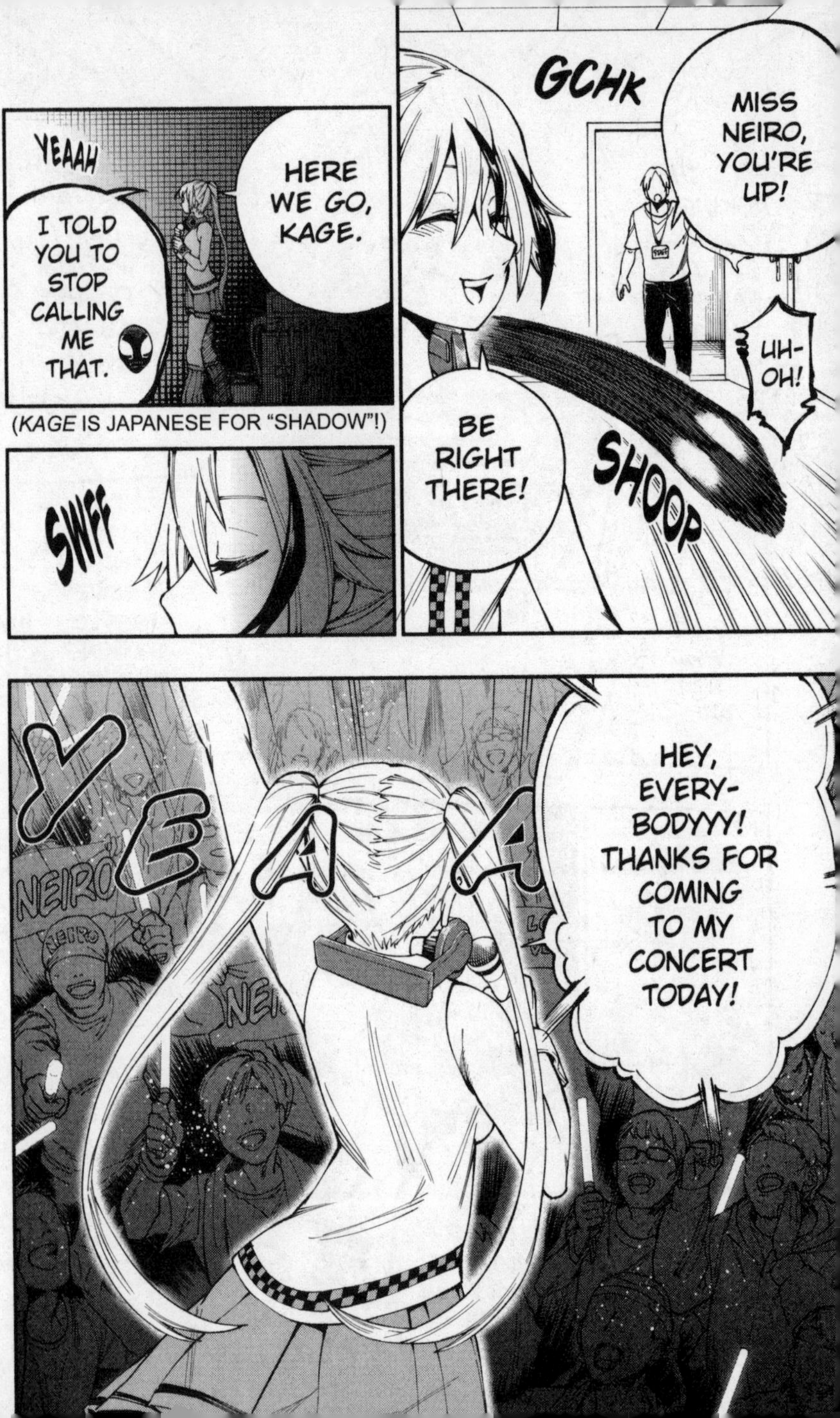
GCHK
MISS NEIRO, YOU'RE UP!
UH-OH!
BE RIGHT THERE!
SHOOP
YEAAH
HERE WE GO, KAGE.
I TOLD YOU TO STOP CALLING ME THAT.
(KAGE IS JAPANESE FOR "SHADOW"!)
SWFF
HEY, EVERY-BODYYY! THANKS FOR COMING TO MY CONCERT TODAY!
YEAA
NEIRO
NEIRO
NEIRO

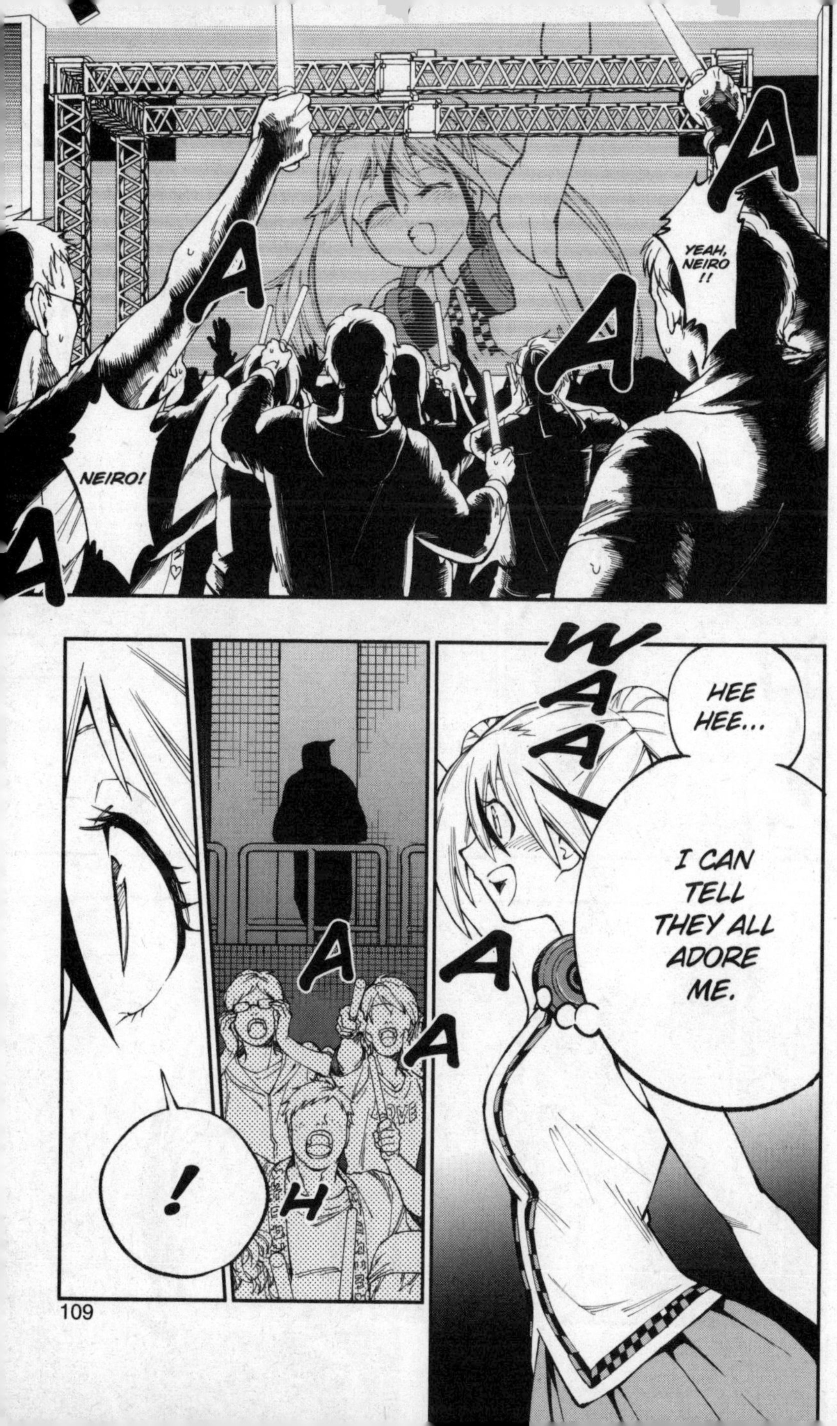
A
YEAH, NEIRO!!
A
A
A
NEIRO!
A
WAAA
HEE HEE...
I CAN TELL THEY ALL ADORE ME.
A
A
A
H
!

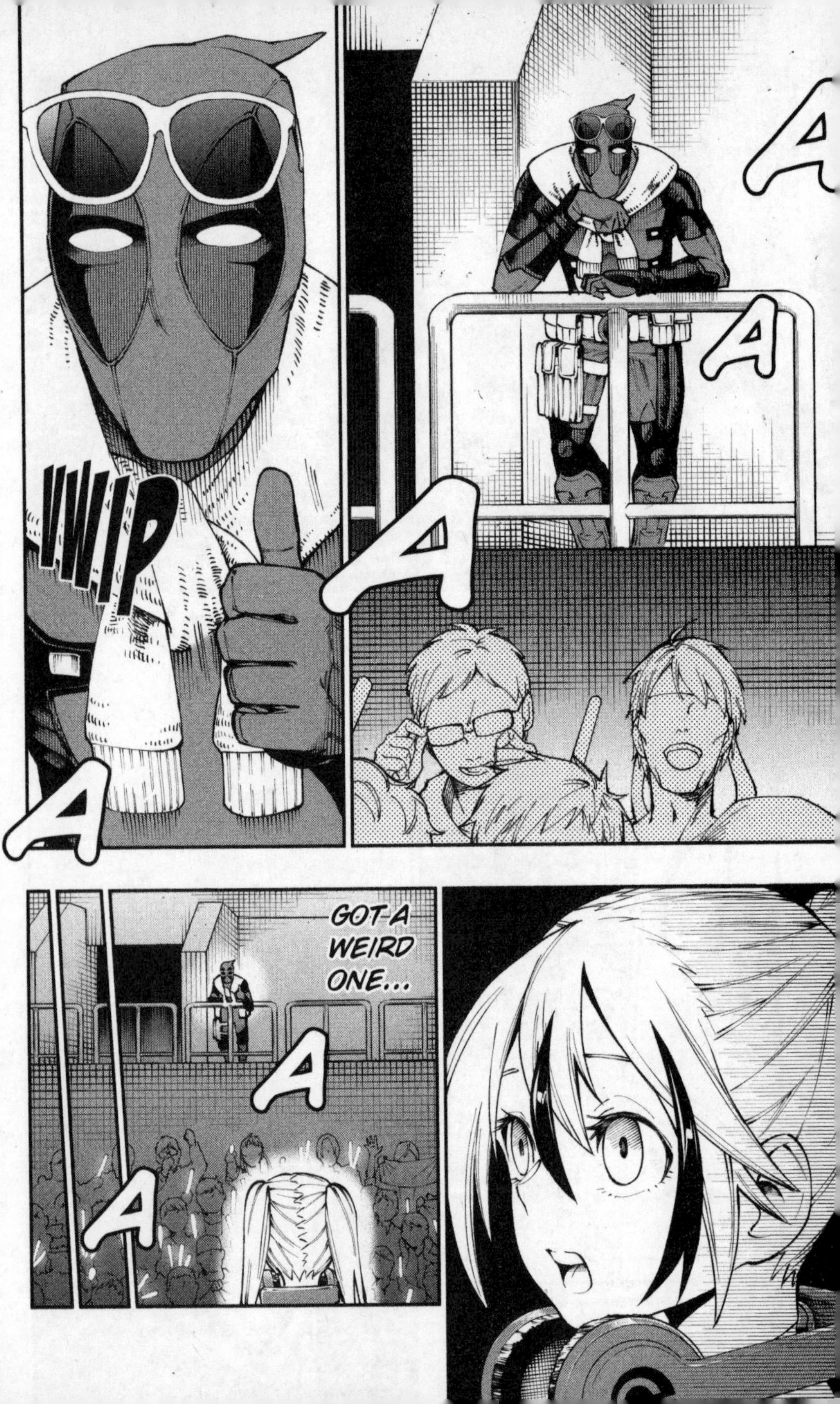
A
A
A
VWIP
A
GOT-A WEIRD ONE...
A
A

BUZZ

THAT GIRL HAS A GIFT.

We goin' to the after-party?

DON'T DO ANYTHING WEIRD, OKAY?

BUZZ

RIGHT. A JOB.

WE'RE HERE BECAUSE WE HAVE A JOB TO DO!

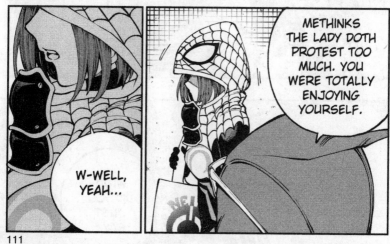

METHINKS THE LADY DOTH PROTEST TOO MUCH. YOU WERE TOTALLY ENJOYING YOURSELF.

W-WELL, YEAH...

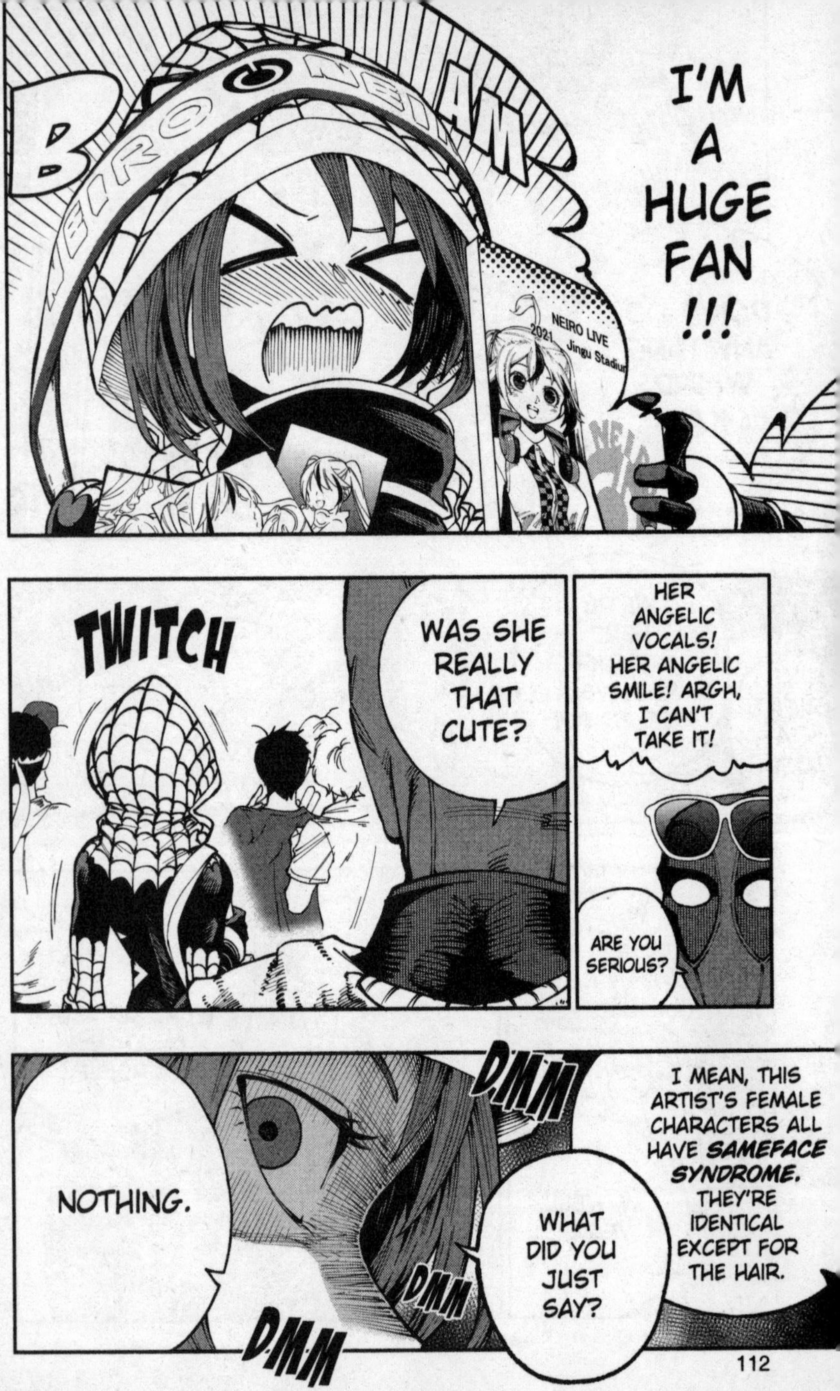
I'M A HUGE FAN!!!
NEIRO LIVE 2021 Jingu Stadiu
HER ANGELIC VOCALS! HER ANGELIC SMILE! ARGH, I CAN'T TAKE IT!
ARE YOU SERIOUS?
WAS SHE REALLY THAT CUTE?
TWITCH
I MEAN, THIS ARTIST'S FEMALE CHARACTERS ALL HAVE **SAMEFACE SYNDROME.** THEY'RE IDENTICAL EXCEPT FOR THE HAIR.
D-MM
WHAT DID YOU JUST SAY?
DMM
D-MM
NOTHING.

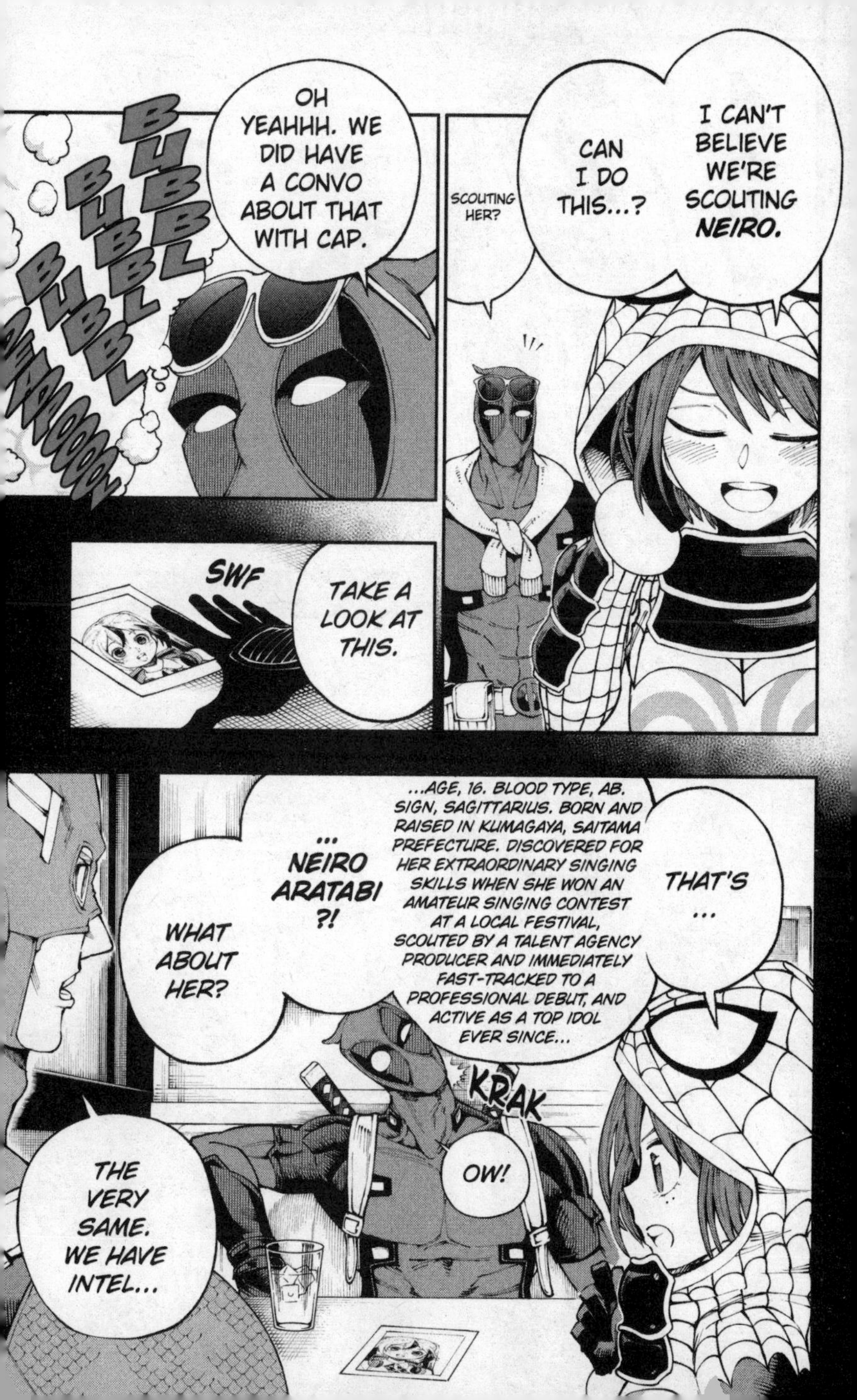

I CAN'T BELIEVE WE'RE SCOUTING NEIRO.
CAN I DO THIS...?
SCOUTING HER?
OH YEAHHH. WE DID HAVE A CONVO ABOUT THAT WITH CAP.
BUBBL BUBBL BUBBBL
SWF
TAKE A LOOK AT THIS.
THAT'S ...
...AGE, 16. BLOOD TYPE, AB. SIGN, SAGITTARIUS. BORN AND RAISED IN KUMAGAYA, SAITAMA PREFECTURE. DISCOVERED FOR HER EXTRAORDINARY SINGING SKILLS WHEN SHE WON AN AMATEUR SINGING CONTEST AT A LOCAL FESTIVAL, SCOUTED BY A TALENT AGENCY PRODUCER AND IMMEDIATELY FAST-TRACKED TO A PROFESSIONAL DEBUT, AND ACTIVE AS A TOP IDOL EVER SINCE...
... NEIRO ARATABI ?!
WHAT ABOUT HER?
KRAK
OW!
THE VERY SAME. WE HAVE INTEL...

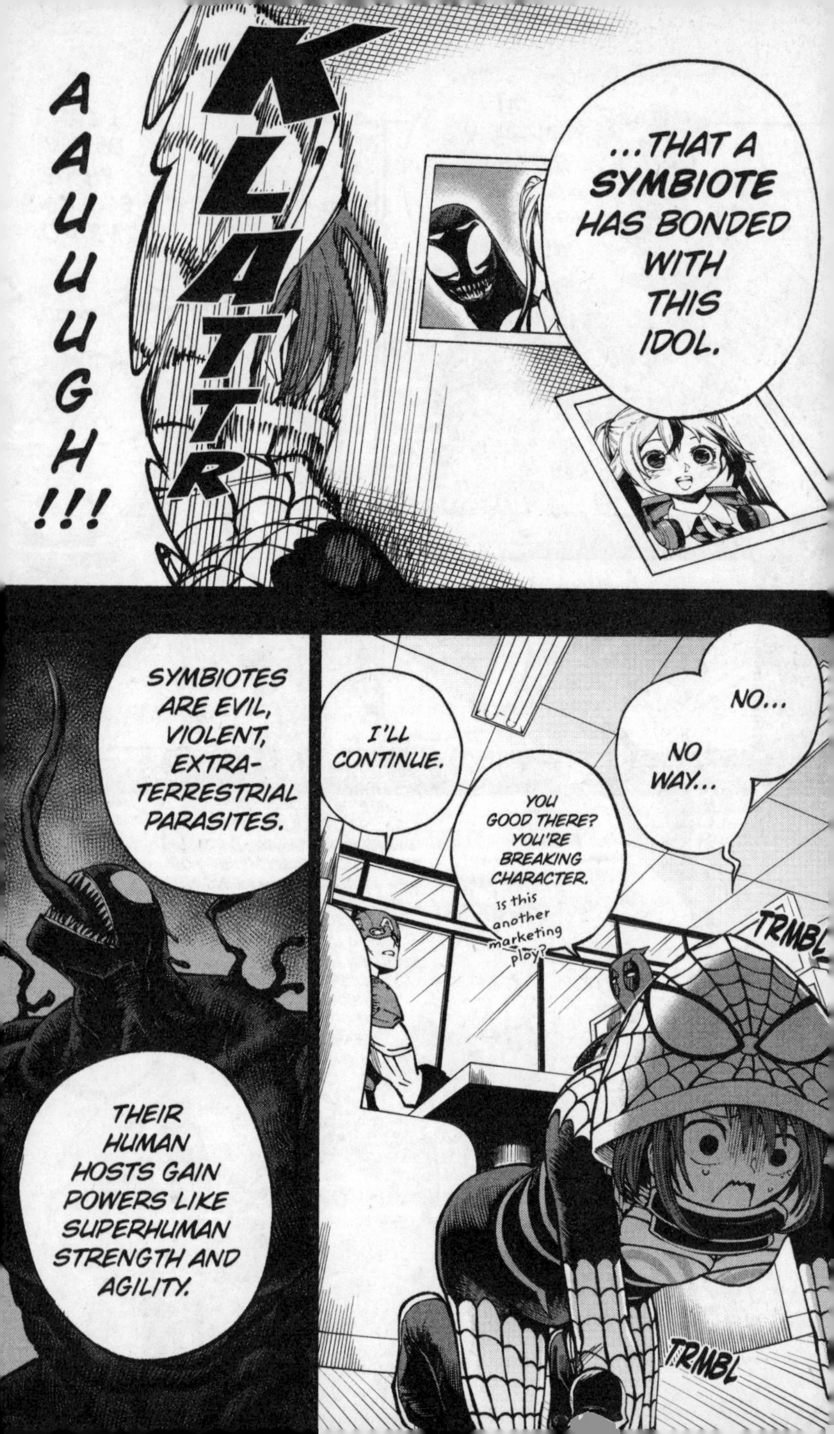
...THAT A SYMBIOTE HAS BONDED WITH THIS IDOL.
KLATTR
AAAUUUGH!!!
NO...
NO WAY...
I'LL CONTINUE.
YOU GOOD THERE? YOU'RE BREAKING CHARACTER.
Is this another marketing ploy?
TRMBL
TRMBL
SYMBIOTES ARE EVIL, VIOLENT, EXTRA-TERRESTRIAL PARASITES.
THEIR HUMAN HOSTS GAIN POWERS LIKE SUPERHUMAN STRENGTH AND AGILITY.

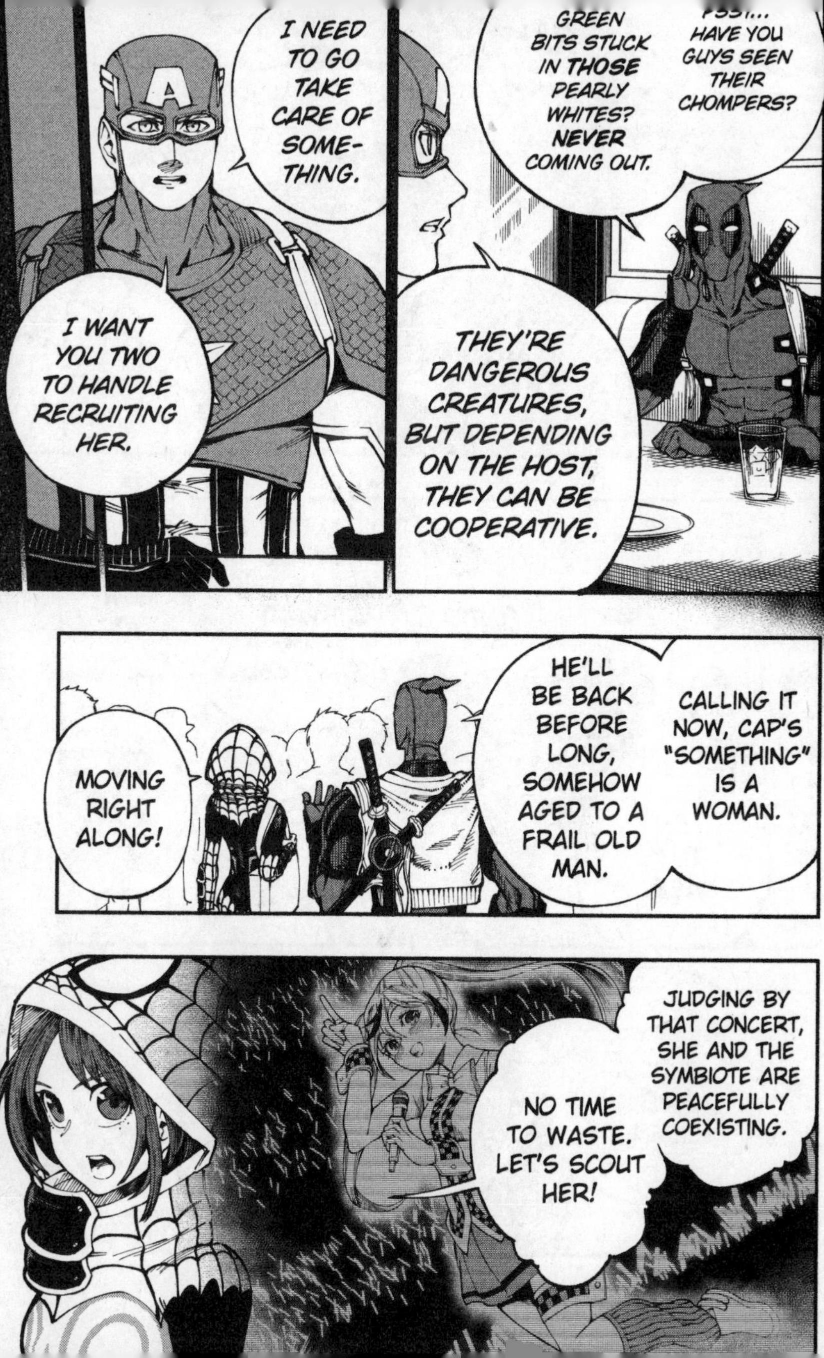
HAVE YOU GUYS SEEN THEIR CHOMPERS?
GREEN BITS STUCK IN THOSE PEARLY WHITES? NEVER COMING OUT.
THEY'RE DANGEROUS CREATURES, BUT DEPENDING ON THE HOST, THEY CAN BE COOPERATIVE.
I NEED TO GO TAKE CARE OF SOME-THING.
I WANT YOU TWO TO HANDLE RECRUITING HER.
CALLING IT NOW, CAP'S "SOMETHING" IS A WOMAN.
HE'LL BE BACK BEFORE LONG, SOMEHOW AGED TO A FRAIL OLD MAN.
MOVING RIGHT ALONG!
JUDGING BY THAT CONCERT, SHE AND THE SYMBIOTE ARE PEACEFULLY COEXISTING.
NO TIME TO WASTE. LET'S SCOUT HER!

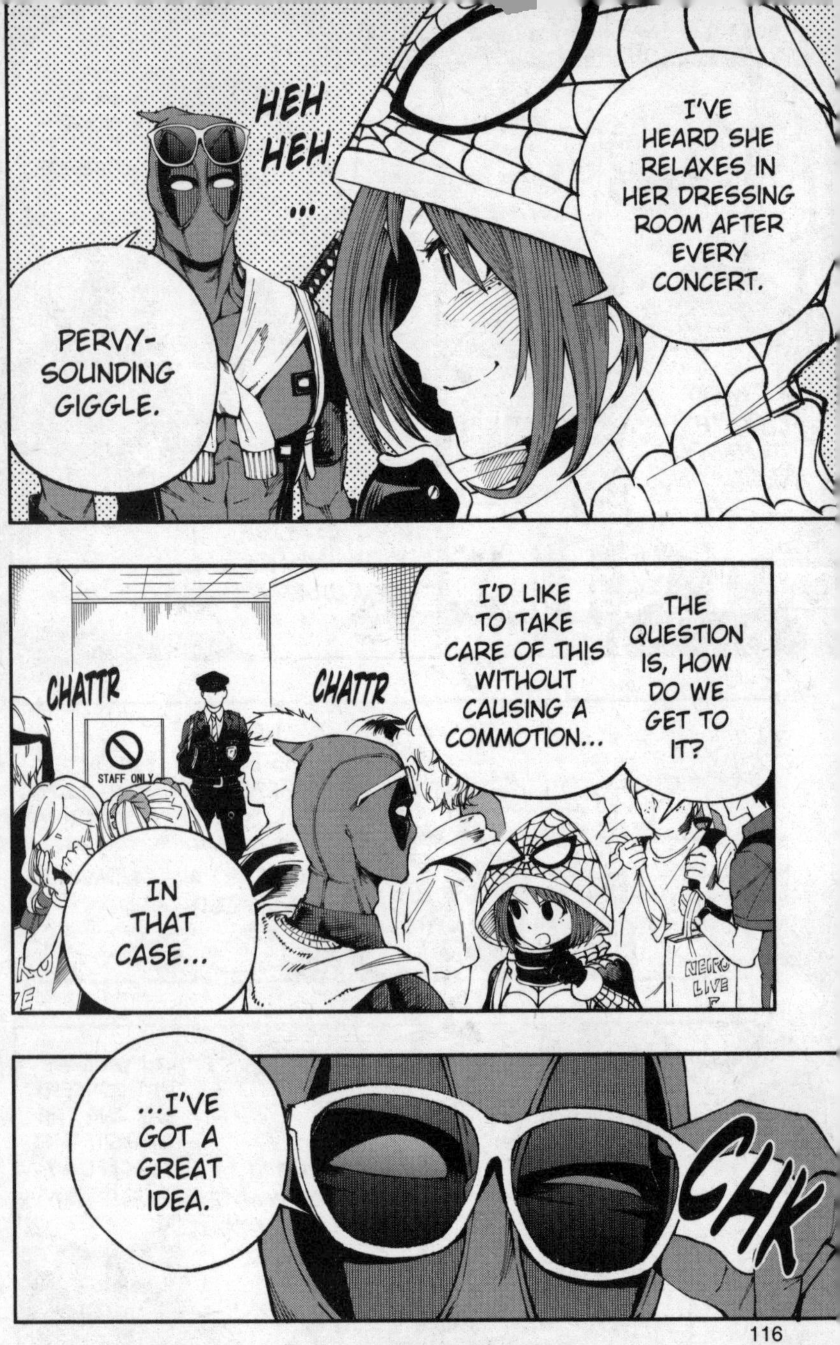
I'VE HEARD SHE RELAXES IN HER DRESSING ROOM AFTER EVERY CONCERT.
HEH HEH ...
PERVY-SOUNDING GIGGLE.
THE QUESTION IS, HOW DO WE GET TO IT?
I'D LIKE TO TAKE CARE OF THIS WITHOUT CAUSING A COMMOTION...
CHATTR
NEIRO LIVE
CHATTR
STAFF ONLY
IN THAT CASE...
CHK
...I'VE GOT A GREAT IDEA.

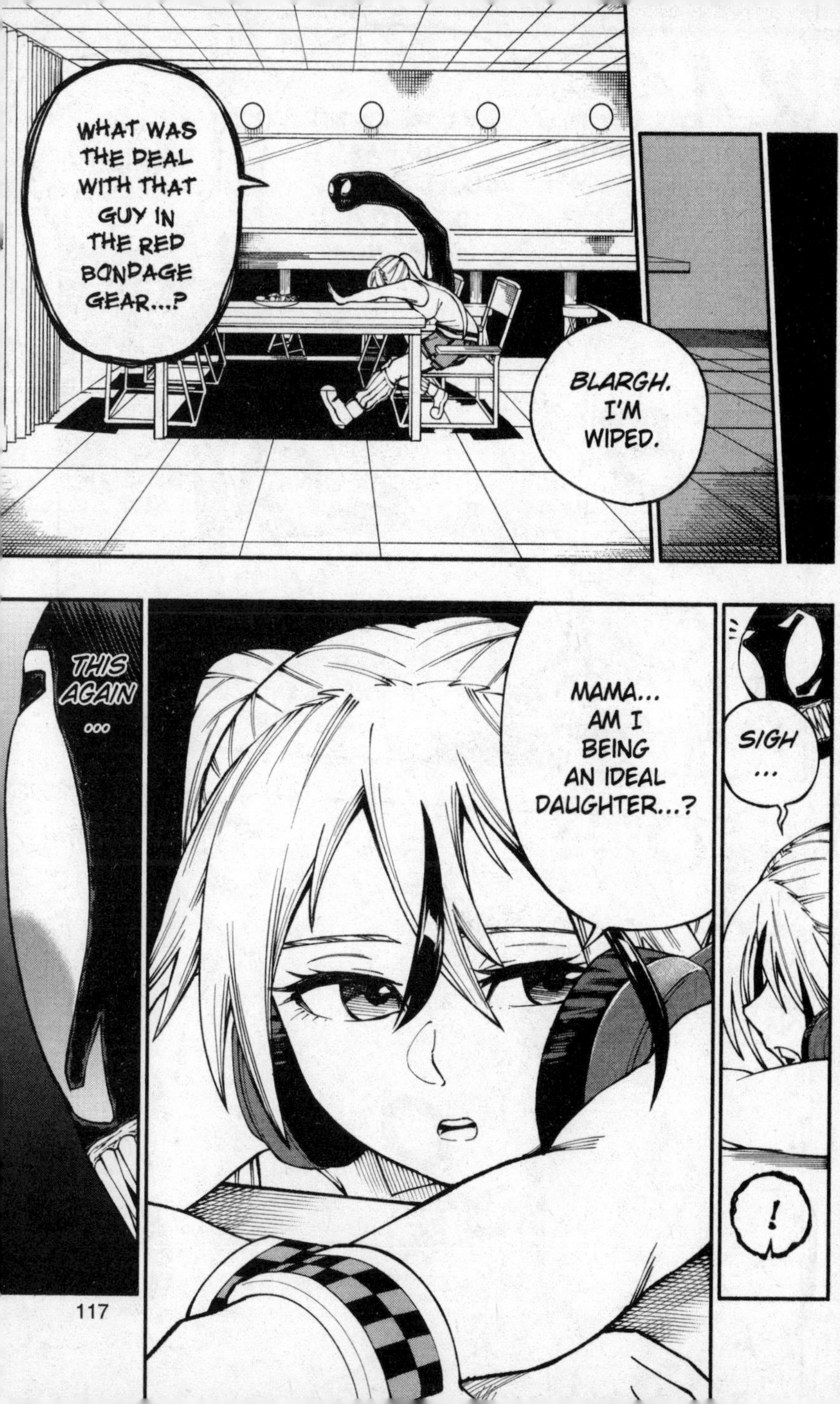
BLARGH. I'M WIPED.
WHAT WAS THE DEAL WITH THAT GUY IN THE RED BONDAGE GEAR...?
SIGH...
!
MAMA... AM I BEING AN IDEAL DAUGHTER...?
THIS AGAIN...

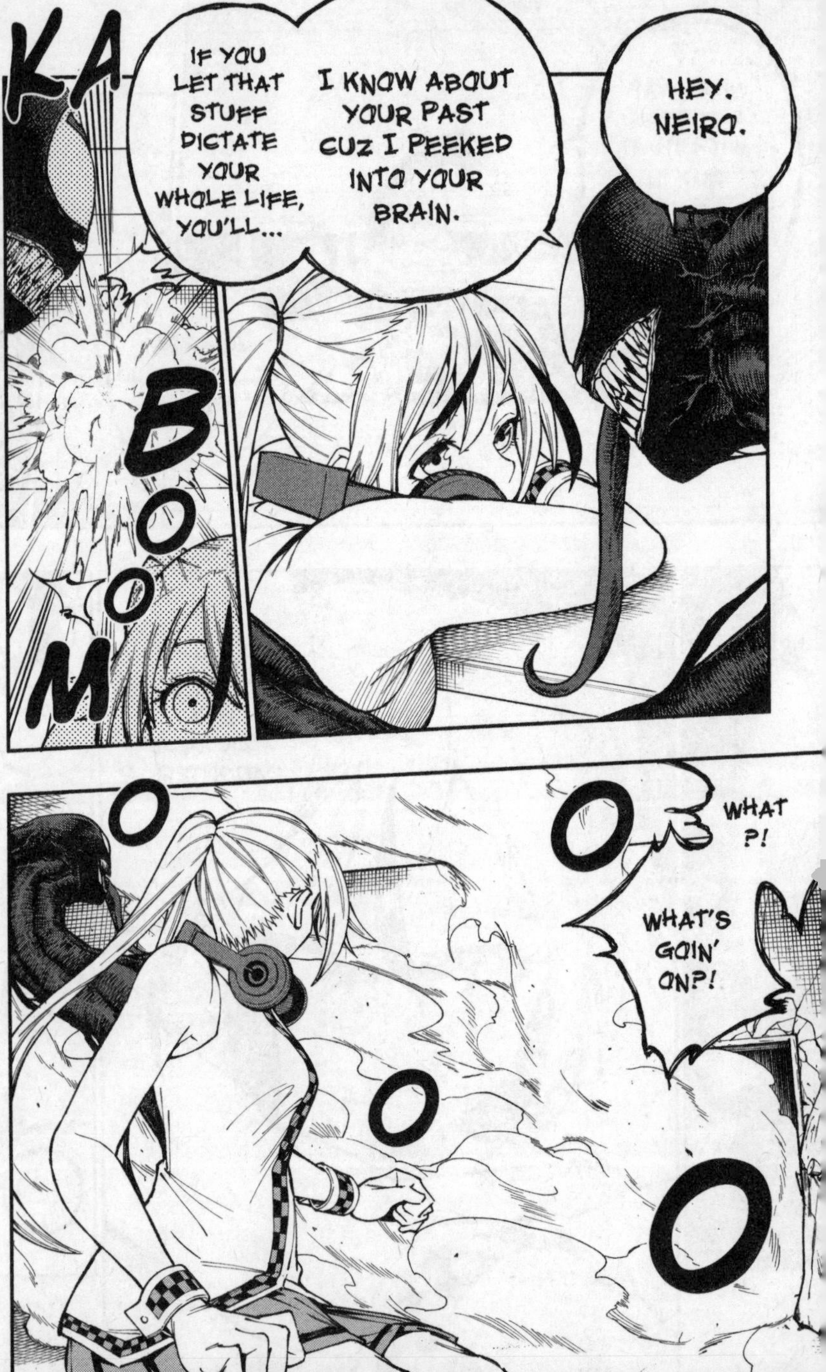
HEY. NEIRO.
I KNOW ABOUT YOUR PAST CUZ I PEEKED INTO YOUR BRAIN.
IF YOU LET THAT STUFF DICTATE YOUR WHOLE LIFE, YOU'LL...
KA
BOOM
OOOO
WHAT?!
WHAT'S GOIN' ON?!

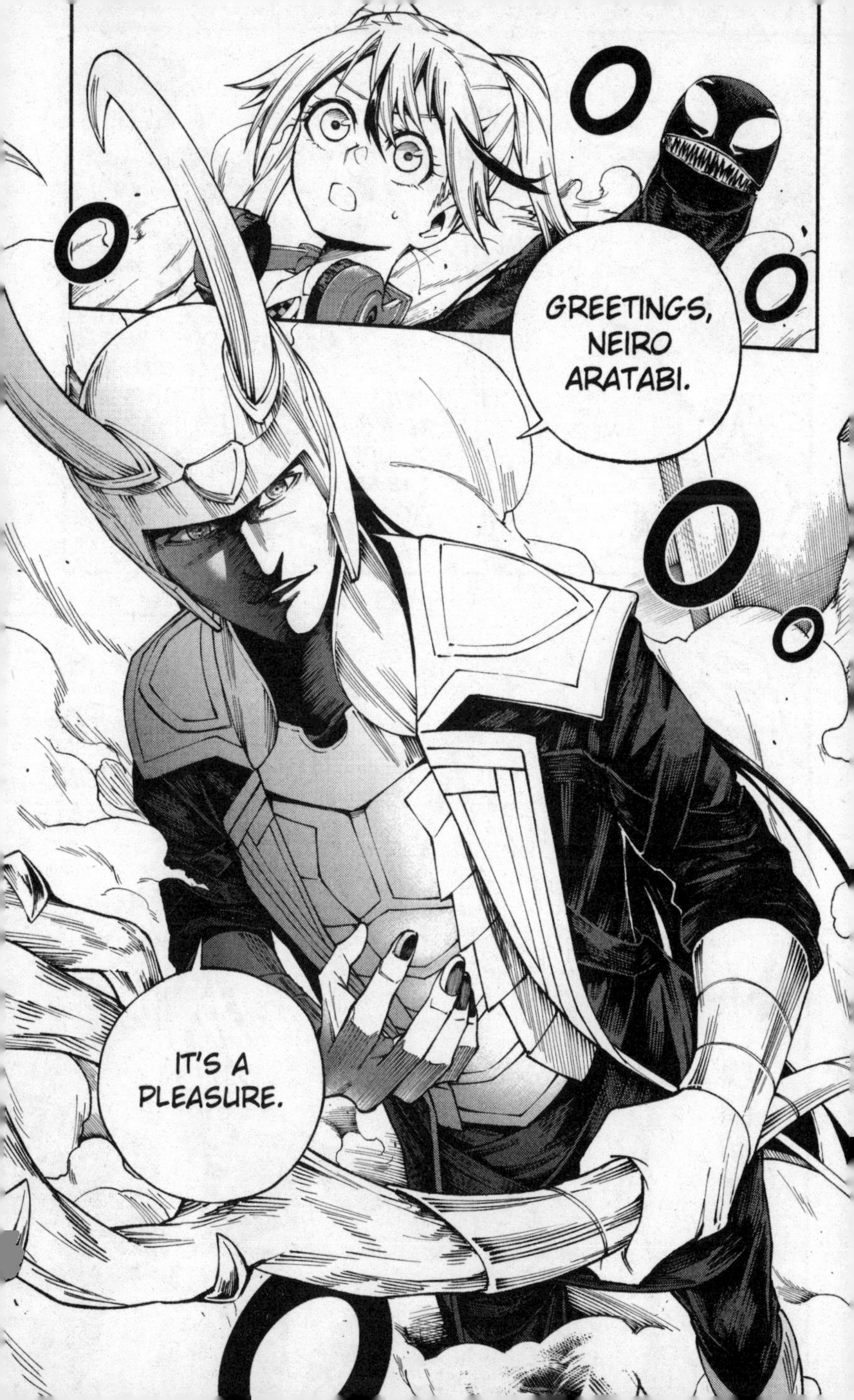
GREETINGS, NEIRO ARATABI.
IT'S A PLEASURE.

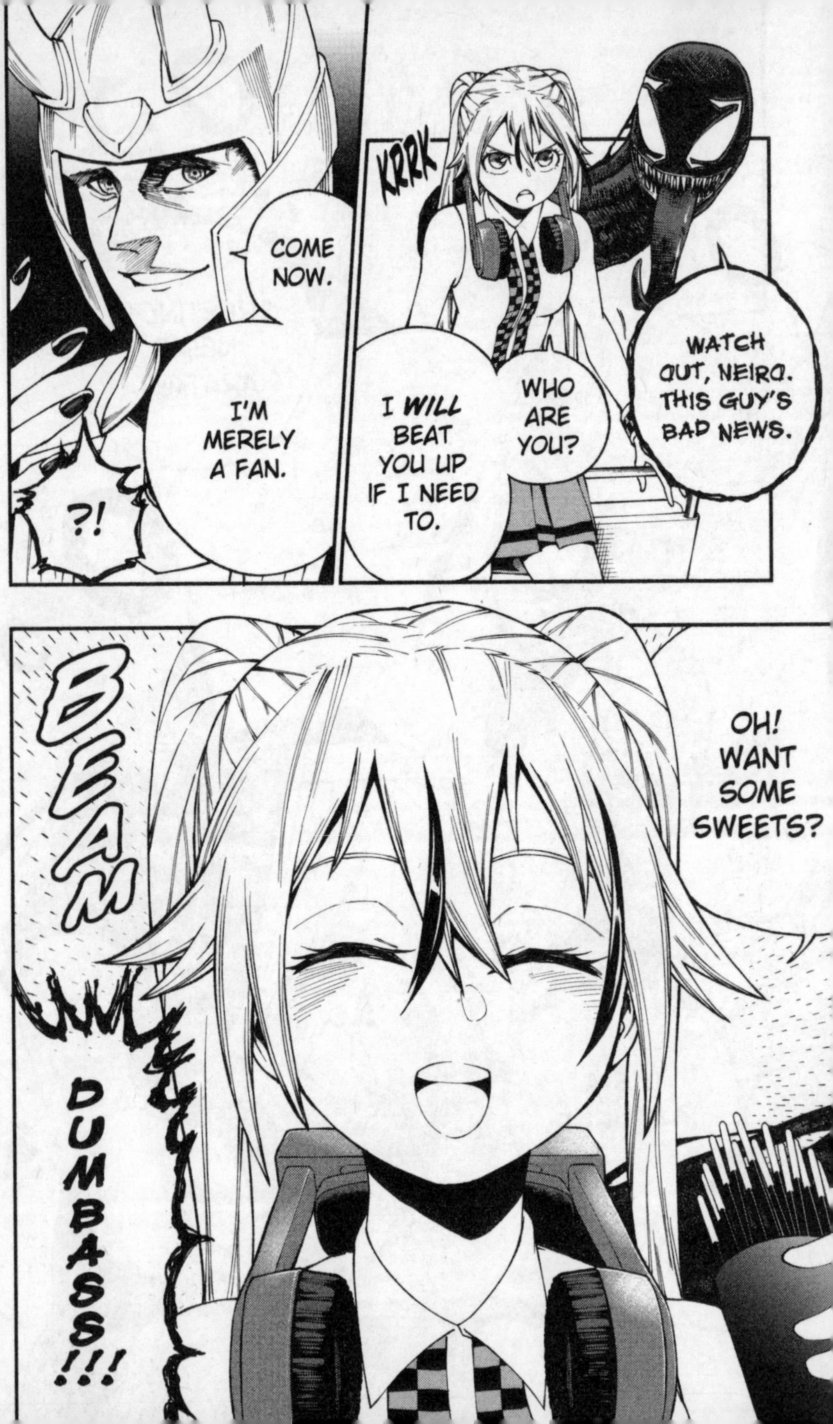
KRRK
WATCH OUT, NEIRO. THIS GUY'S BAD NEWS.
WHO ARE YOU?
I WILL BEAT YOU UP IF I NEED TO.
COME NOW.
I'M MERELY A FAN.
?!
OH! WANT SOME SWEETS?
BEAM
DUMBASS!!!

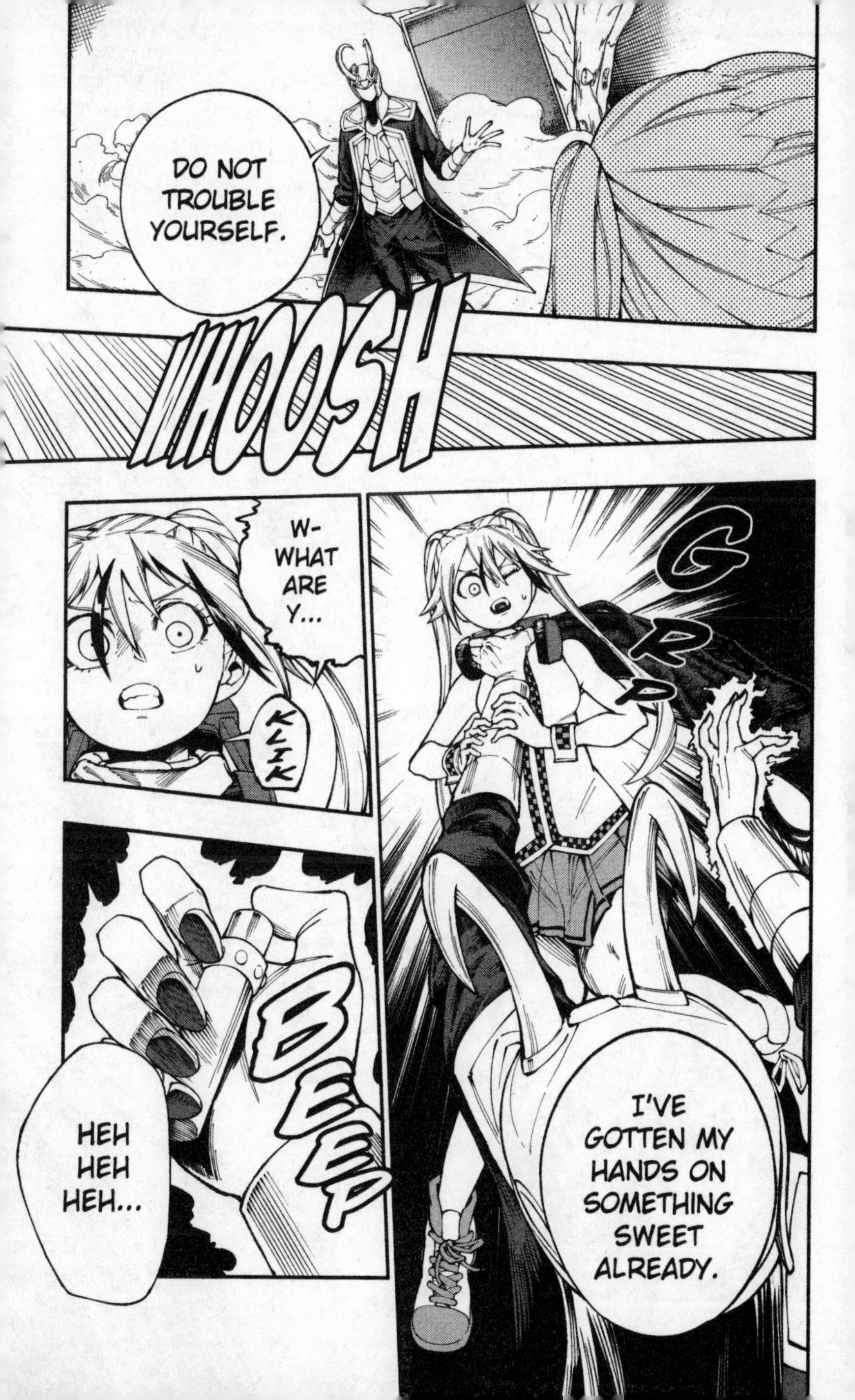
DO NOT TROUBLE YOURSELF.
WHOOSH
GRPP
I'VE GOTTEN MY HANDS ON SOMETHING SWEET ALREADY.
W- WHAT ARE Y...
KLIK
BEEEP
HEH HEH HEH...

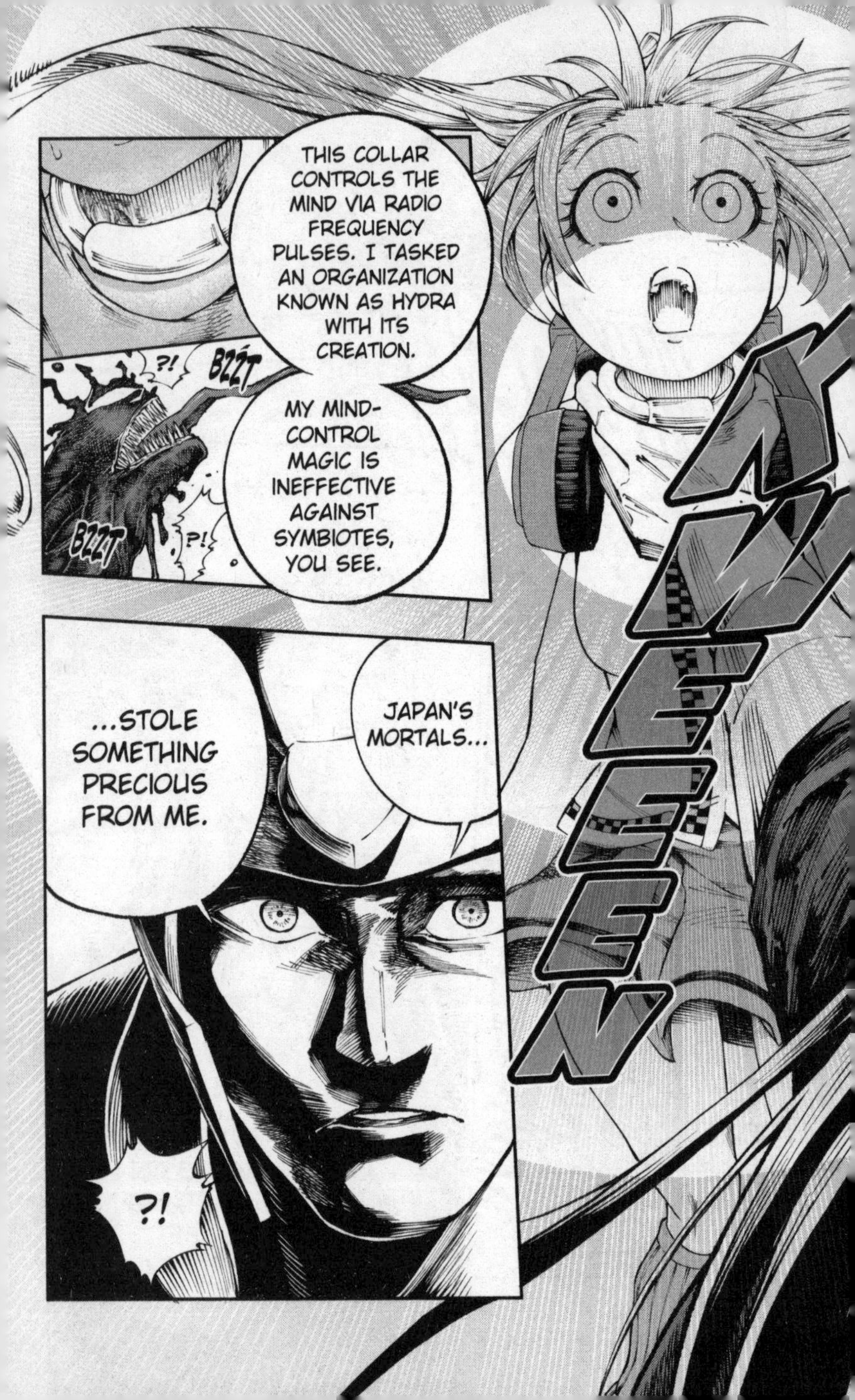
THIS COLLAR CONTROLS THE MIND VIA RADIO FREQUENCY PULSES. I TASKED AN ORGANIZATION KNOWN AS HYDRA WITH ITS CREATION.
?!
BZZT
MY MIND-CONTROL MAGIC IS INEFFECTIVE AGAINST SYMBIOTES, YOU SEE.
?!
BZZT
KWEEEEN
JAPAN'S MORTALS...
...STOLE SOMETHING PRECIOUS FROM ME.
?!

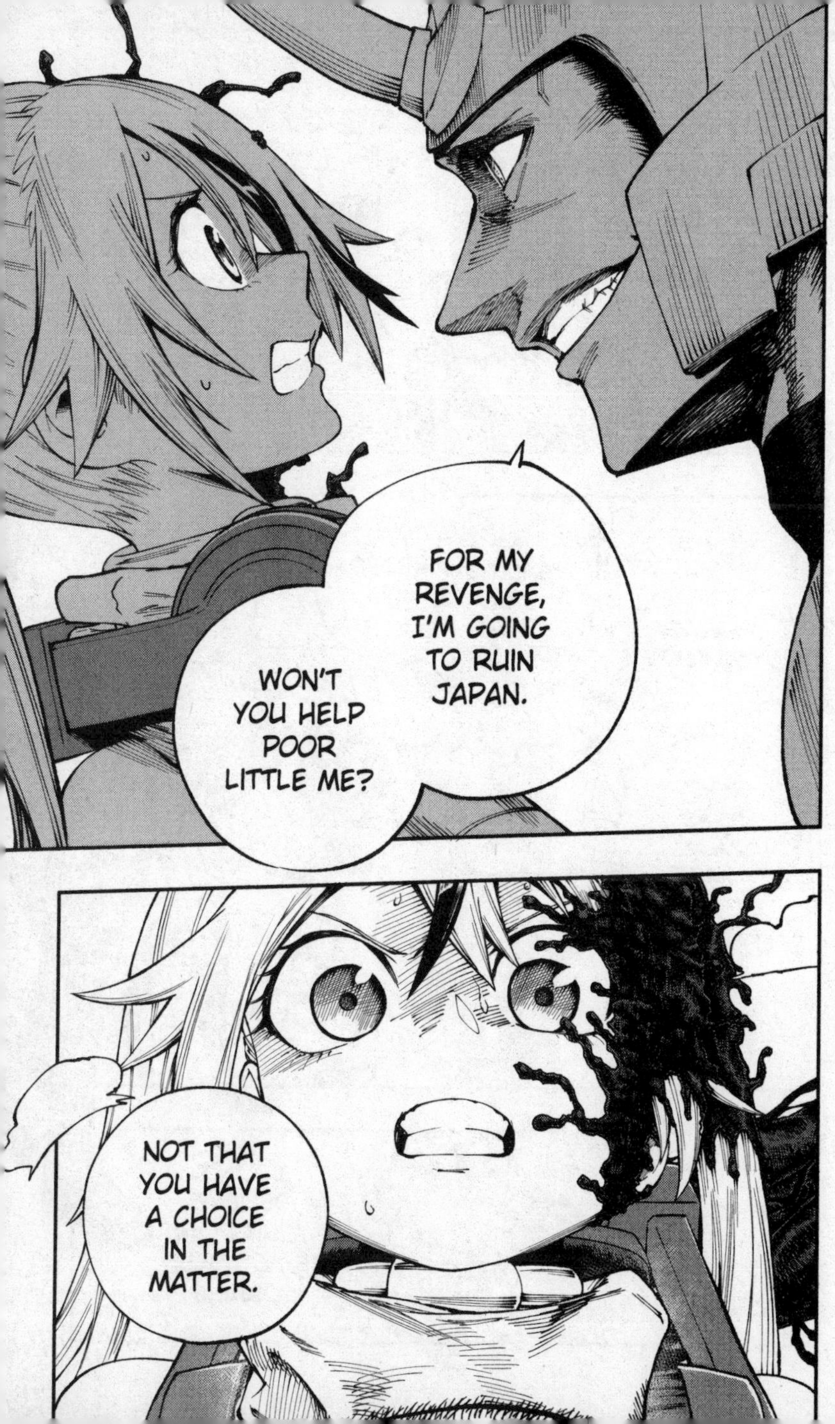
FOR MY REVENGE, I'M GOING TO RUIN JAPAN.
WON'T YOU HELP POOR LITTLE ME?
NOT THAT YOU HAVE A CHOICE IN THE MATTER.

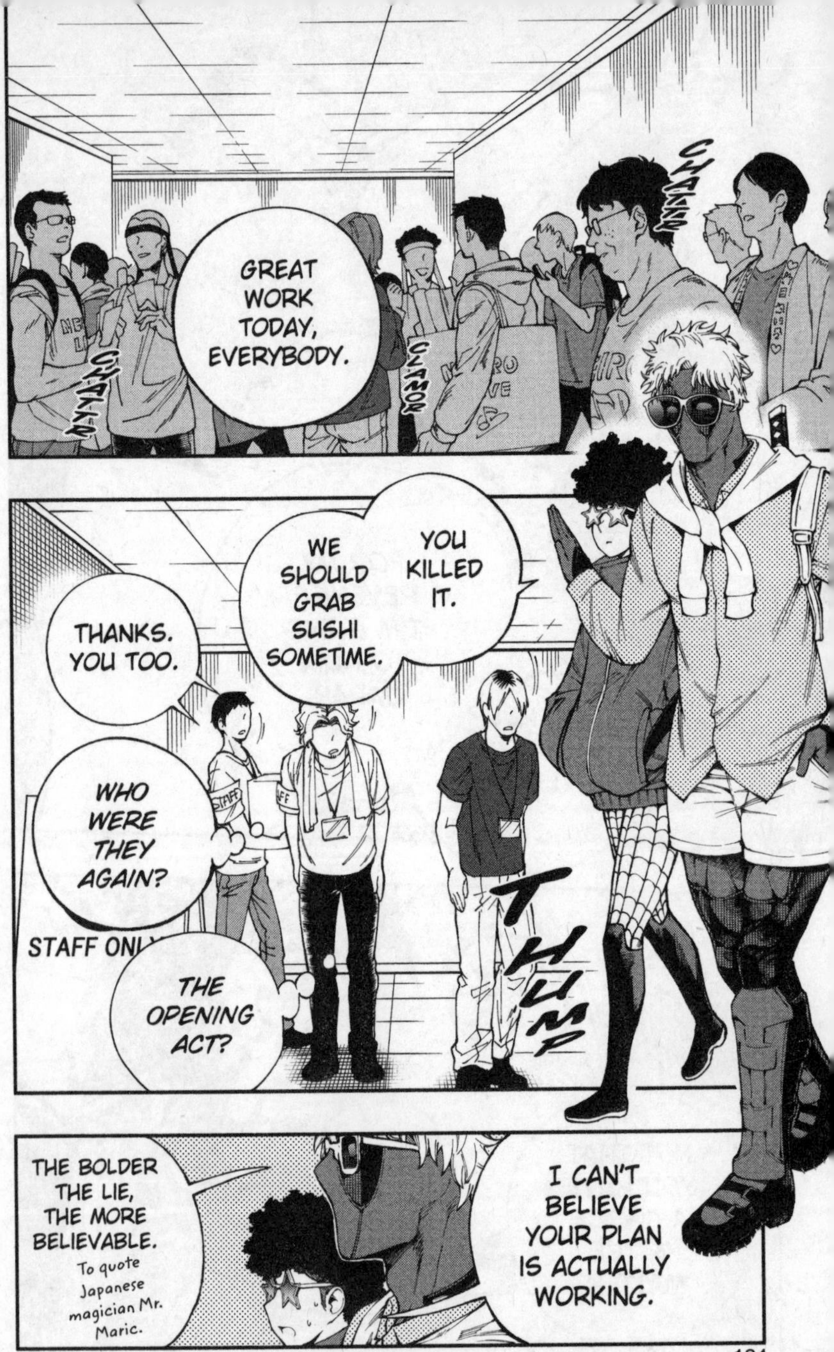
CHATTER
GREAT WORK TODAY, EVERYBODY.
CLAMOR
CHATTER
YOU KILLED IT.
WE SHOULD GRAB SUSHI SOMETIME.
THANKS. YOU TOO.
WHO WERE THEY AGAIN?
STAFF ONL
THE OPENING ACT?
THUMP
I CAN'T BELIEVE YOUR PLAN IS ACTUALLY WORKING.
THE BOLDER THE LIE, THE MORE BELIEVABLE.
To quote Japanese magician Mr. Maric.

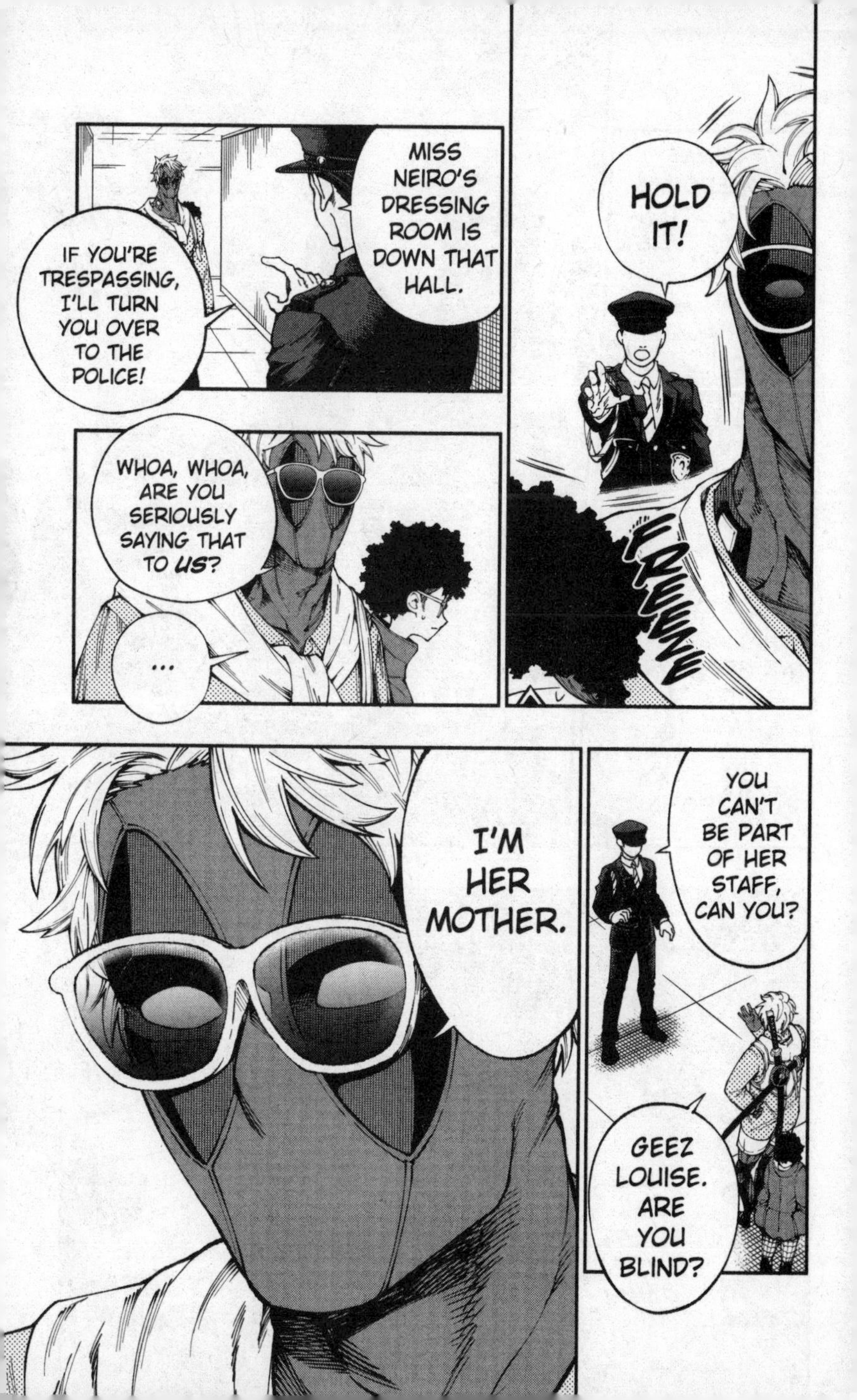
HOLD IT!
FREEZE
MISS NEIRO'S DRESSING ROOM IS DOWN THAT HALL.
IF YOU'RE TRESPASSING, I'LL TURN YOU OVER TO THE POLICE!
WHOA, WHOA, ARE YOU SERIOUSLY SAYING THAT TO *US*?
...
YOU CAN'T BE PART OF HER STAFF, CAN YOU?
GEEZ LOUISE. ARE YOU BLIND?
I'M HER MOTHER.

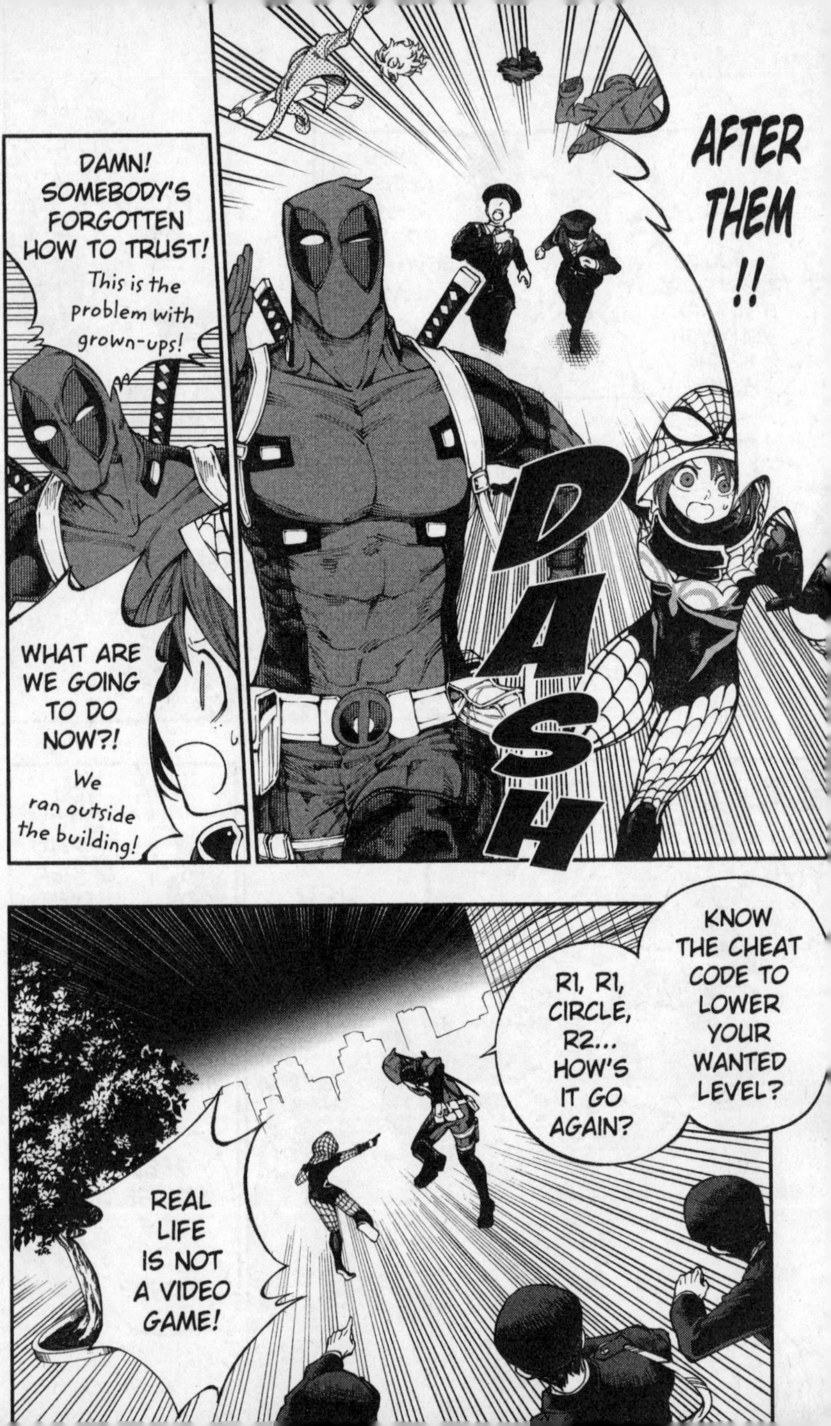
AFTER THEM!!
DASH
DAMN! SOMEBODY'S FORGOTTEN HOW TO TRUST!
This is the problem with grown-ups!
WHAT ARE WE GOING TO DO NOW?!
We ran outside the building!
KNOW THE CHEAT CODE TO LOWER YOUR WANTED LEVEL?
R1, R1, CIRCLE, R2... HOW'S IT GO AGAIN?
REAL LIFE IS NOT A VIDEO GAME!

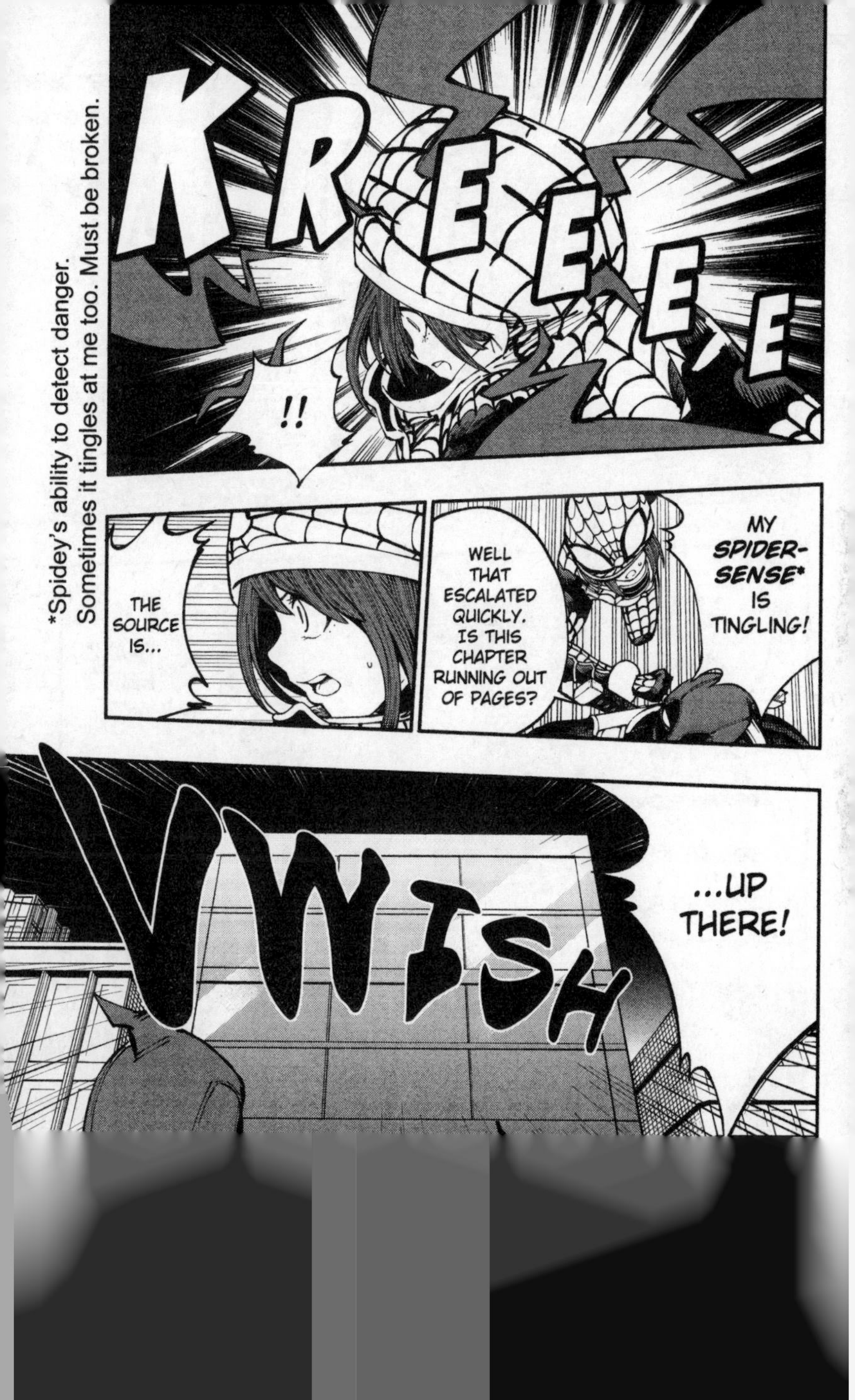
KREEEEE
!!
MY SPIDER-SENSE* IS TINGLING!
WELL THAT ESCALATED QUICKLY. IS THIS CHAPTER RUNNING OUT OF PAGES?
THE SOURCE IS...
...UP THERE!
VWISH

*Spidey's ability to detect danger. Sometimes it tingles at me too. Must be broken.

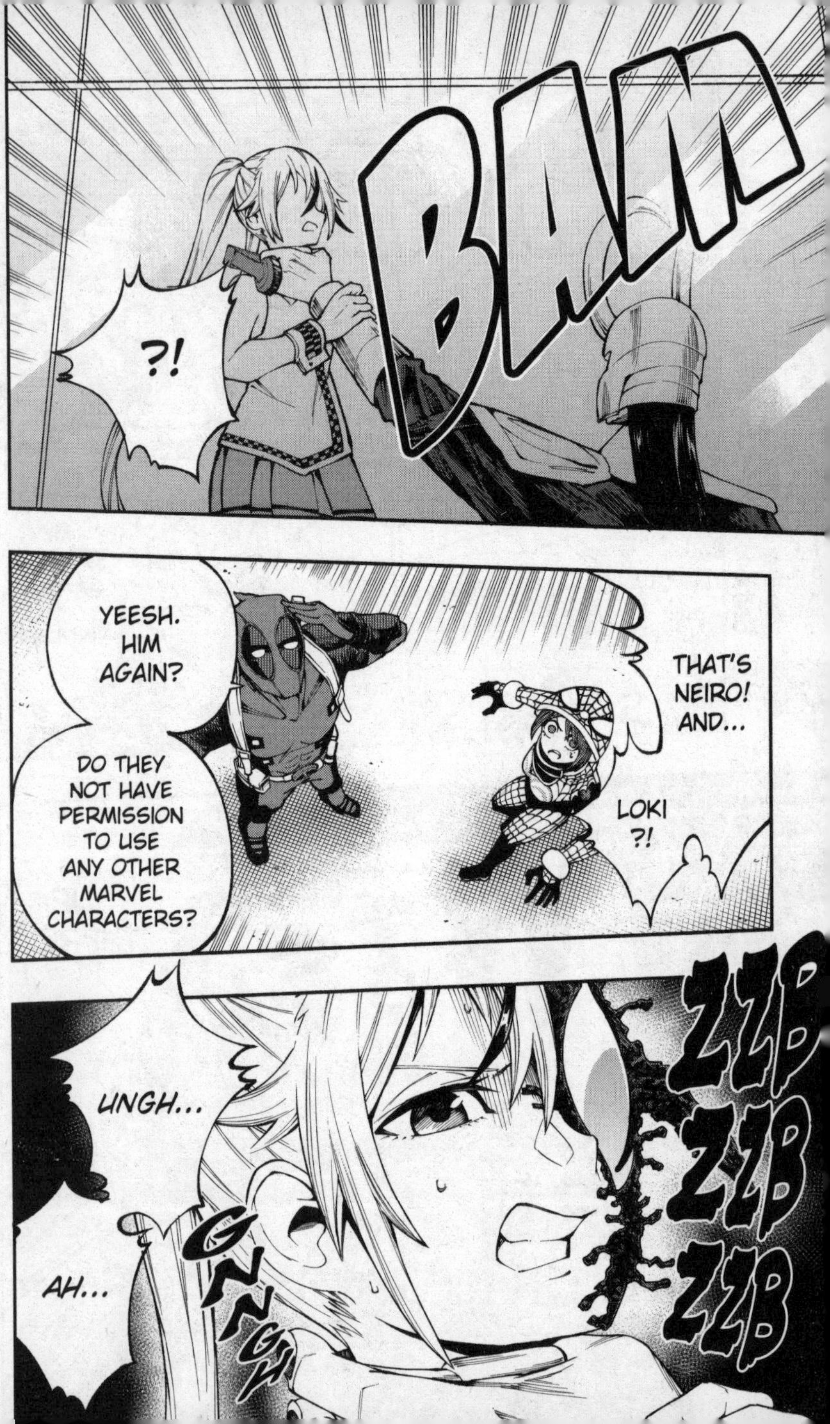
BAM
?!
THAT'S NEIRO! AND...
LOKI ?!
YEESH. HIM AGAIN?
DO THEY NOT HAVE PERMISSION TO USE ANY OTHER MARVEL CHARACTERS?
ZZB ZZB ZZB
UNGH...
GNNGH
AH...

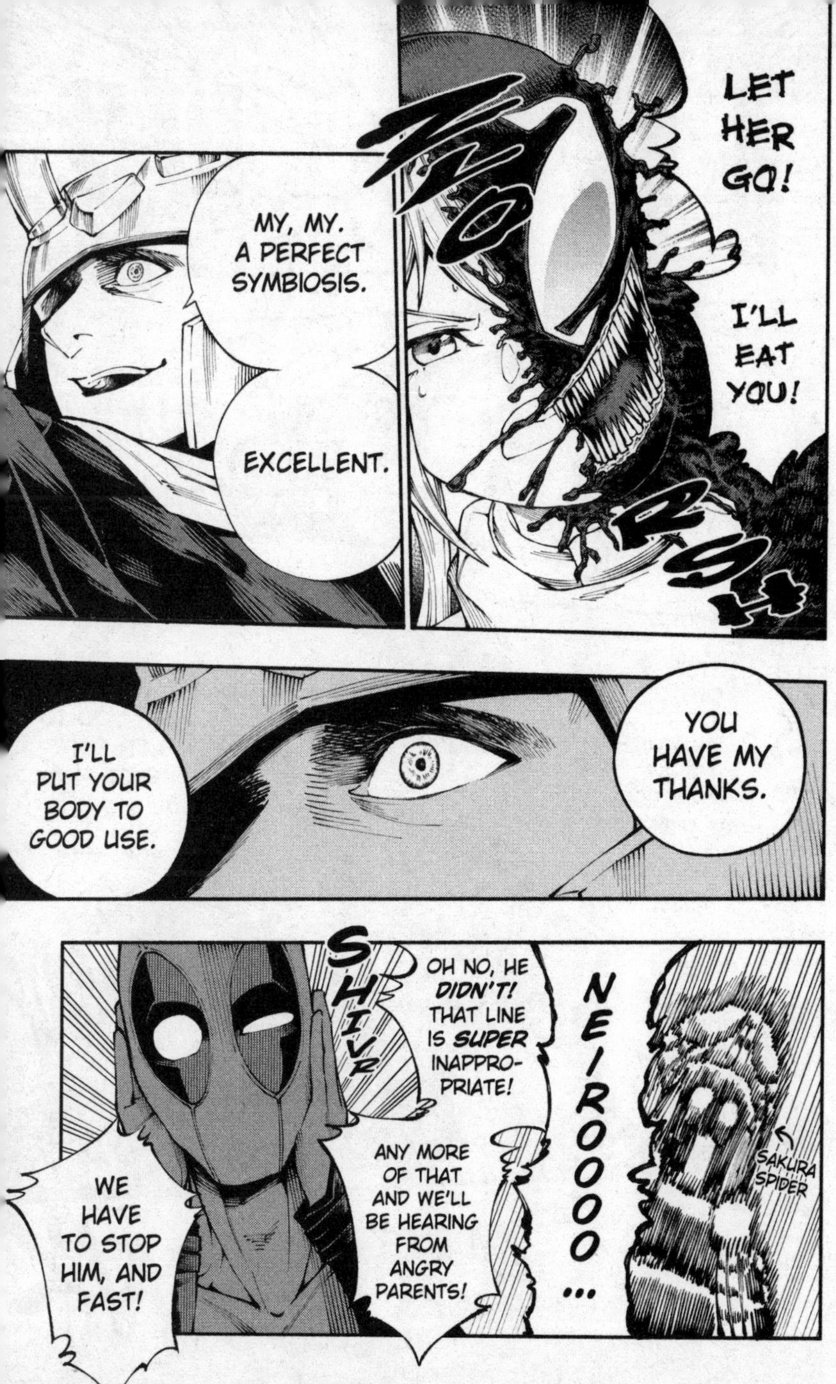
LET HER GO!
I'LL EAT YOU!
MY, MY. A PERFECT SYMBIOSIS.
EXCELLENT.
YOU HAVE MY THANKS.
I'LL PUT YOUR BODY TO GOOD USE.
NEIROOOOO...
SAKURA SPIDER
OH NO, HE *DIDN'T!* THAT LINE IS *SUPER* INAPPROPRIATE!
ANY MORE OF THAT AND WE'LL BE HEARING FROM ANGRY PARENTS!
SHIVR
WE HAVE TO STOP HIM, AND FAST!

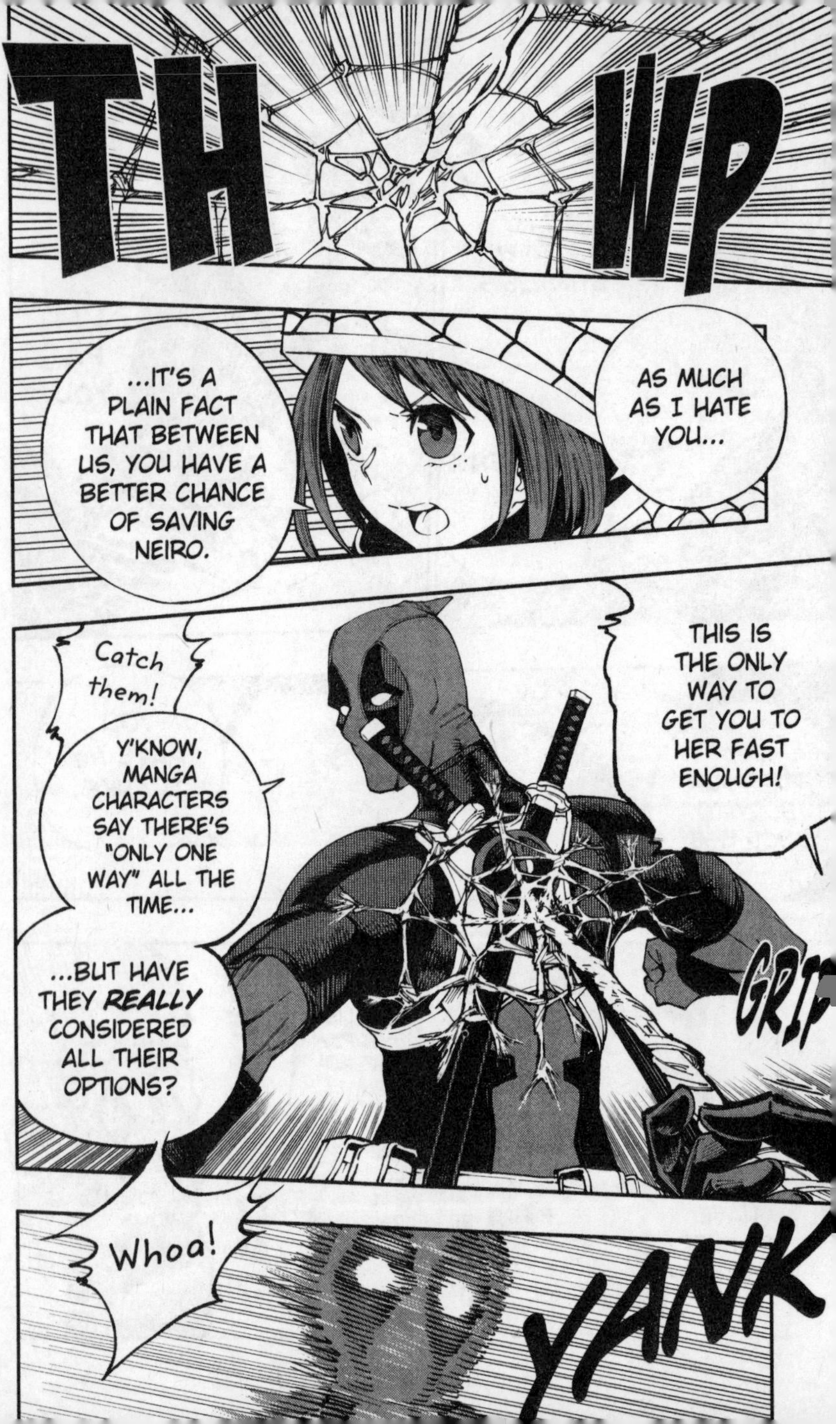
THWP
AS MUCH AS I HATE YOU...
...IT'S A PLAIN FACT THAT BETWEEN US, YOU HAVE A BETTER CHANCE OF SAVING NEIRO.
THIS IS THE ONLY WAY TO GET YOU TO HER FAST ENOUGH!
GRIP
Catch them!
Y'KNOW, MANGA CHARACTERS SAY THERE'S "ONLY ONE WAY" ALL THE TIME...
...BUT HAVE THEY **REALLY** CONSIDERED ALL THEIR OPTIONS?
YANK
Whoa!

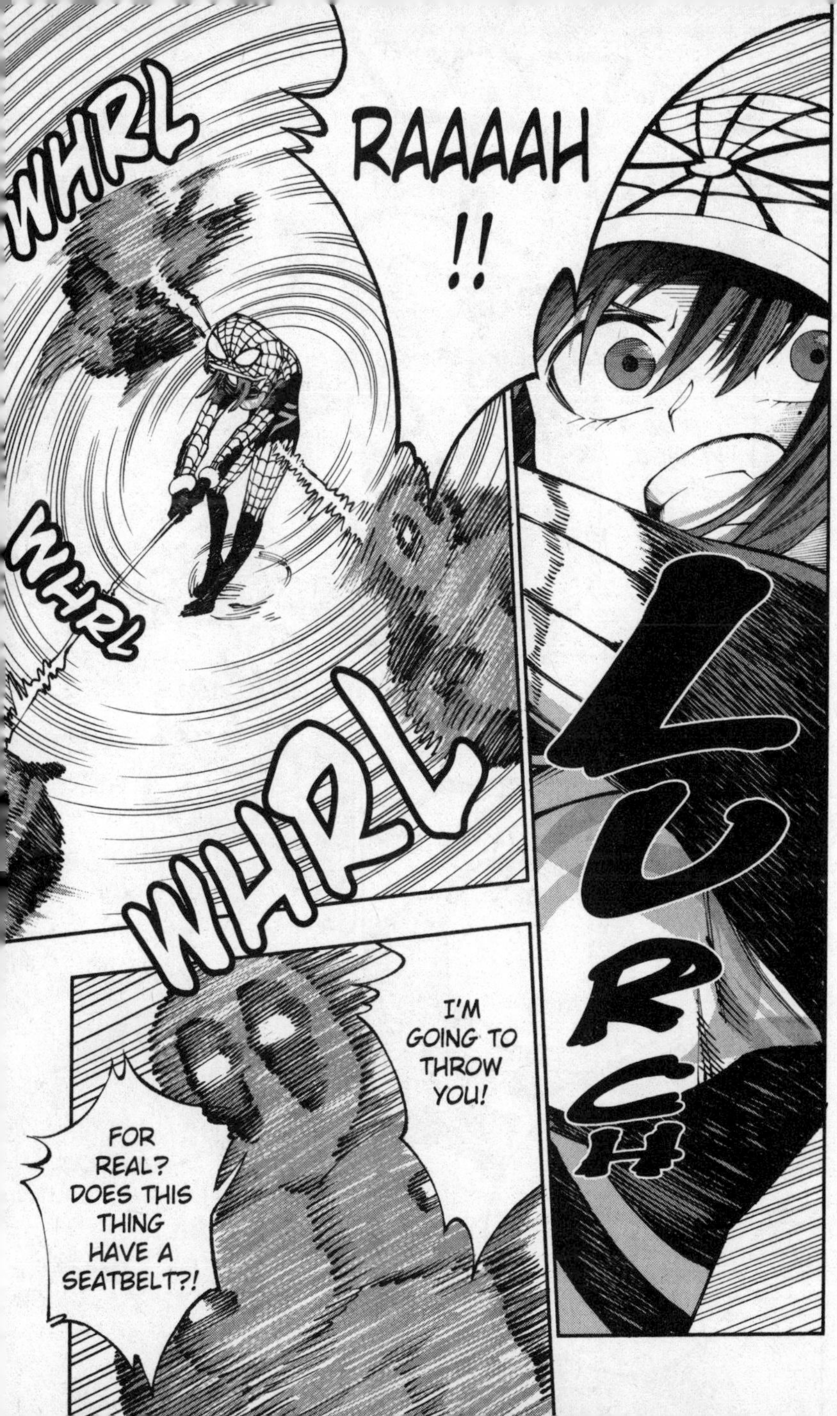
RAAAAH !!
WHRL
WHRL
WHRL
LURCH
I'M GOING TO THROW YOU!
FOR REAL? DOES THIS THING HAVE A SEATBELT?!

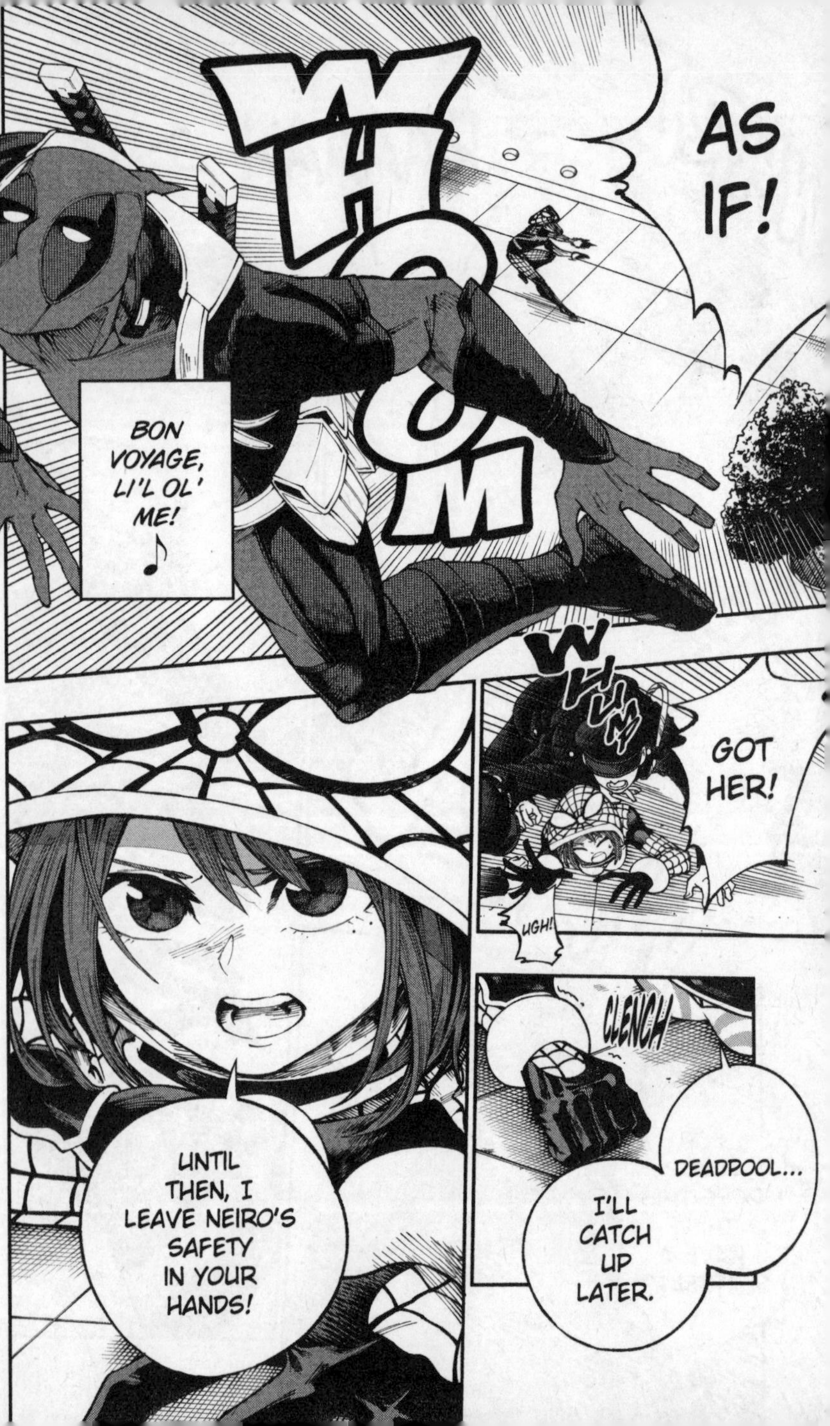
AS IF!
WHOOM
BON VOYAGE, LI'L OL' ME! ♪
GOT HER!
UGH!
CLENCH
DEADPOOL...
I'LL CATCH UP LATER.
UNTIL THEN, I LEAVE NEIRO'S SAFETY IN YOUR HANDS!

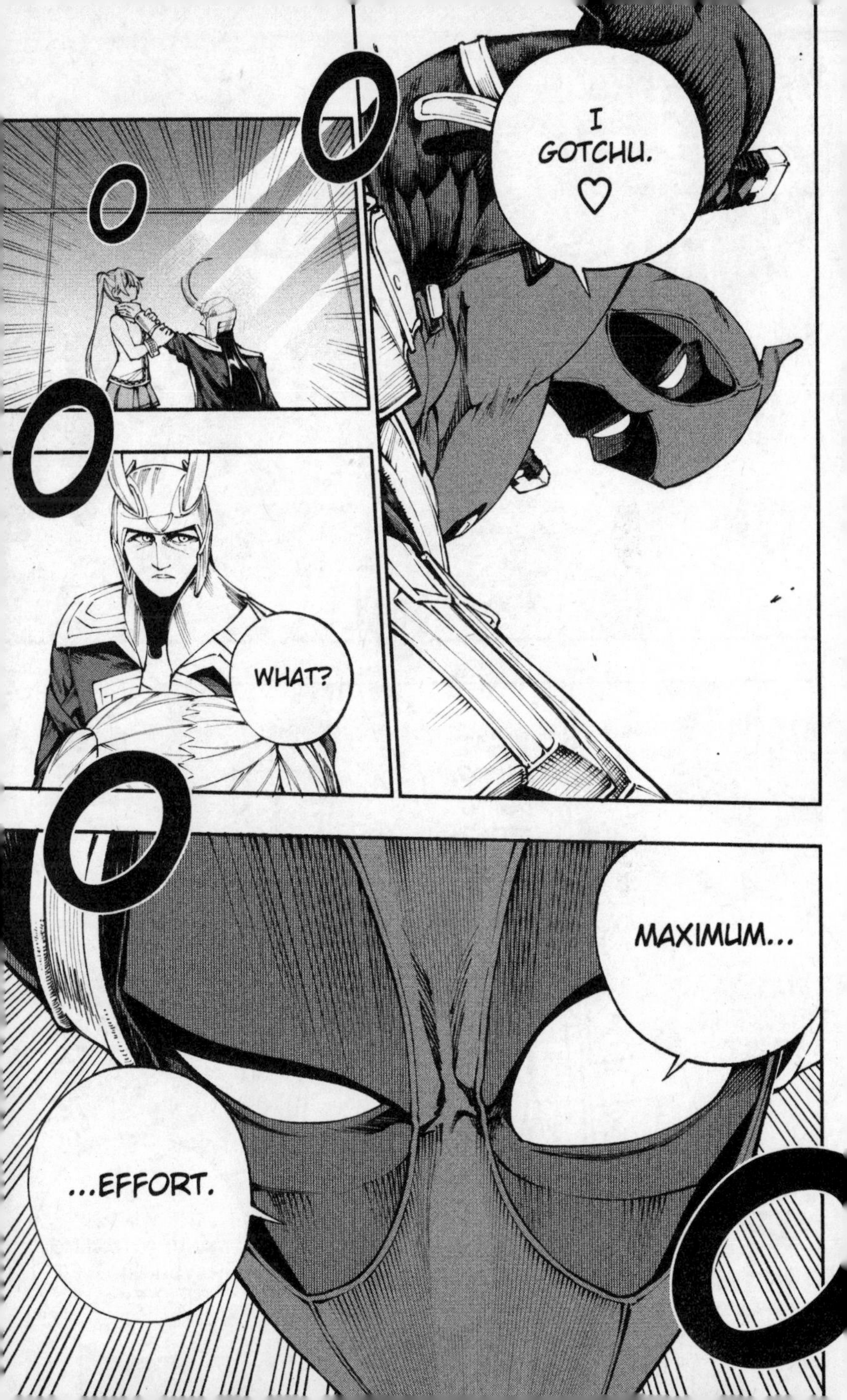
I GOTCHU. ♡
WHAT?
MAXIMUM...
...EFFORT.

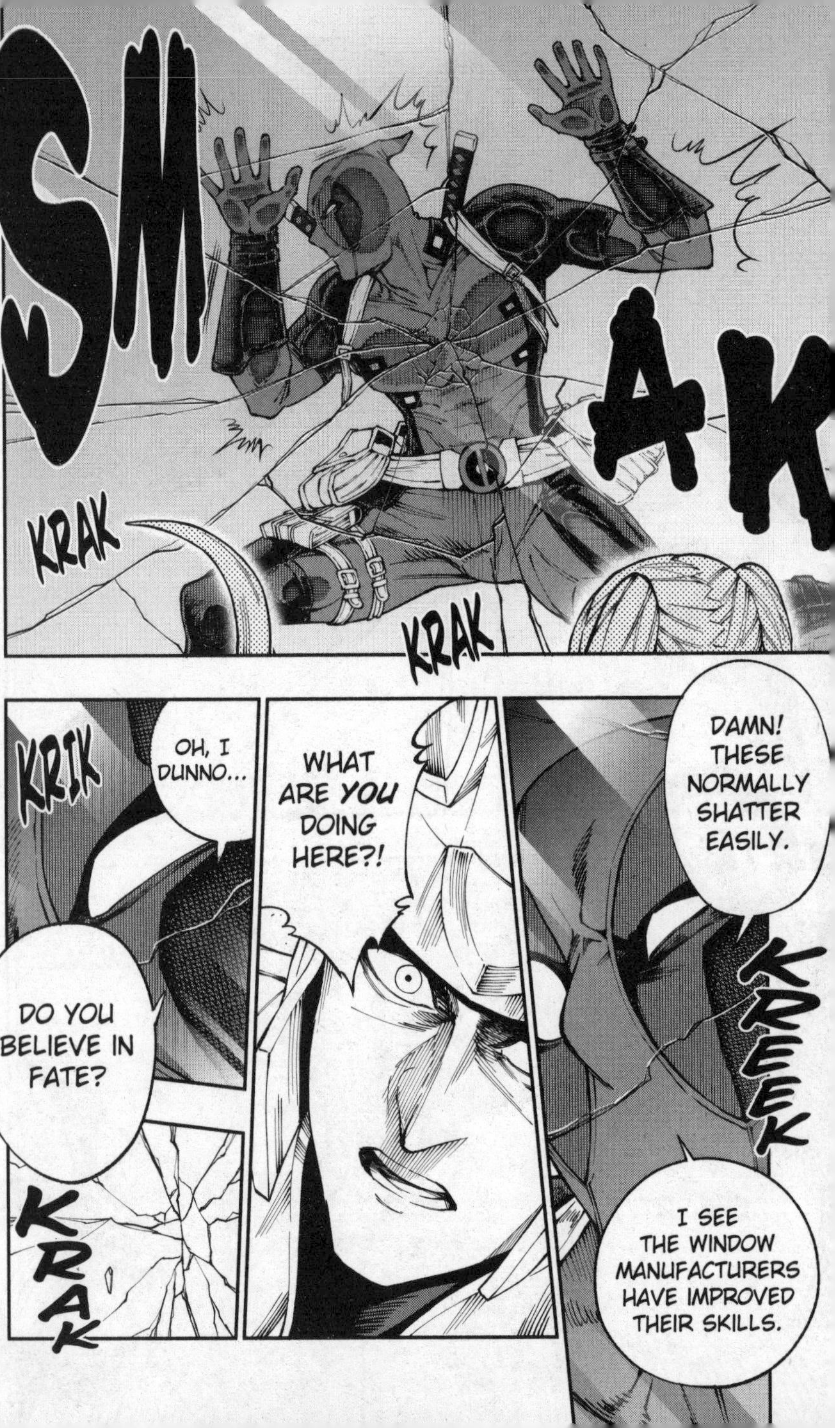
SMAK
KRAK
KRAK
DAMN! THESE NORMALLY SHATTER EASILY.
KREEK
I SEE THE WINDOW MANUFACTURERS HAVE IMPROVED THEIR SKILLS.
WHAT ARE YOU DOING HERE?!
KRIK
OH, I DUNNO...
DO YOU BELIEVE IN FATE?
KRAK

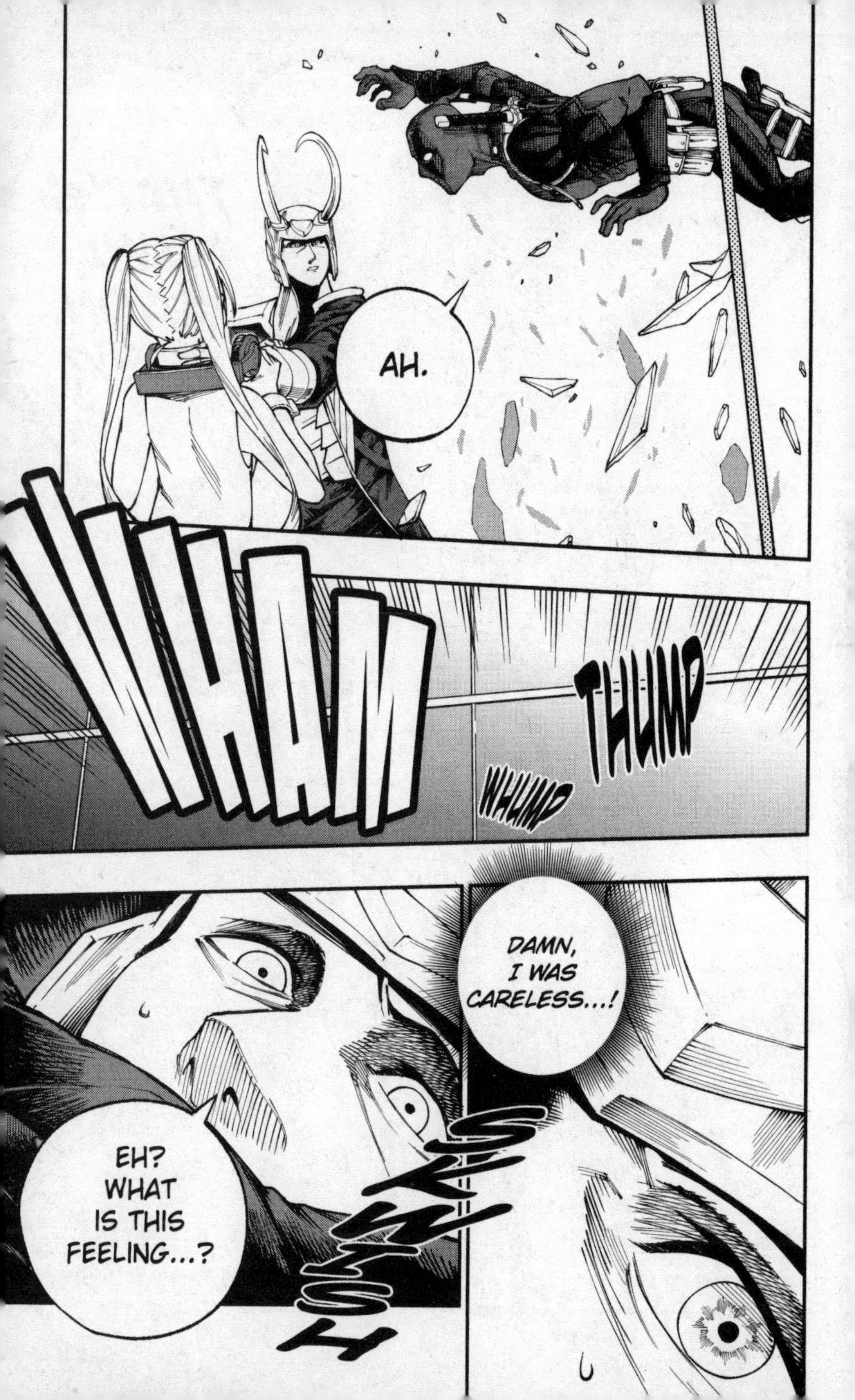
AH.
THUMP
WHUMP
WHAM
DAMN, I WAS CARELESS...!
SWISH
EH? WHAT IS THIS FEELING...?

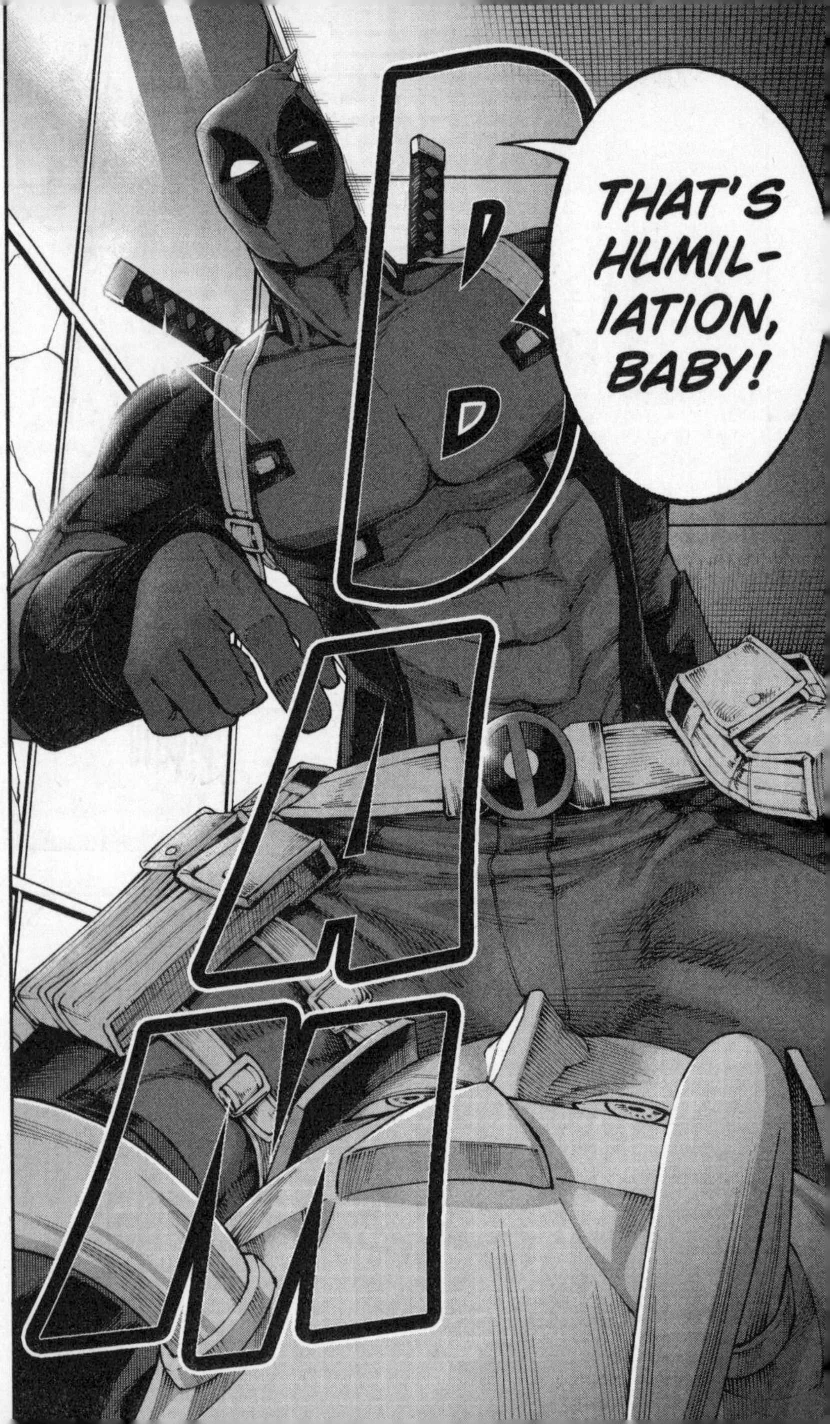
THAT'S HUMIL-IATION, BABY!
DAM

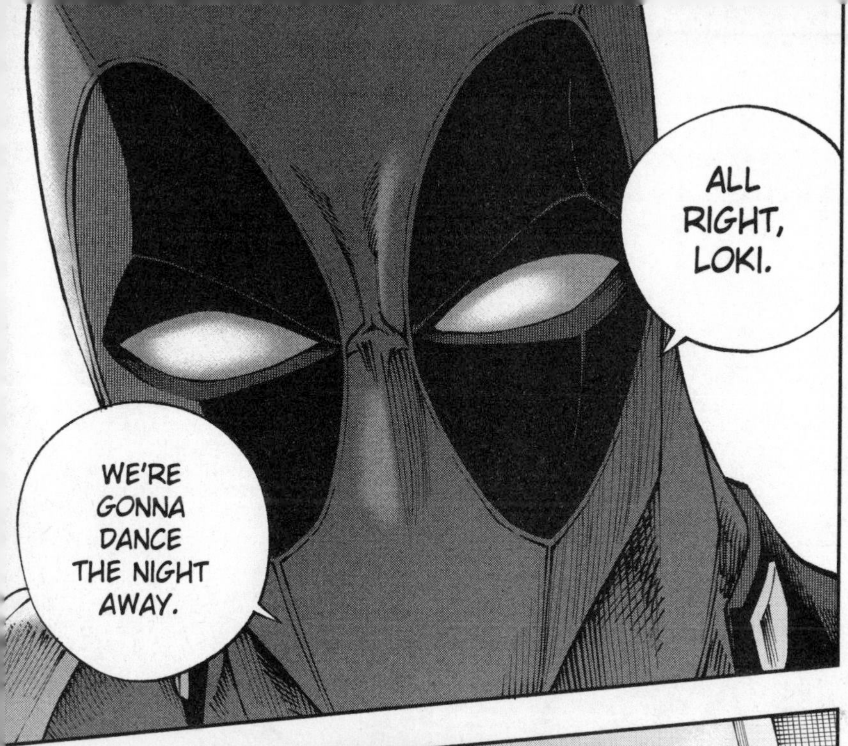
ALL RIGHT, LOKI.
WE'RE GONNA DANCE THE NIGHT AWAY.
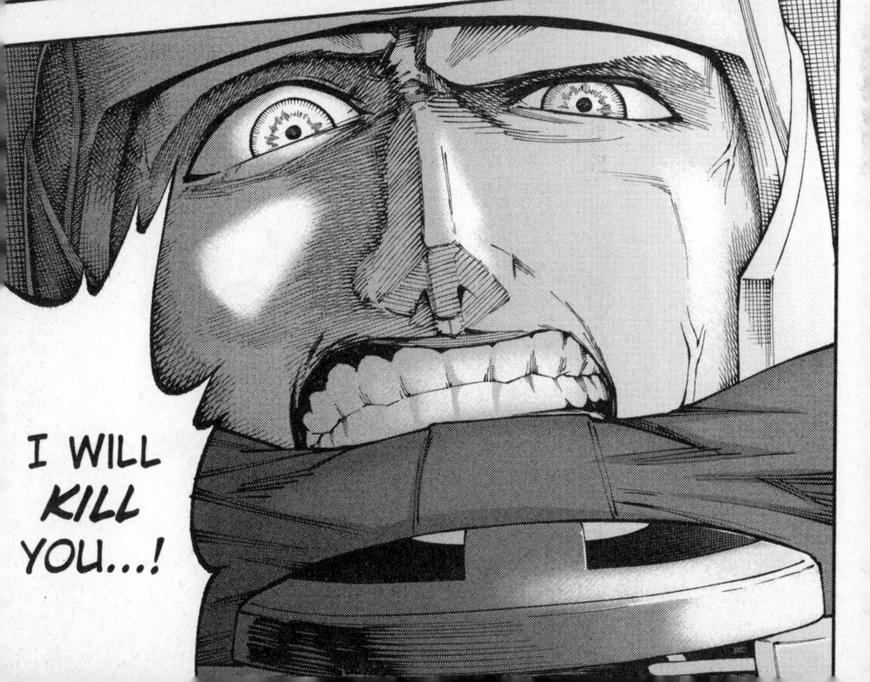
I WILL *KILL* YOU...!

REAL NAME: HARUKA HIDA

POWERS: NEARLY IDENTICAL TO SPIDER-MAN'S

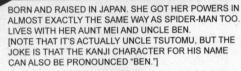

BORN AND RAISED IN JAPAN. SHE GOT HER POWERS IN ALMOST EXACTLY THE SAME WAY AS SPIDER-MAN TOO. LIVES WITH HER AUNT MEI AND UNCLE BEN.
[NOTE THAT IT'S ACTUALLY UNCLE TSUTOMU, BUT THE JOKE IS THAT THE KANJI CHARACTER FOR HIS NAME CAN ALSO BE PRONOUNCED "BEN."]

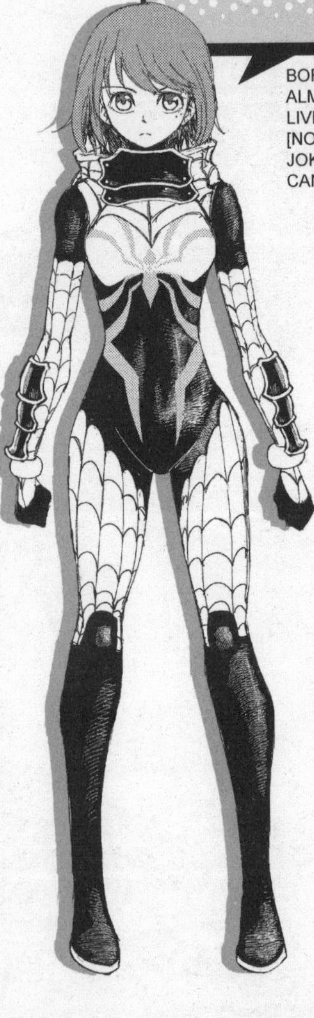

Web shooter

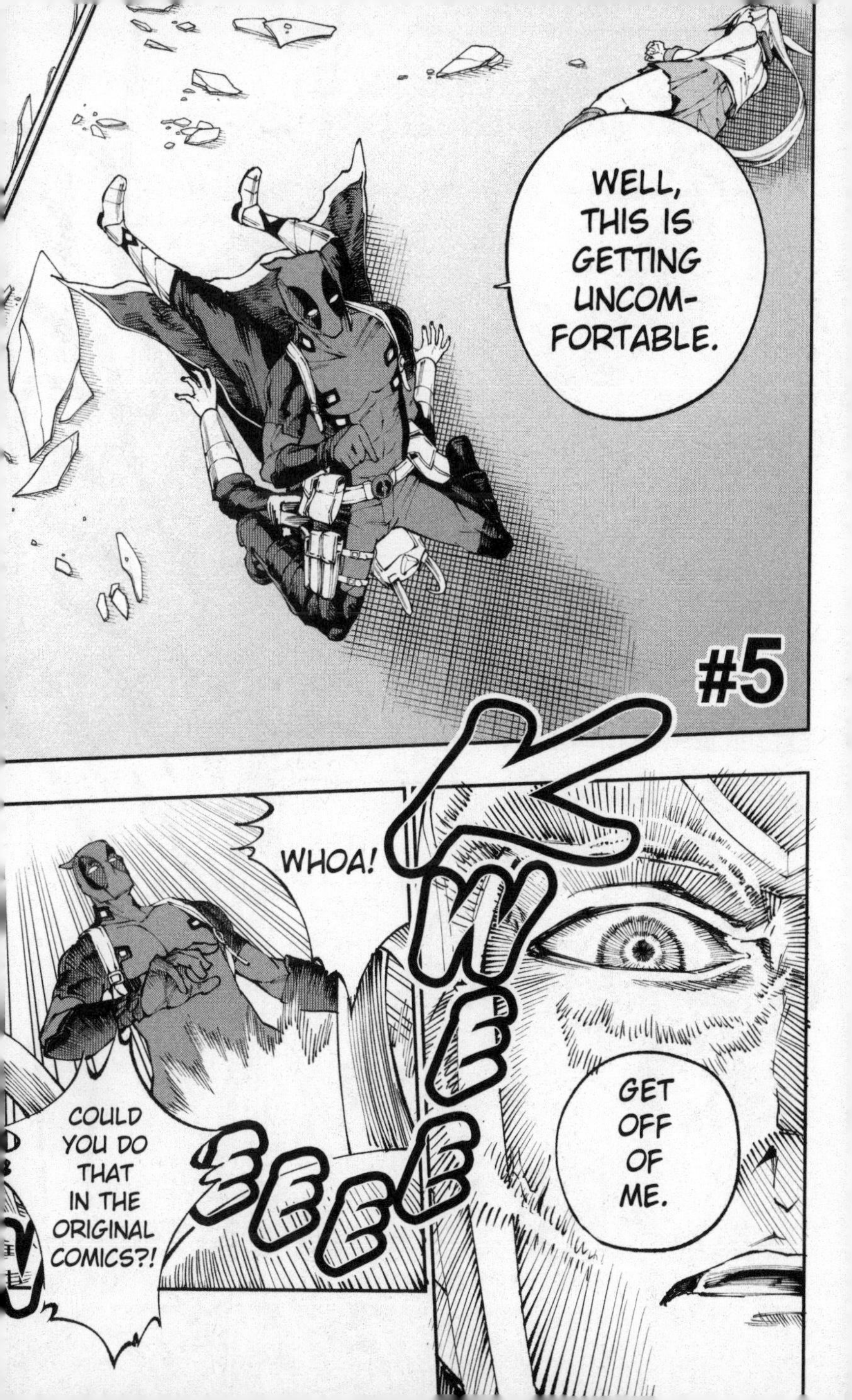
WELL, THIS IS GETTING UNCOM-FORTABLE.
#5
WHOA!
GET OFF OF ME.
COULD YOU DO THAT IN THE ORIGINAL COMICS?!

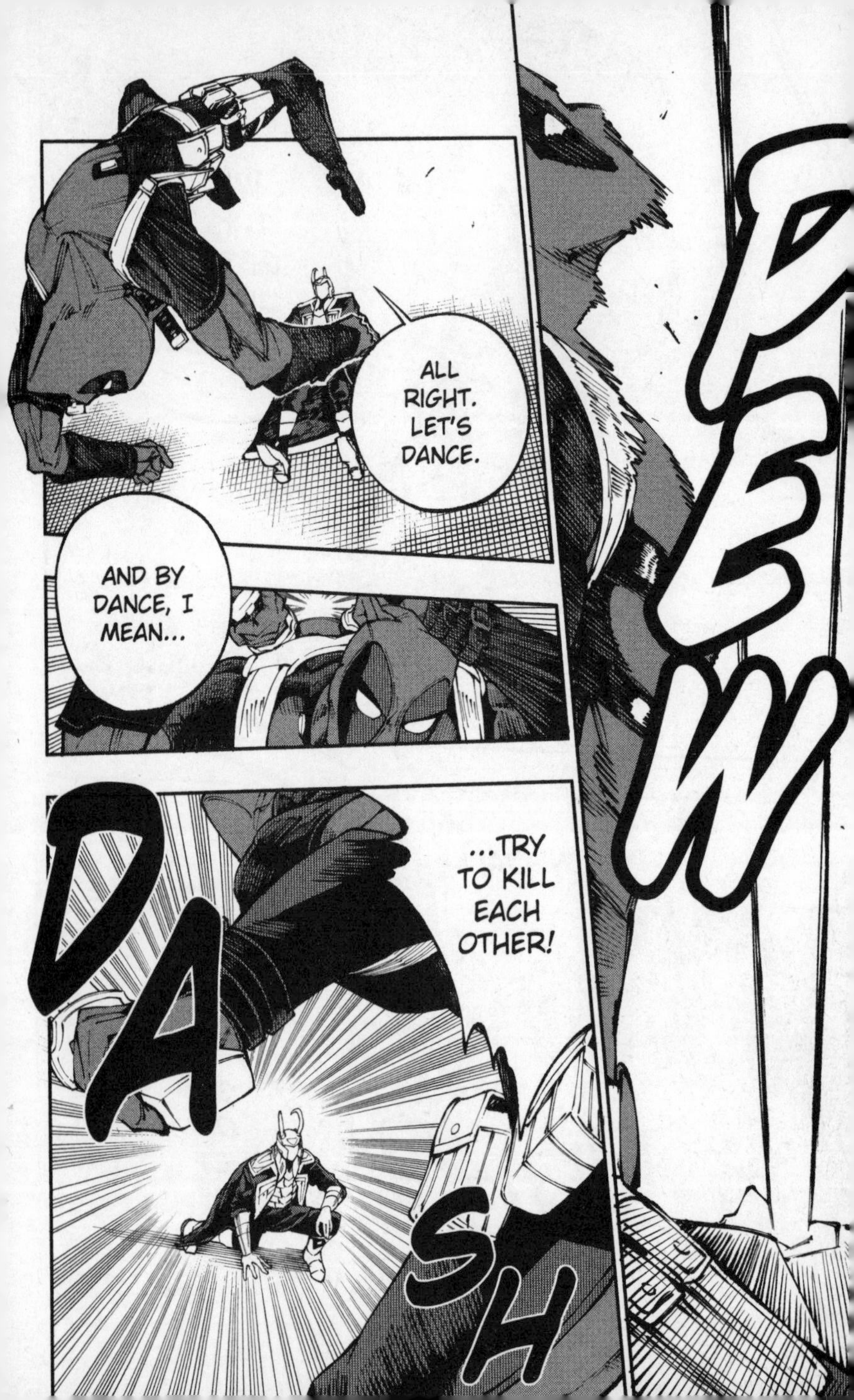
ALL RIGHT. LET'S DANCE.
AND BY DANCE, I MEAN...
...TRY TO KILL EACH OTHER!
DA
SH

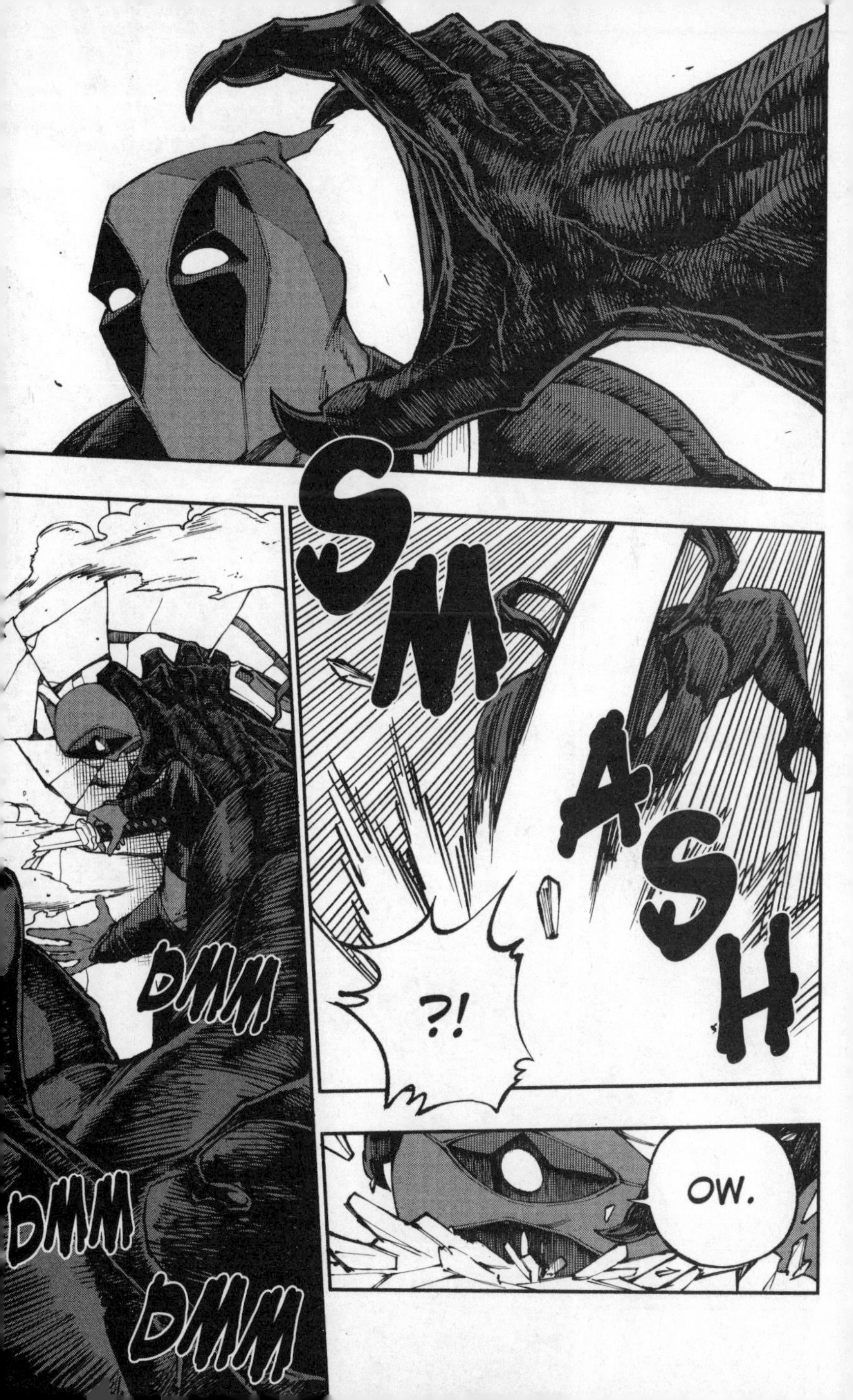
SMASH
?!
OW.
DMM
DMM
DMM

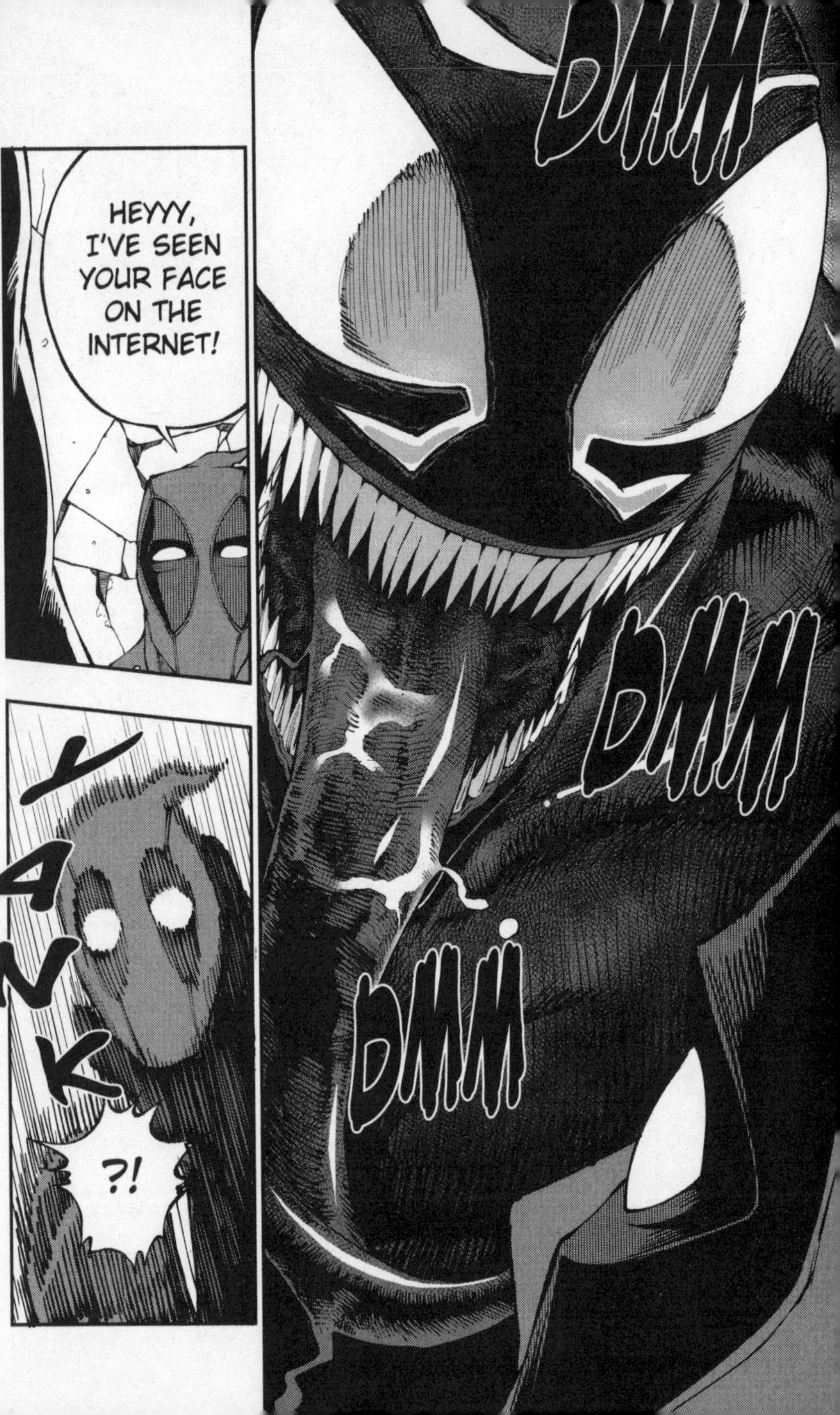
HEYYY, I'VE SEEN YOUR FACE ON THE INTERNET!
YANK
?!

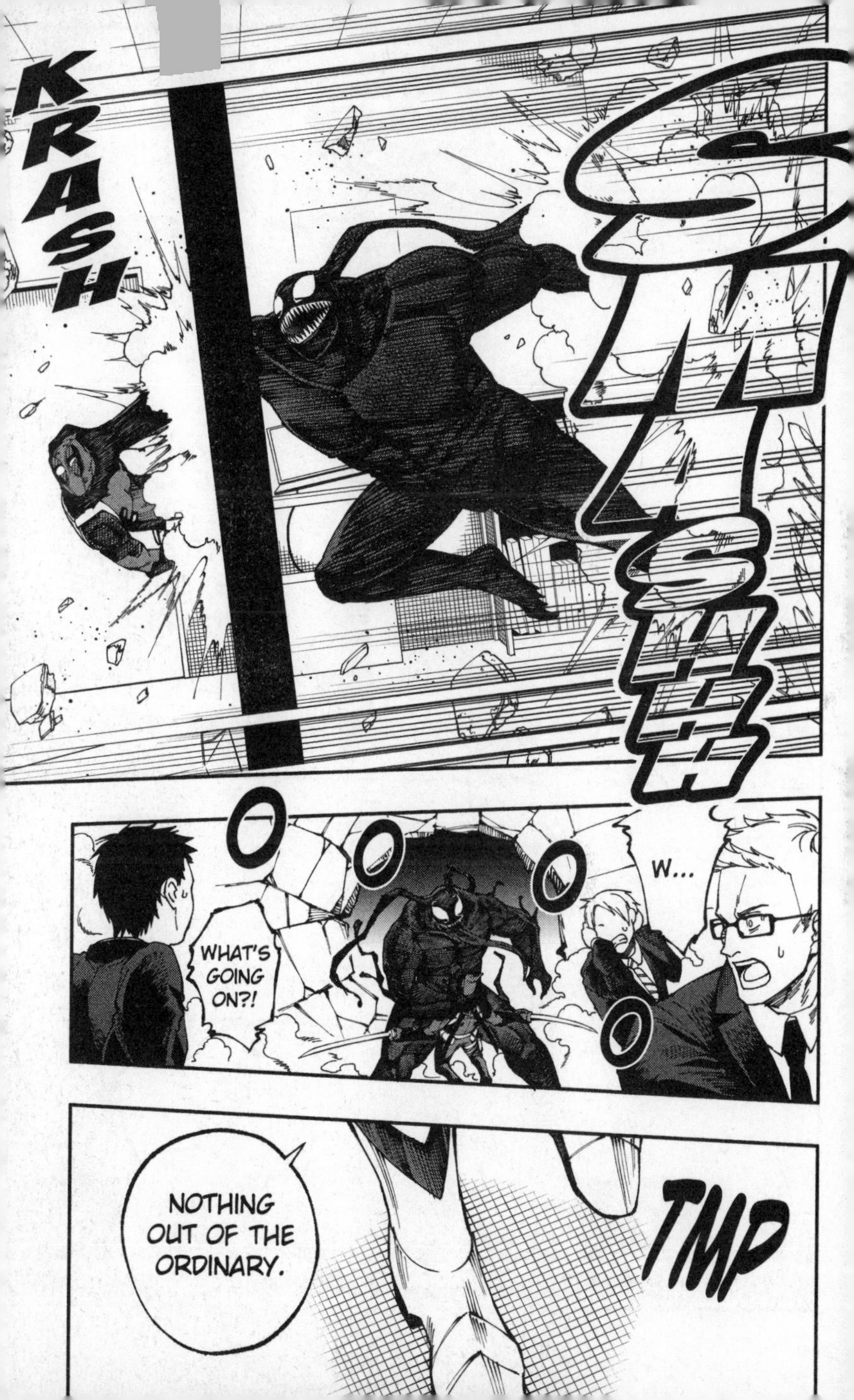
SMASHHHH
KRASH
W...
WHAT'S GOING ON?!
TMP
NOTHING OUT OF THE ORDINARY.

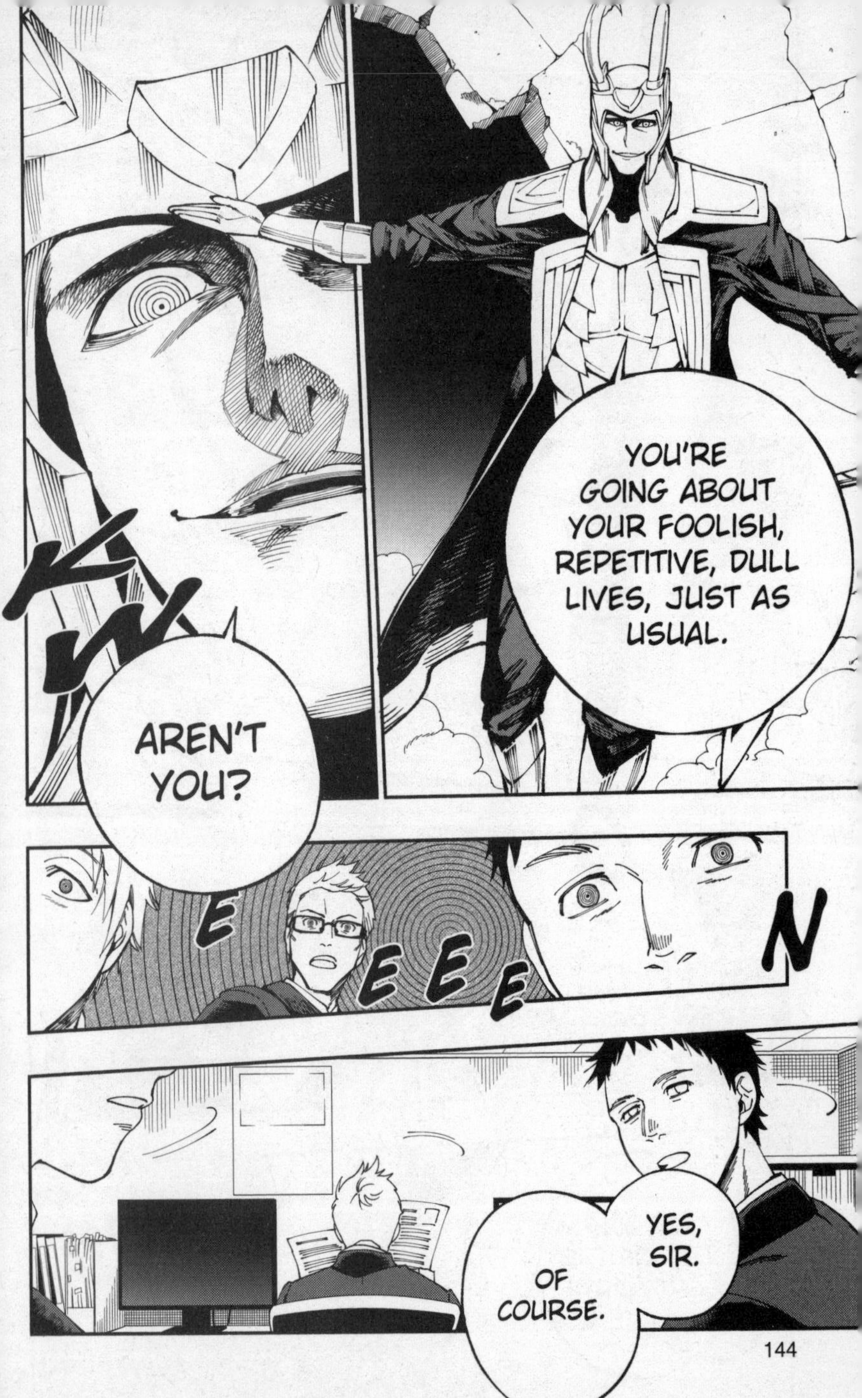
YOU'RE GOING ABOUT YOUR FOOLISH, REPETITIVE, DULL LIVES, JUST AS USUAL.
KW
AREN'T YOU?
EEEEN
YES, SIR.
OF COURSE.

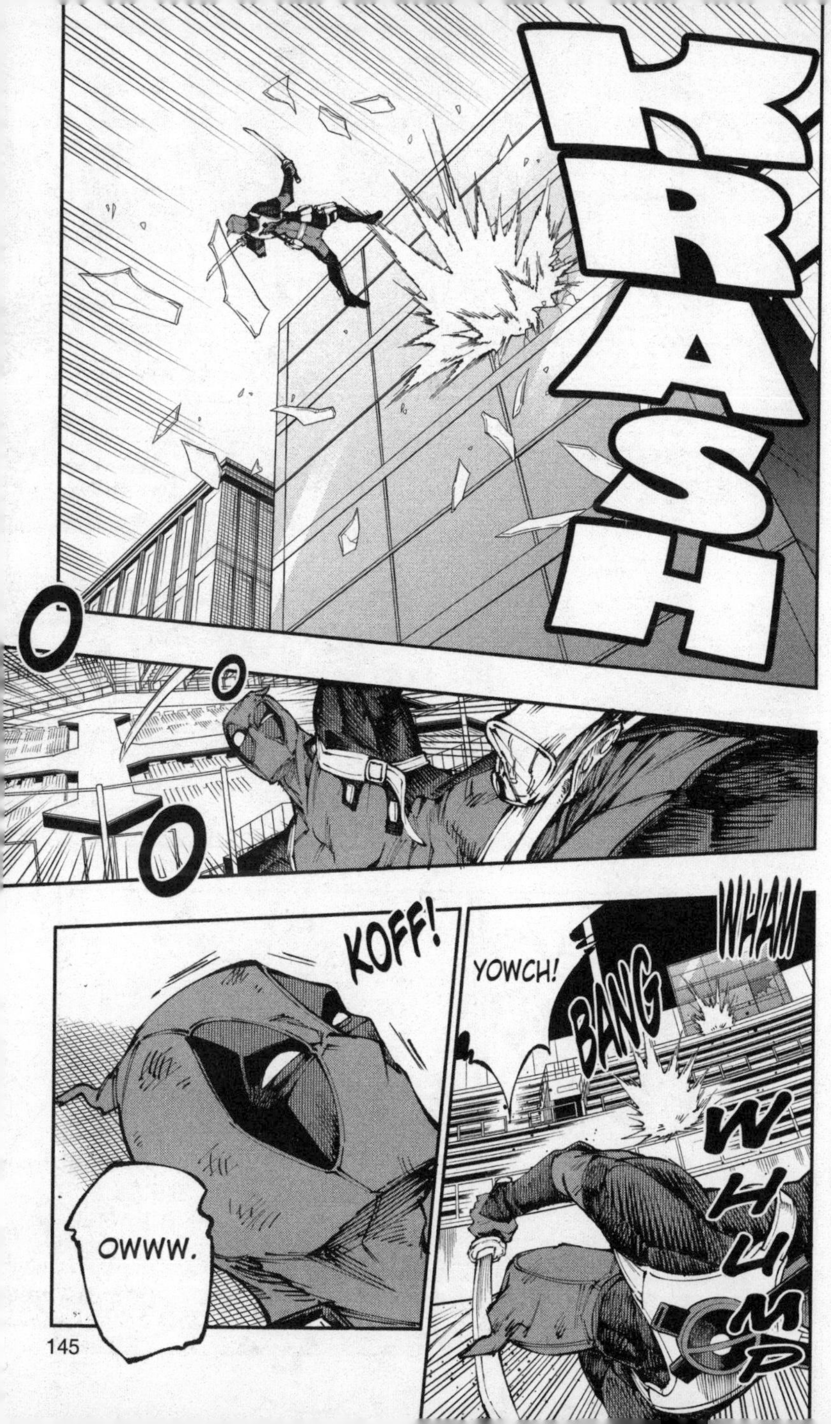
KRASH
WHAM
YOWCH!
BANG
WHUMP
KOFF!
OWWW.

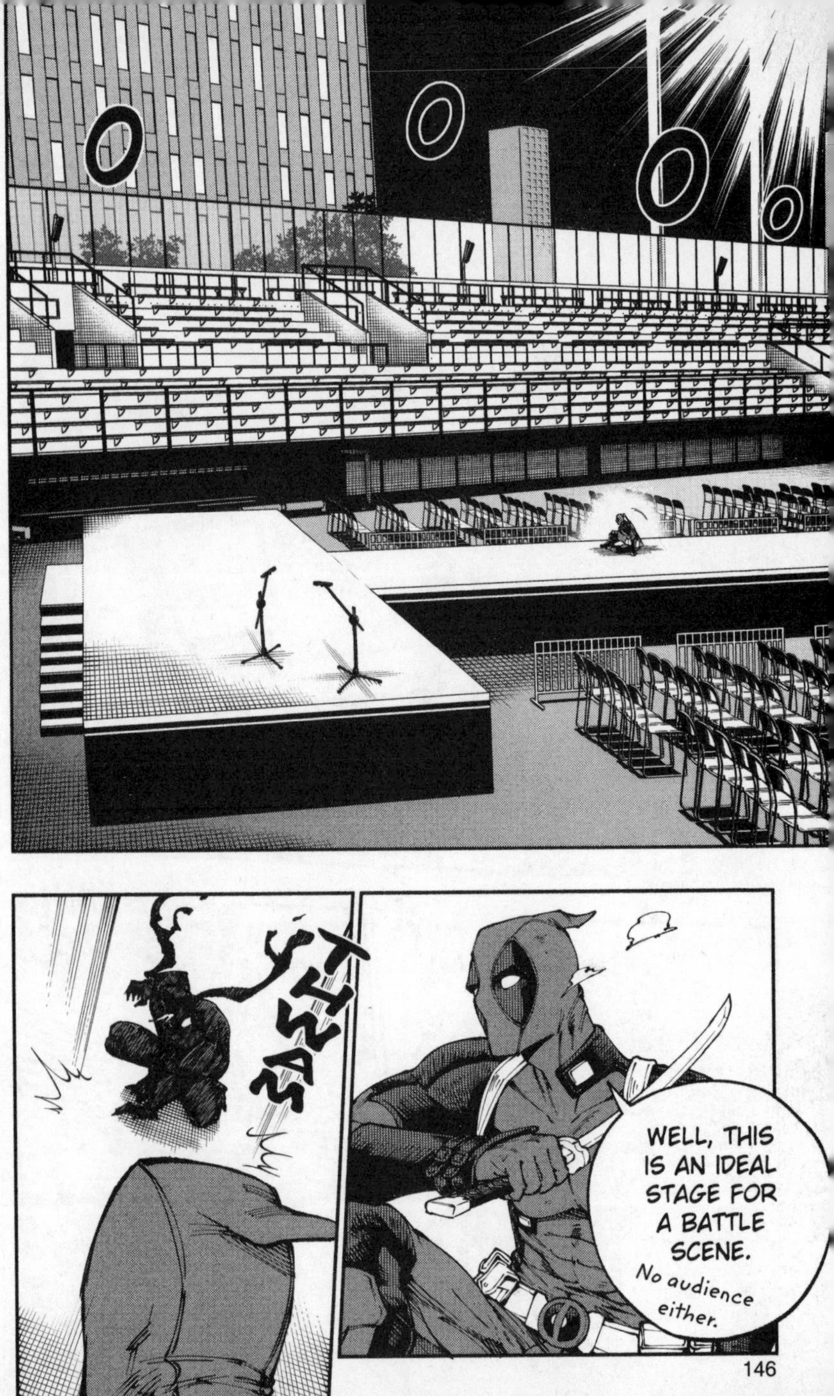
WELL, THIS IS AN IDEAL STAGE FOR A BATTLE SCENE.
No audience either.
THWAM

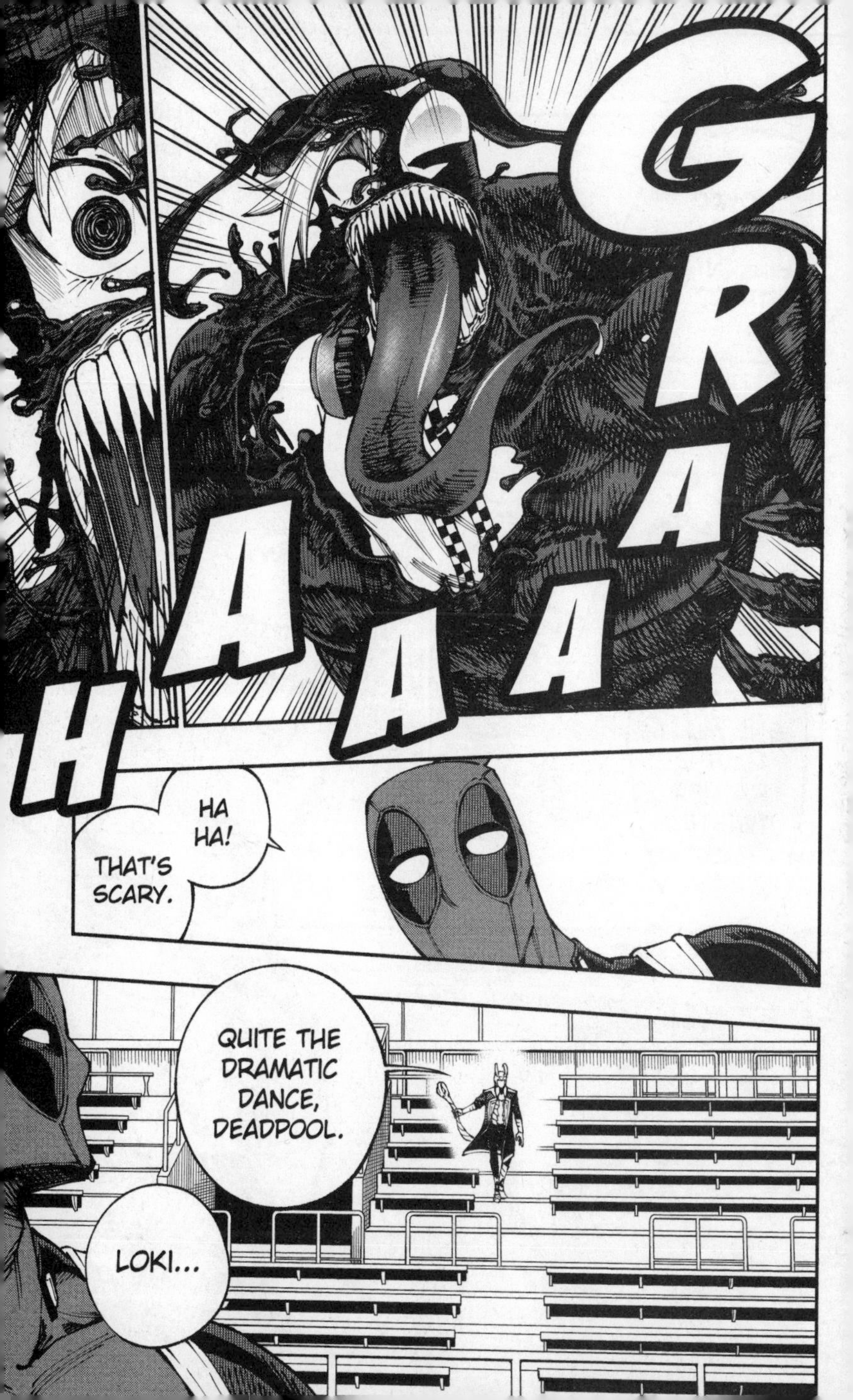
GRAAAAH
HA HA! THAT'S SCARY.
QUITE THE DRAMATIC DANCE, DEADPOOL.
LOKI...

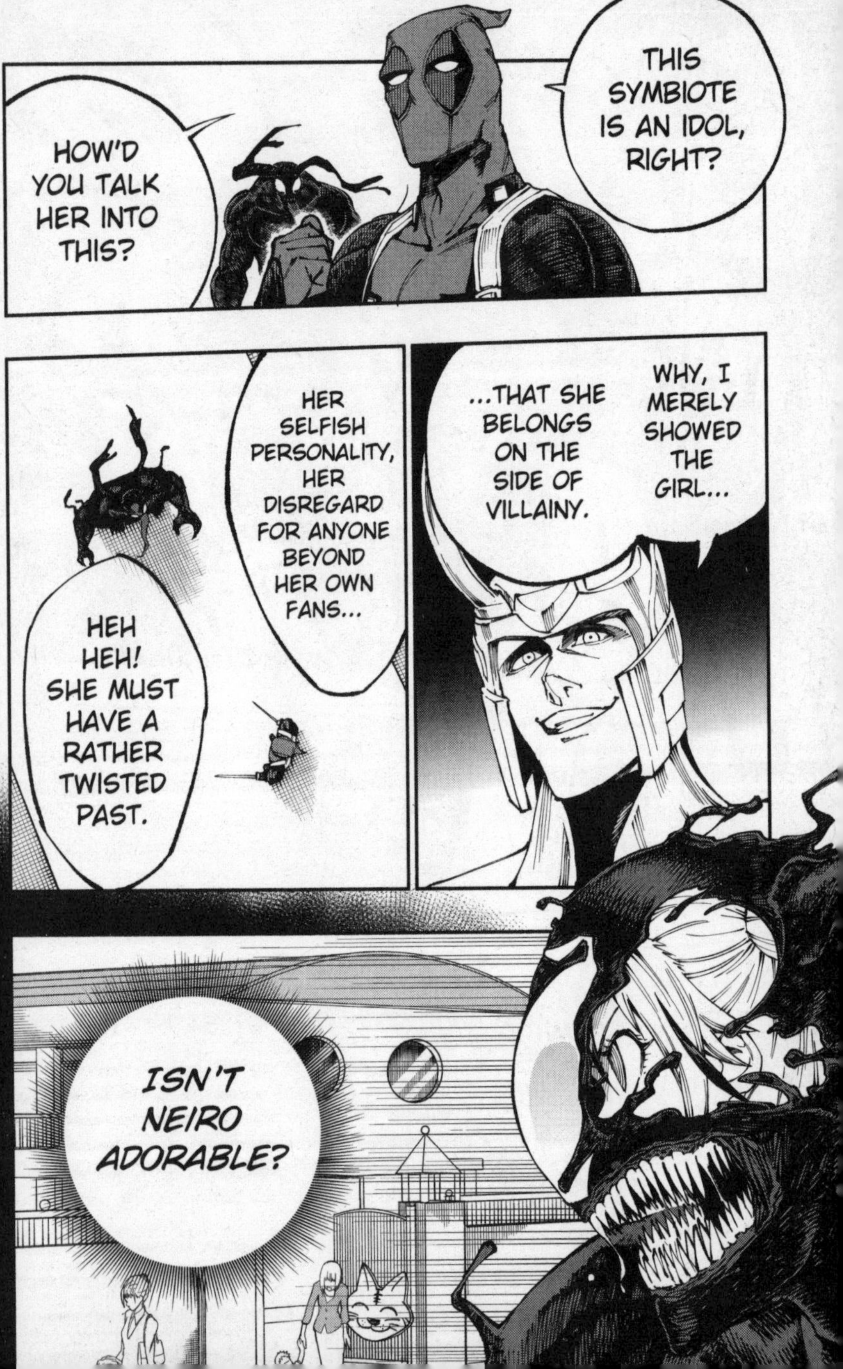
THIS SYMBIOTE IS AN IDOL, RIGHT?
HOW'D YOU TALK HER INTO THIS?
WHY, I MERELY SHOWED THE GIRL...
...THAT SHE BELONGS ON THE SIDE OF VILLAINY.
HER SELFISH PERSONALITY, HER DISREGARD FOR ANYONE BEYOND HER OWN FANS...
HEH HEH! SHE MUST HAVE A RATHER TWISTED PAST.
ISN'T NEIRO ADORABLE?

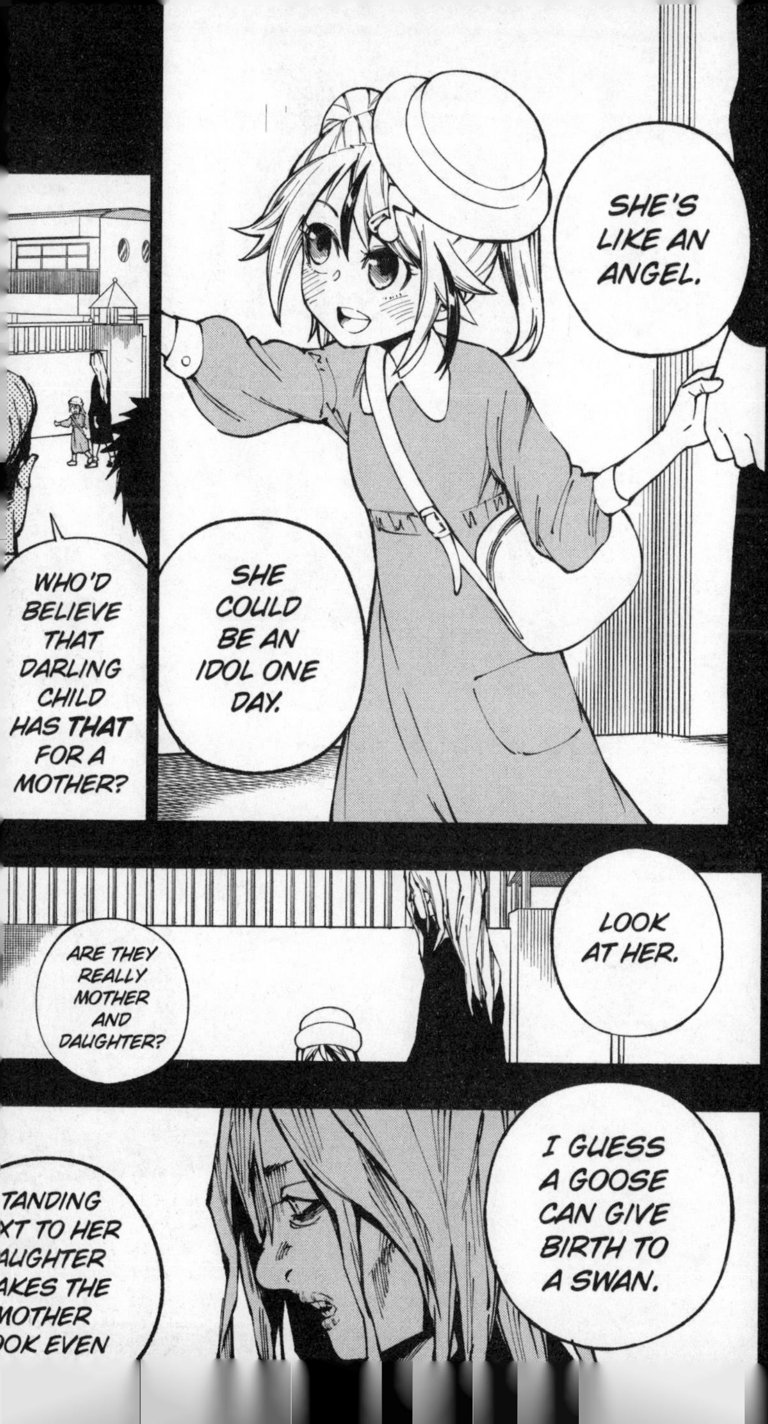
SHE'S LIKE AN ANGEL.
SHE COULD BE AN IDOL ONE DAY.
WHO'D BELIEVE THAT DARLING CHILD HAS THAT FOR A MOTHER?
LOOK AT HER.
ARE THEY REALLY MOTHER AND DAUGHTER?
I GUESS A GOOSE CAN GIVE BIRTH TO A SWAN.
TANDING XT TO HER AUGHTER AKES THE MOTHER OOK EVEN

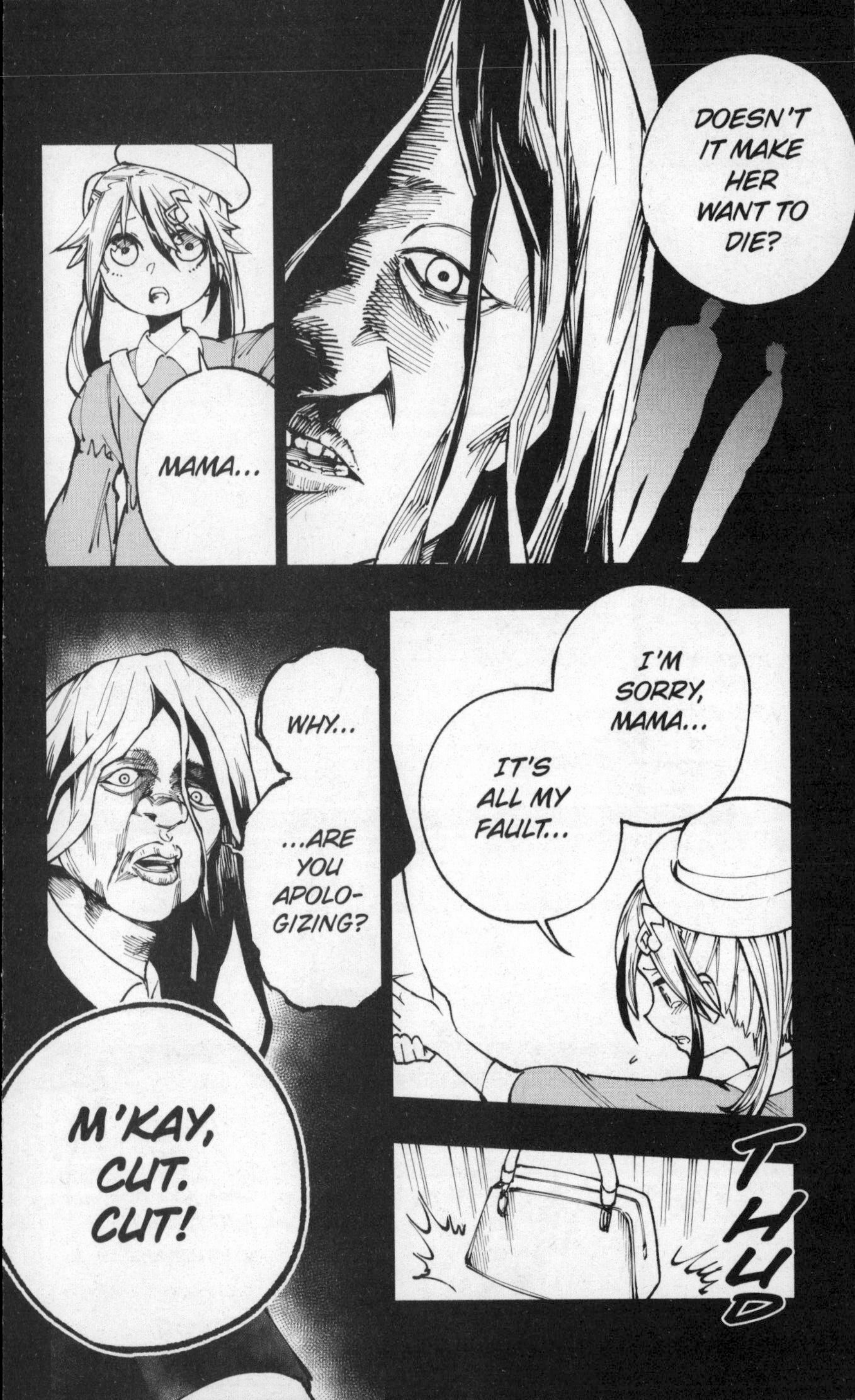
DOESN'T IT MAKE HER WANT TO DIE?
MAMA...
I'M SORRY, MAMA...
IT'S ALL MY FAULT...
THUD
WHY...
...ARE YOU APOLOGIZING?
M'KAY, CUT. CUT!

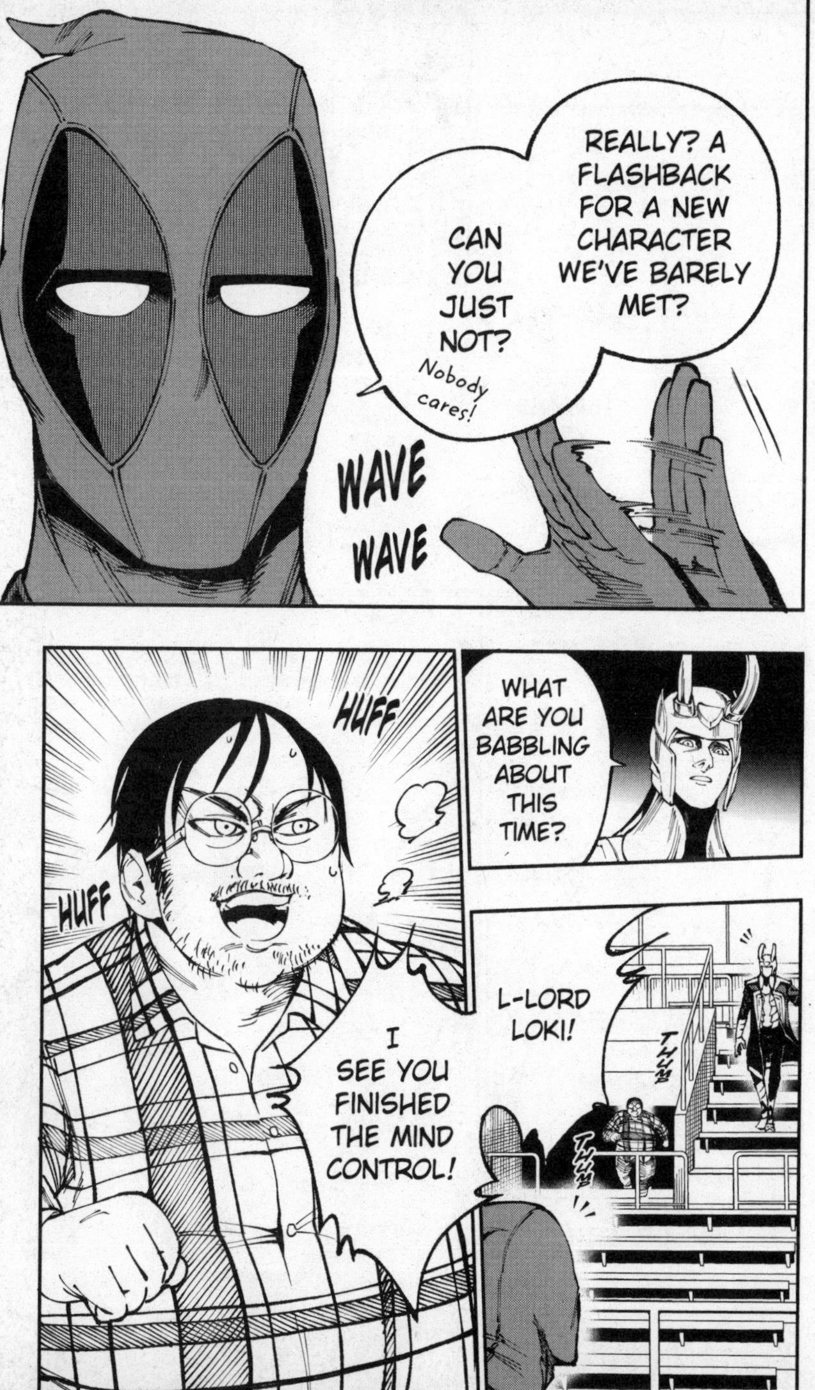
REALLY? A FLASHBACK FOR A NEW CHARACTER WE'VE BARELY MET?
CAN YOU JUST NOT?
Nobody cares!
WAVE
WAVE
WHAT ARE YOU BABBLING ABOUT THIS TIME?
L-LORD LOKI!
THUMP
THUMP
HUFF
HUFF
I SEE YOU FINISHED THE MIND CONTROL!

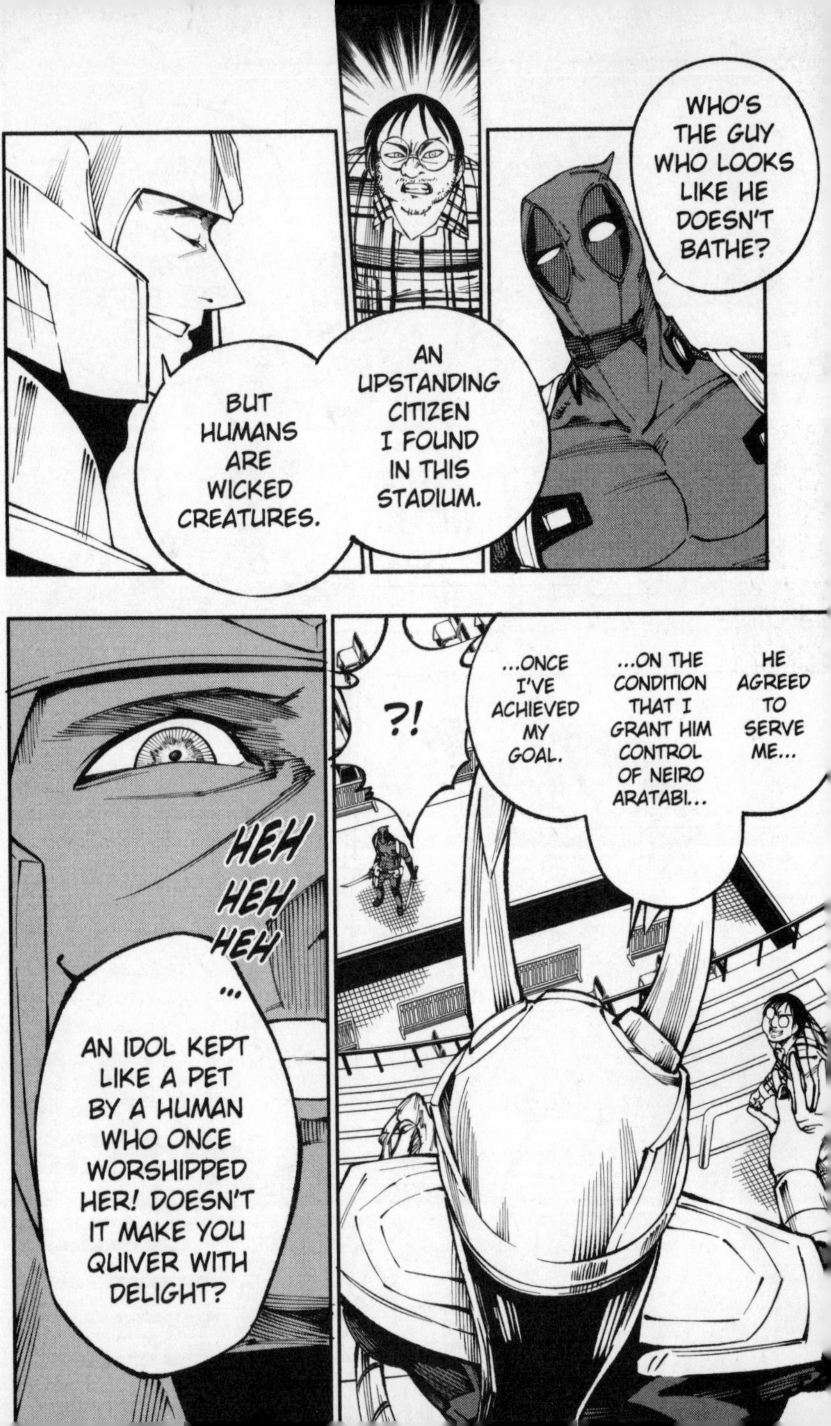
WHO'S THE GUY WHO LOOKS LIKE HE DOESN'T BATHE?
AN UPSTANDING CITIZEN I FOUND IN THIS STADIUM.
BUT HUMANS ARE WICKED CREATURES.
HE AGREED TO SERVE ME...
...ON THE CONDITION THAT I GRANT HIM CONTROL OF NEIRO ARATABI...
...ONCE I'VE ACHIEVED MY GOAL.
?!
HEH HEH HEH
...
AN IDOL KEPT LIKE A PET BY A HUMAN WHO ONCE WORSHIPPED HER! DOESN'T IT MAKE YOU QUIVER WITH DELIGHT?

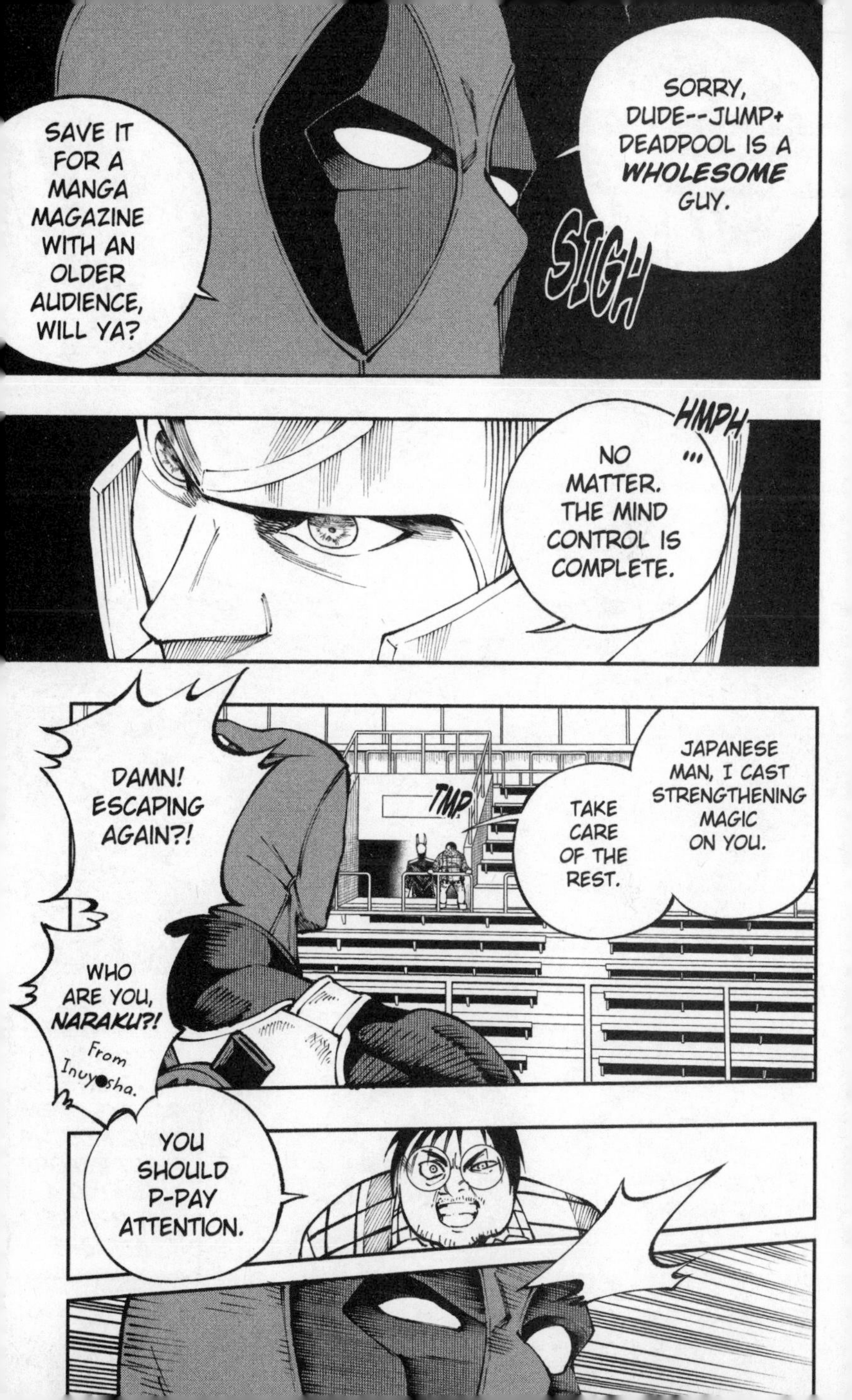
SORRY, DUDE--JUMP+ DEADPOOL IS A WHOLESOME GUY.
SIGH
SAVE IT FOR A MANGA MAGAZINE WITH AN OLDER AUDIENCE, WILL YA?
HMPH
...
NO MATTER. THE MIND CONTROL IS COMPLETE.
JAPANESE MAN, I CAST STRENGTHENING MAGIC ON YOU.
TAKE CARE OF THE REST.
TMP
DAMN! ESCAPING AGAIN?!
WHO ARE YOU, NARAKU?!
From Inuyasha.
YOU SHOULD P-PAY ATTENTION.

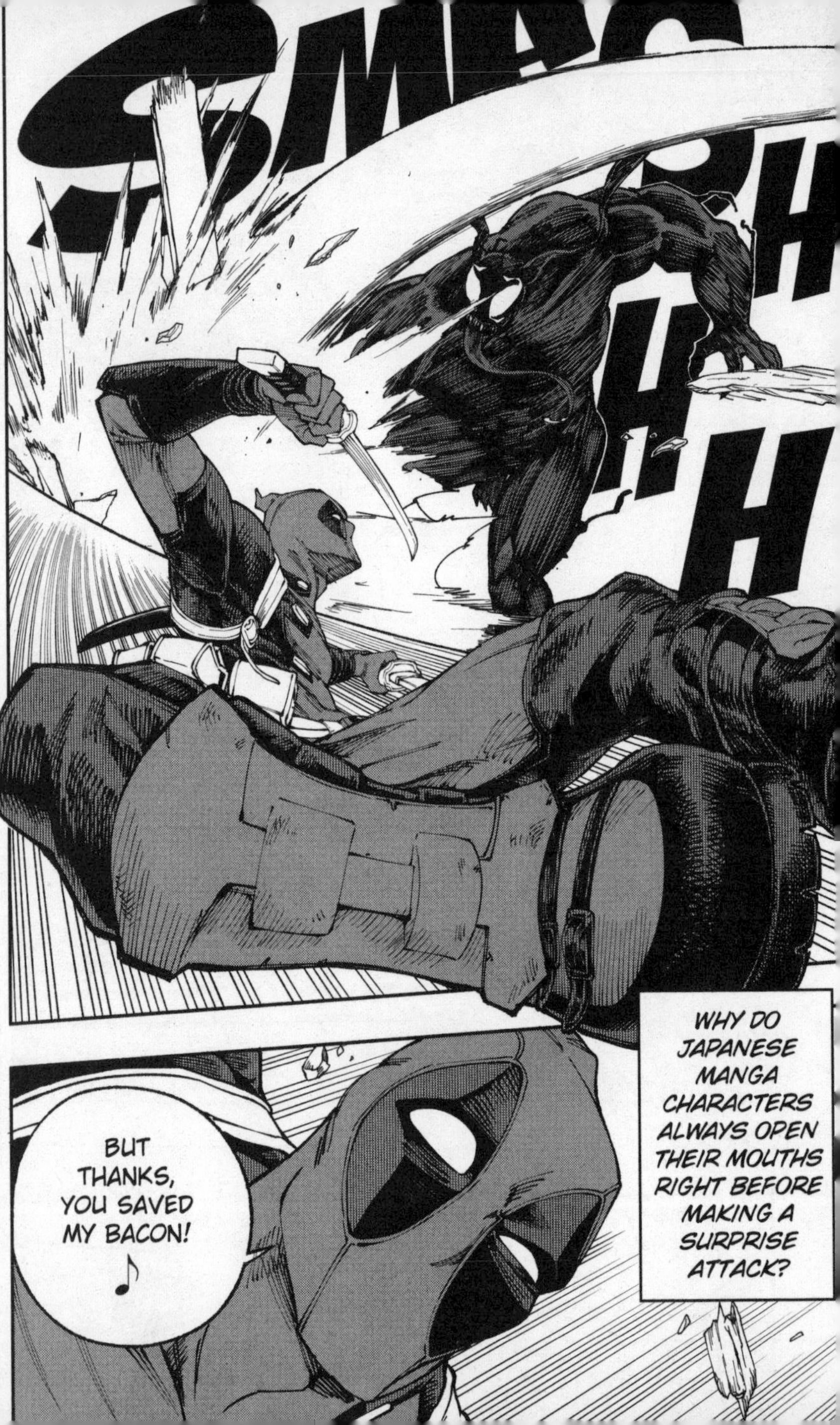
WHY DO JAPANESE MANGA CHARACTERS ALWAYS OPEN THEIR MOUTHS RIGHT BEFORE MAKING A SURPRISE ATTACK?
BUT THANKS, YOU SAVED MY BACON! ♪

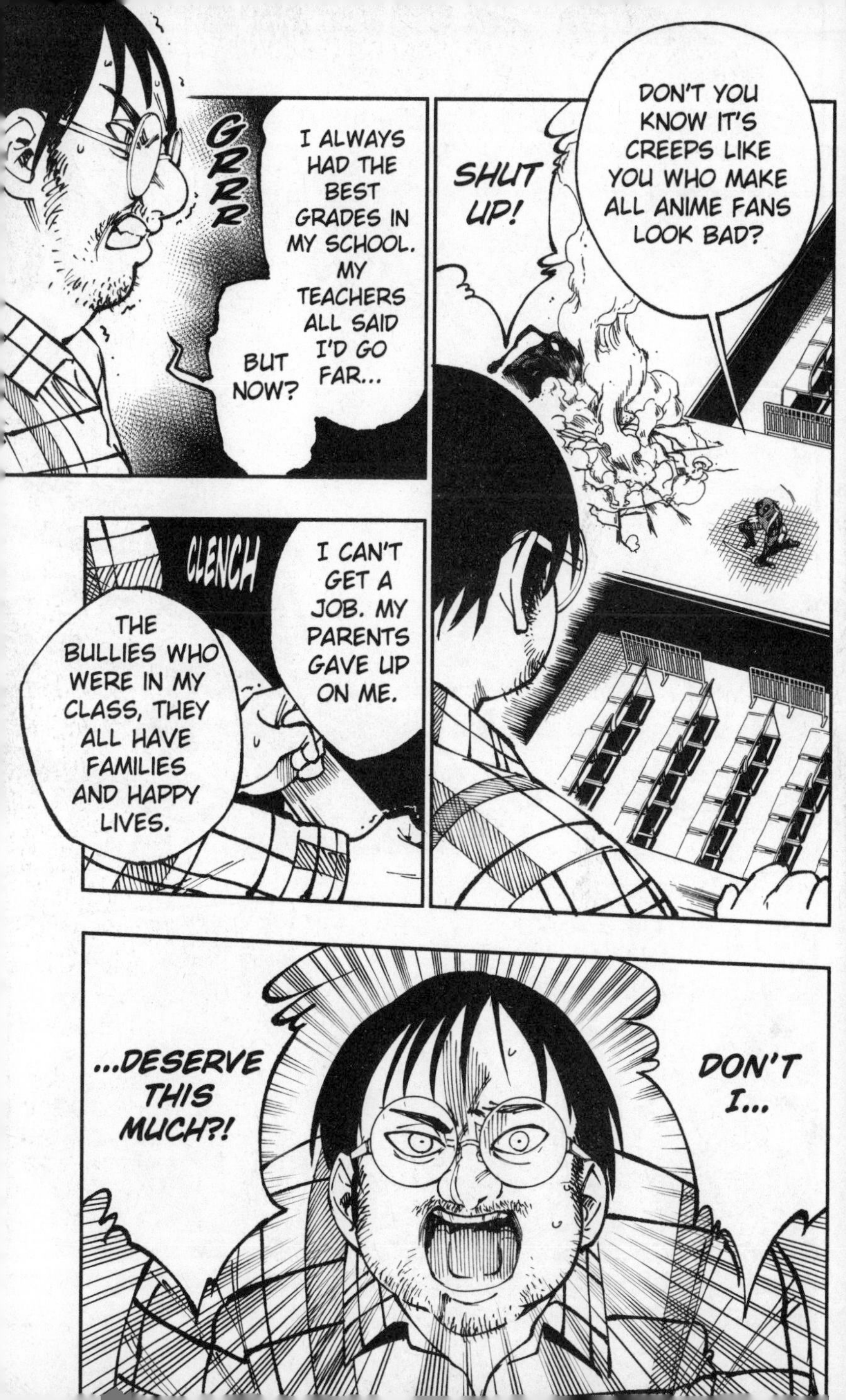
DON'T YOU KNOW IT'S CREEPS LIKE YOU WHO MAKE ALL ANIME FANS LOOK BAD?
SHUT UP!
GRRR
I ALWAYS HAD THE BEST GRADES IN MY SCHOOL. MY TEACHERS ALL SAID I'D GO FAR...
BUT NOW?
I CAN'T GET A JOB. MY PARENTS GAVE UP ON ME.
CLENCH
THE BULLIES WHO WERE IN MY CLASS, THEY ALL HAVE FAMILIES AND HAPPY LIVES.
DON'T I...
...DESERVE THIS MUCH?!

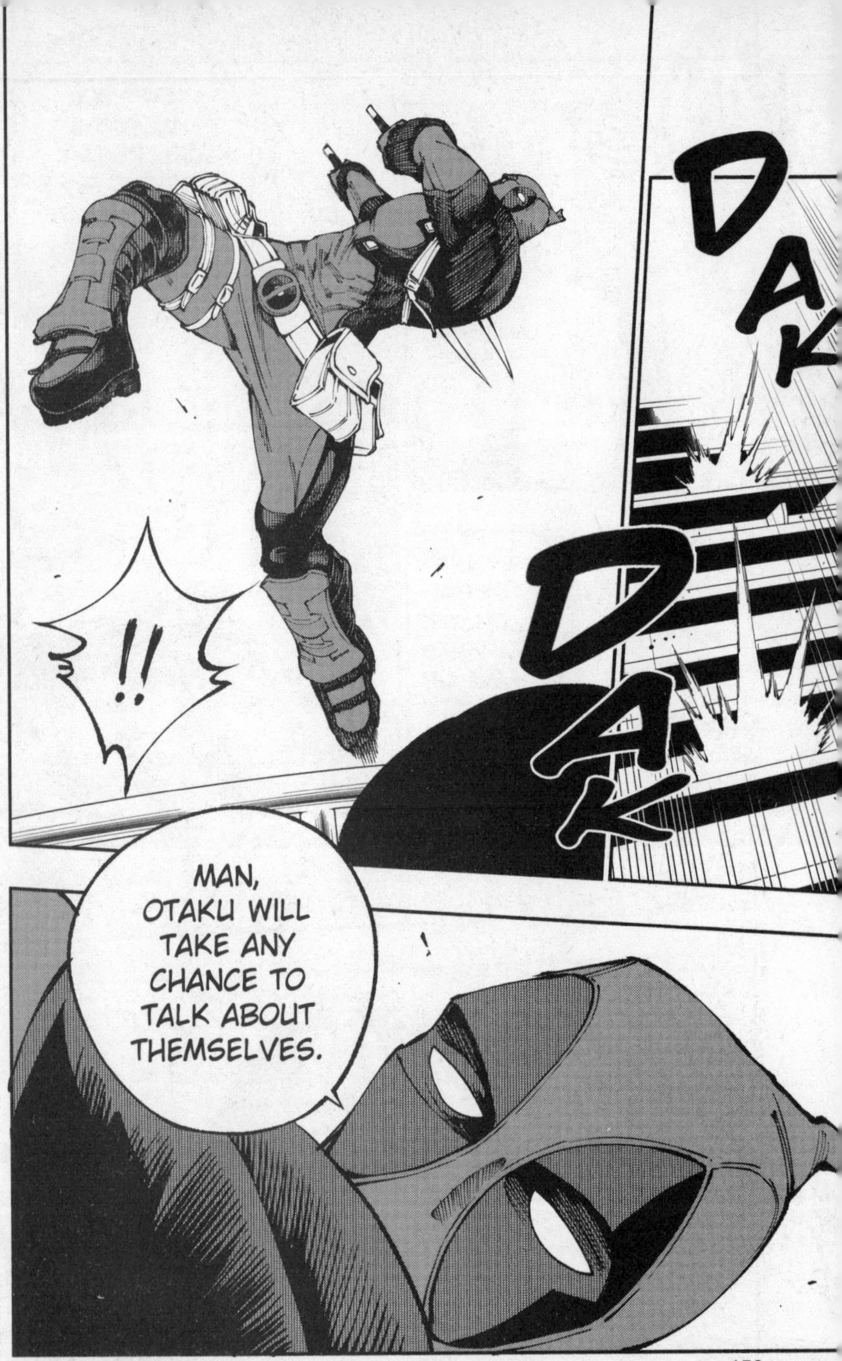
DAK
DAK
!!
MAN, OTAKU WILL TAKE ANY CHANCE TO TALK ABOUT THEMSELVES.
!

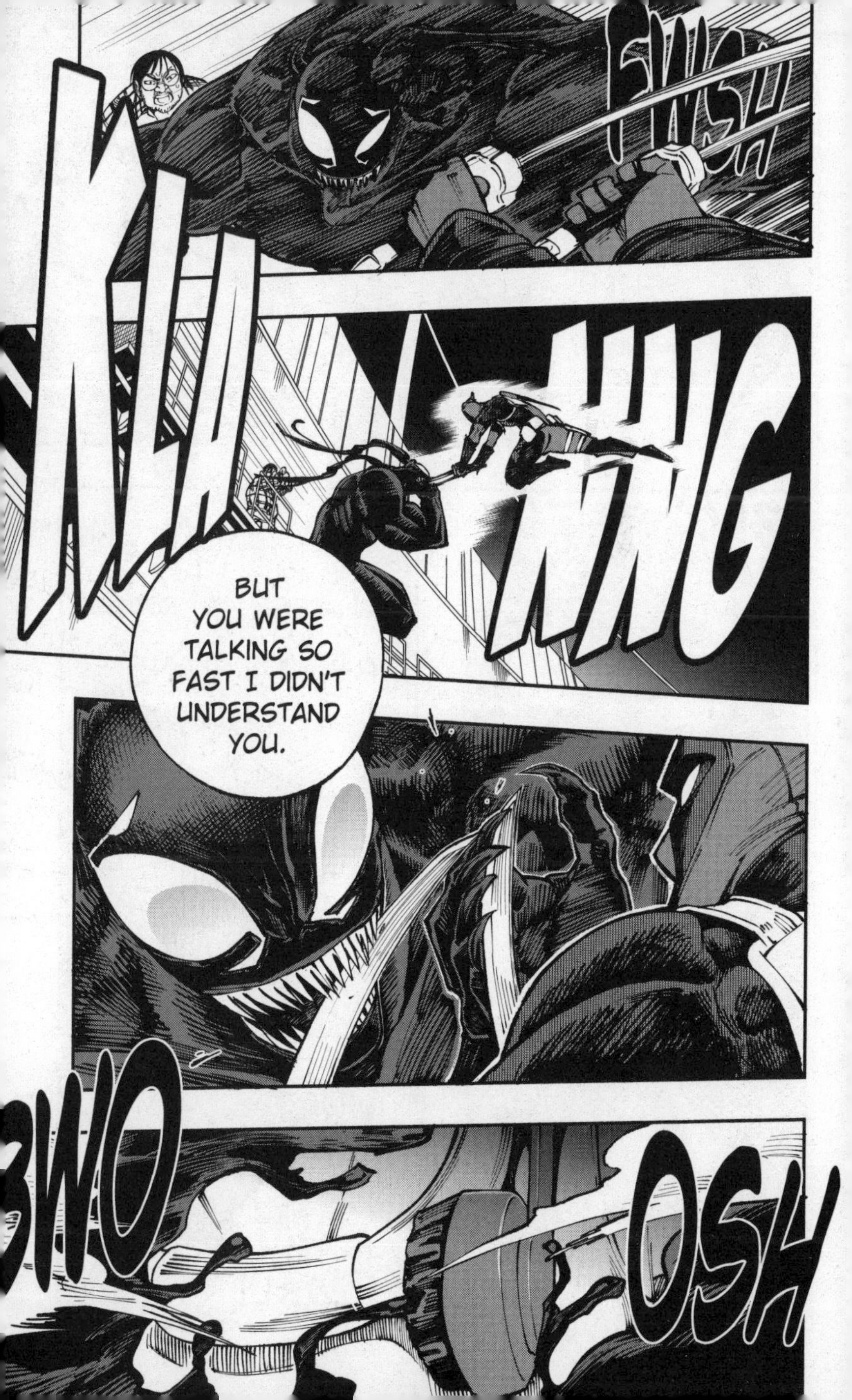
FWSH
KLANNG
BUT YOU WERE TALKING SO FAST I DIDN'T UNDERSTAND YOU.
SWOOSH

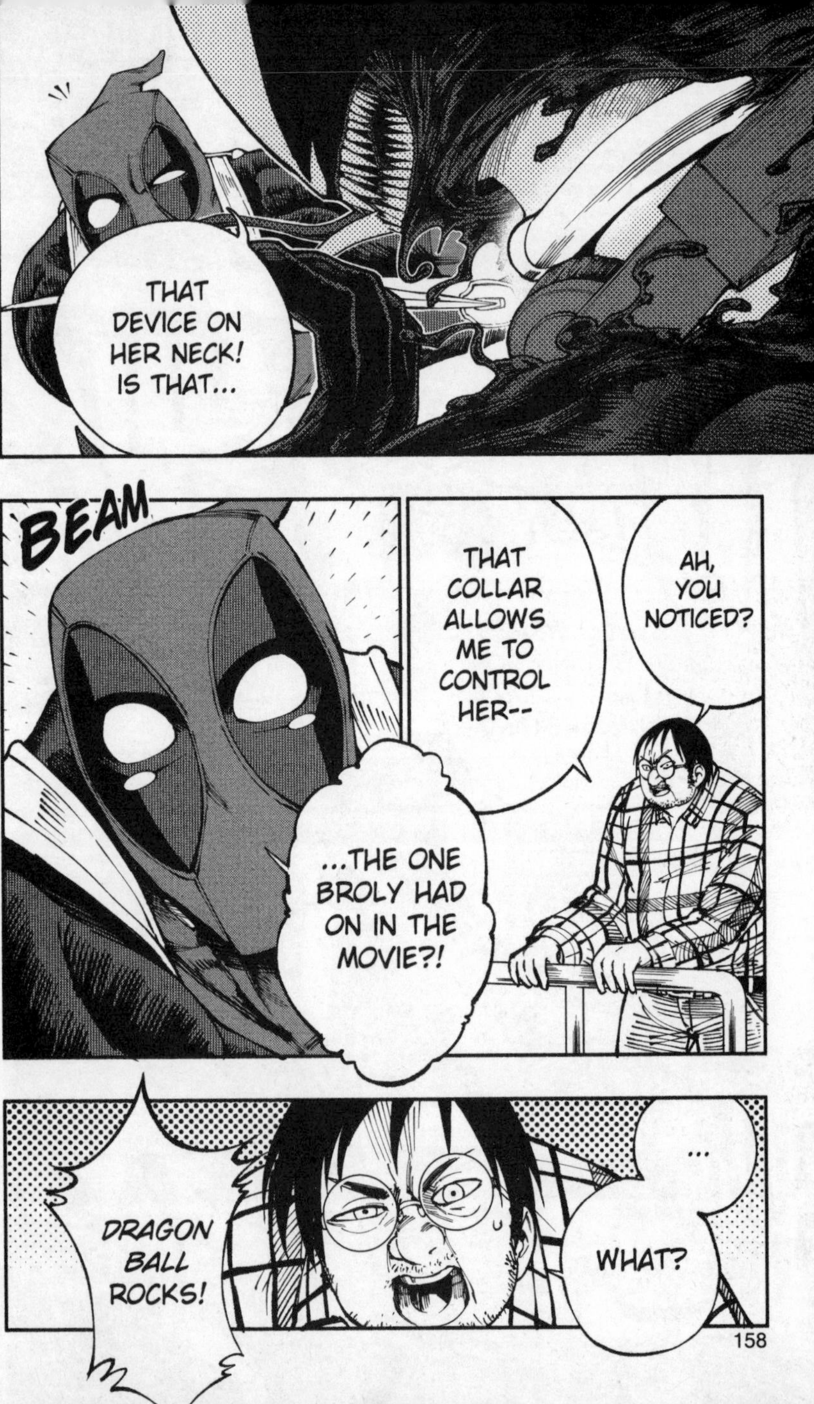
THAT DEVICE ON HER NECK! IS THAT...
AH, YOU NOTICED?
THAT COLLAR ALLOWS ME TO CONTROL HER--
BEAM
...THE ONE BROLY HAD ON IN THE MOVIE?!
... WHAT?
DRAGON BALL ROCKS!

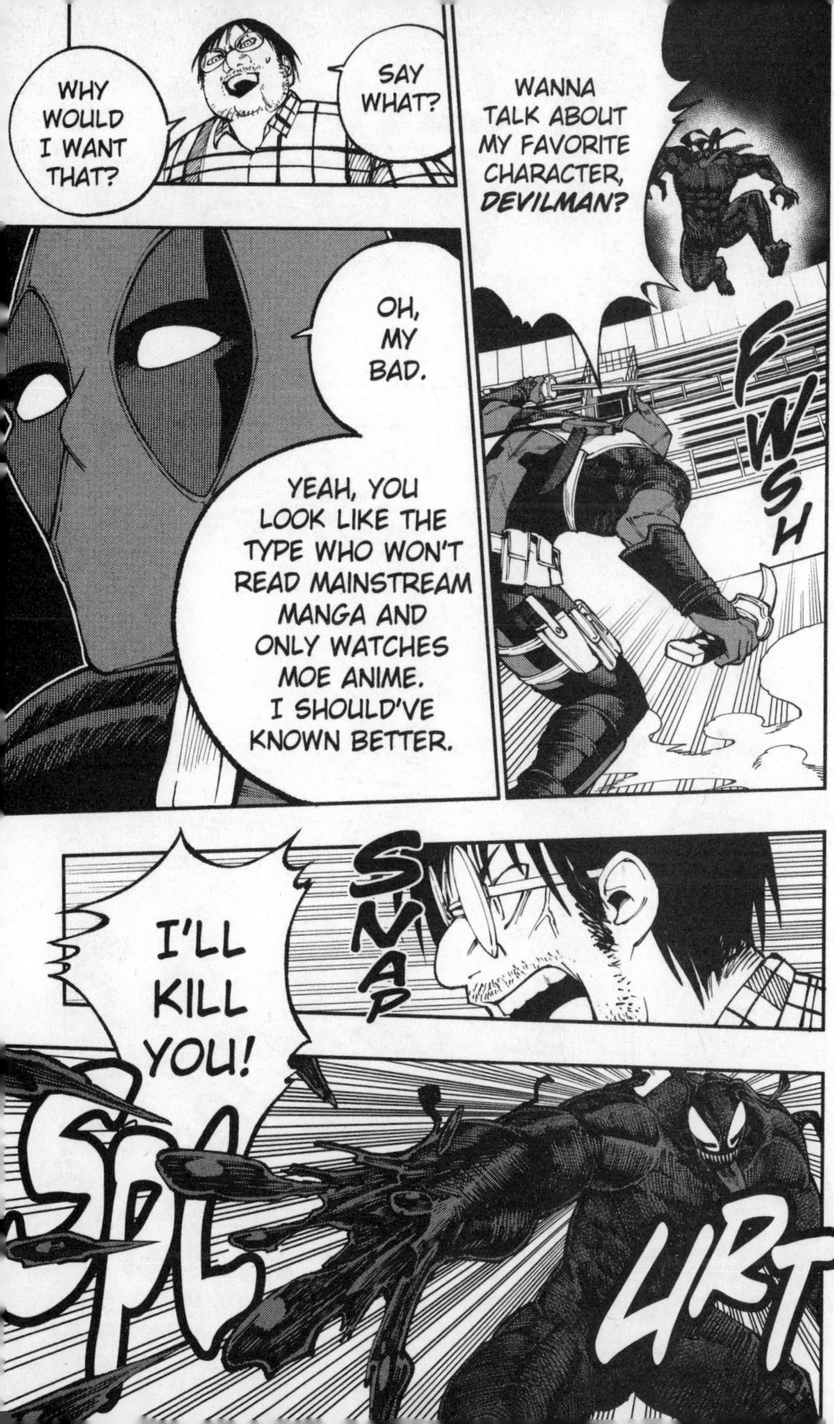
WANNA TALK ABOUT MY FAVORITE CHARACTER, *DEVILMAN?*
FWSH
SAY WHAT?
WHY WOULD I WANT THAT?
OH, MY BAD.
YEAH, YOU LOOK LIKE THE TYPE WHO WON'T READ MAINSTREAM MANGA AND ONLY WATCHES MOE ANIME. I SHOULD'VE KNOWN BETTER.
SNAP
I'LL KILL YOU!
SPLURT

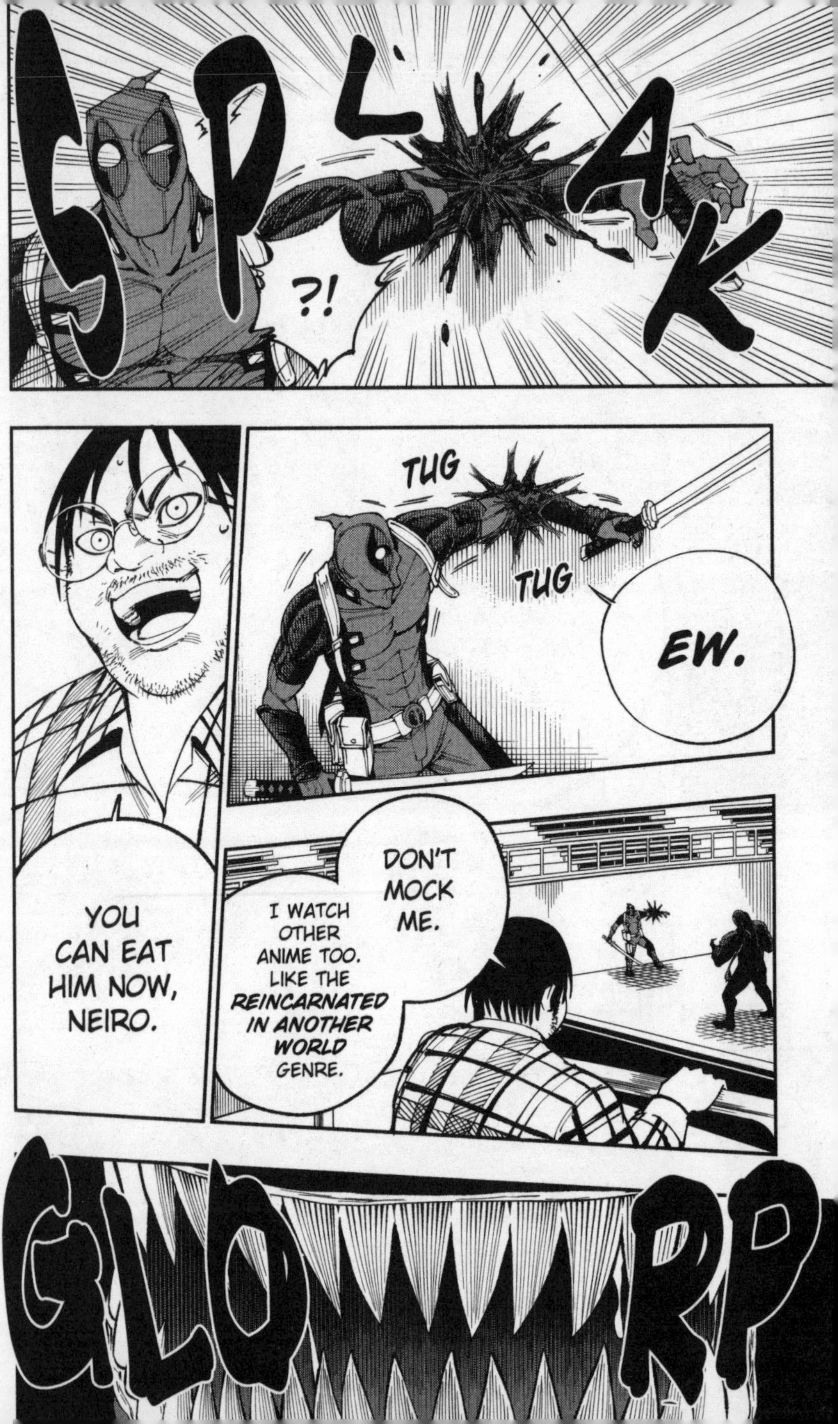
SPLAK
?!
TUG
TUG
EW.
DON'T MOCK ME.
I WATCH OTHER ANIME TOO. LIKE THE *REINCARNATED IN ANOTHER WORLD* GENRE.
YOU CAN EAT HIM NOW, NEIRO.
GLORP

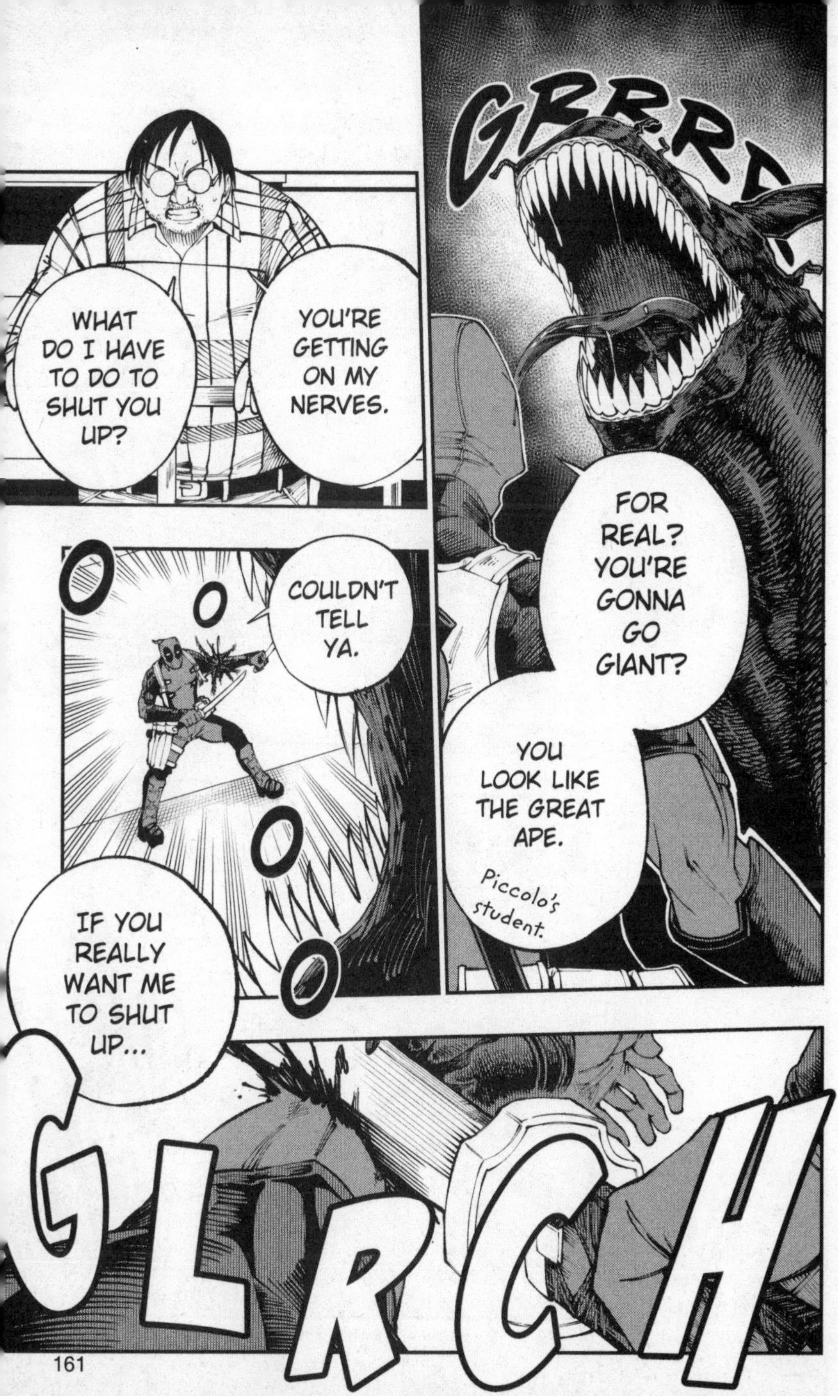
GRRRR
FOR REAL? YOU'RE GONNA GO GIANT?
YOU LOOK LIKE THE GREAT APE.
Piccolo's student.
YOU'RE GETTING ON MY NERVES.
WHAT DO I HAVE TO DO TO SHUT YOU UP?
COULDN'T TELL YA.
IF YOU REALLY WANT ME TO SHUT UP...
GLRCH

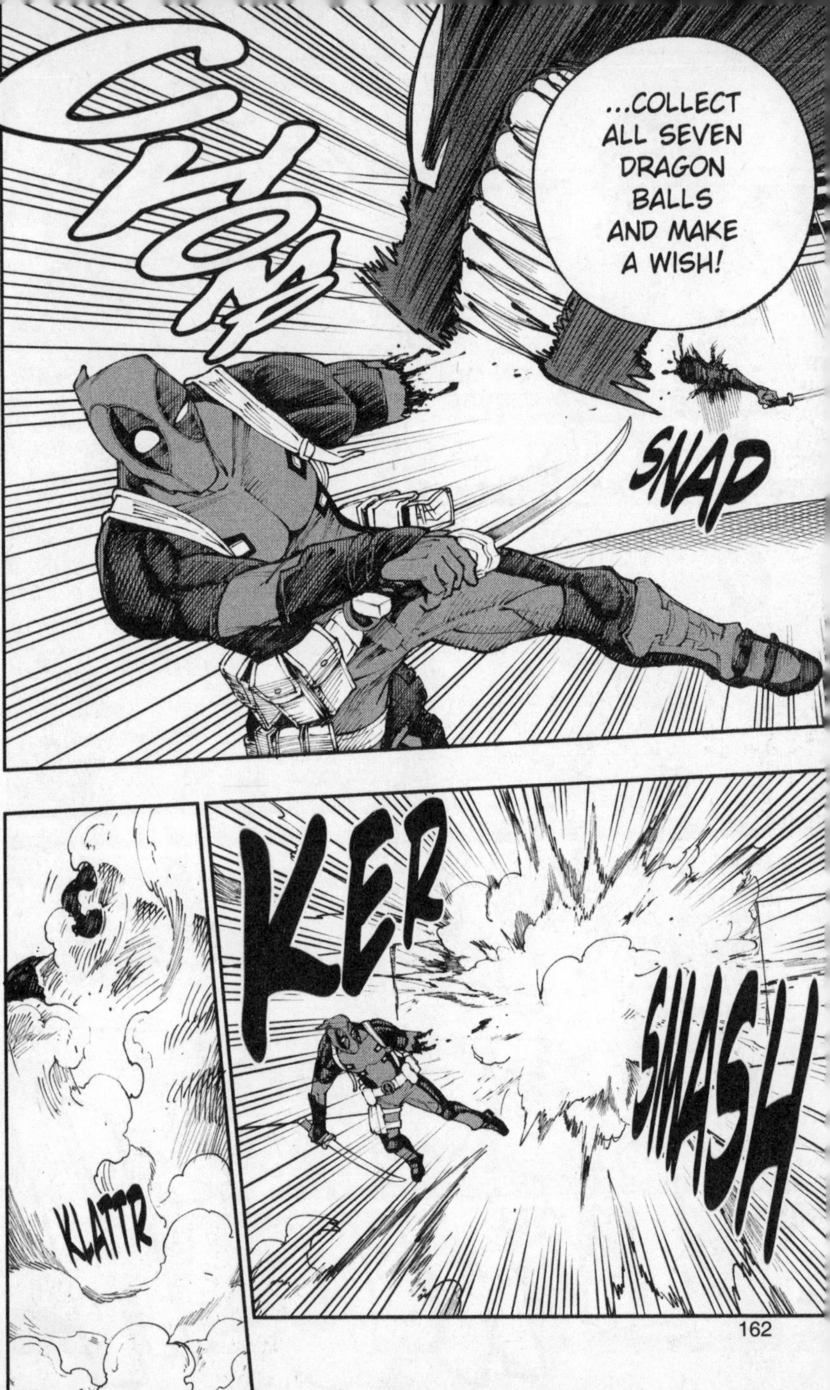
...COLLECT ALL SEVEN DRAGON BALLS AND MAKE A WISH!
CHOM
SNAP
KER
SMASH
KLATTR

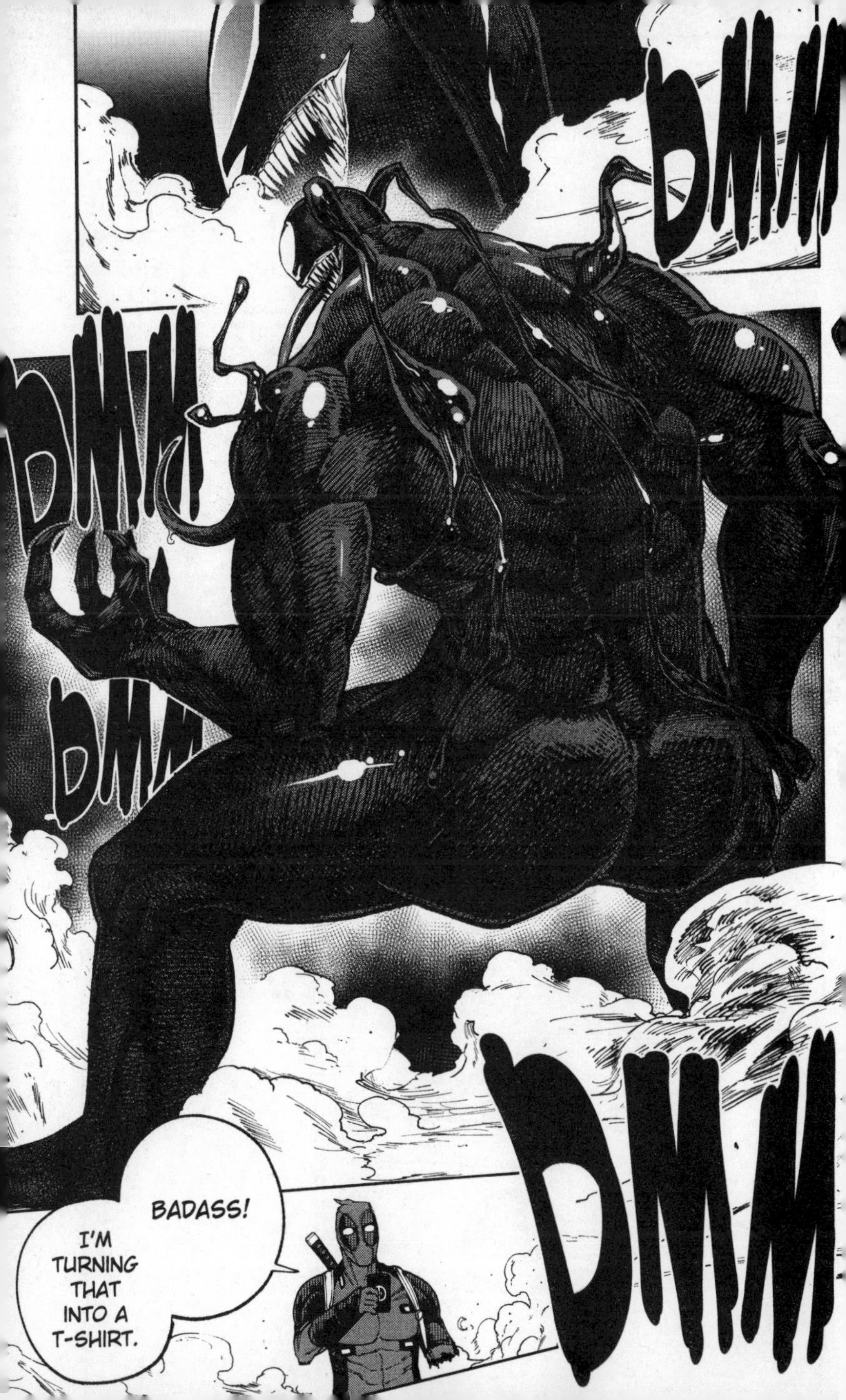
DMM
DMM
DMM
DMM
BADASS!
I'M TURNING THAT INTO A T-SHIRT.

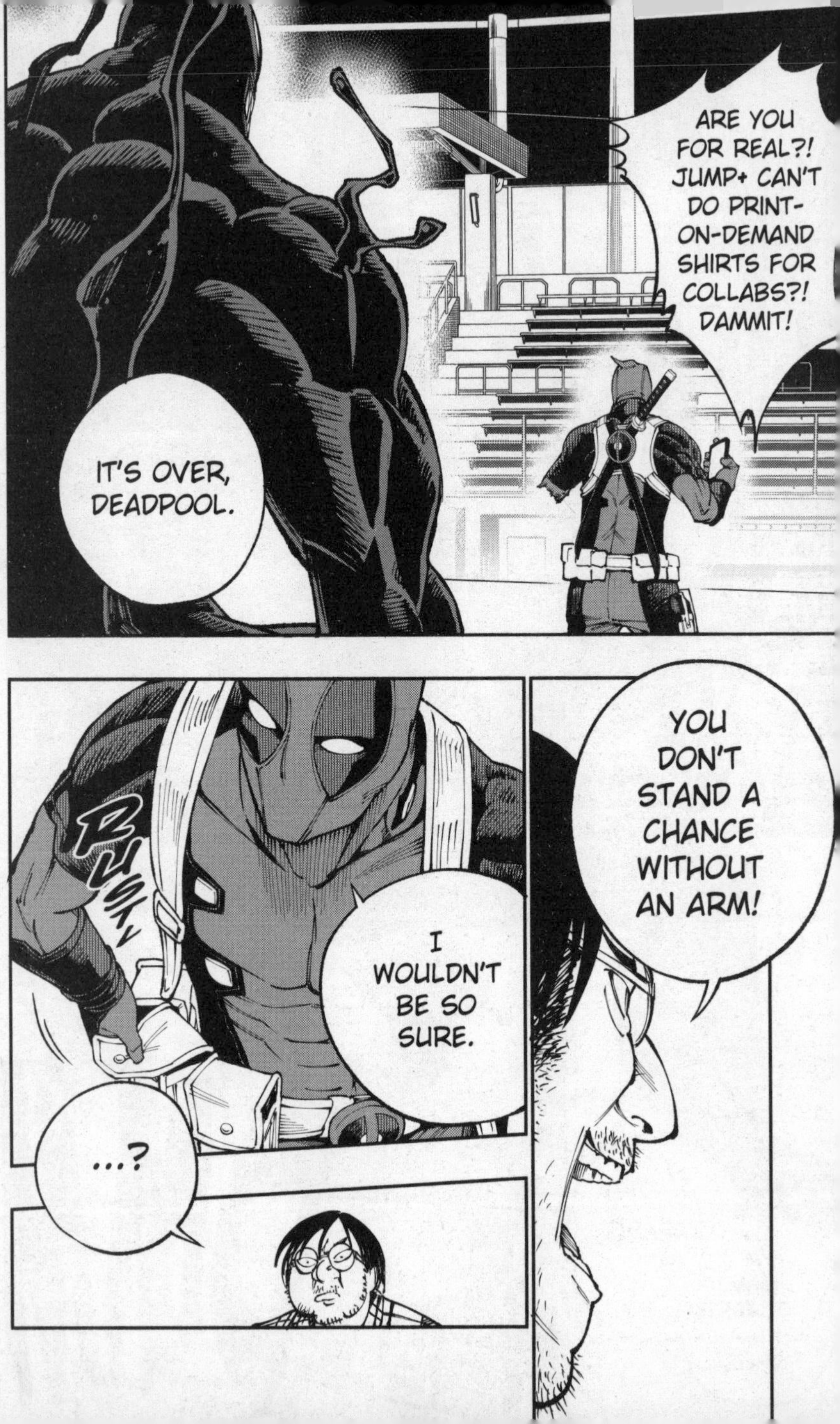
ARE YOU FOR REAL?! JUMP+ CAN'T DO PRINT-ON-DEMAND SHIRTS FOR COLLABS?! DAMMIT!
IT'S OVER, DEADPOOL.
YOU DON'T STAND A CHANCE WITHOUT AN ARM!
I WOULDN'T BE SO SURE.
...?

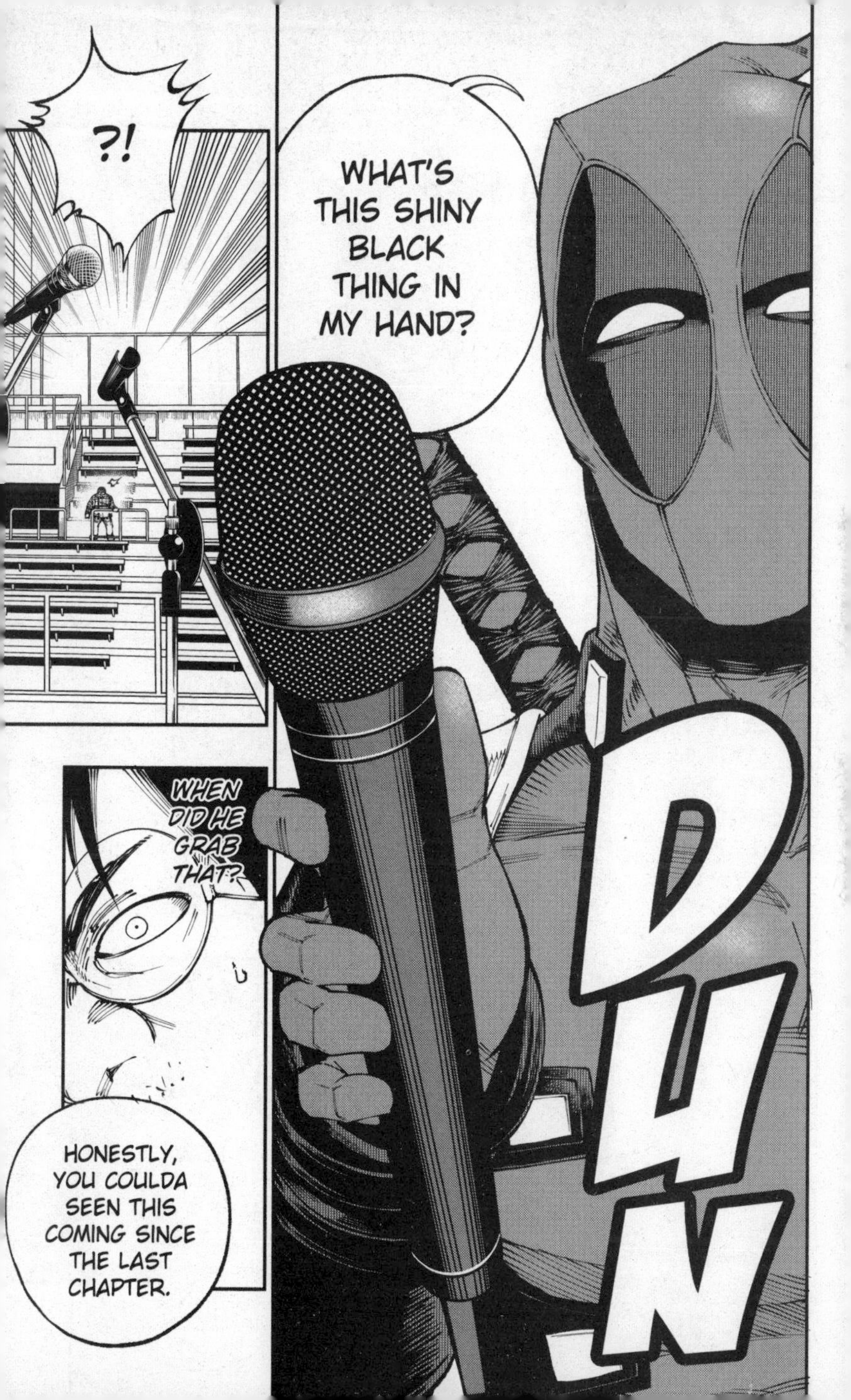
WHAT'S THIS SHINY BLACK THING IN MY HAND?
DUN
?!
WHEN DID HE GRAB THAT?
HONESTLY, YOU COULDA SEEN THIS COMING SINCE THE LAST CHAPTER.

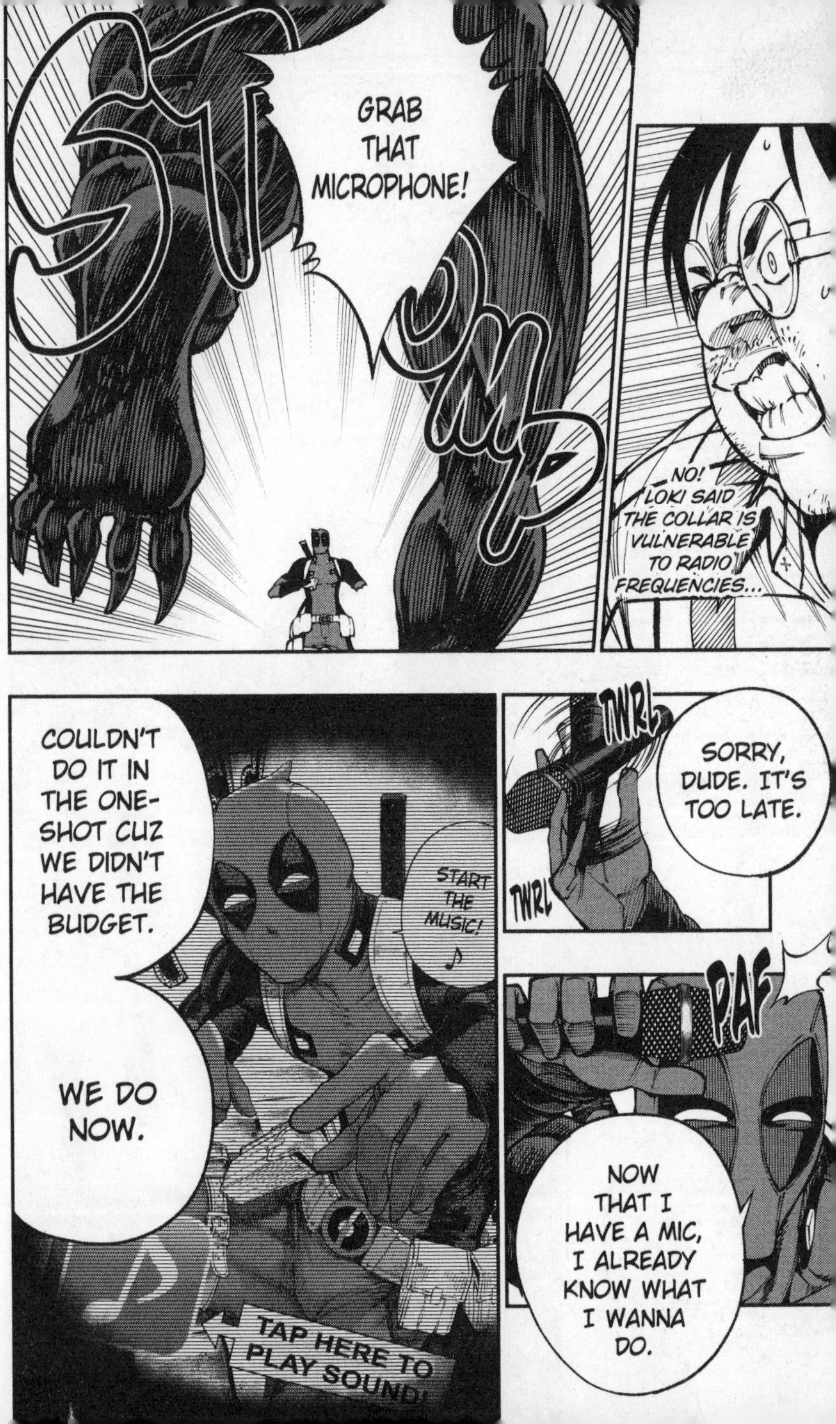
NO! LOKI SAID THE COLLAR IS VULNERABLE TO RADIO FREQUENCIES...
STOMP
GRAB THAT MICROPHONE!
TWRL
SORRY, DUDE. IT'S TOO LATE.
TWRL
PAF
NOW THAT I HAVE A MIC, I ALREADY KNOW WHAT I WANNA DO.
COULDN'T DO IT IN THE ONE-SHOT CUZ WE DIDN'T HAVE THE BUDGET.
START THE MUSIC!
WE DO NOW.
TAP HERE TO PLAY SOUND!

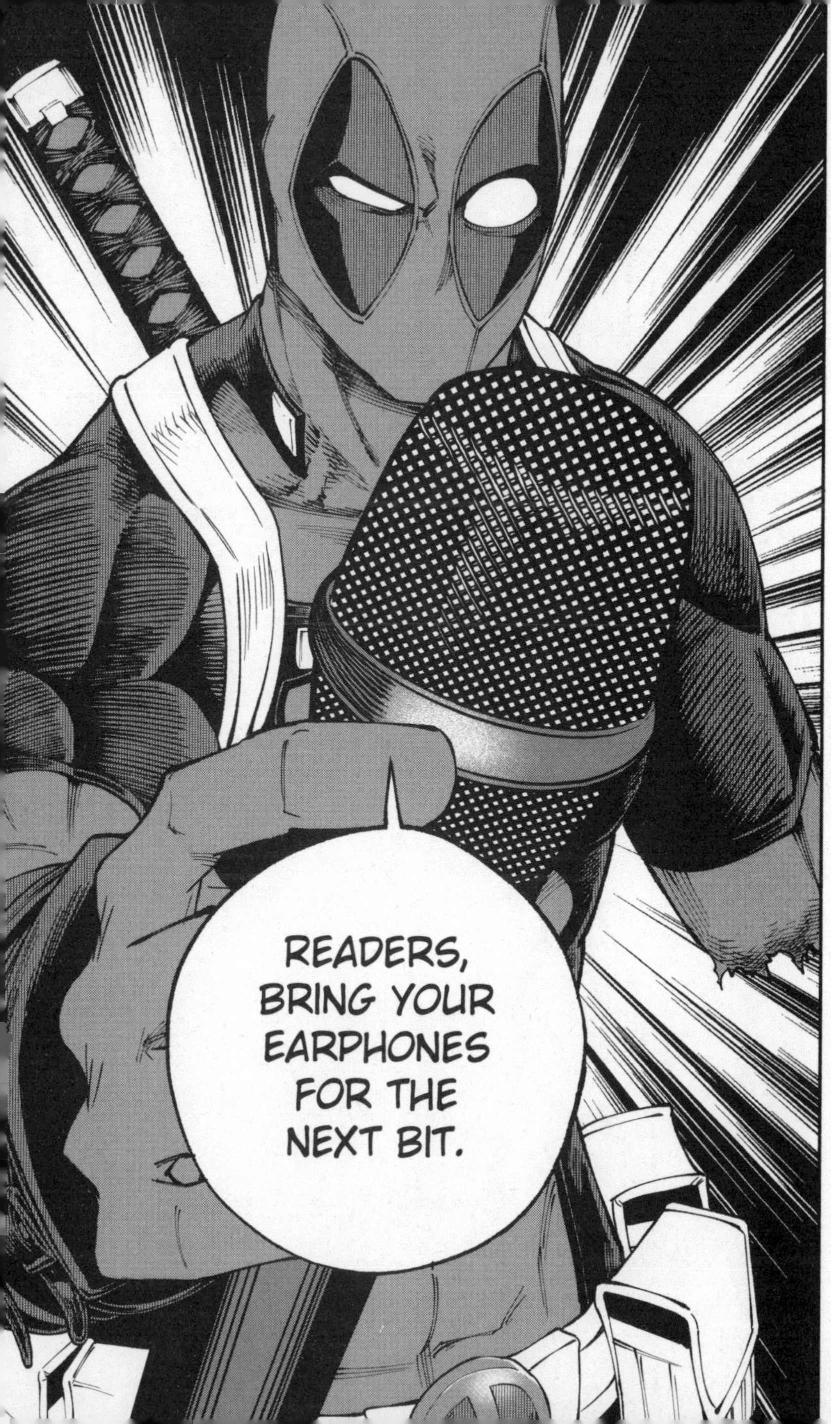
READERS, BRING YOUR EARPHONES FOR THE NEXT BIT.

Character Profile

DANGEROUS CREEP

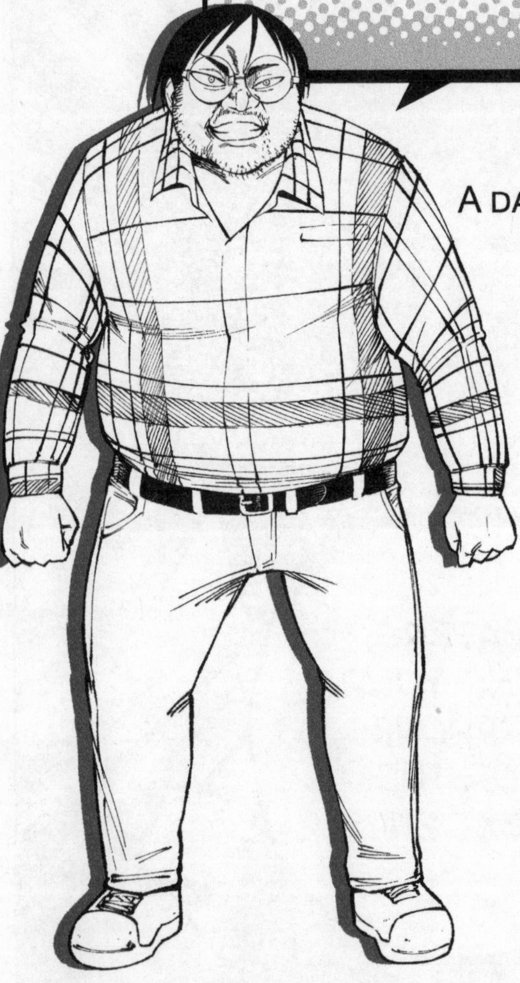

A DANGEROUS CREEP.

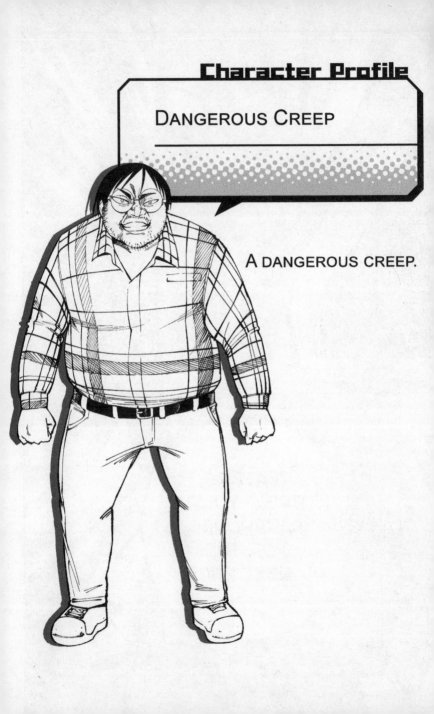

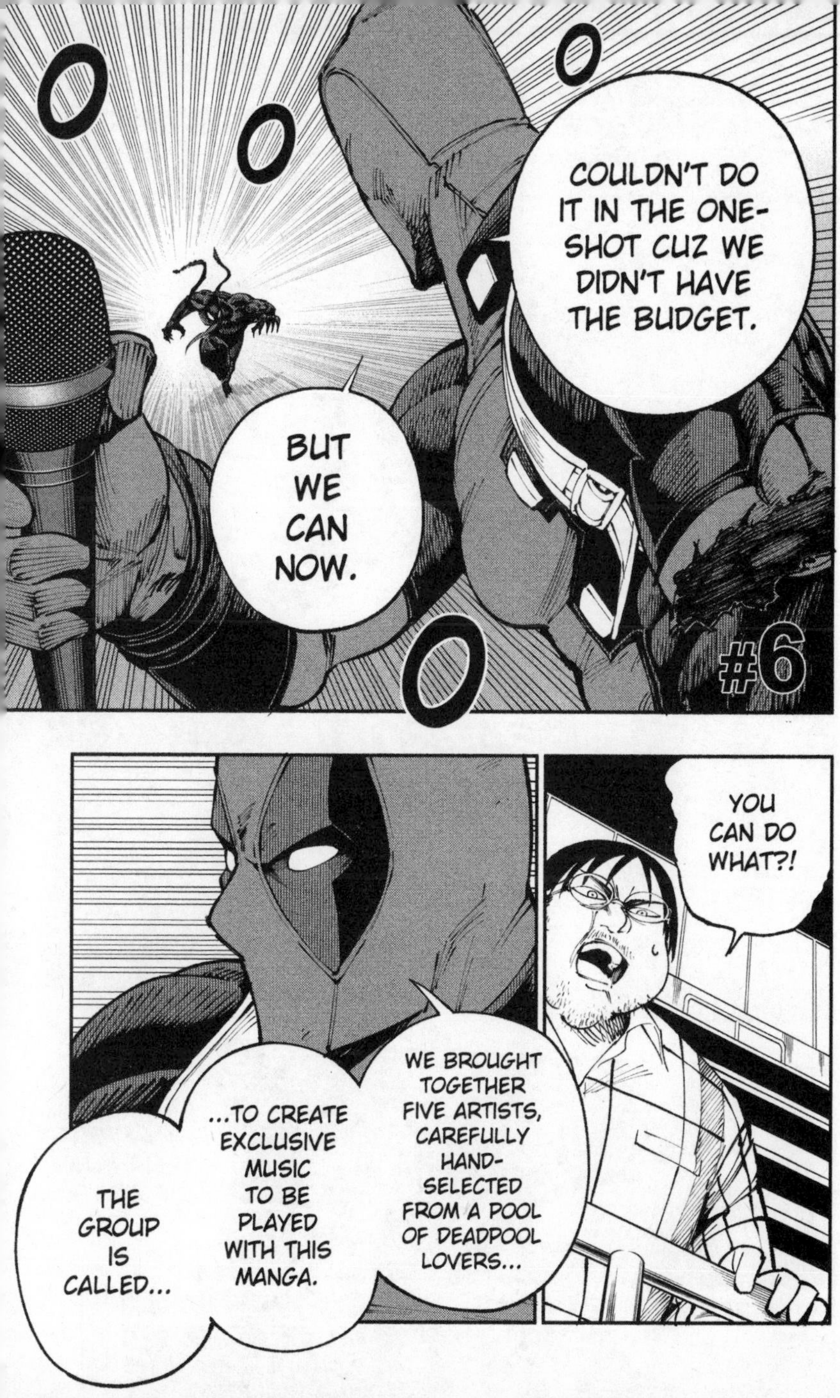
COULDN'T DO IT IN THE ONE-SHOT CUZ WE DIDN'T HAVE THE BUDGET.
BUT WE CAN NOW.
#6
YOU CAN DO WHAT?!
WE BROUGHT TOGETHER FIVE ARTISTS, CAREFULLY HAND-SELECTED FROM A POOL OF DEADPOOL LOVERS...
...TO CREATE EXCLUSIVE MUSIC TO BE PLAYED WITH THIS MANGA.
THE GROUP IS CALLED...

THE DEADPOOL BAND!

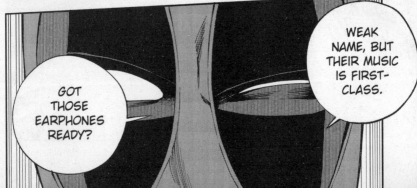

WEAK NAME, BUT THEIR MUSIC IS FIRST-CLASS.

GOT THOSE EARPHONES READY?

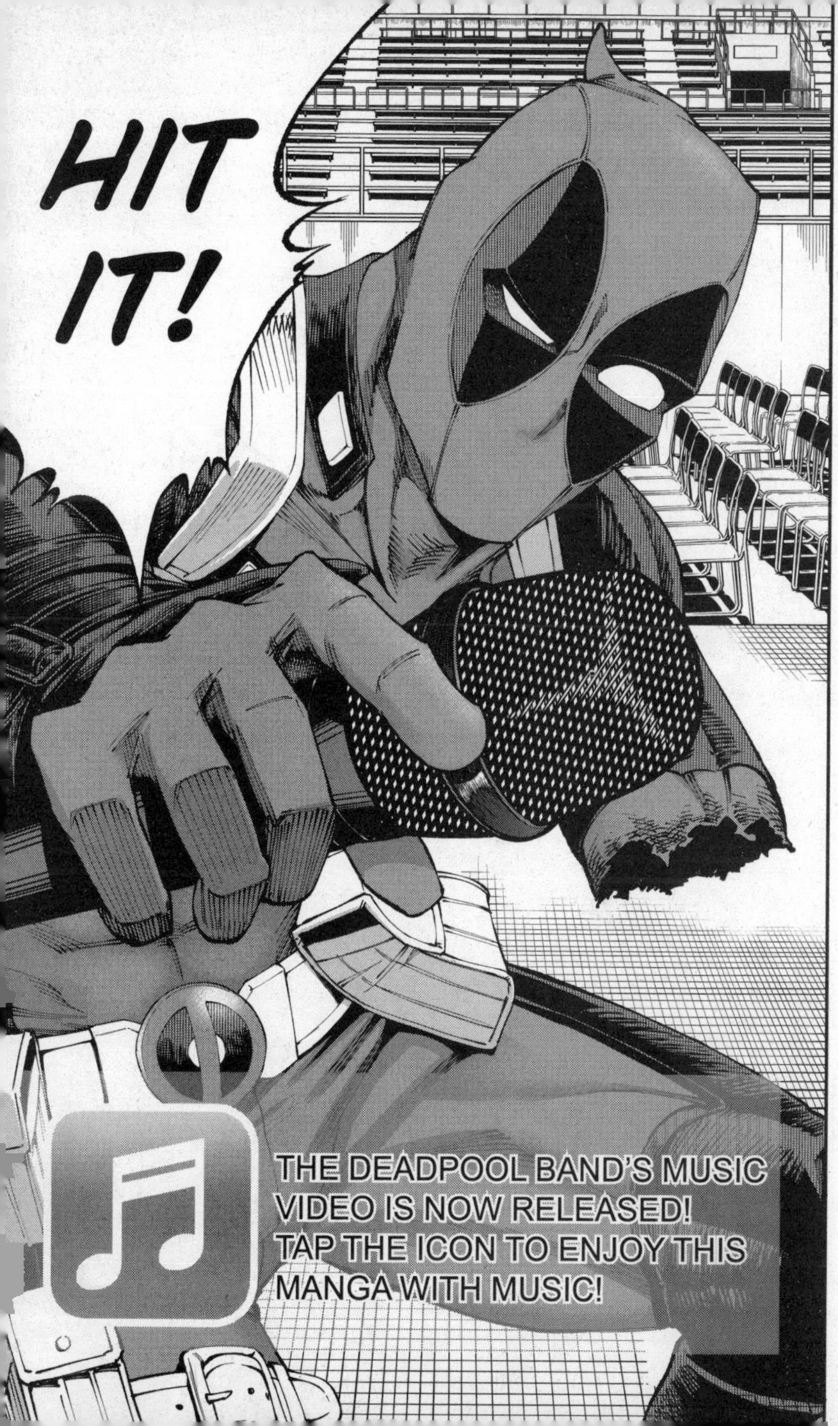
HIT IT!
THE DEADPOOL BAND'S MUSIC VIDEO IS NOW RELEASED! TAP THE ICON TO ENJOY THIS MANGA WITH MUSIC!

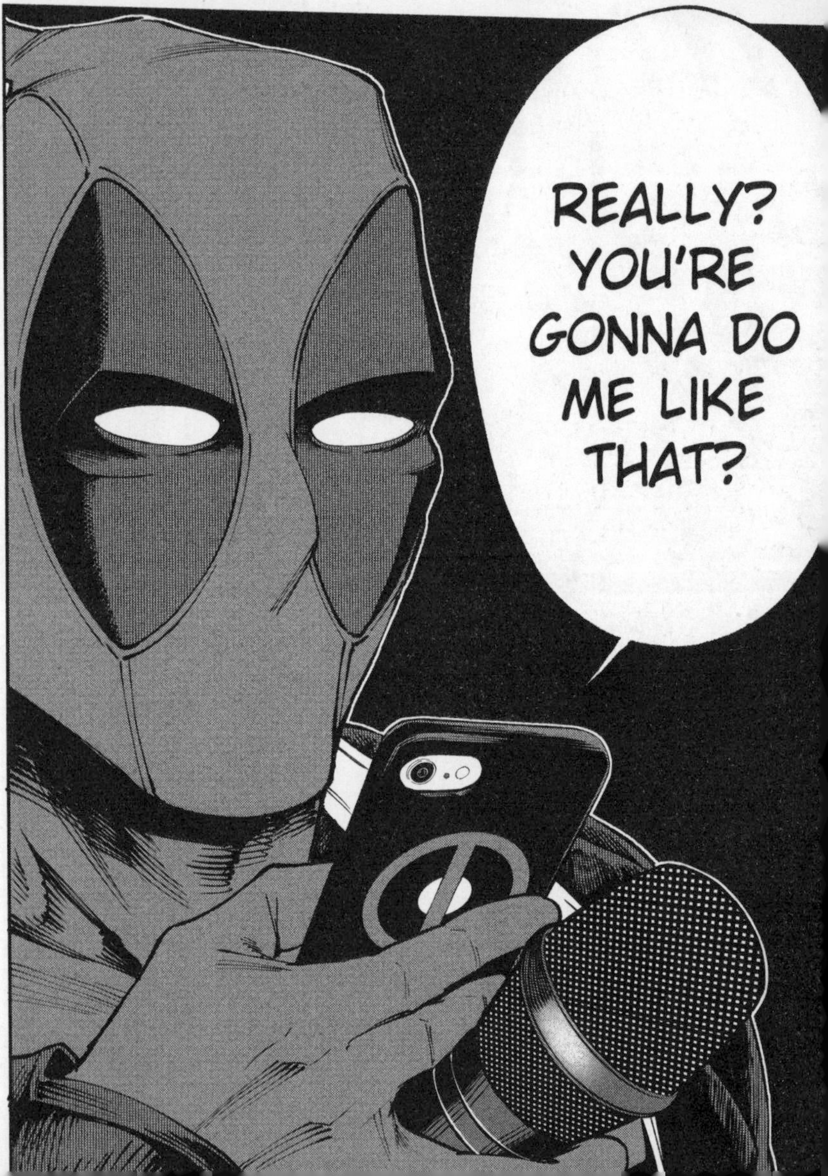
REALLY? YOU'RE GONNA DO ME LIKE THAT?

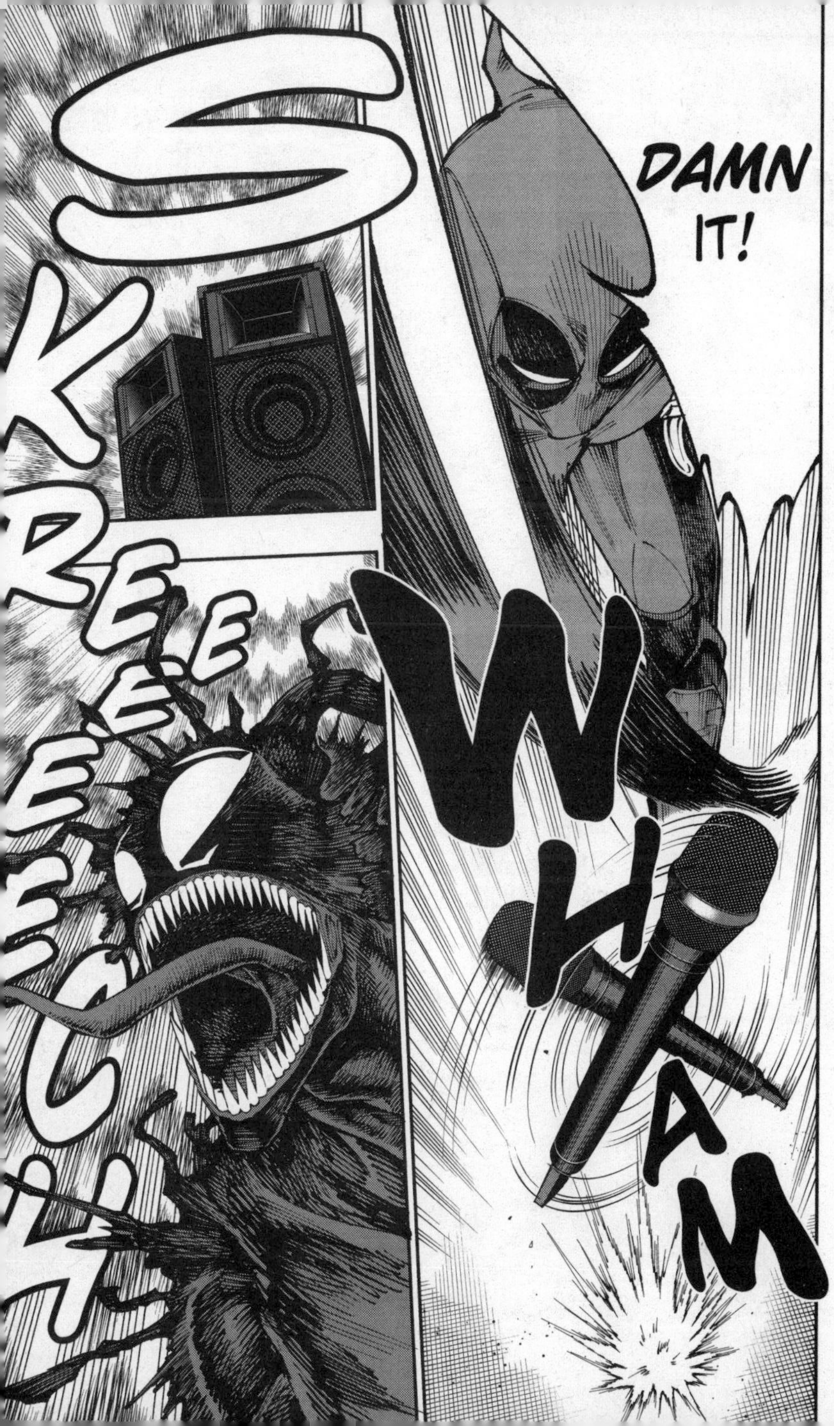
DAMN IT!
WHAM

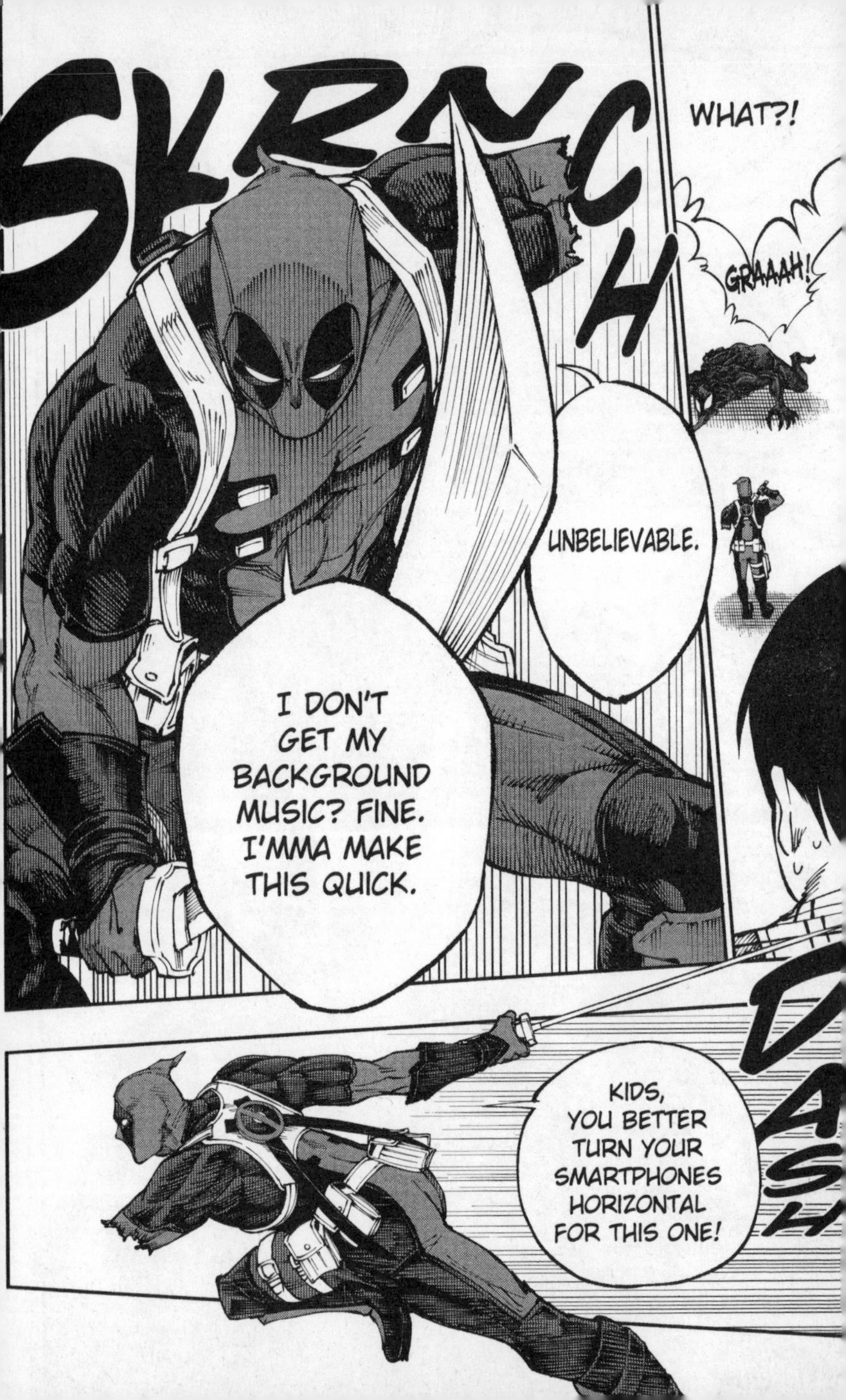
SKRNCH
WHAT?!
GRAAAH!
UNBELIEVABLE.
I DON'T GET MY BACKGROUND MUSIC? FINE. I'MMA MAKE THIS QUICK.
DASH
KIDS, YOU BETTER TURN YOUR SMARTPHONES HORIZONTAL FOR THIS ONE!

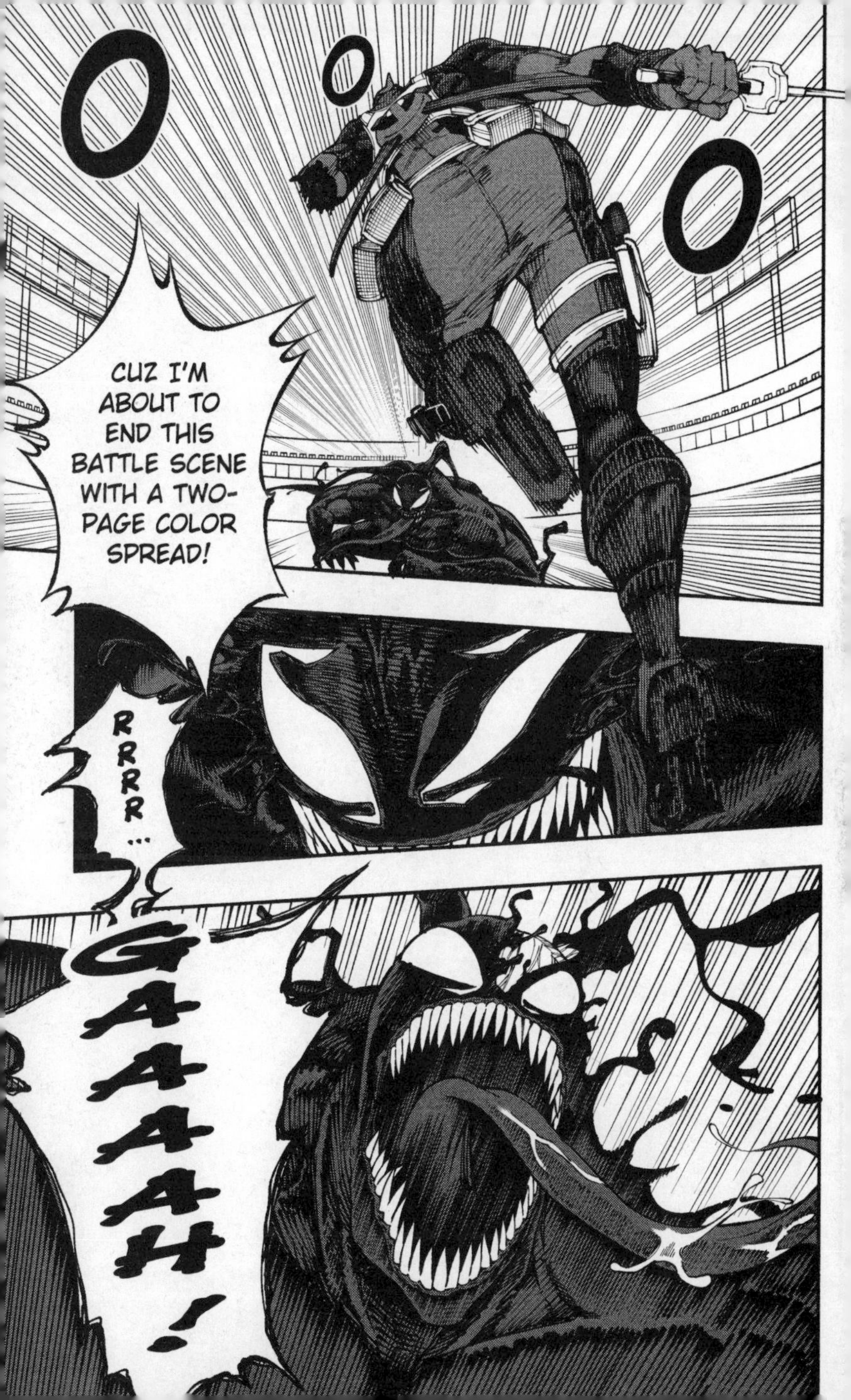
OOO
CUZ I'M ABOUT TO END THIS BATTLE SCENE WITH A TWO-PAGE COLOR SPREAD!
RRRR...
GAAAAH!!

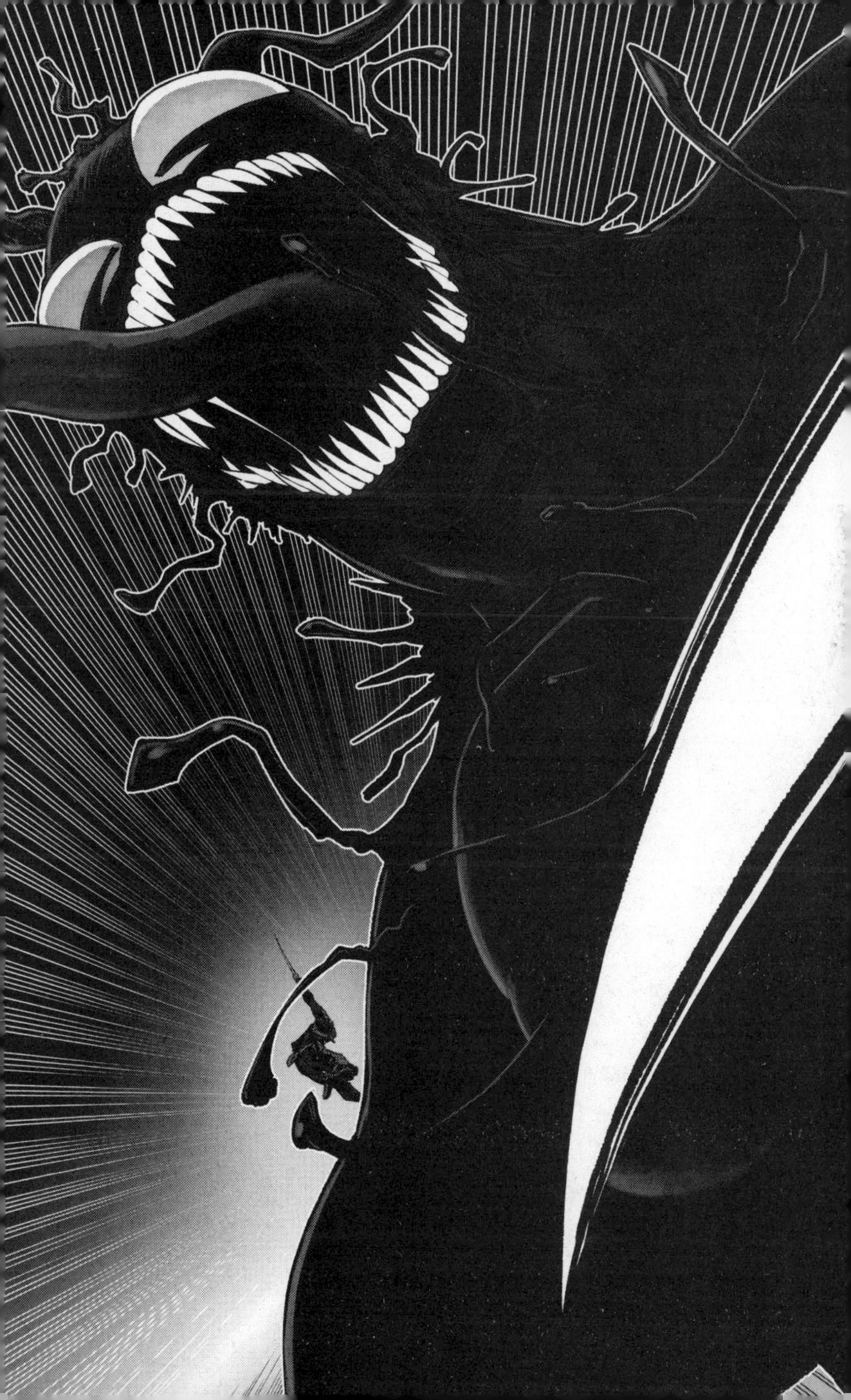

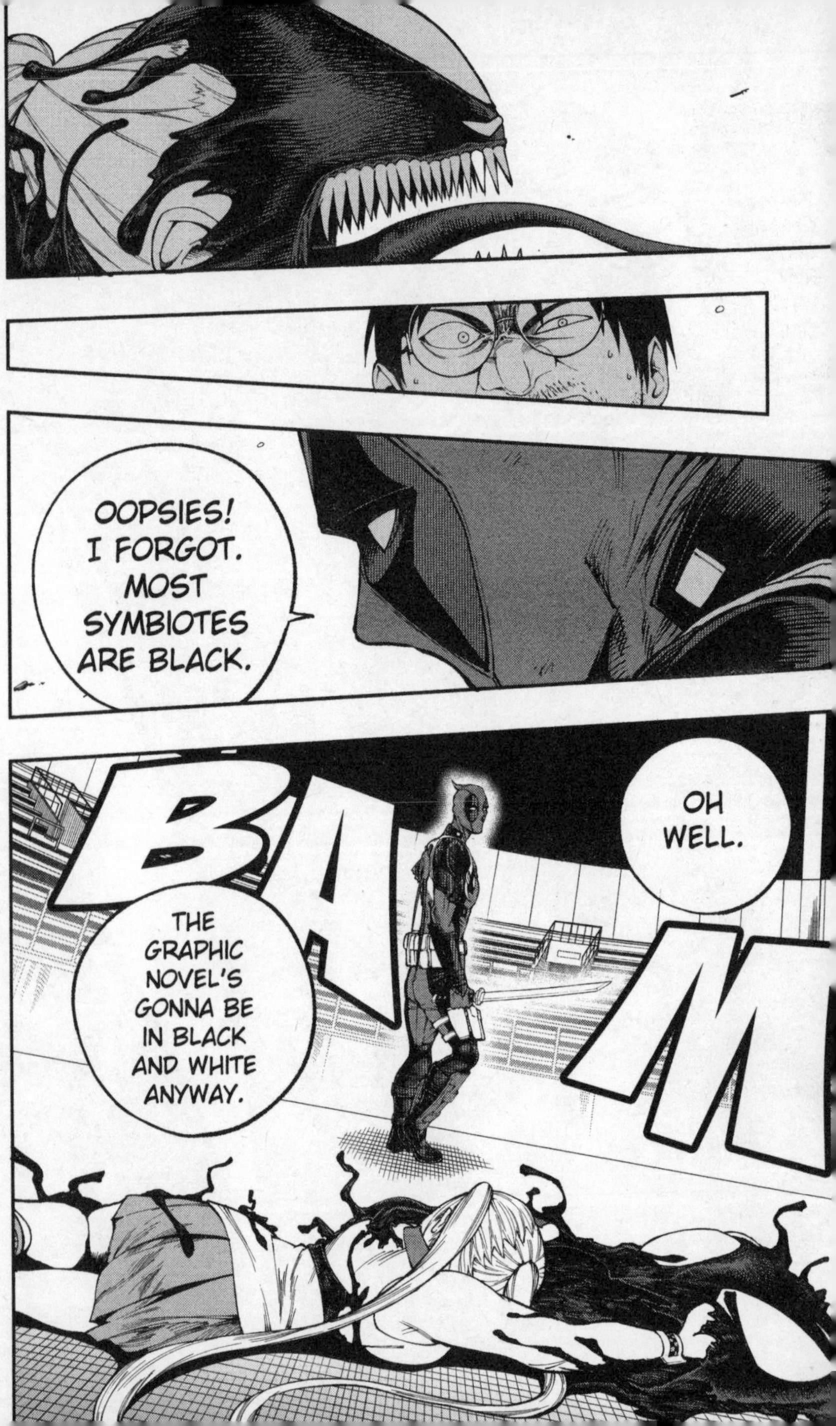
OOPSIES! I FORGOT. MOST SYMBIOTES ARE BLACK.
OH WELL.
BAM
THE GRAPHIC NOVEL'S GONNA BE IN BLACK AND WHITE ANYWAY.

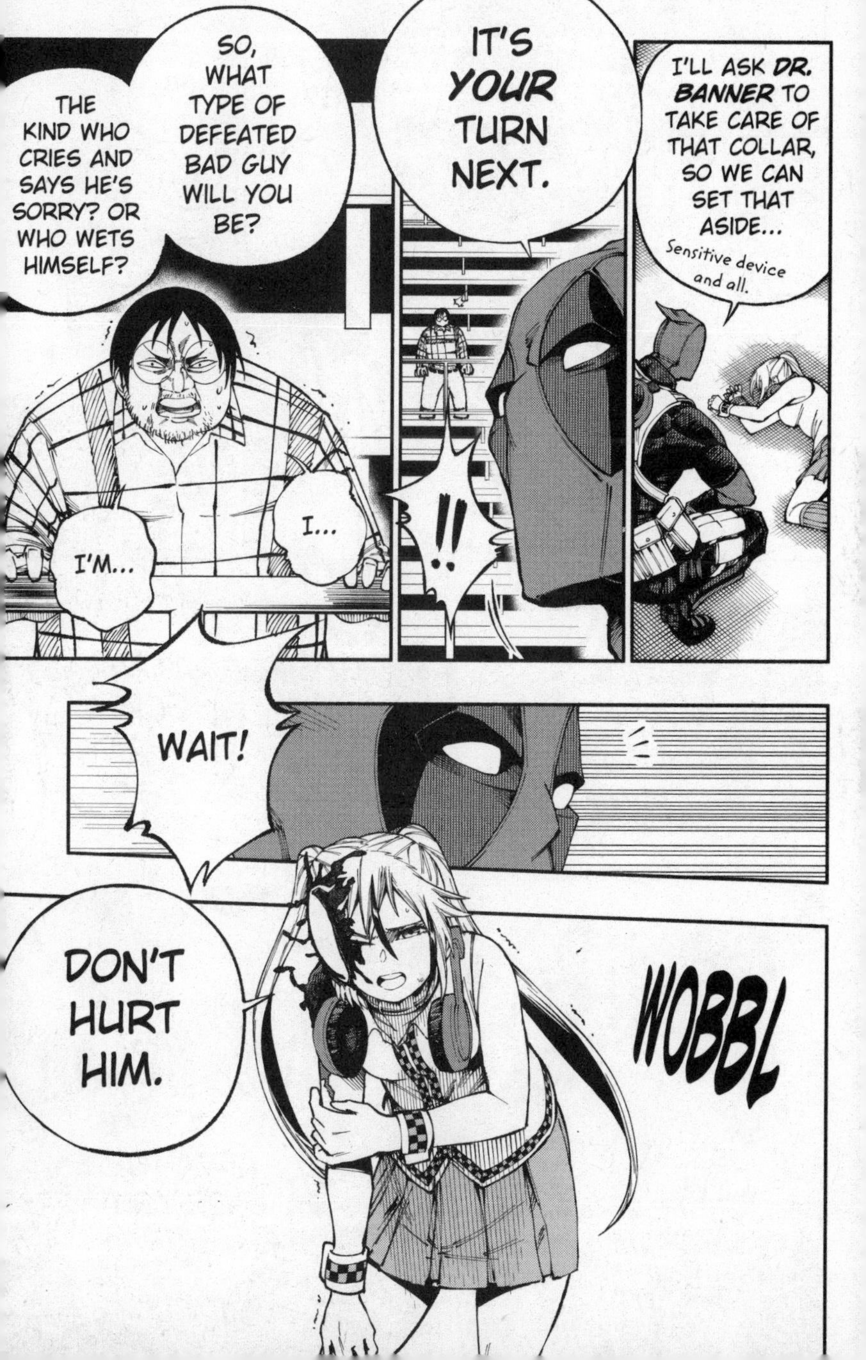
I'LL ASK DR. BANNER TO TAKE CARE OF THAT COLLAR, SO WE CAN SET THAT ASIDE...
Sensitive device and all.
IT'S YOUR TURN NEXT.
!!
SO, WHAT TYPE OF DEFEATED BAD GUY WILL YOU BE?
THE KIND WHO CRIES AND SAYS HE'S SORRY? OR WHO WETS HIMSELF?
I...
I'M...
WAIT!
DON'T HURT HIM.
WOBBL

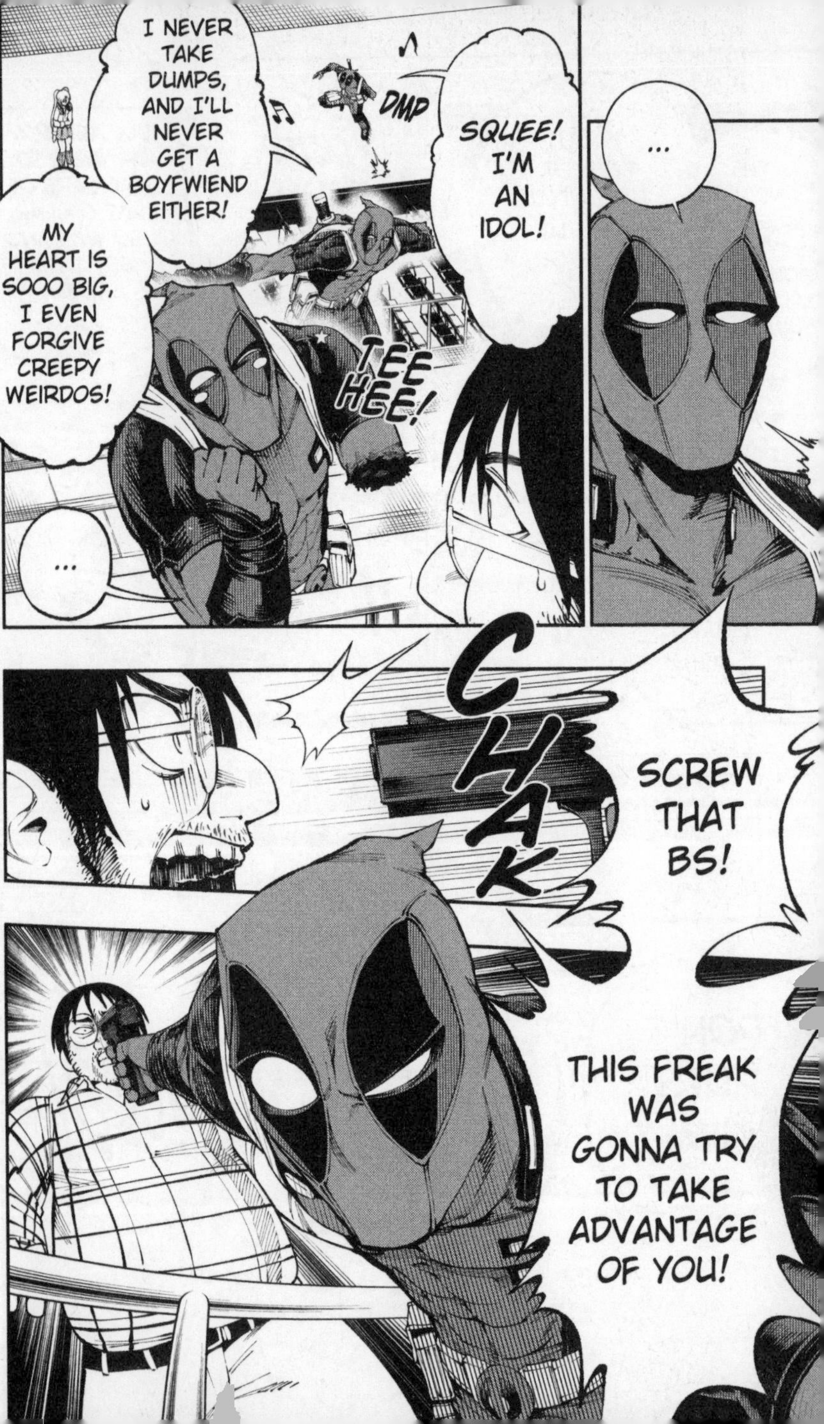
...
SQUEE! I'M AN IDOL!
DMP
I NEVER TAKE DUMPS, AND I'LL NEVER GET A BOYFWIEND EITHER!
MY HEART IS SOOO BIG, I EVEN FORGIVE CREEPY WEIRDOS!
TEE HEE!
...
SCREW THAT BS!
CHAK
THIS FREAK WAS GONNA TRY TO TAKE ADVANTAGE OF YOU!

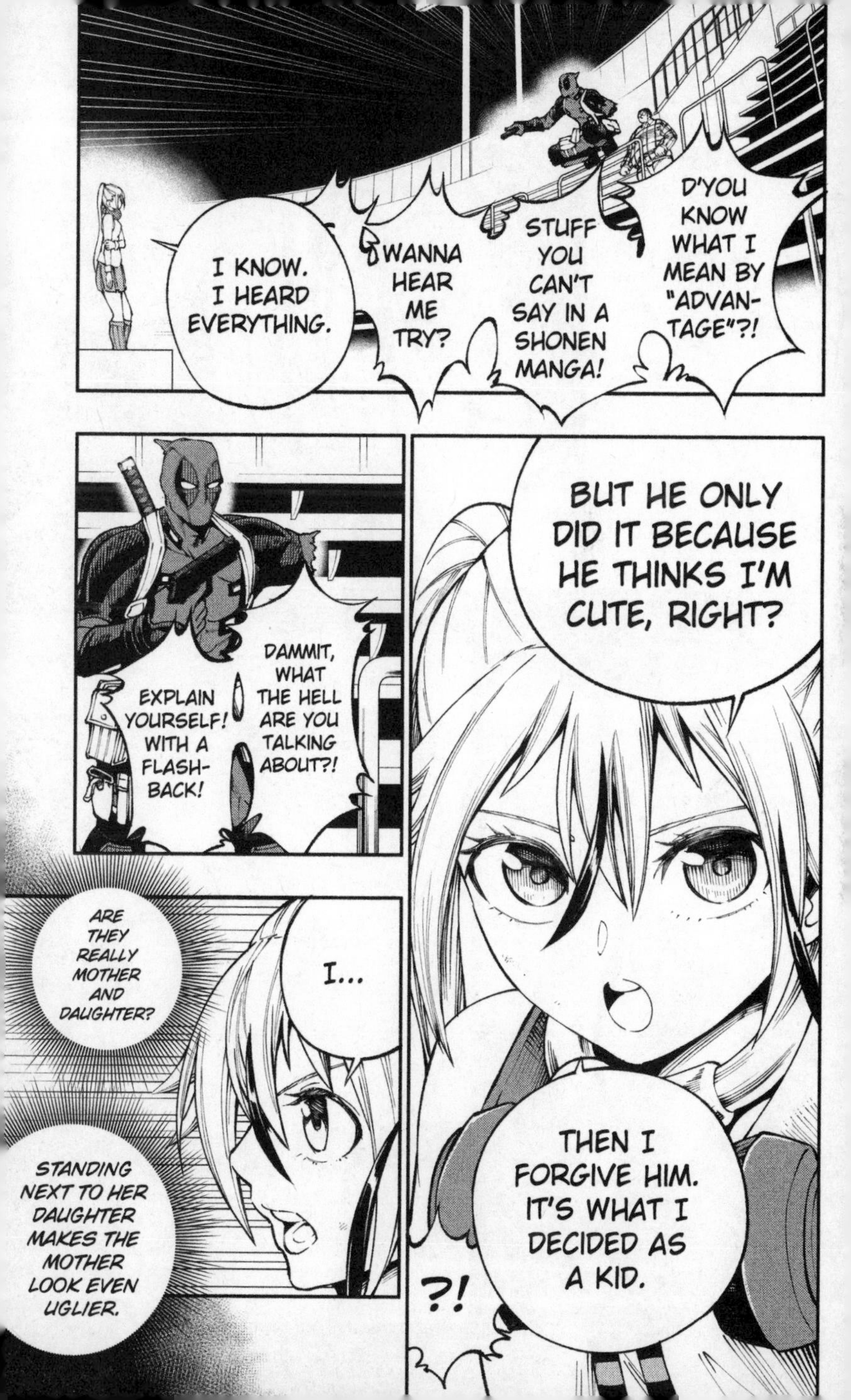
D'YOU KNOW WHAT I MEAN BY "ADVANTAGE"?!
STUFF YOU CAN'T SAY IN A SHONEN MANGA!
WANNA HEAR ME TRY?
I KNOW. I HEARD EVERYTHING.
BUT HE ONLY DID IT BECAUSE HE THINKS I'M CUTE, RIGHT?
THEN I FORGIVE HIM. IT'S WHAT I DECIDED AS A KID.
?!
DAMMIT, WHAT THE HELL ARE YOU TALKING ABOUT?!
EXPLAIN YOURSELF! WITH A FLASH-BACK!
I...
ARE THEY REALLY MOTHER AND DAUGHTER?
STANDING NEXT TO HER DAUGHTER MAKES THE MOTHER LOOK EVEN UGLIER.

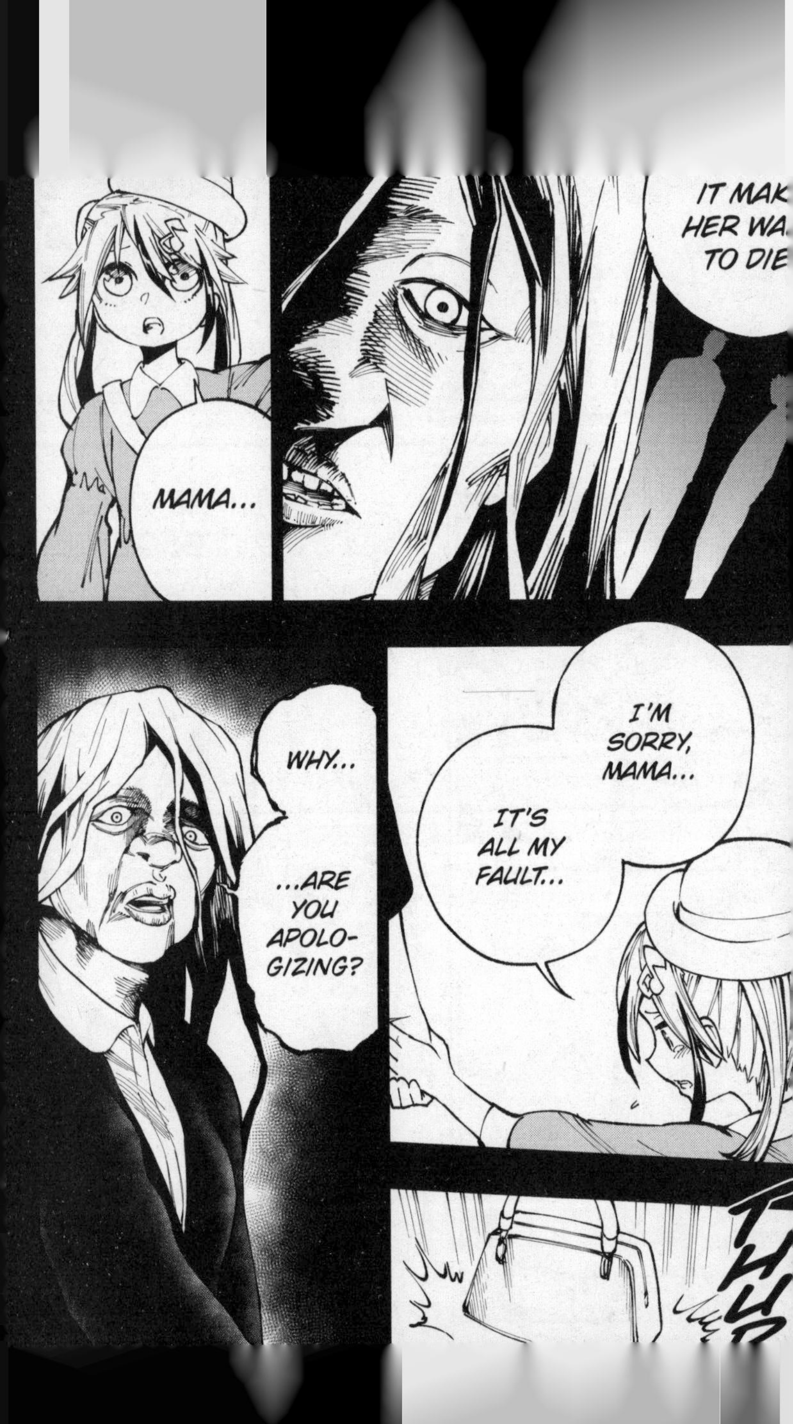
IT MAK
HER WA
TO DIE
MAMA...
I'M SORRY, MAMA...
IT'S ALL MY FAULT...
THU
WHY...
...ARE YOU APOLO-GIZING?

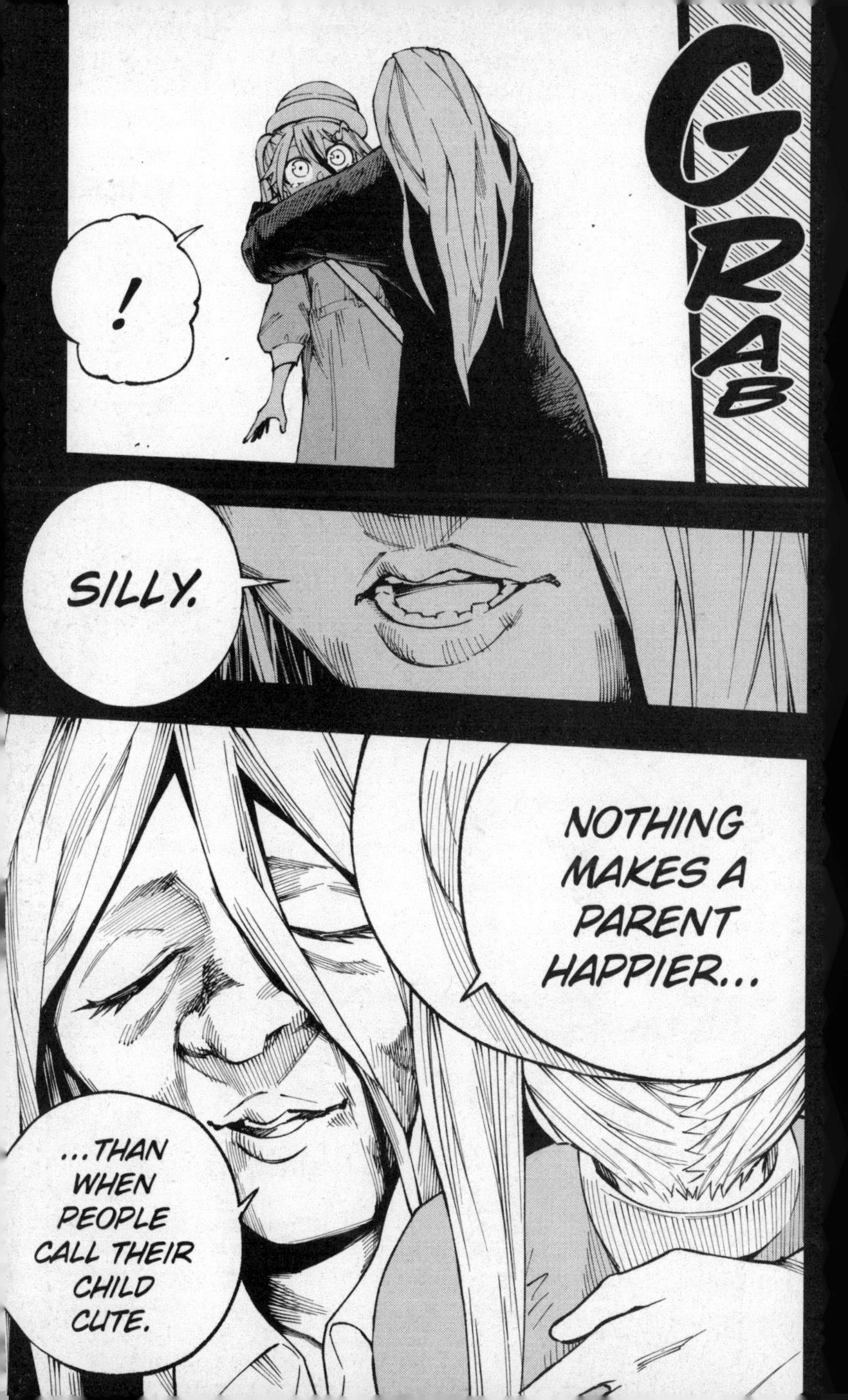
GRAB
!
SILLY.
NOTHING MAKES A PARENT HAPPIER...
...THAN WHEN PEOPLE CALL THEIR CHILD CUTE.

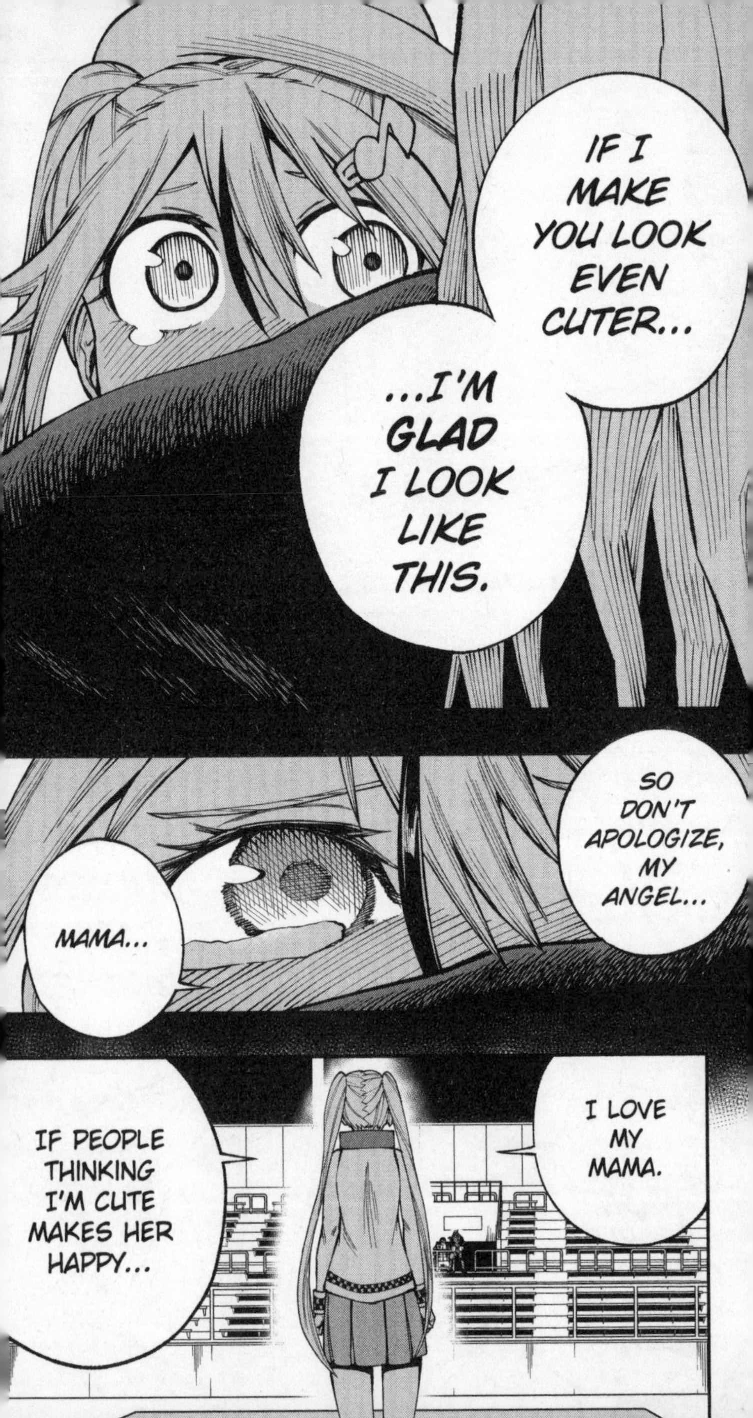
IF I MAKE YOU LOOK EVEN CUTER...
...I'M **GLAD** I LOOK LIKE THIS.
SO DON'T APOLOGIZE, MY ANGEL...
MAMA...
I LOVE MY MAMA.
IF PEOPLE THINKING I'M CUTE MAKES HER HAPPY...

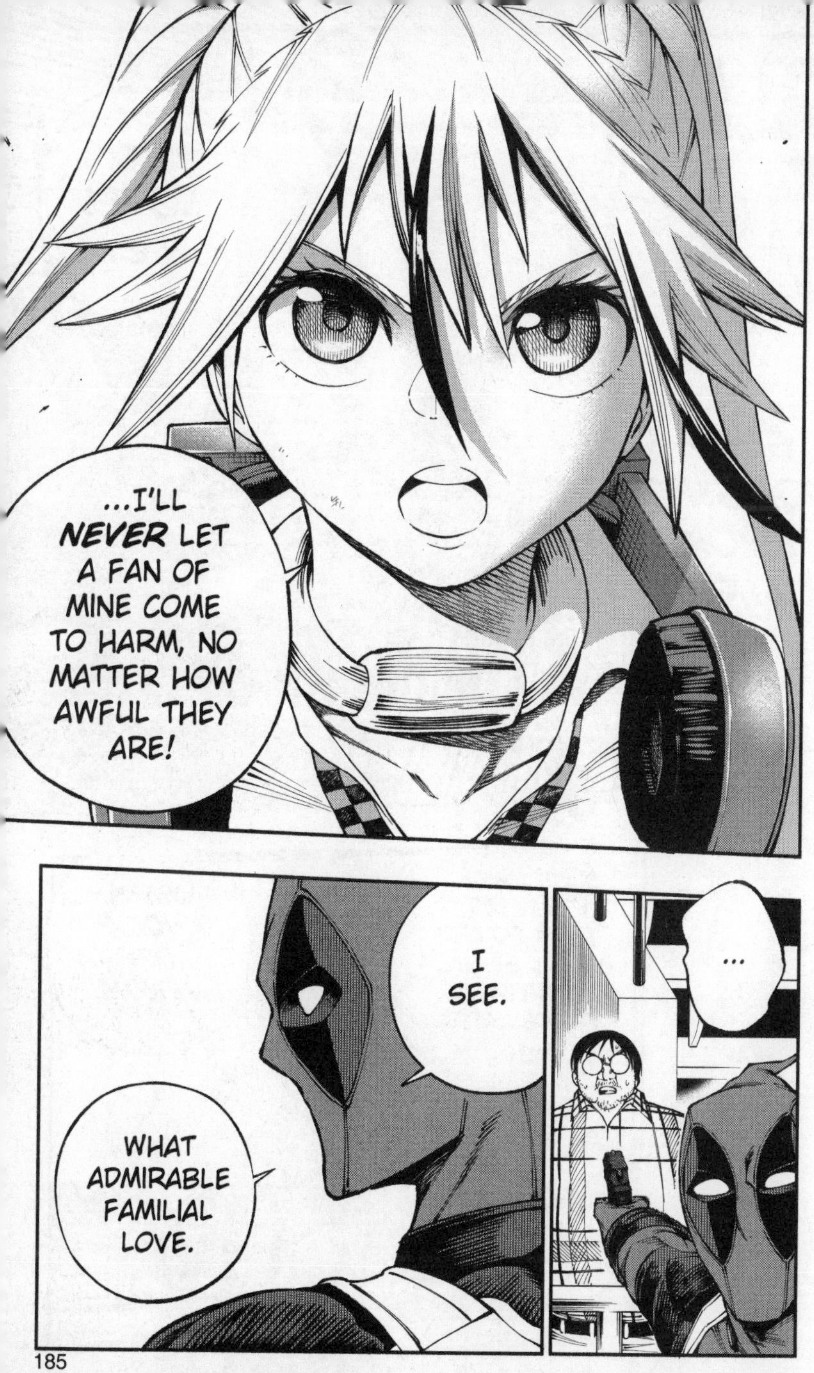
...I'LL NEVER LET A FAN OF MINE COME TO HARM, NO MATTER HOW AWFUL THEY ARE!
...
I SEE.
WHAT ADMIRABLE FAMILIAL LOVE.

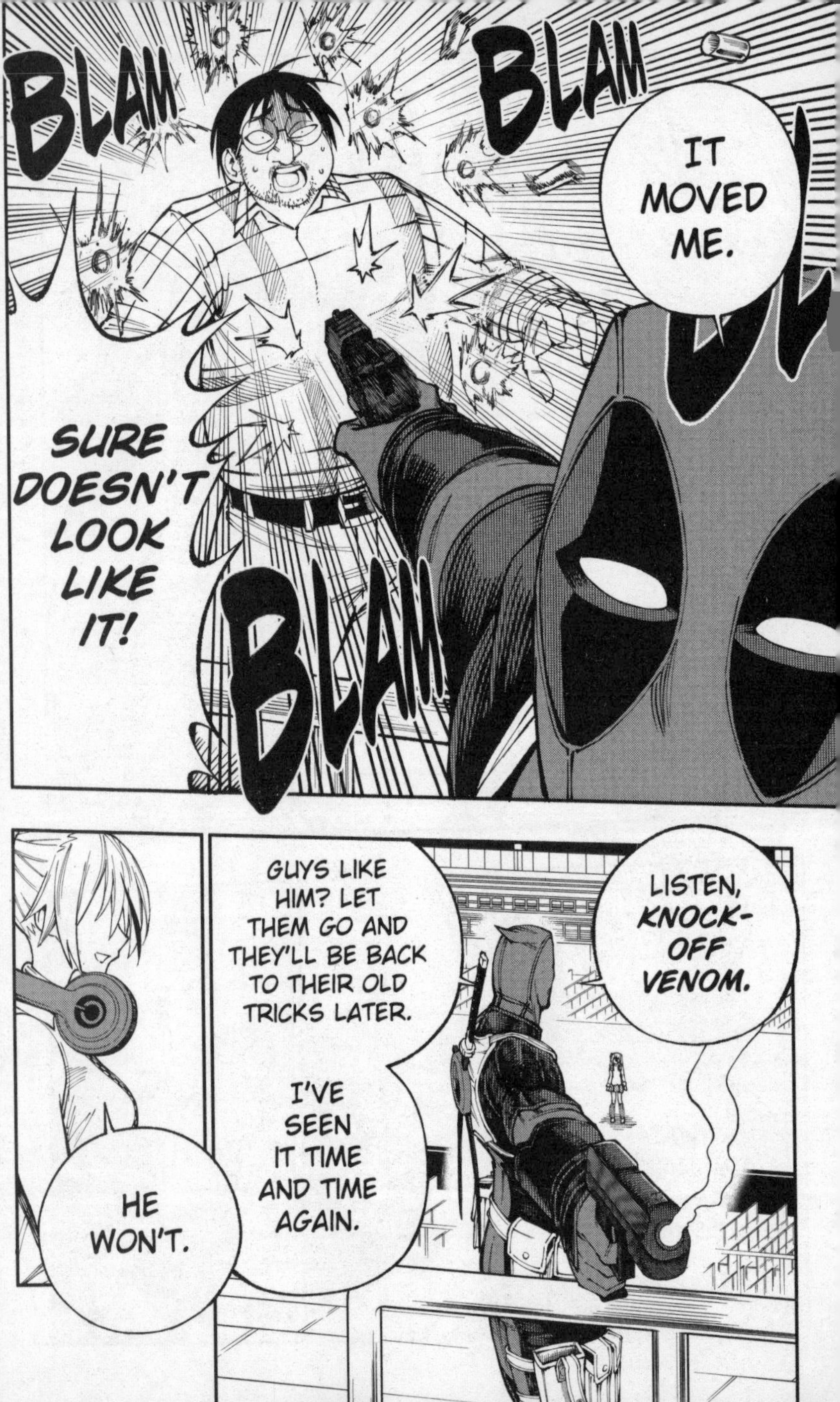
BLAM
IT MOVED ME.
BLAM
SURE DOESN'T LOOK LIKE IT!
BLAM
LISTEN, KNOCK-OFF VENOM.
GUYS LIKE HIM? LET THEM GO AND THEY'LL BE BACK TO THEIR OLD TRICKS LATER.
I'VE SEEN IT TIME AND TIME AGAIN.
HE WON'T.

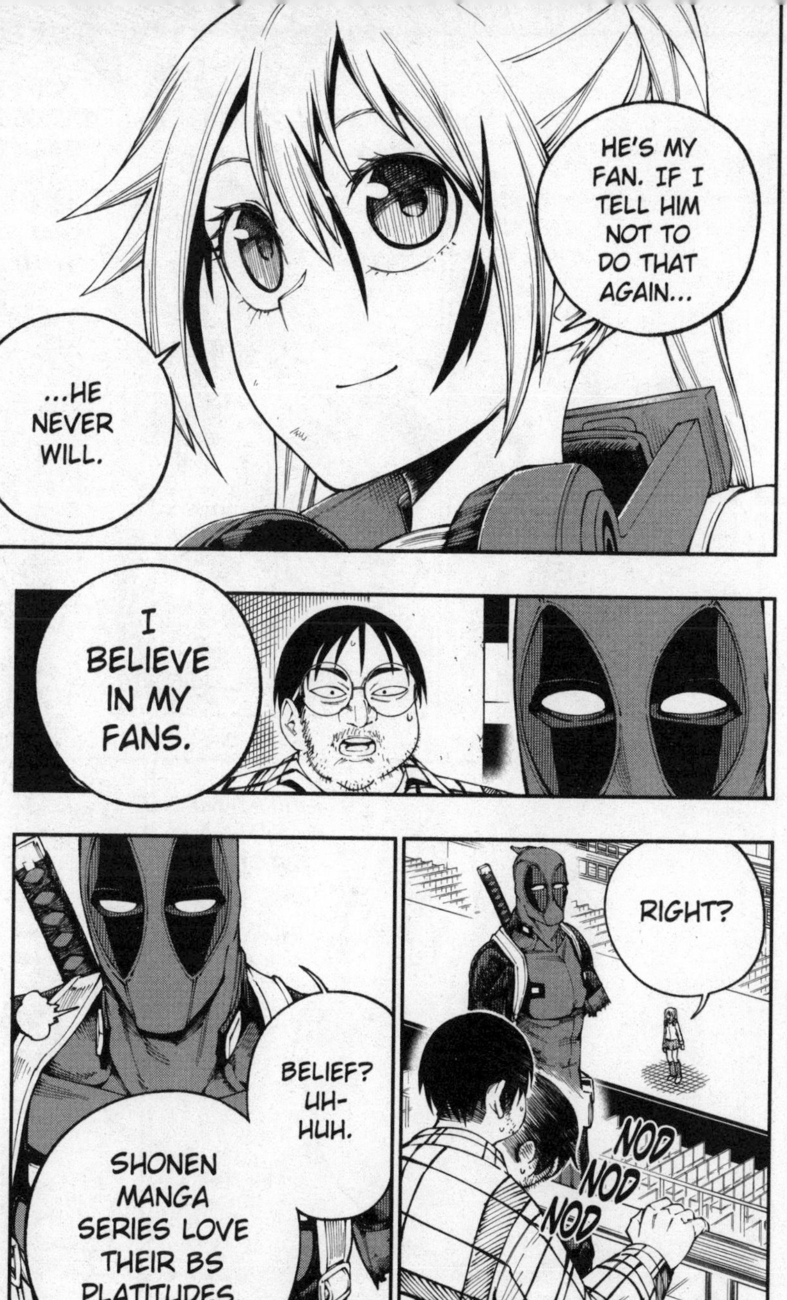
HE'S MY FAN. IF I TELL HIM NOT TO DO THAT AGAIN...
...HE NEVER WILL.
I BELIEVE IN MY FANS.
RIGHT?
NOD NOD NOD
BELIEF? UH-HUH.
SHONEN MANGA SERIES LOVE THEIR BS PLATITUDES.

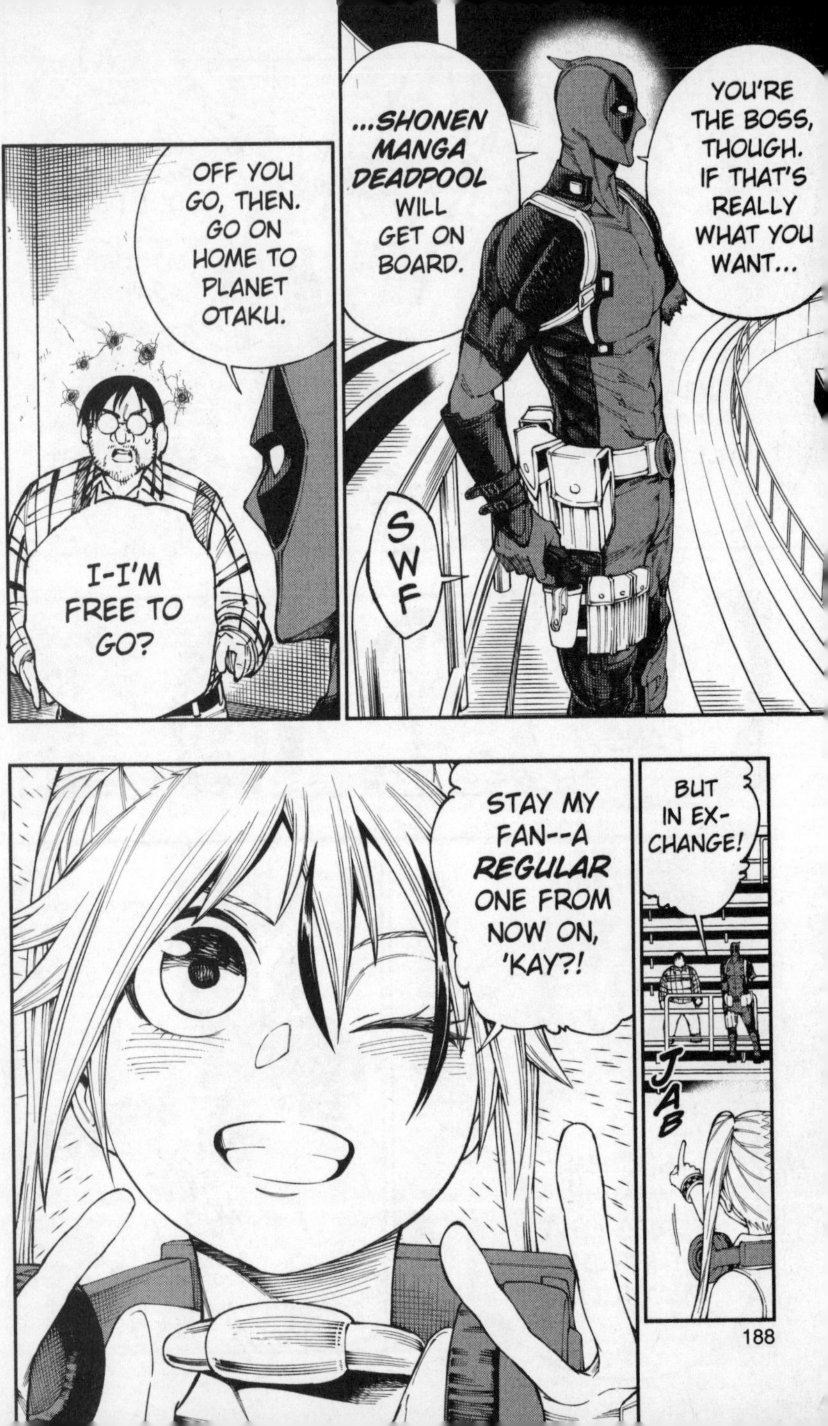
YOU'RE THE BOSS, THOUGH. IF THAT'S REALLY WHAT YOU WANT...
...SHONEN MANGA DEADPOOL WILL GET ON BOARD.
SWF
OFF YOU GO, THEN. GO ON HOME TO PLANET OTAKU.
I-I'M FREE TO GO?
BUT IN EX-CHANGE!
JAB
STAY MY FAN--A REGULAR ONE FROM NOW ON, 'KAY?!

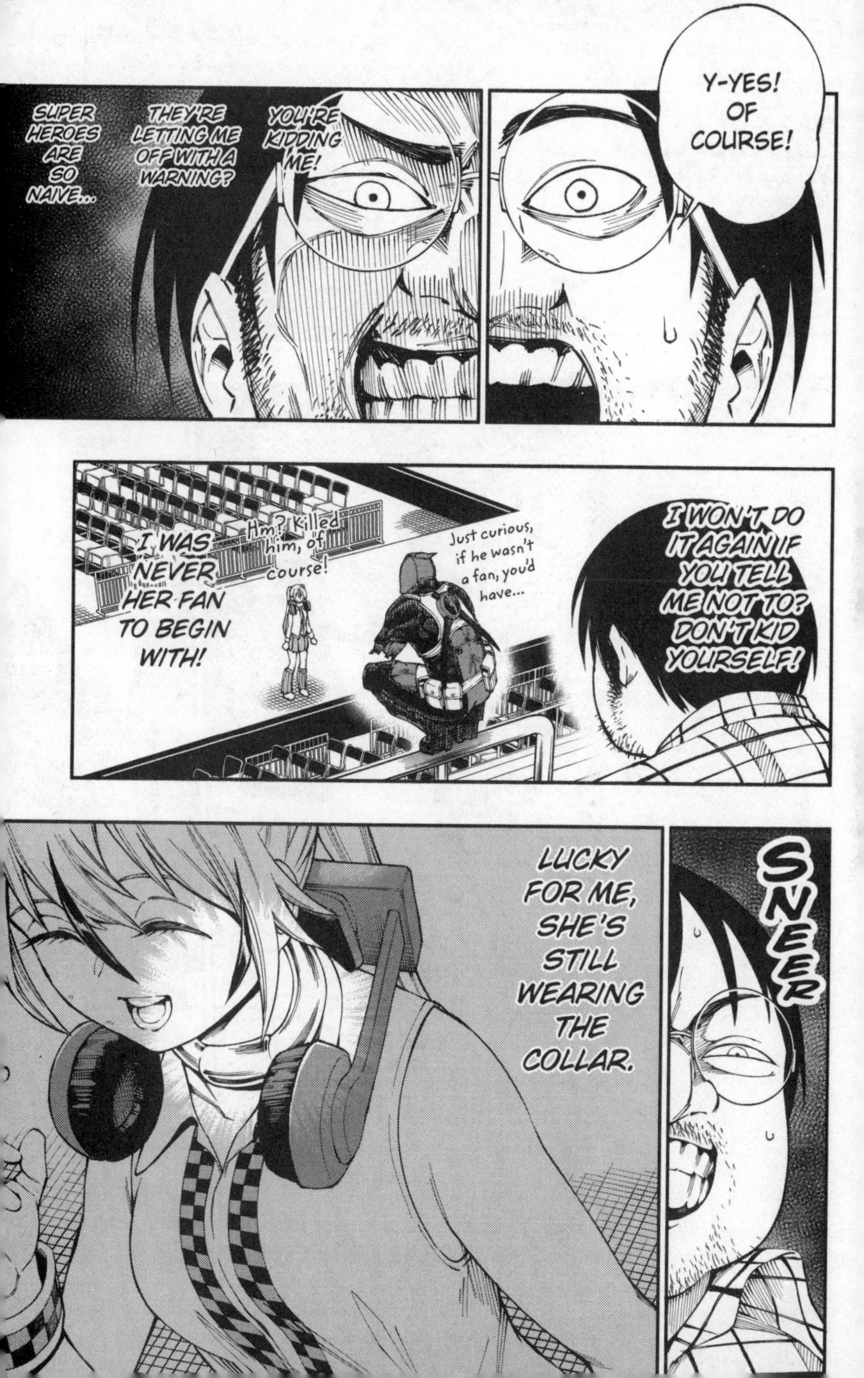
Y-YES! OF COURSE!
YOU'RE KIDDING ME!
THEY'RE LETTING ME OFF WITH A WARNING?
SUPER HEROES ARE SO NAIVE...
I WON'T DO IT AGAIN IF YOU TELL ME NOT TO? DON'T KID YOURSELF!
Just curious, if he wasn't a fan, you'd have...
Hm? Killed him, of course!
I WAS NEVER HER FAN TO BEGIN WITH!
SNEER
LUCKY FOR ME, SHE'S STILL WEARING THE COLLAR.

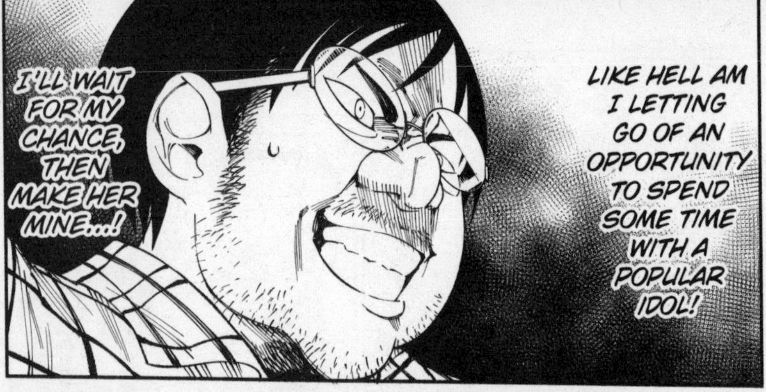
LIKE HELL AM I LETTING GO OF AN OPPORTUNITY TO SPEND SOME TIME WITH A POPULAR IDOL!
I'LL WAIT FOR MY CHANCE, THEN MAKE HER MINE...!
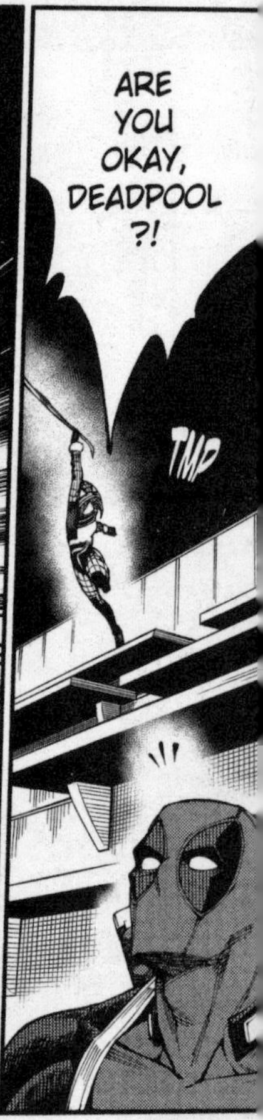
ARE YOU OKAY, DEADPOOL ?!
TMP
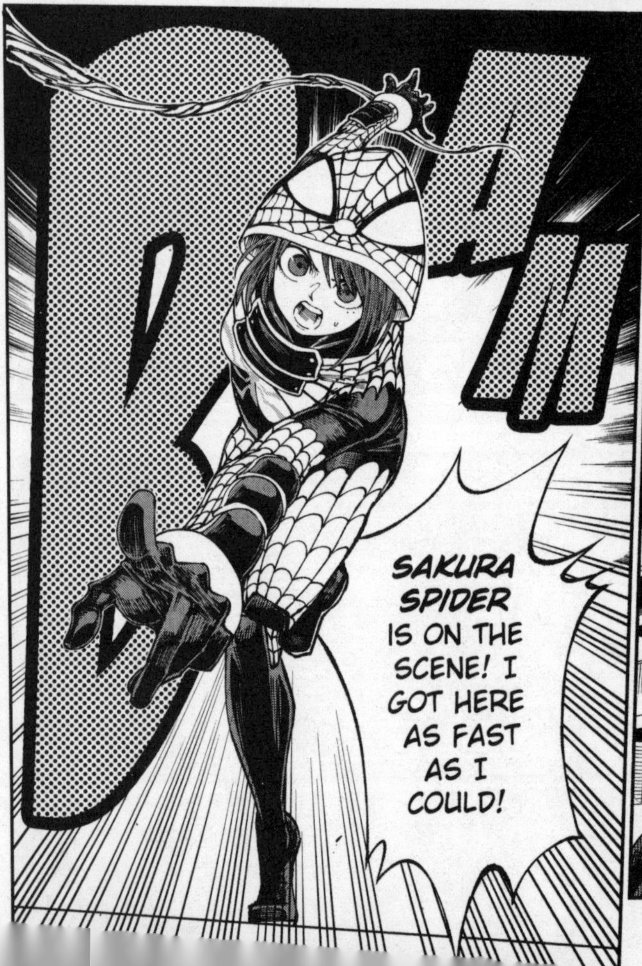
SAKURA SPIDER IS ON THE SCENE! I GOT HERE AS FAST AS I COULD!

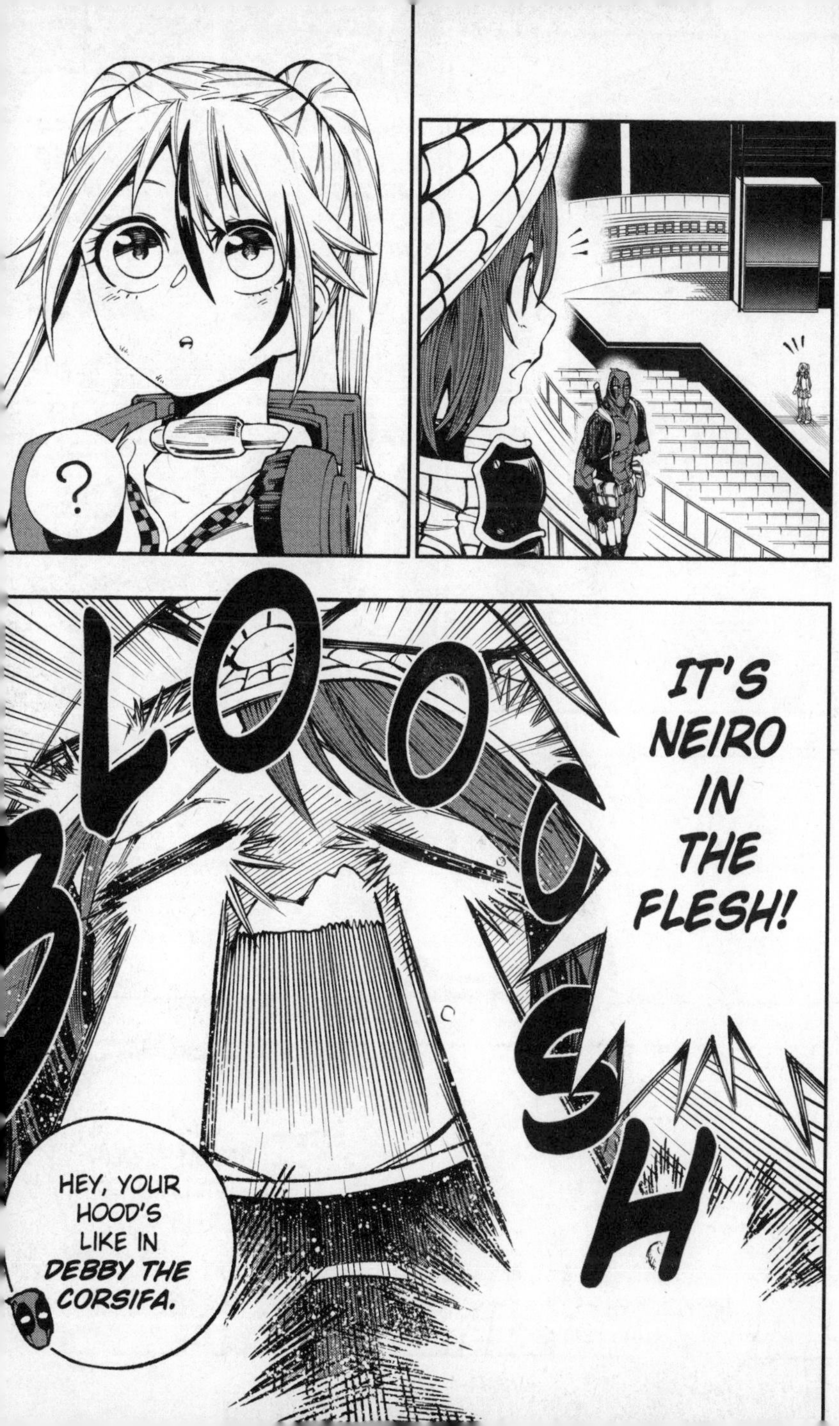
?
BLOOOSH
IT'S NEIRO IN THE FLESH!
HEY, YOUR HOOD'S LIKE IN *DEBBY THE CORSIFA.*

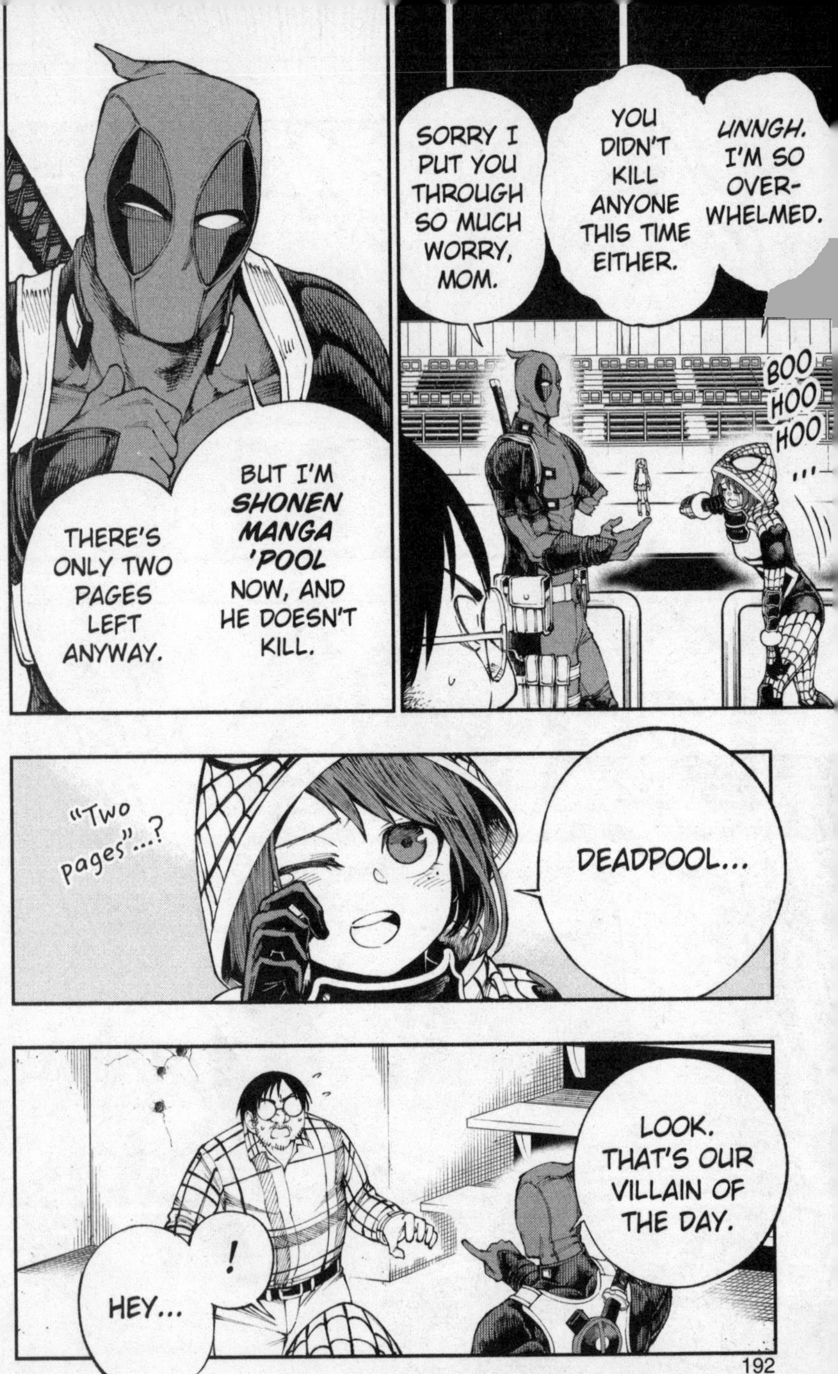
UNNGH. I'M SO OVER-WHELMED.
YOU DIDN'T KILL ANYONE THIS TIME EITHER.
SORRY I PUT YOU THROUGH SO MUCH WORRY, MOM.
BOO HOO HOO...
BUT I'M *SHONEN MANGA 'POOL* NOW, AND HE DOESN'T KILL.
THERE'S ONLY TWO PAGES LEFT ANYWAY.
DEADPOOL...
"Two pages"...?
LOOK. THAT'S OUR VILLAIN OF THE DAY.
!
HEY...

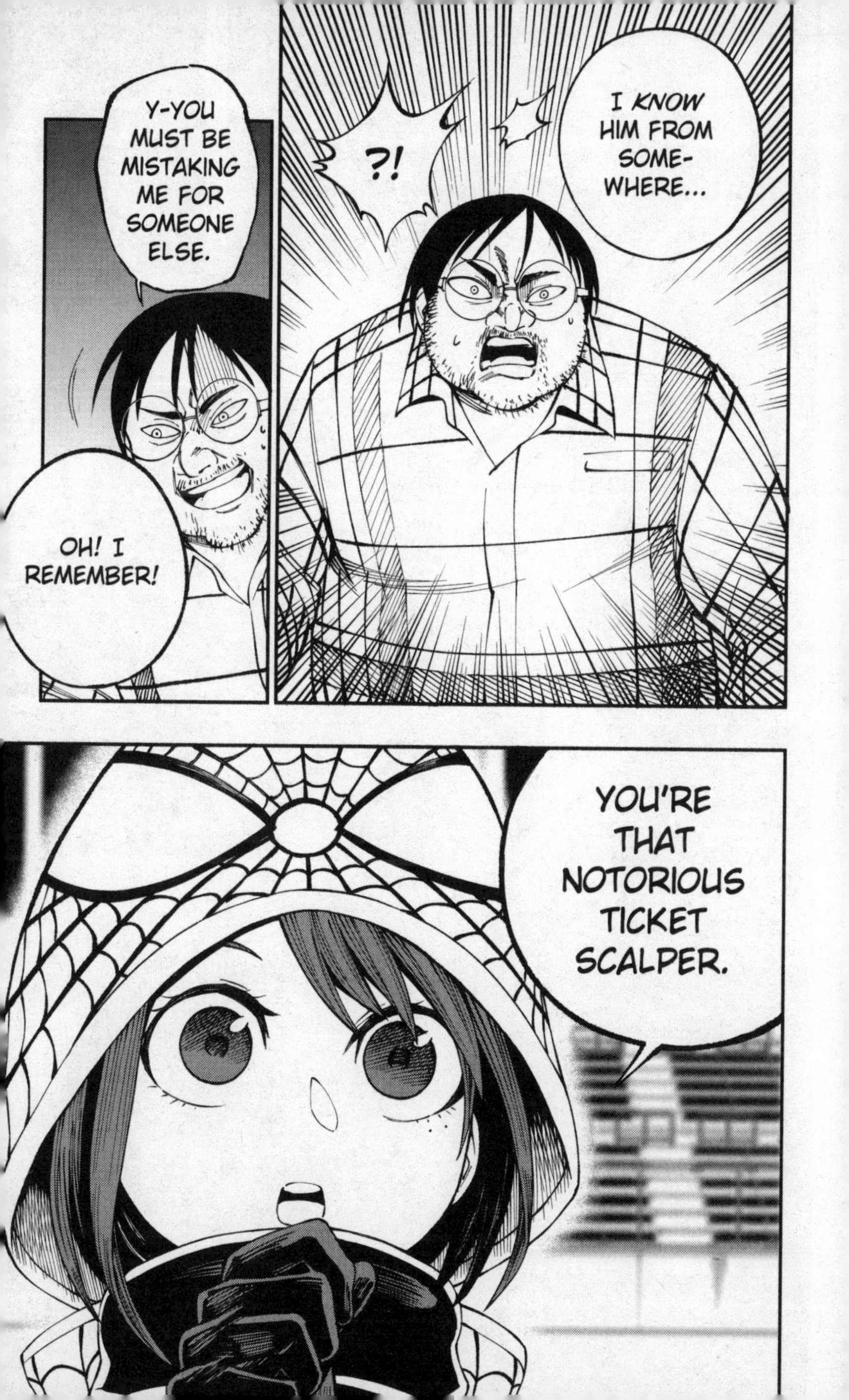
I KNOW HIM FROM SOME-WHERE...
?!
Y-YOU MUST BE MISTAKING ME FOR SOMEONE ELSE.
OH! I REMEMBER!
YOU'RE THAT NOTORIOUS TICKET SCALPER.

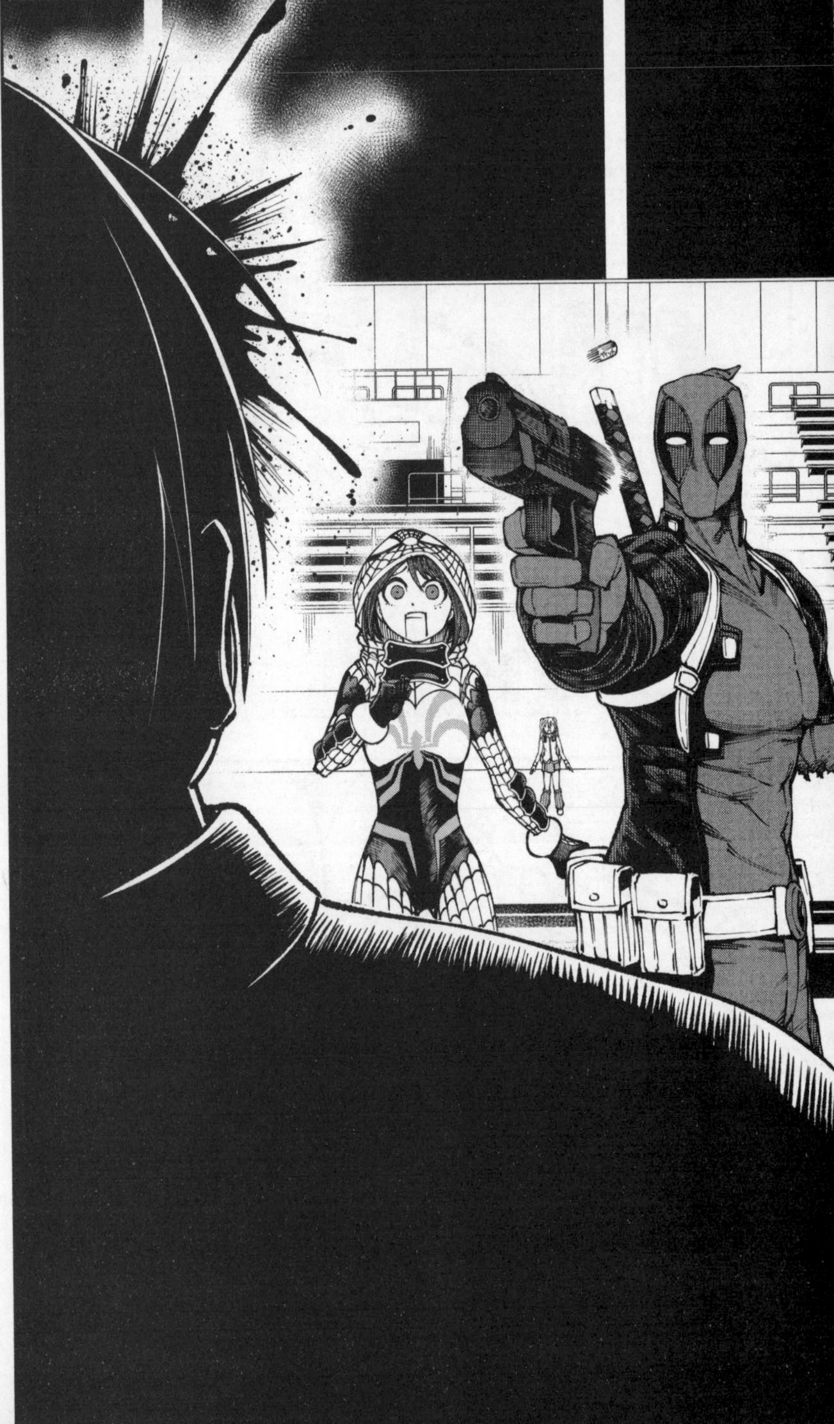

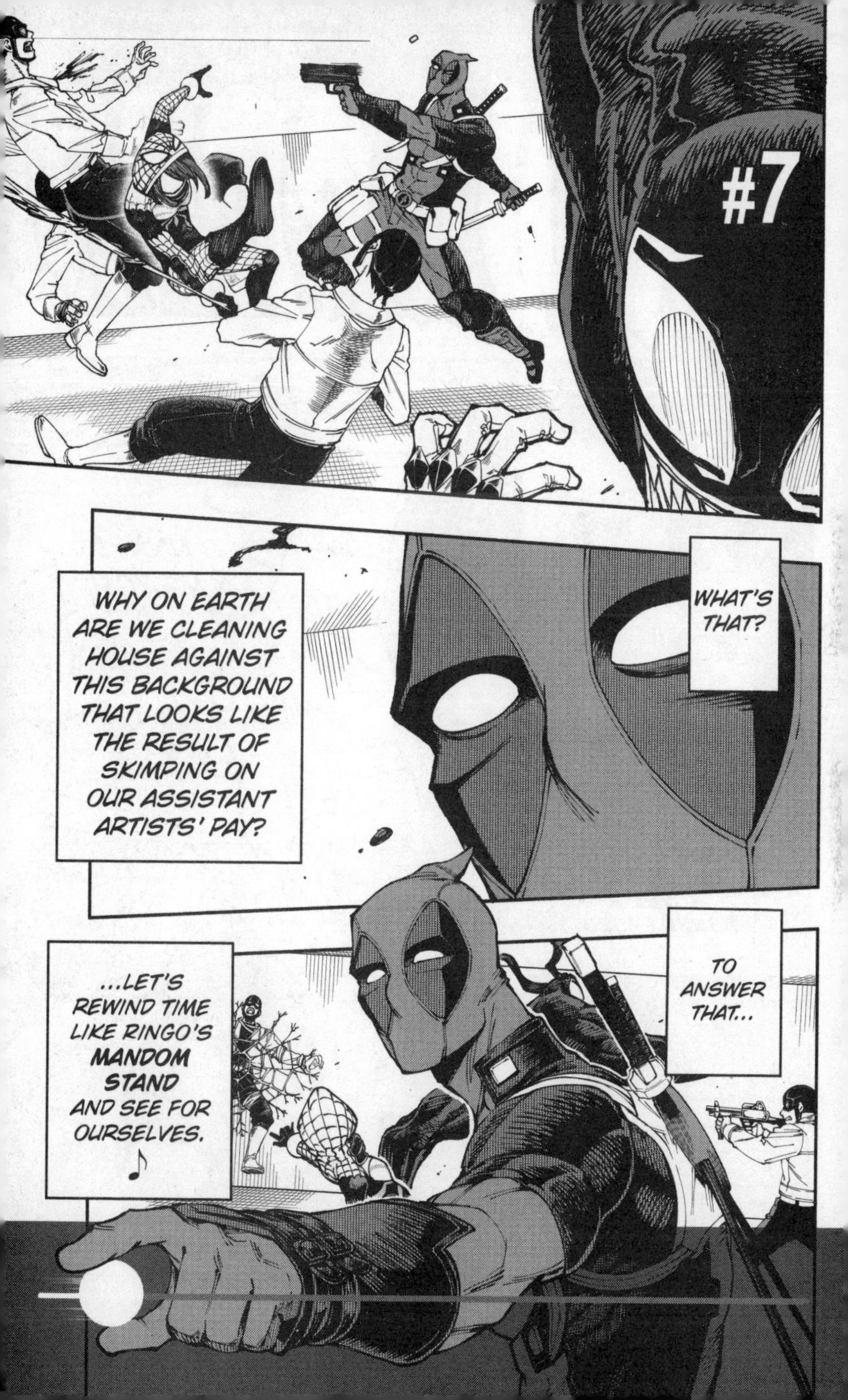
#7
WHAT'S THAT?
WHY ON EARTH ARE WE CLEANING HOUSE AGAINST THIS BACKGROUND THAT LOOKS LIKE THE RESULT OF SKIMPING ON OUR ASSISTANT ARTISTS' PAY?
TO ANSWER THAT...
...LET'S REWIND TIME LIKE RINGO'S **MANDOM STAND** AND SEE FOR OURSELVES. ♪

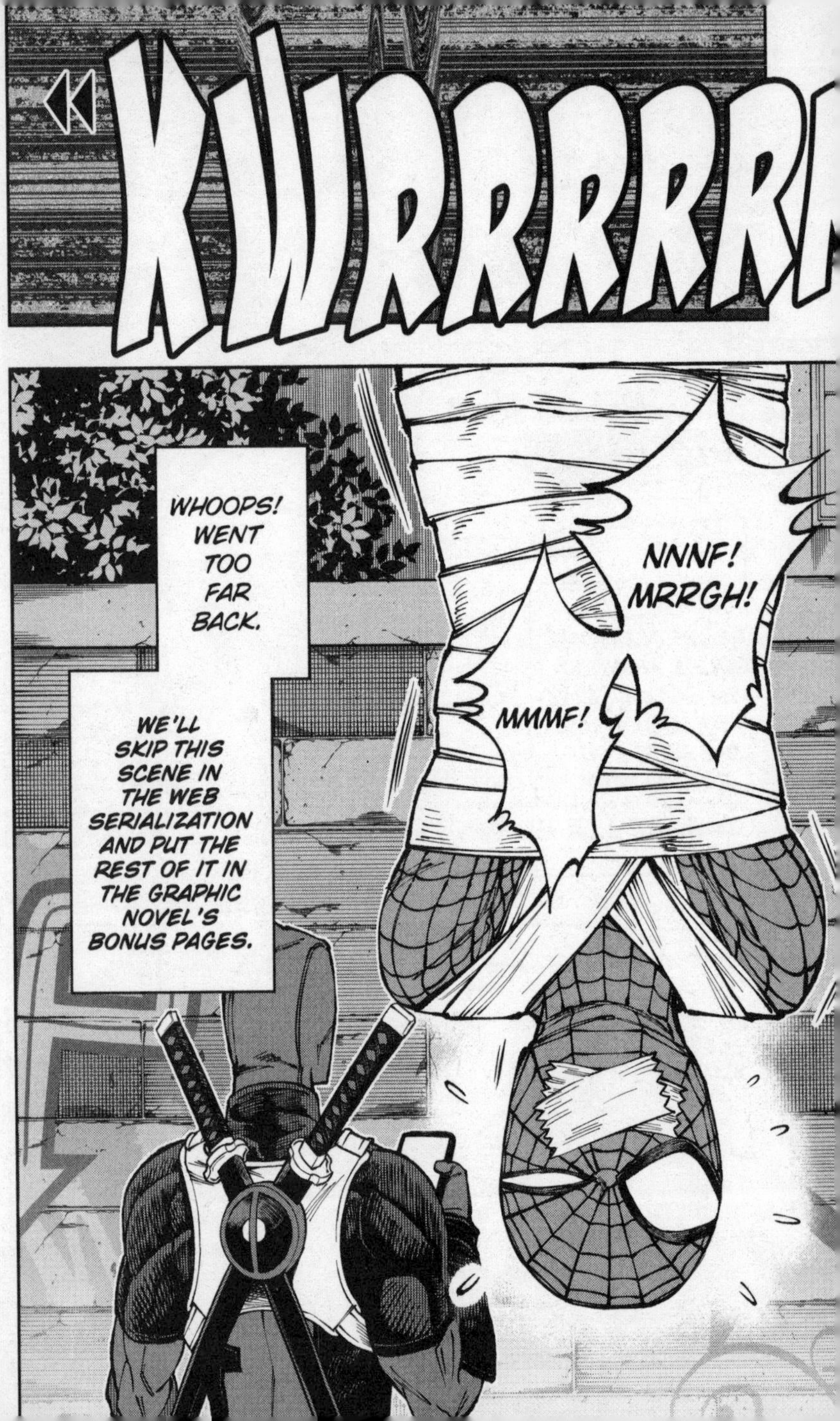
KWRRRRRR
NNNF! MRRGH!
WHOOPS! WENT TOO FAR BACK.
MMMF!
WE'LL SKIP THIS SCENE IN THE WEB SERIALIZATION AND PUT THE REST OF IT IN THE GRAPHIC NOVEL'S BONUS PAGES.

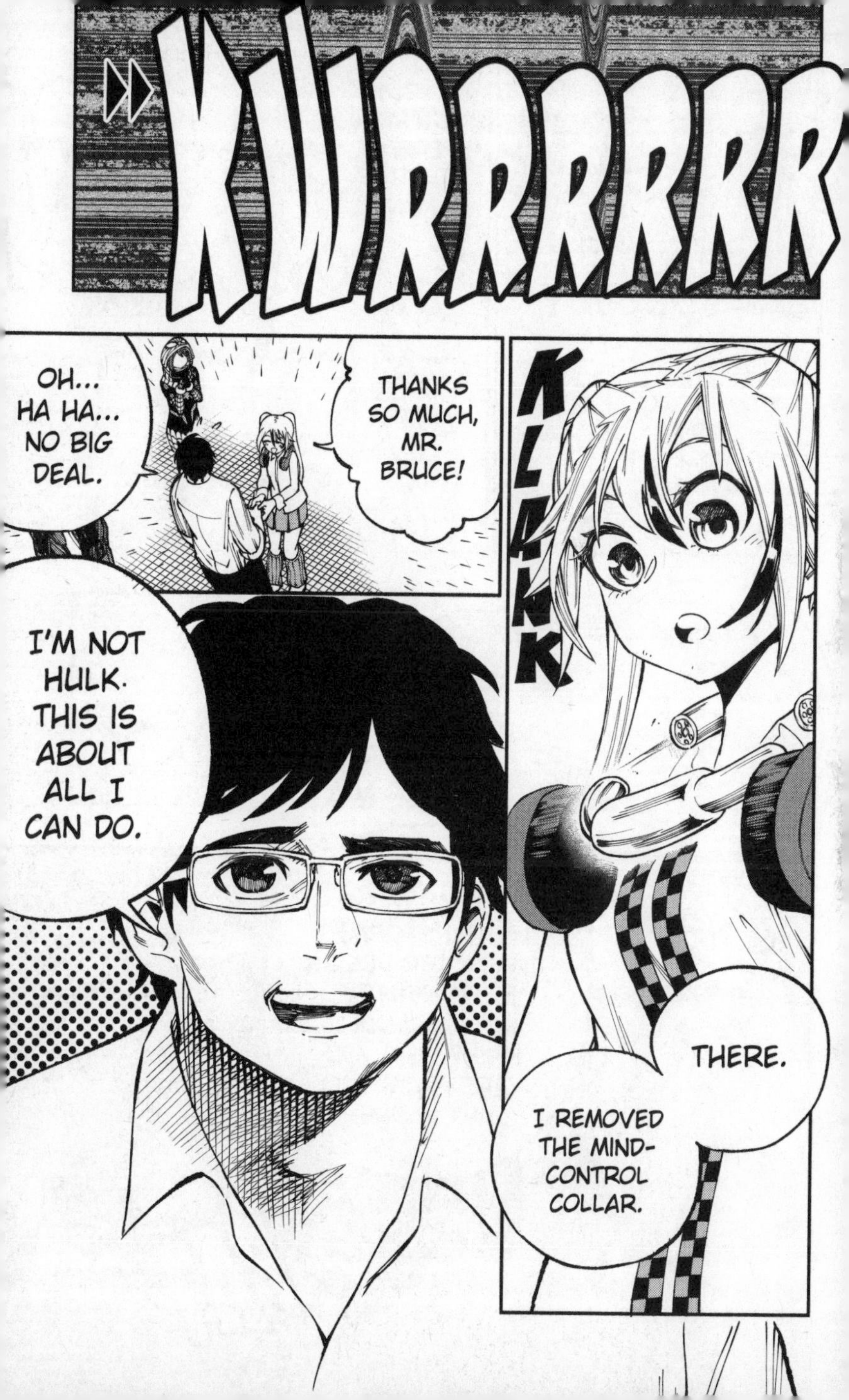
KWRRRRRR
KLANK
THERE.
I REMOVED THE MIND-CONTROL COLLAR.
THANKS SO MUCH, MR. BRUCE!
OH... HA HA... NO BIG DEAL.
I'M NOT HULK. THIS IS ABOUT ALL I CAN DO.

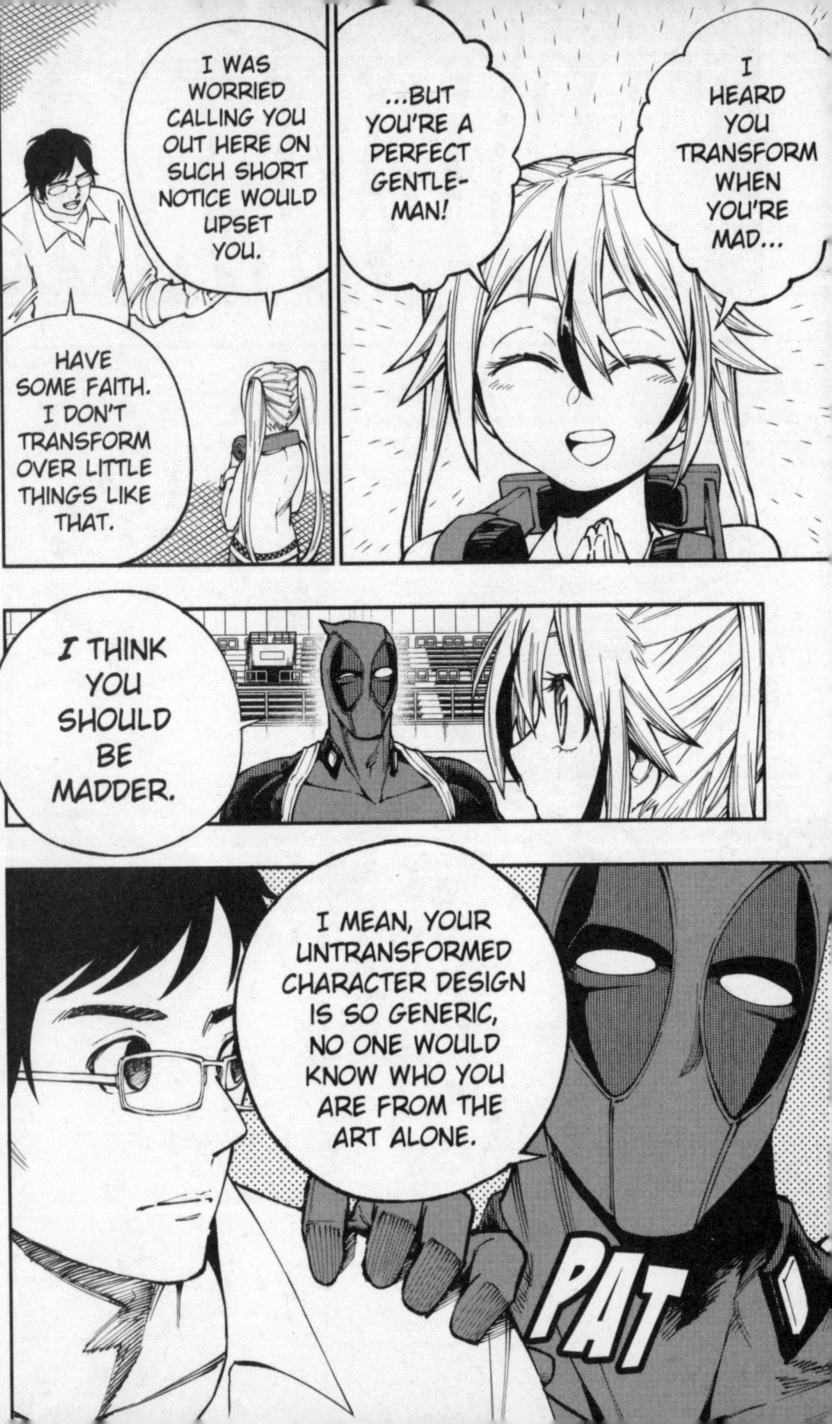
I HEARD YOU TRANSFORM WHEN YOU'RE MAD...
...BUT YOU'RE A PERFECT GENTLE-MAN!
I WAS WORRIED CALLING YOU OUT HERE ON SUCH SHORT NOTICE WOULD UPSET YOU.
HAVE SOME FAITH. I DON'T TRANSFORM OVER LITTLE THINGS LIKE THAT.
I THINK YOU SHOULD BE MADDER.
I MEAN, YOUR UNTRANSFORMED CHARACTER DESIGN IS SO GENERIC, NO ONE WOULD KNOW WHO YOU ARE FROM THE ART ALONE.
PAT

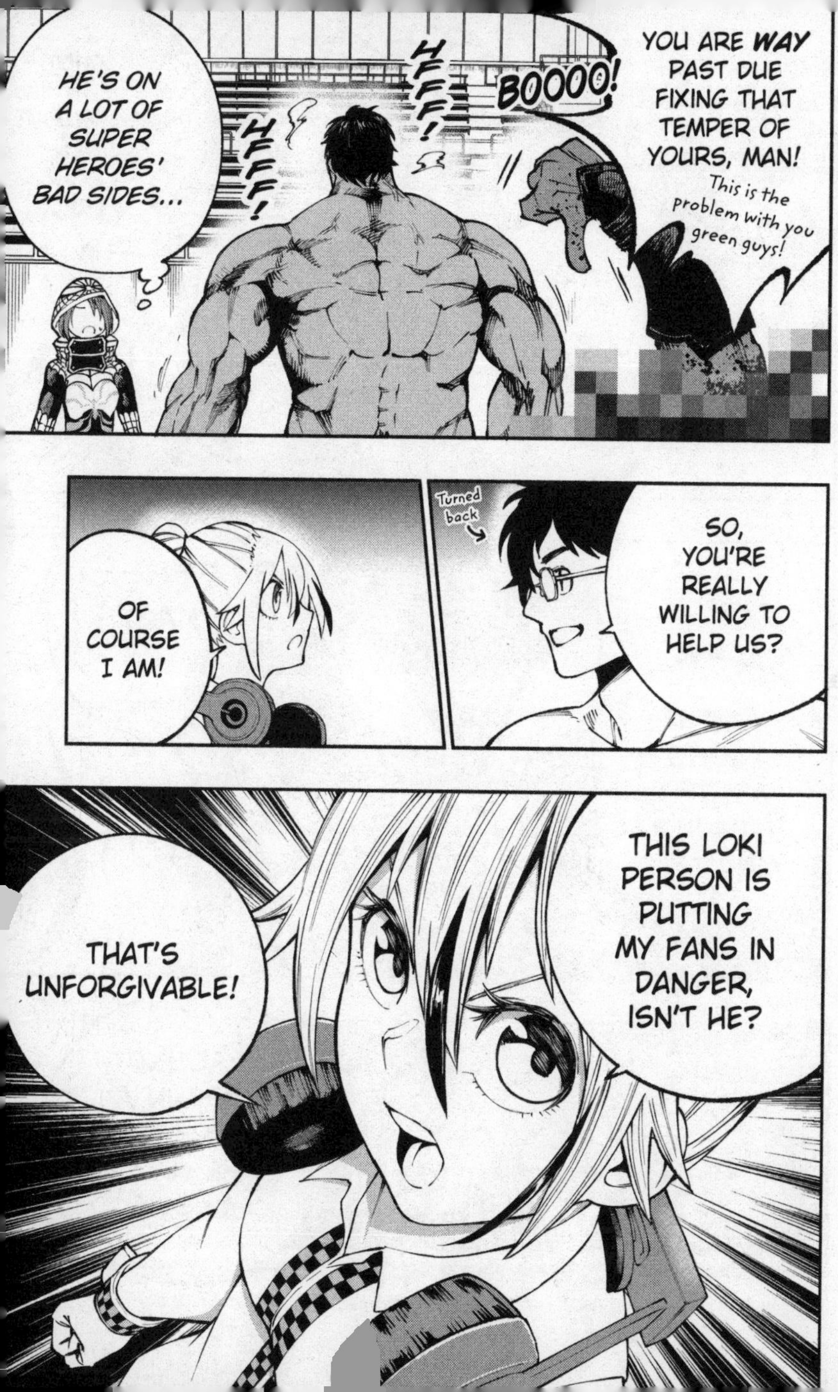
YOU ARE WAY PAST DUE FIXING THAT TEMPER OF YOURS, MAN!
This is the problem with you green guys!
BOOOO!
HFFF!
HFFF!
HE'S ON A LOT OF SUPER HEROES' BAD SIDES...
Turned back
SO, YOU'RE REALLY WILLING TO HELP US?
OF COURSE I AM!
THIS LOKI PERSON IS PUTTING MY FANS IN DANGER, ISN'T HE?
THAT'S UNFORGIVABLE!

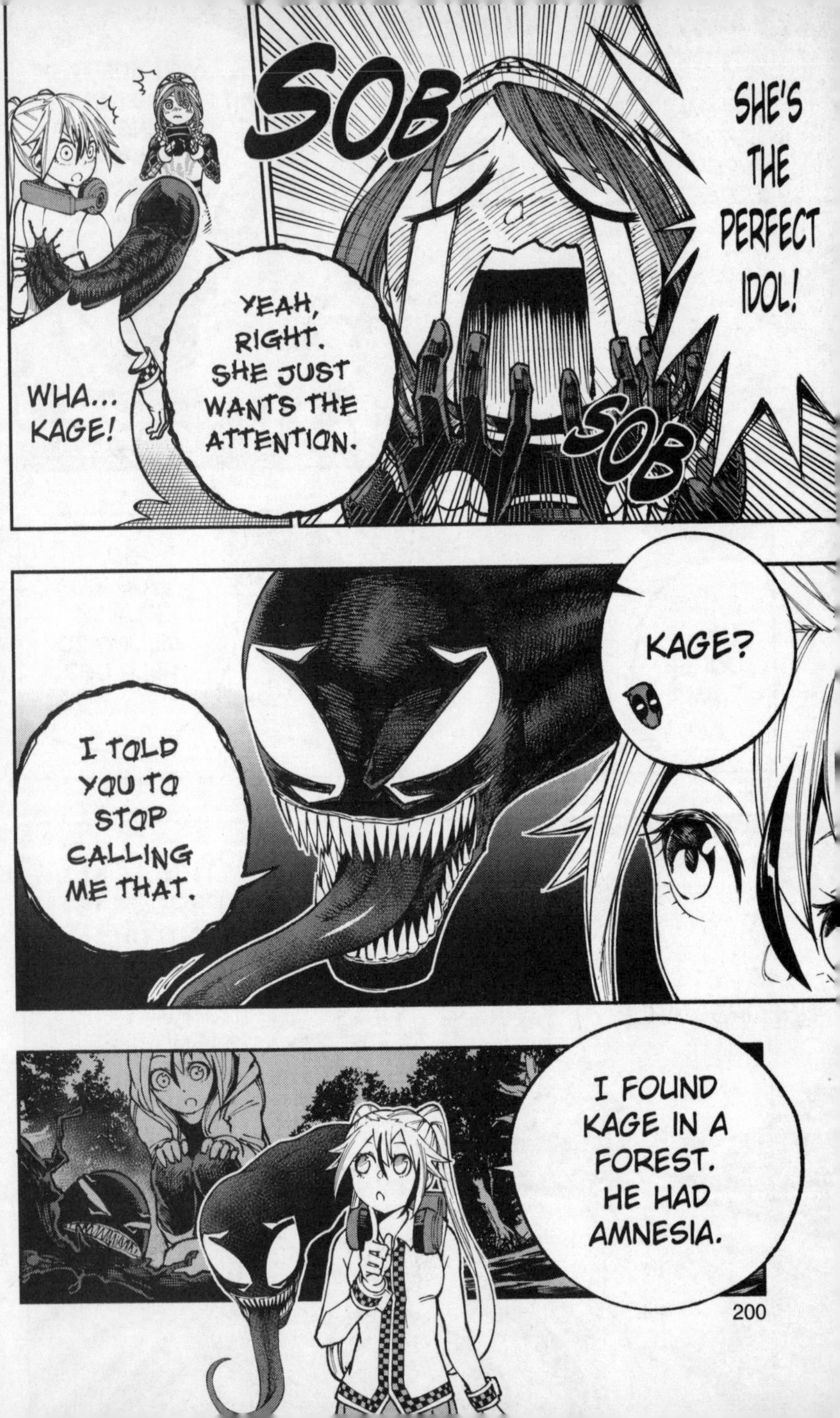
SOB
SHE'S THE PERFECT IDOL!
SOB
YEAH, RIGHT. SHE JUST WANTS THE ATTENTION.
WHA... KAGE!
KAGE?
I TOLD YOU TO STOP CALLING ME THAT.
I FOUND KAGE IN A FOREST. HE HAD AMNESIA.

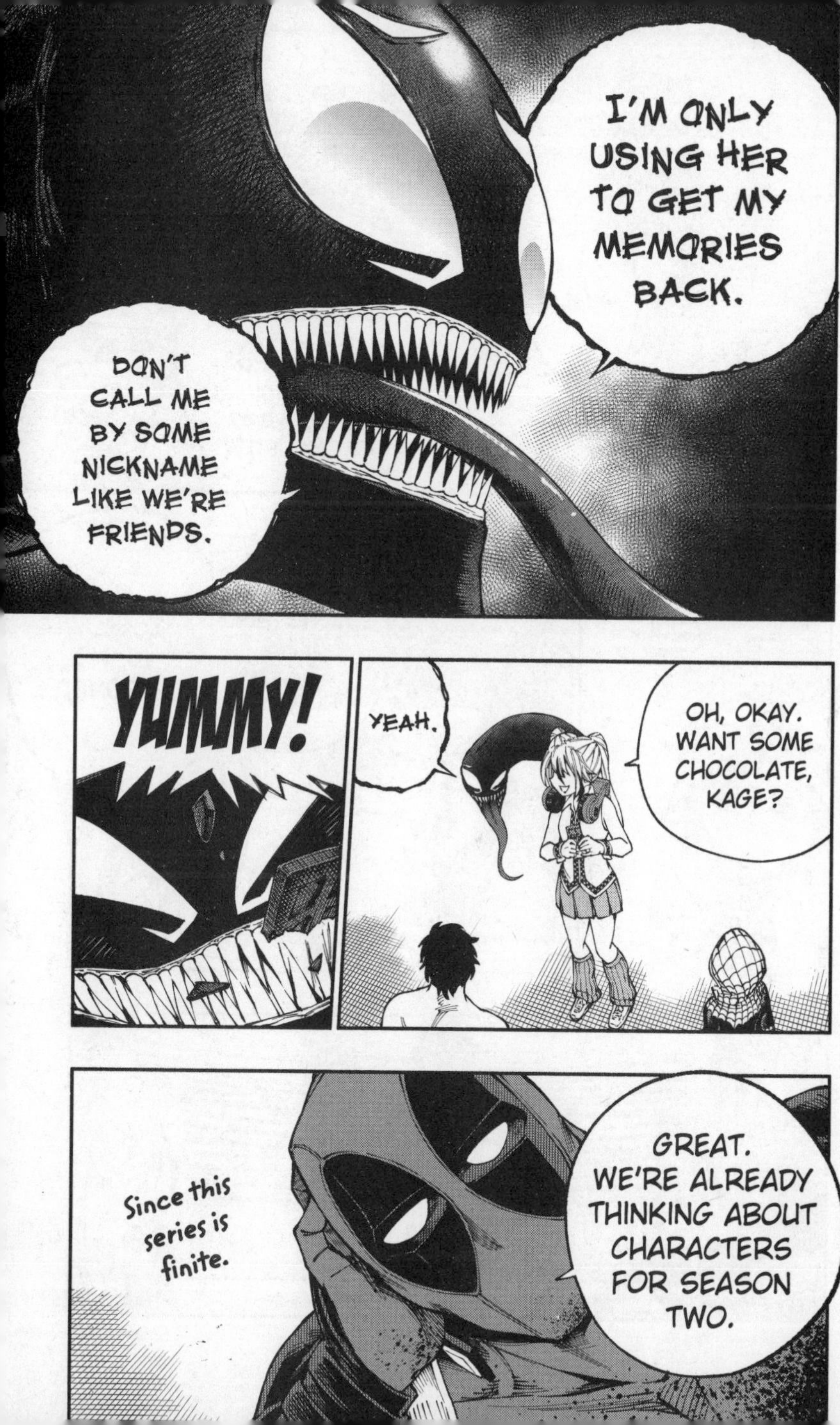
I'M ONLY USING HER TO GET MY MEMORIES BACK.
DON'T CALL ME BY SOME NICKNAME LIKE WE'RE FRIENDS.
OH, OKAY. WANT SOME CHOCOLATE, KAGE?
YEAH.
YUMMY!
GREAT. WE'RE ALREADY THINKING ABOUT CHARACTERS FOR SEASON TWO.
Since this series is finite.

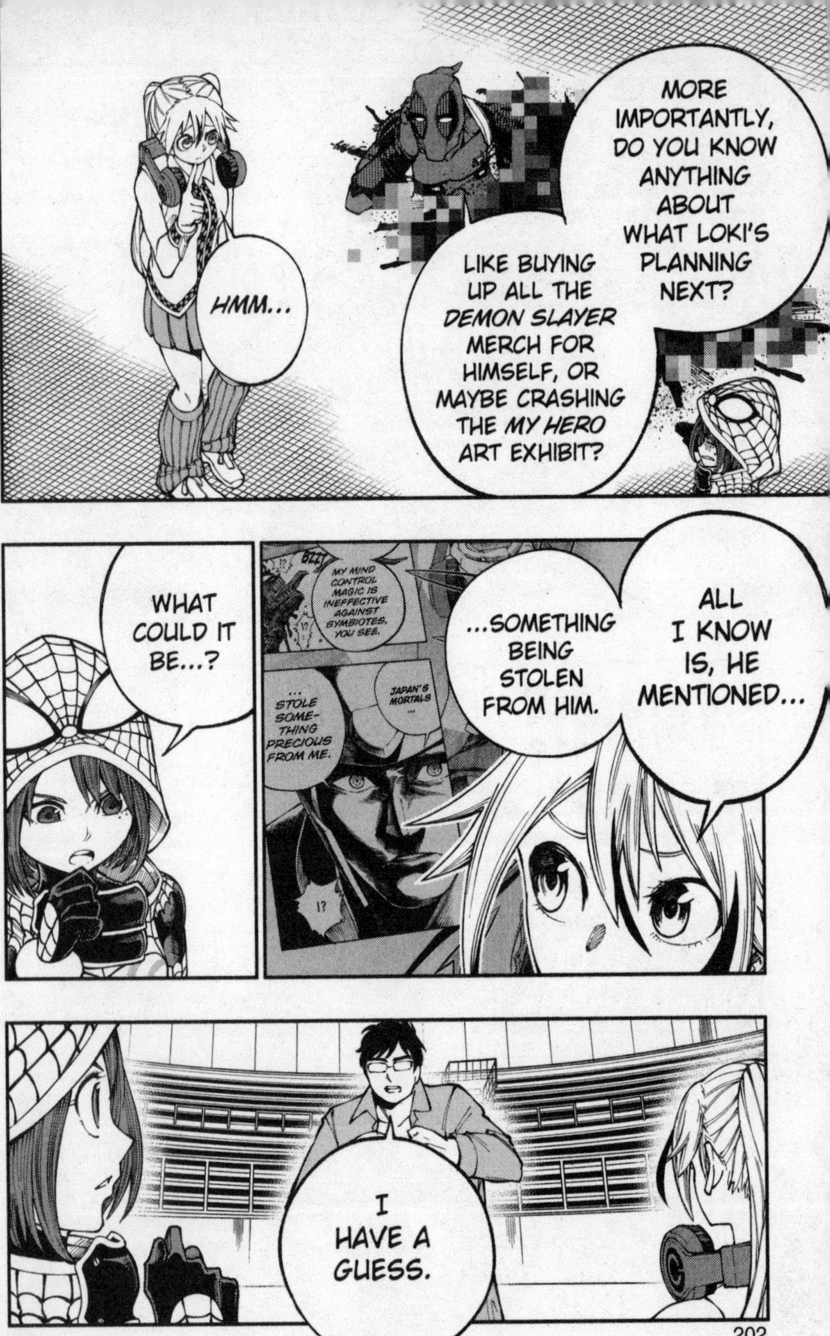
MORE IMPORTANTLY, DO YOU KNOW ANYTHING ABOUT WHAT LOKI'S PLANNING NEXT?
LIKE BUYING UP ALL THE *DEMON SLAYER* MERCH FOR HIMSELF, OR MAYBE CRASHING THE *MY HERO* ART EXHIBIT?
HMM...
ALL I KNOW IS, HE MENTIONED...
...SOMETHING BEING STOLEN FROM HIM.
MY MIND CONTROL MAGIC IS INEFFECTIVE AGAINST SYMBIOTES, YOU SEE.
!?
JAPAN'S MORTALS...
...STOLE SOMETHING PRECIOUS FROM ME.
!?
WHAT COULD IT BE...?
I HAVE A GUESS.

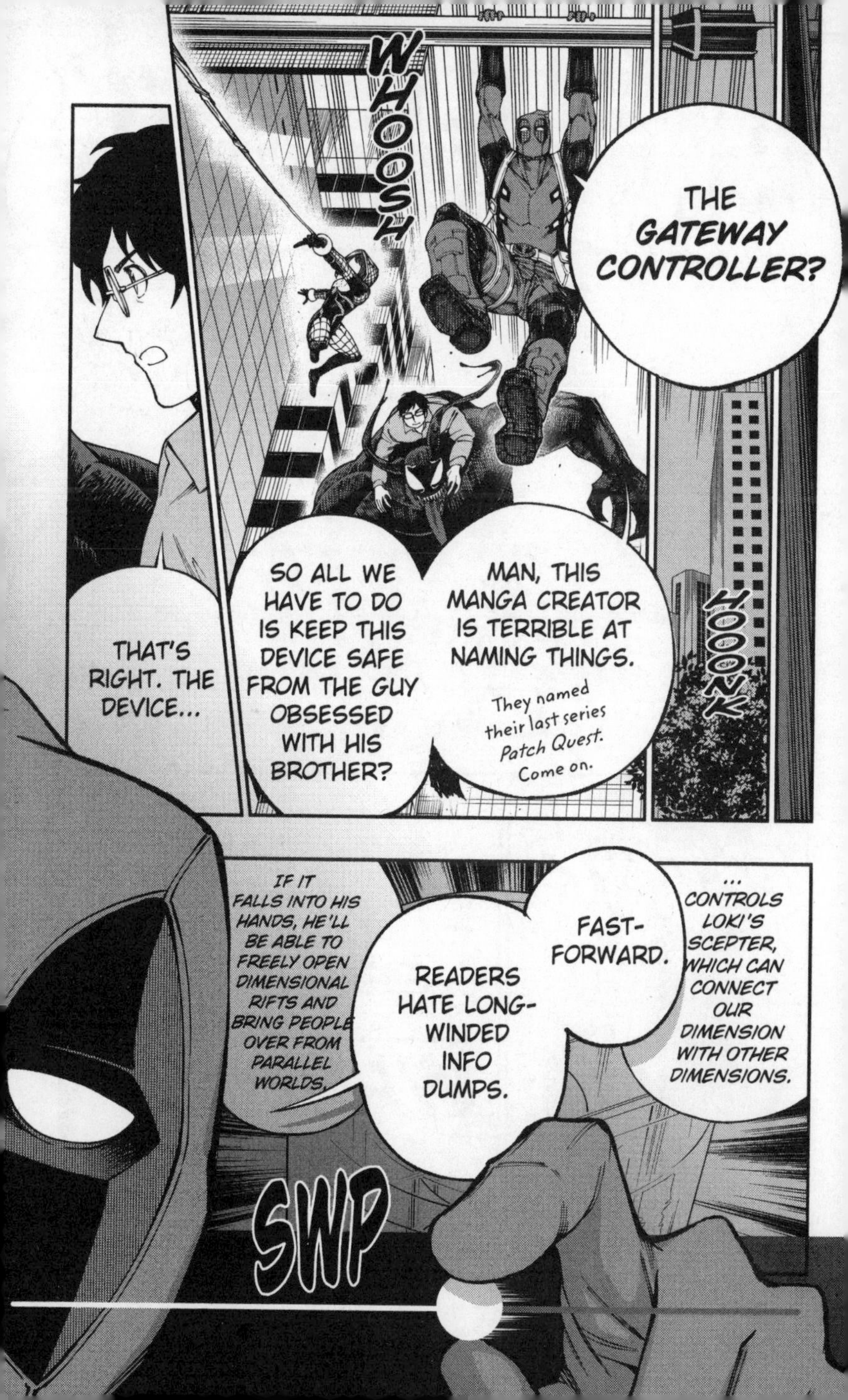
WHOOSH
THE GATEWAY CONTROLLER?
HOOONK
MAN, THIS MANGA CREATOR IS TERRIBLE AT NAMING THINGS.
They named their last series Patch Quest. Come on.
SO ALL WE HAVE TO DO IS KEEP THIS DEVICE SAFE FROM THE GUY OBSESSED WITH HIS BROTHER?
THAT'S RIGHT. THE DEVICE...
...CONTROLS LOKI'S SCEPTER, WHICH CAN CONNECT OUR DIMENSION WITH OTHER DIMENSIONS.
FAST-FORWARD.
READERS HATE LONG-WINDED INFO DUMPS.
IF IT FALLS INTO HIS HANDS, HE'LL BE ABLE TO FREELY OPEN DIMENSIONAL RIFTS AND BRING PEOPLE OVER FROM PARALLEL WORLDS,
SWP

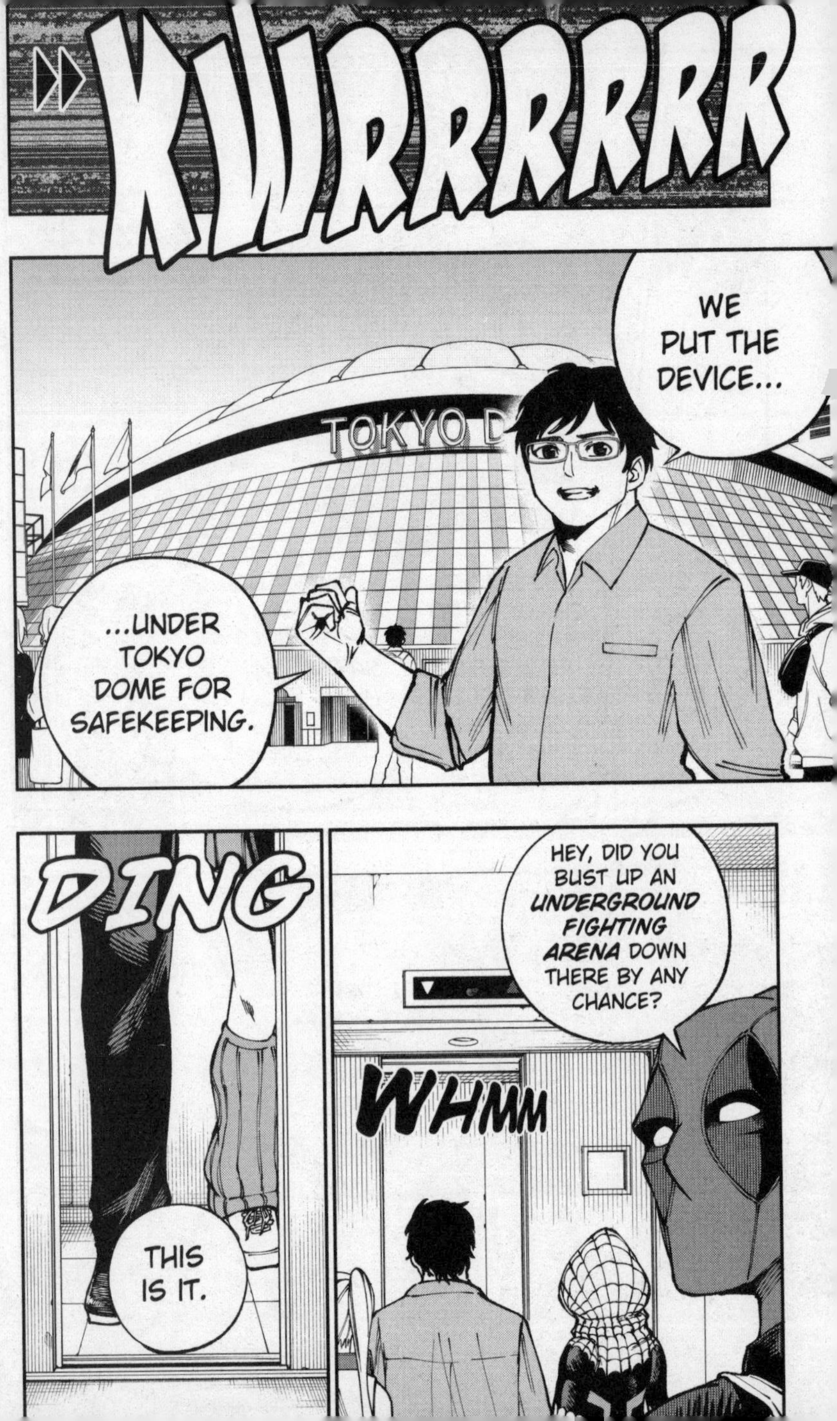
KWRRRRRR
WE PUT THE DEVICE...
...UNDER TOKYO DOME FOR SAFEKEEPING.
TOKYO D
HEY, DID YOU BUST UP AN *UNDERGROUND FIGHTING ARENA* DOWN THERE BY ANY CHANCE?
WHMM
DING
THIS IS IT.

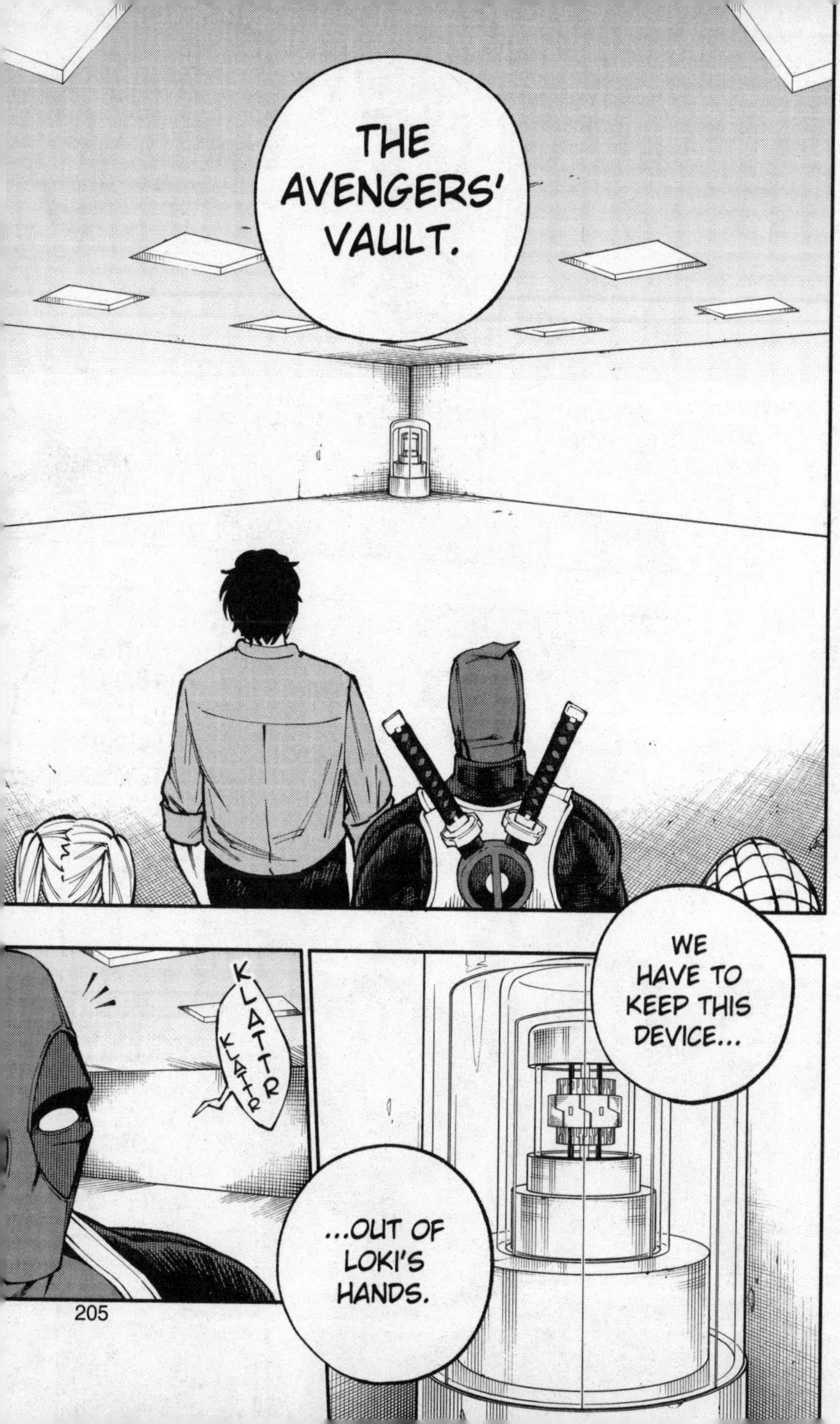
THE AVENGERS' VAULT.
WE HAVE TO KEEP THIS DEVICE...
...OUT OF LOKI'S HANDS.
KLATTR
KLATTR

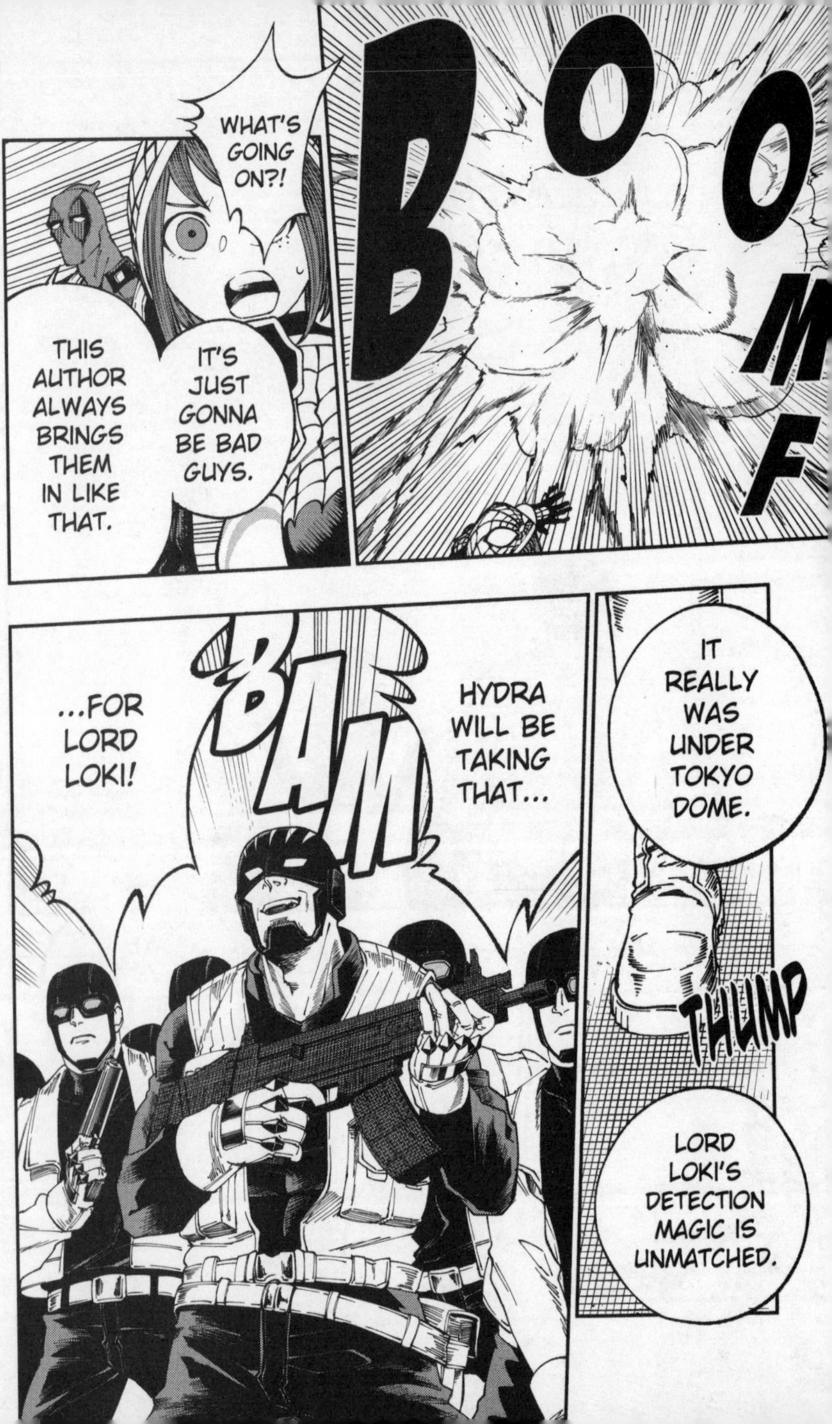
BOOOMF
WHAT'S GOING ON?!
IT'S JUST GONNA BE BAD GUYS.
THIS AUTHOR ALWAYS BRINGS THEM IN LIKE THAT.
IT REALLY WAS UNDER TOKYO DOME.
THUMP
LORD LOKI'S DETECTION MAGIC IS UNMATCHED.
BAM
HYDRA WILL BE TAKING THAT...
...FOR LORD LOKI!

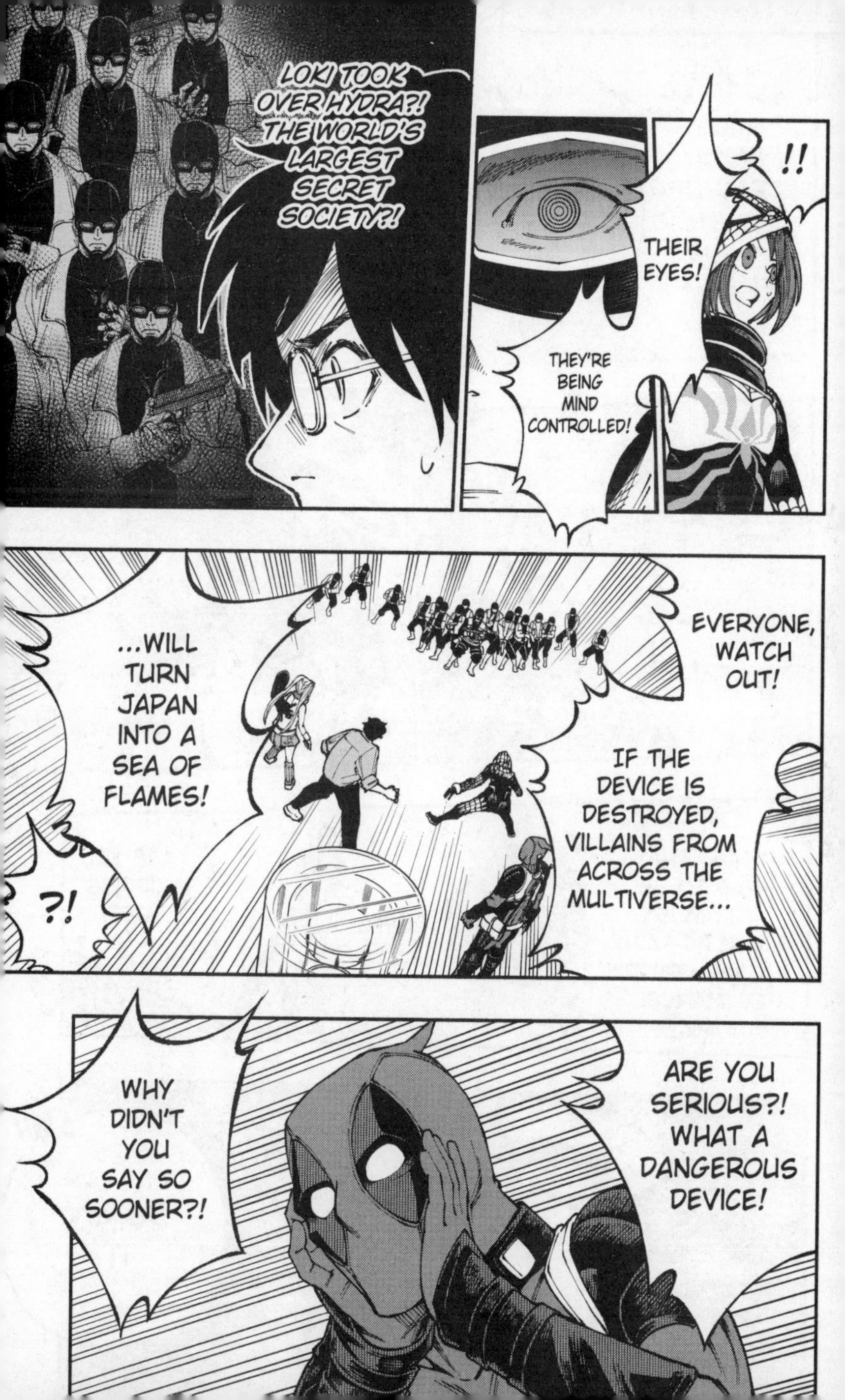
!!
THEIR EYES!
THEY'RE BEING MIND CONTROLLED!
LOKI TOOK OVER HYDRA?! THE WORLD'S LARGEST SECRET SOCIETY?!
EVERYONE, WATCH OUT!
IF THE DEVICE IS DESTROYED, VILLAINS FROM ACROSS THE MULTIVERSE...
...WILL TURN JAPAN INTO A SEA OF FLAMES!
?!
ARE YOU SERIOUS?! WHAT A DANGEROUS DEVICE!
WHY DIDN'T YOU SAY SO SOONER?!

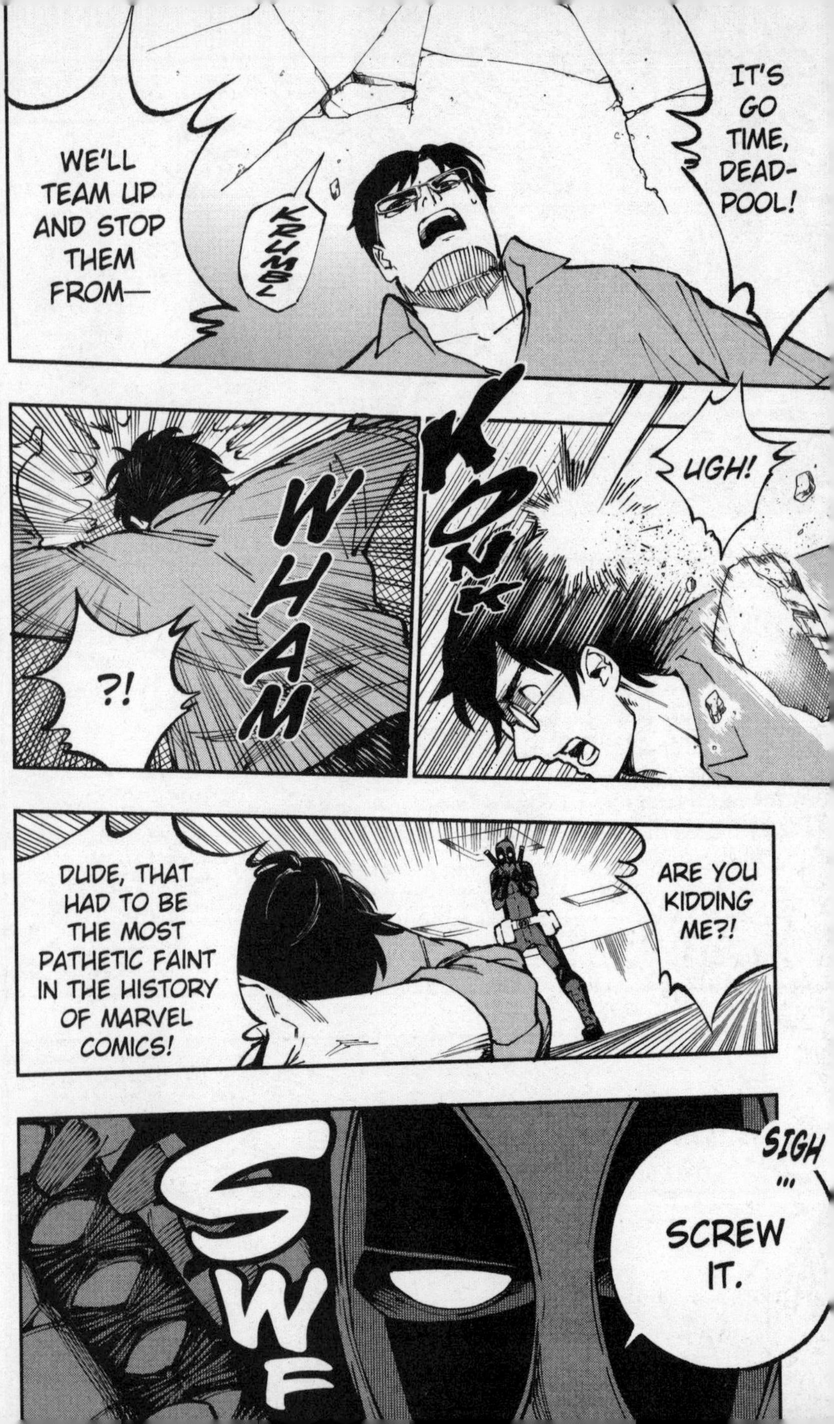
IT'S GO TIME, DEAD-POOL!
KRUMBL
WE'LL TEAM UP AND STOP THEM FROM—
KONK
UGH!
WHAM
?!
ARE YOU KIDDING ME?!
DUDE, THAT HAD TO BE THE MOST PATHETIC FAINT IN THE HISTORY OF MARVEL COMICS!
SIGH... SCREW IT.
SWF

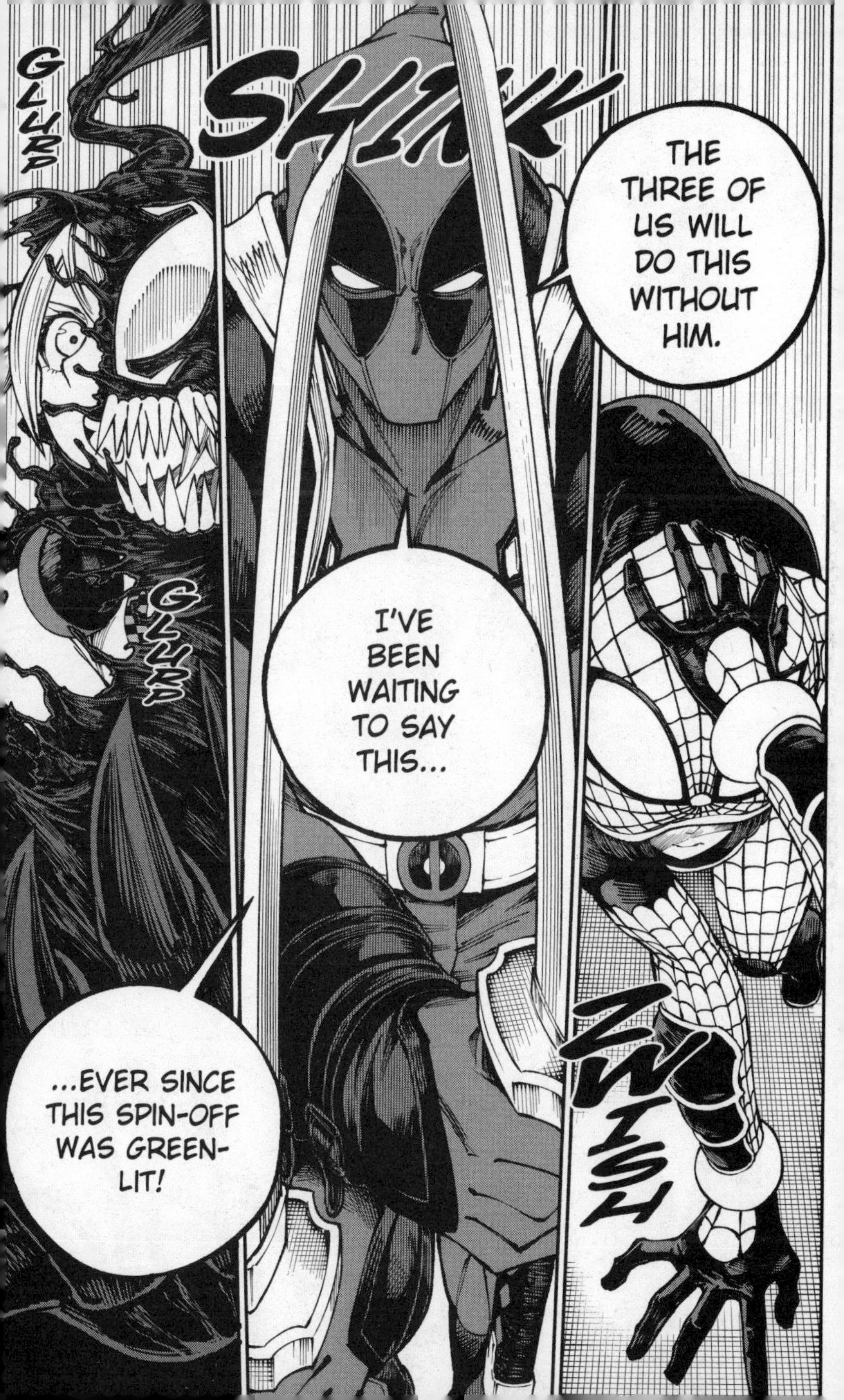
THE THREE OF US WILL DO THIS WITHOUT HIM.
SWISH
I'VE BEEN WAITING TO SAY THIS...
GLURP
GLURP
...EVER SINCE THIS SPIN-OFF WAS GREEN-LIT!

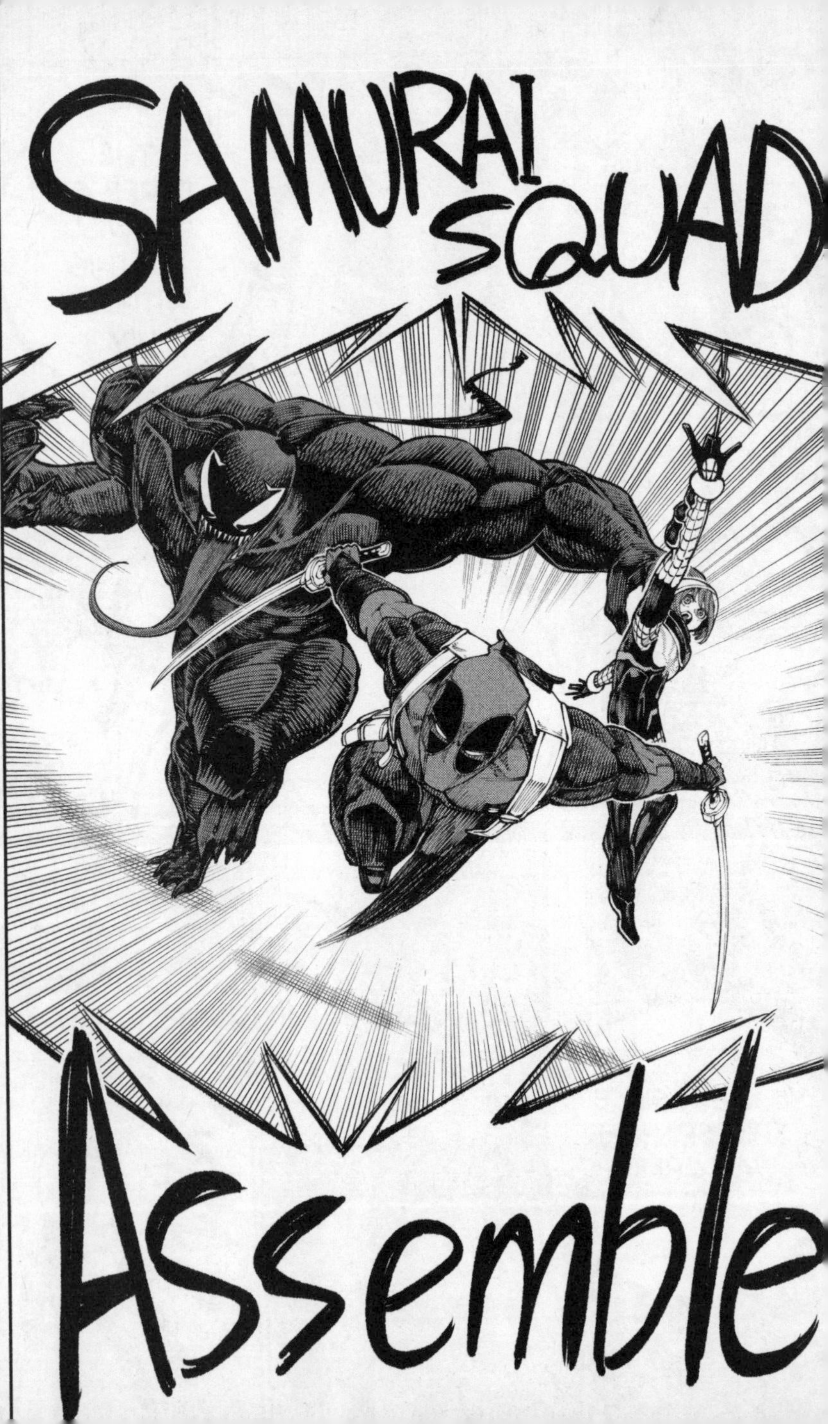
SAMURAI SQUAD
Assemble

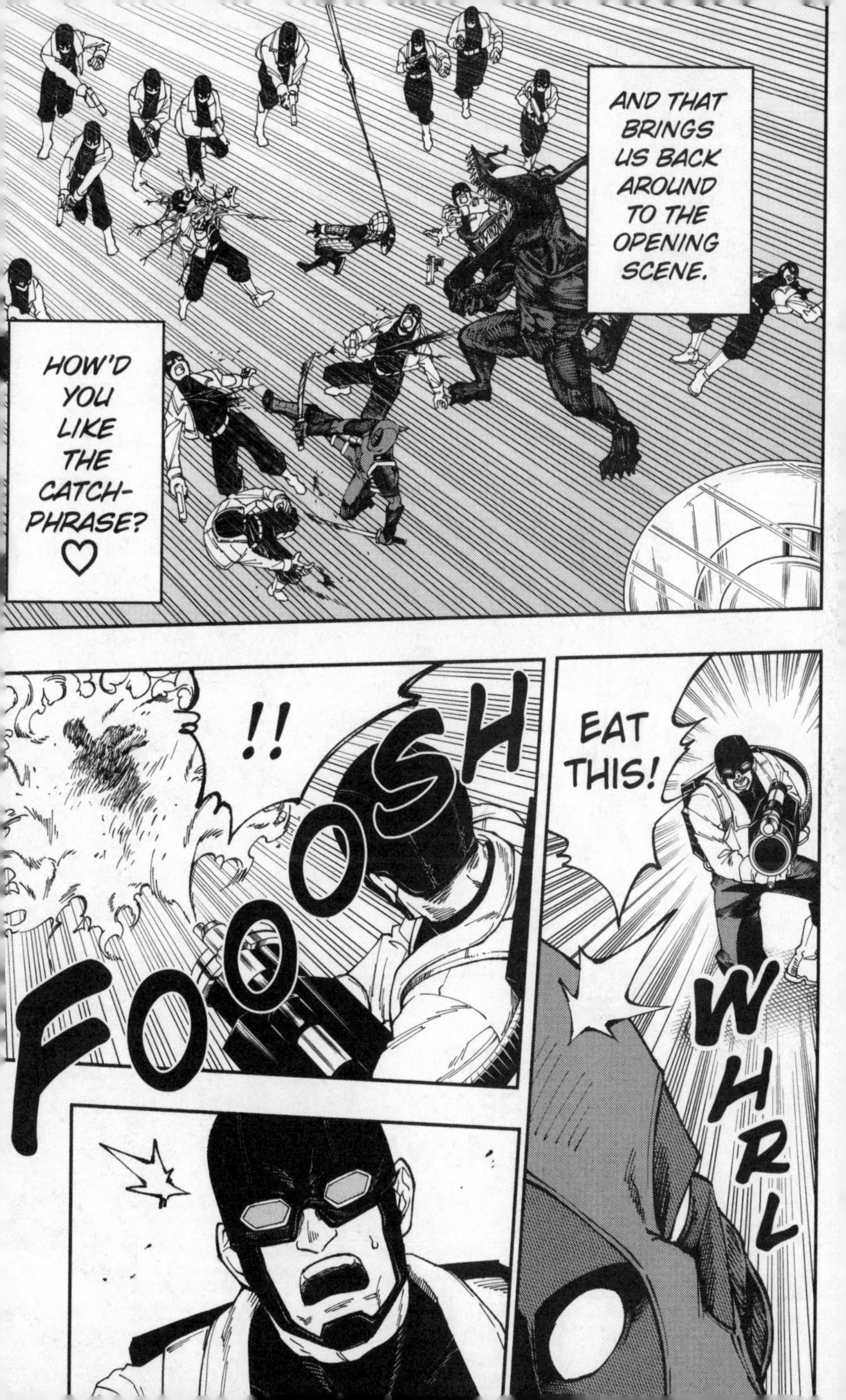
AND THAT BRINGS US BACK AROUND TO THE OPENING SCENE.
HOW'D YOU LIKE THE CATCH-PHRASE? ♡
EAT THIS!
WHRL
!!
FOOOOSH

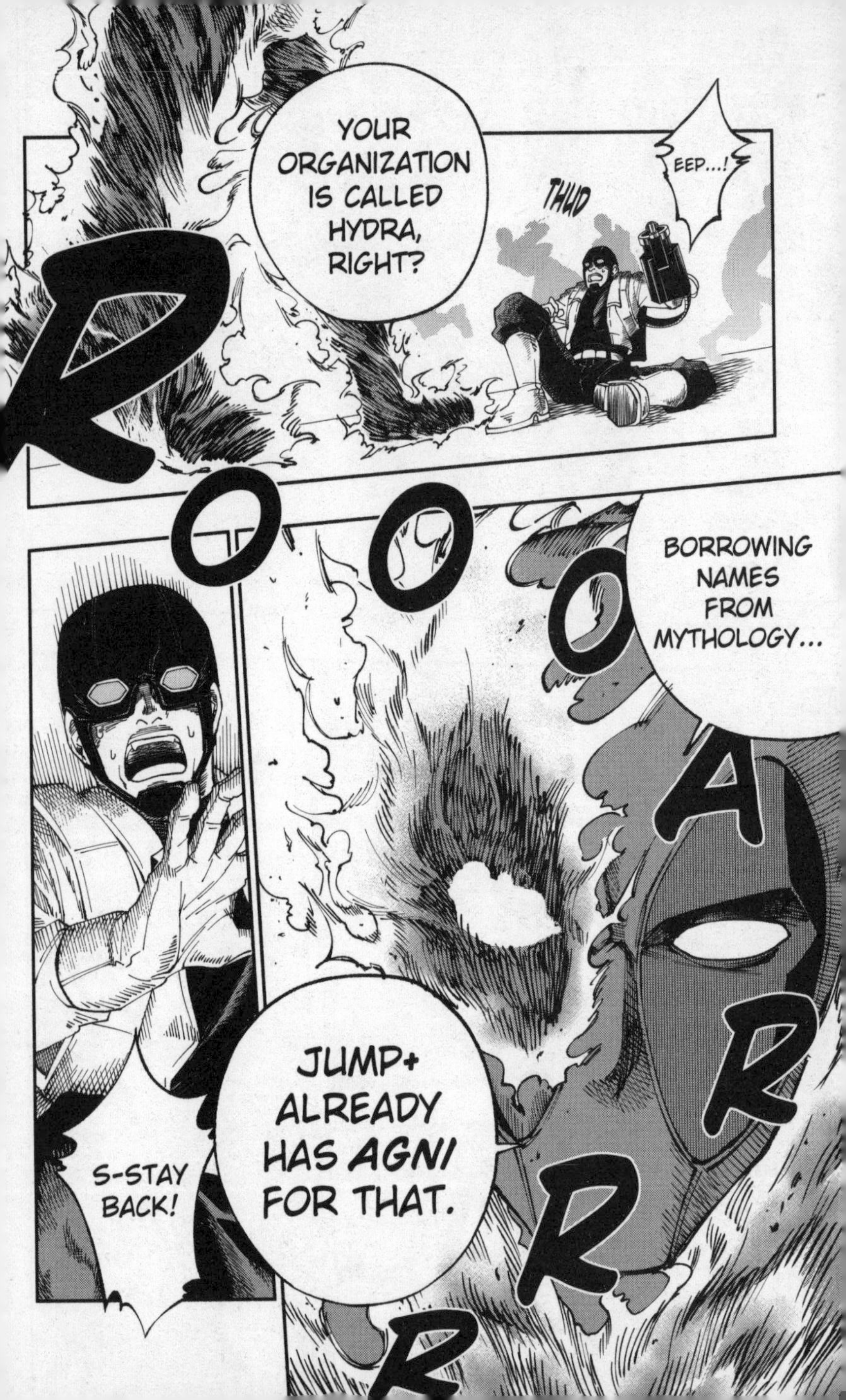
EEP...!
THUD
YOUR ORGANIZATION IS CALLED HYDRA, RIGHT?
ROOOARRR
BORROWING NAMES FROM MYTHOLOGY...
JUMP+ ALREADY HAS *AGNI* FOR THAT.
S-STAY BACK!

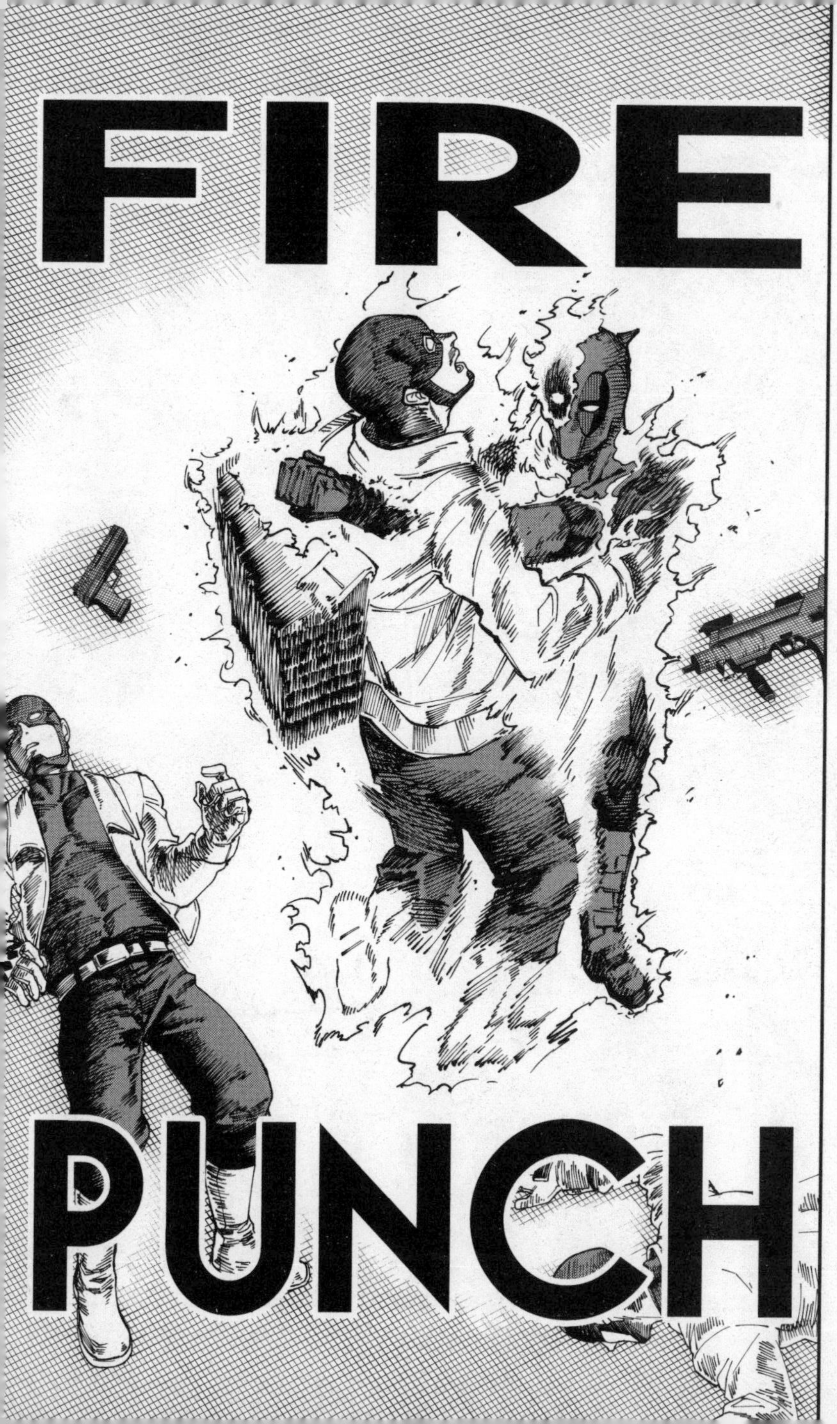
FIRE
PUNCH

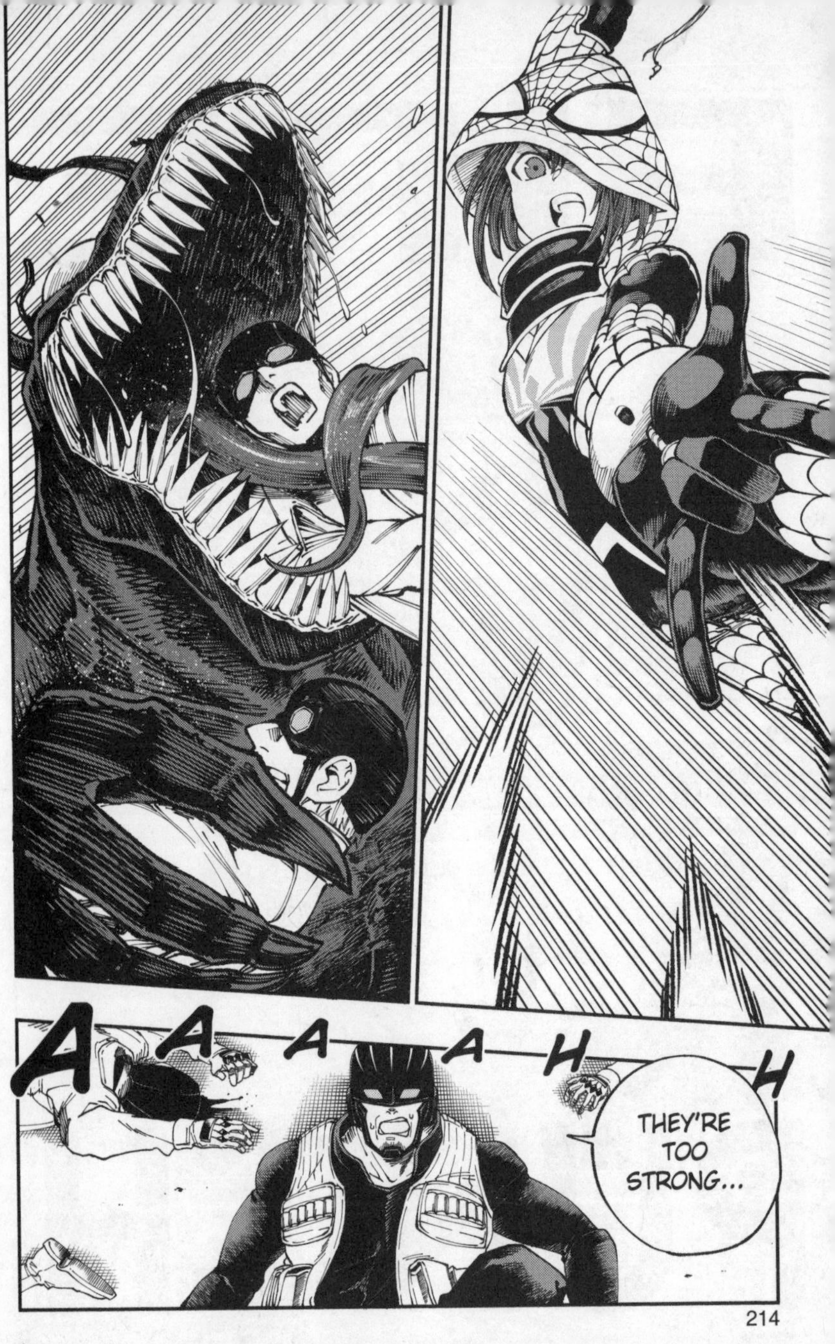

AAAAAHH
THEY'RE TOO STRONG...

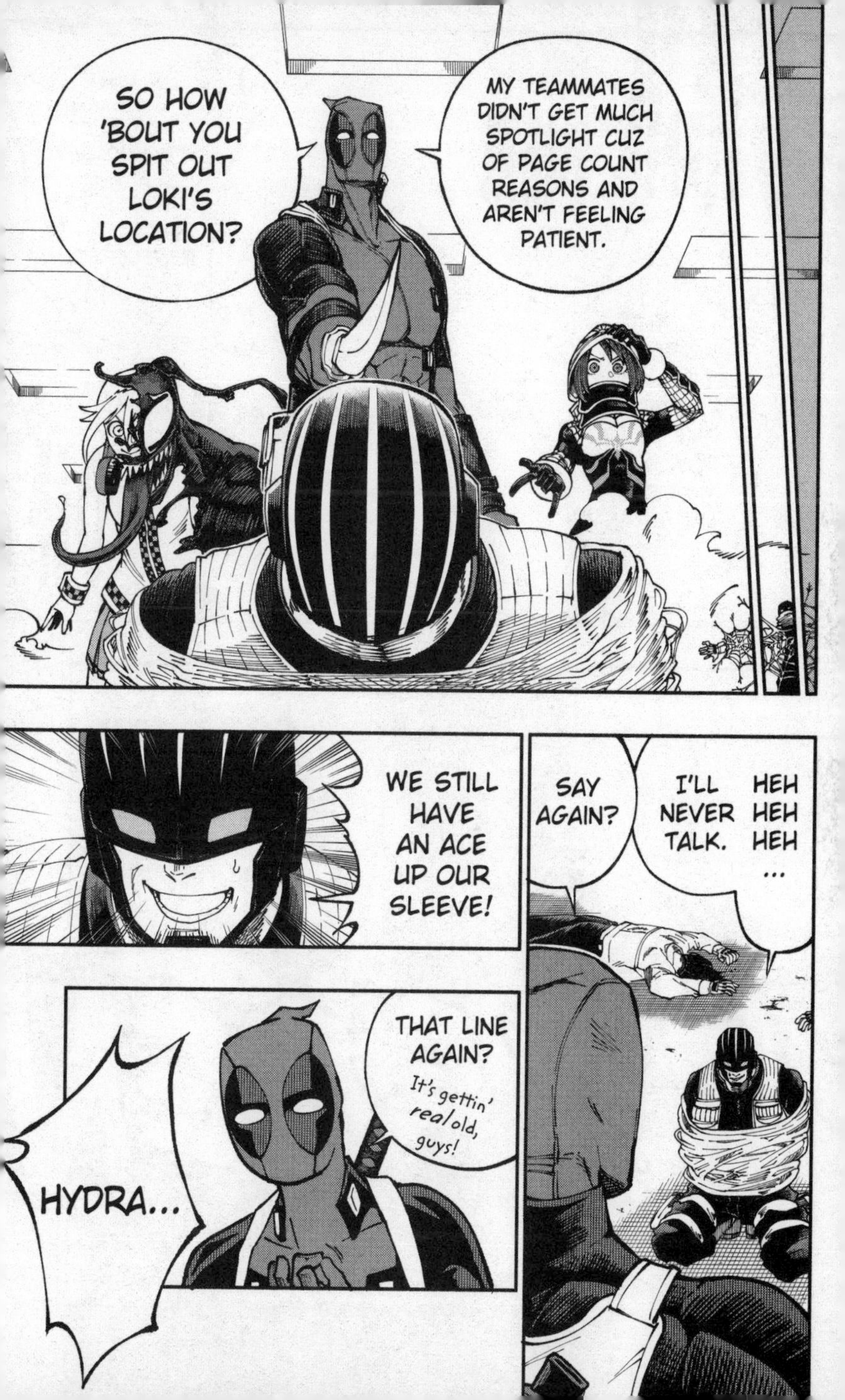
MY TEAMMATES DIDN'T GET MUCH SPOTLIGHT CUZ OF PAGE COUNT REASONS AND AREN'T FEELING PATIENT.
SO HOW 'BOUT YOU SPIT OUT LOKI'S LOCATION?
HEH HEH HEH ...
I'LL NEVER TALK.
SAY AGAIN?
WE STILL HAVE AN ACE UP OUR SLEEVE!
THAT LINE AGAIN?
It's gettin' real old, guys!
HYDRA...

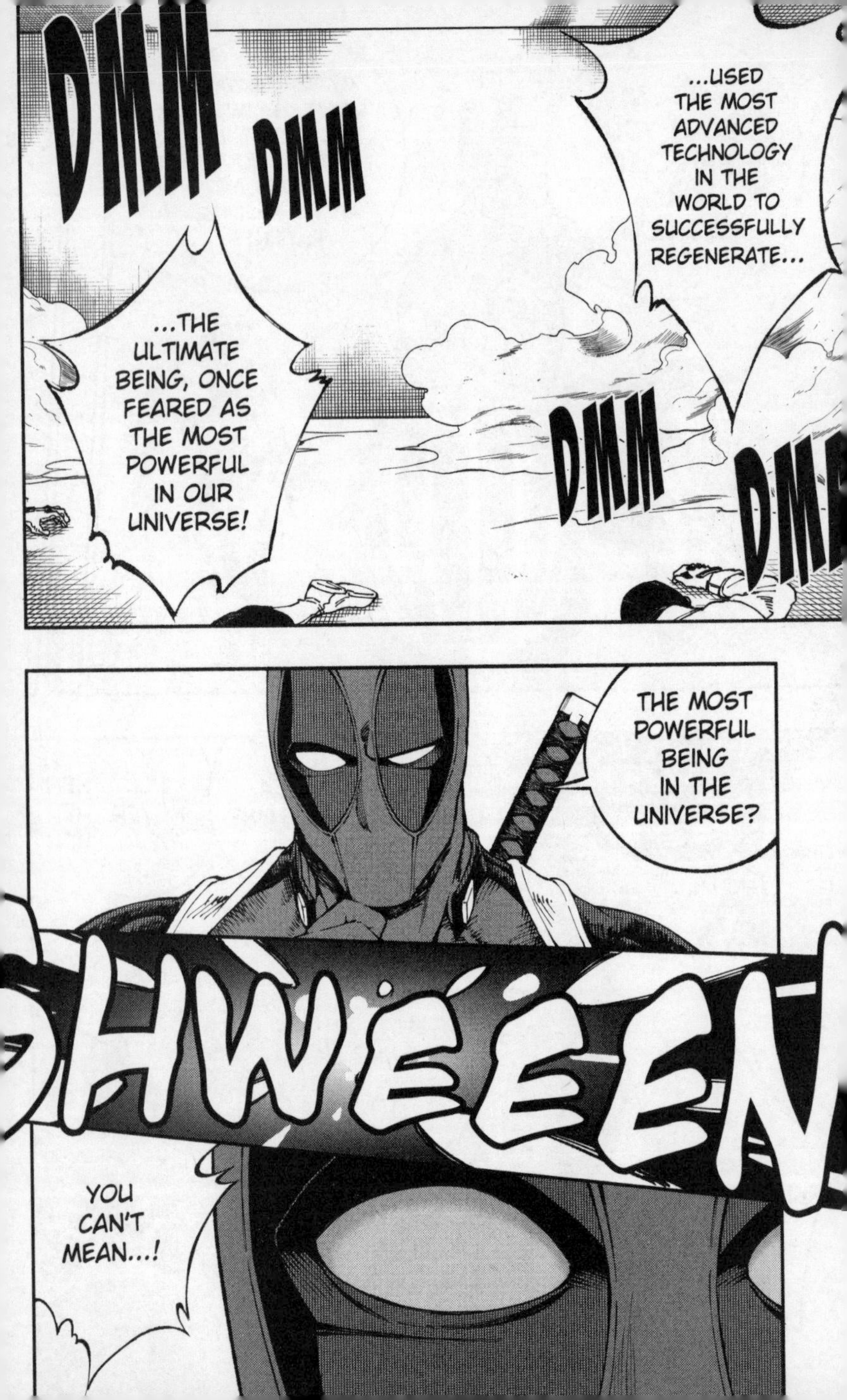

DMM DMM
...USED THE MOST ADVANCED TECHNOLOGY IN THE WORLD TO SUCCESSFULLY REGENERATE...
...THE ULTIMATE BEING, ONCE FEARED AS THE MOST POWERFUL IN OUR UNIVERSE!
DMM
THE MOST POWERFUL BEING IN THE UNIVERSE?
HWEEEN
YOU CAN'T MEAN...!

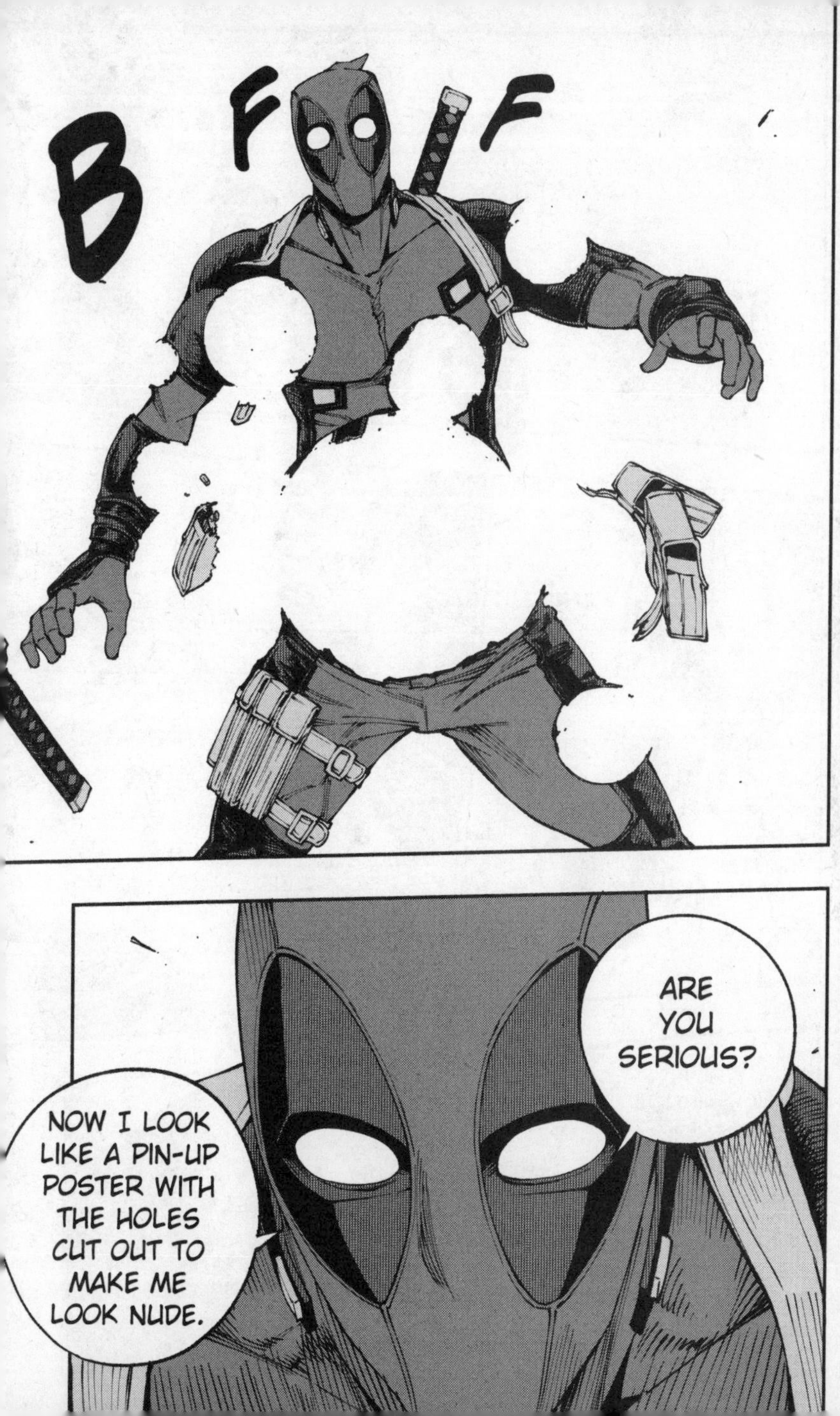
BFF
ARE YOU SERIOUS?
NOW I LOOK LIKE A PIN-UP POSTER WITH THE HOLES CUT OUT TO MAKE ME LOOK NUDE.

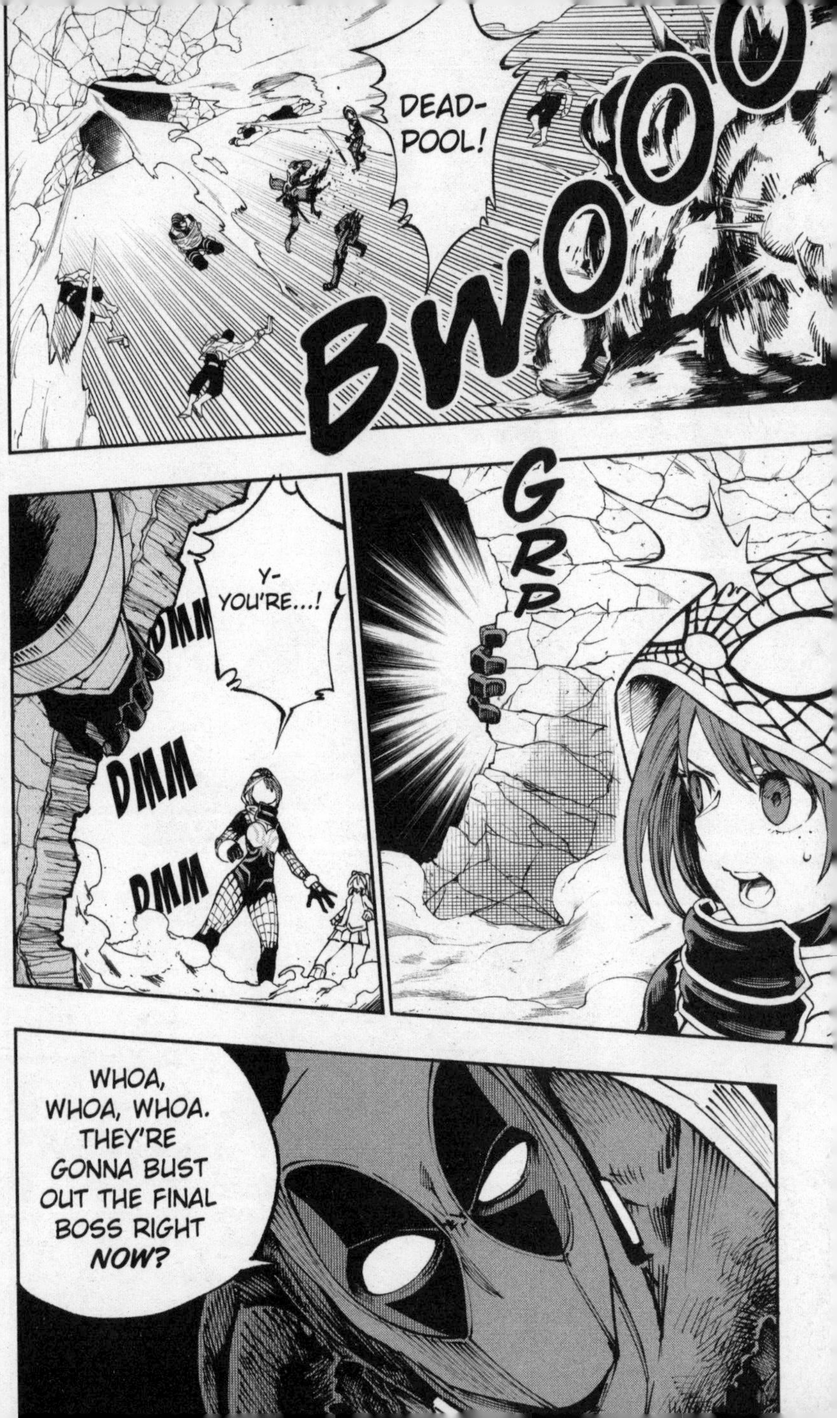
BWOOOOO
DEAD-POOL!
GRP
Y-YOU'RE...!
DMM
DMM
DMM
WHOA, WHOA, WHOA. THEY'RE GONNA BUST OUT THE FINAL BOSS RIGHT NOW?

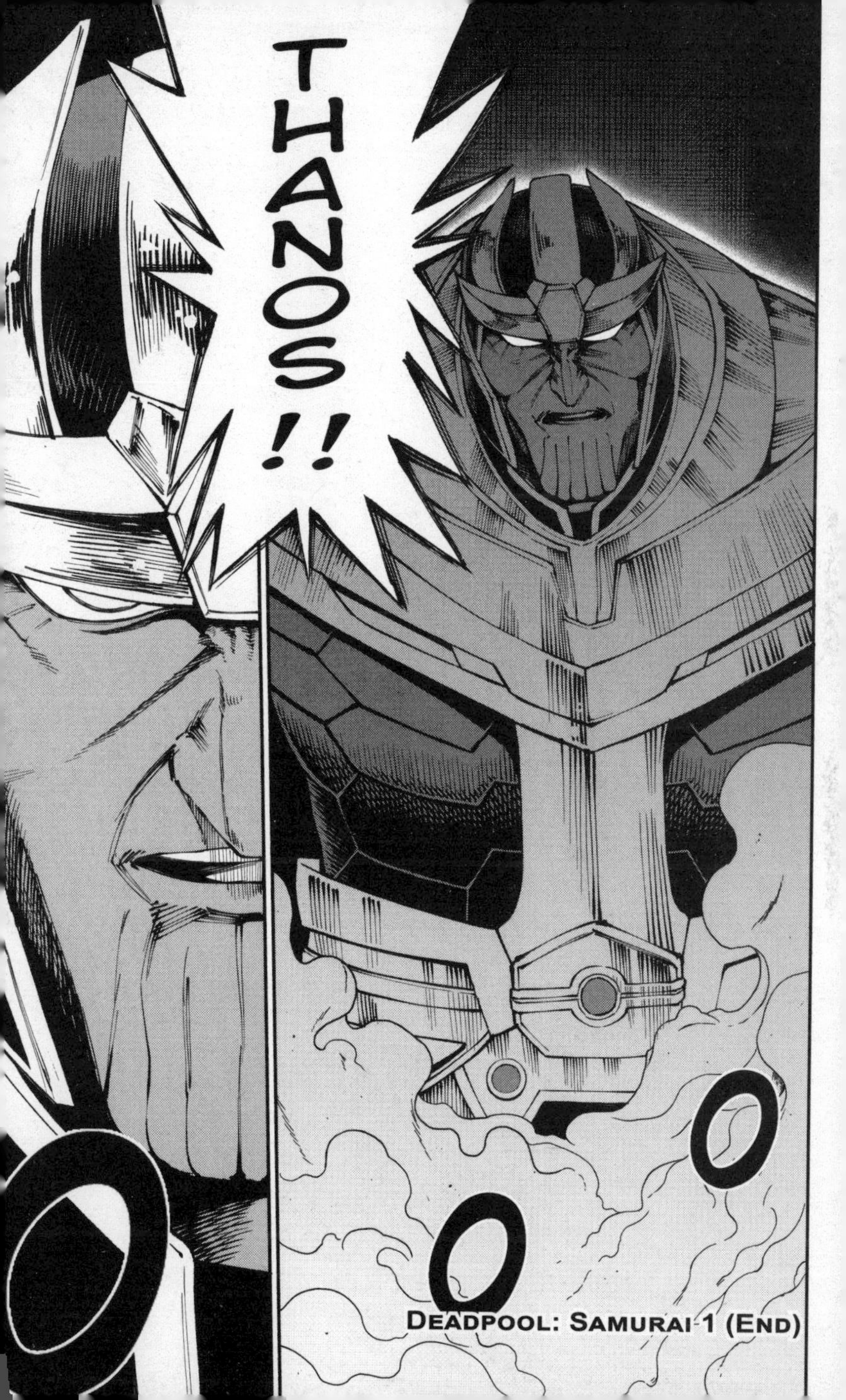
THANOS!!
DEADPOOL: SAMURAI 1 (END)

DEADPOOL
SAMURAI

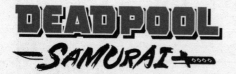

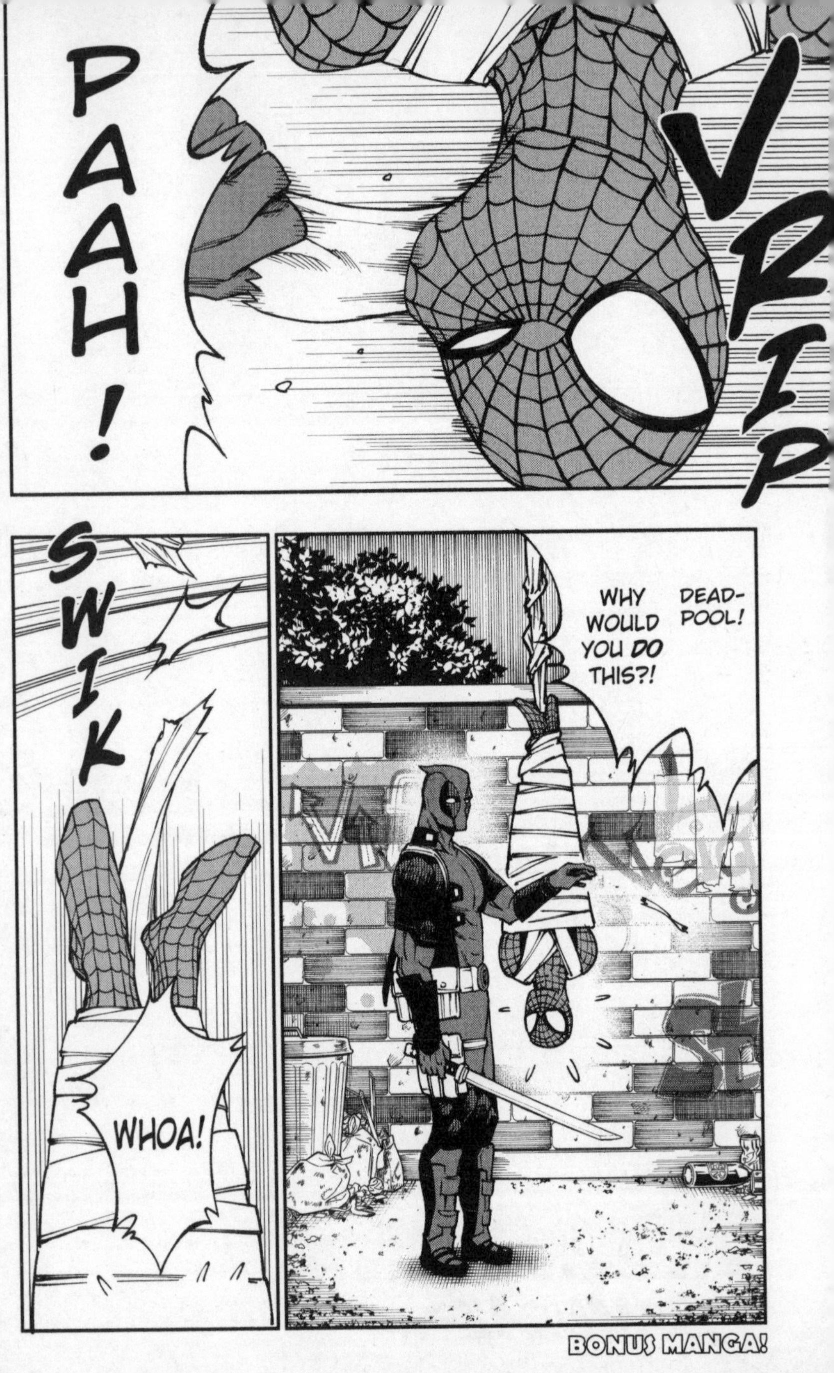
VRIP
PAAH!
DEAD-POOL!
WHY WOULD YOU DO THIS?!
SWIK
WHOA!

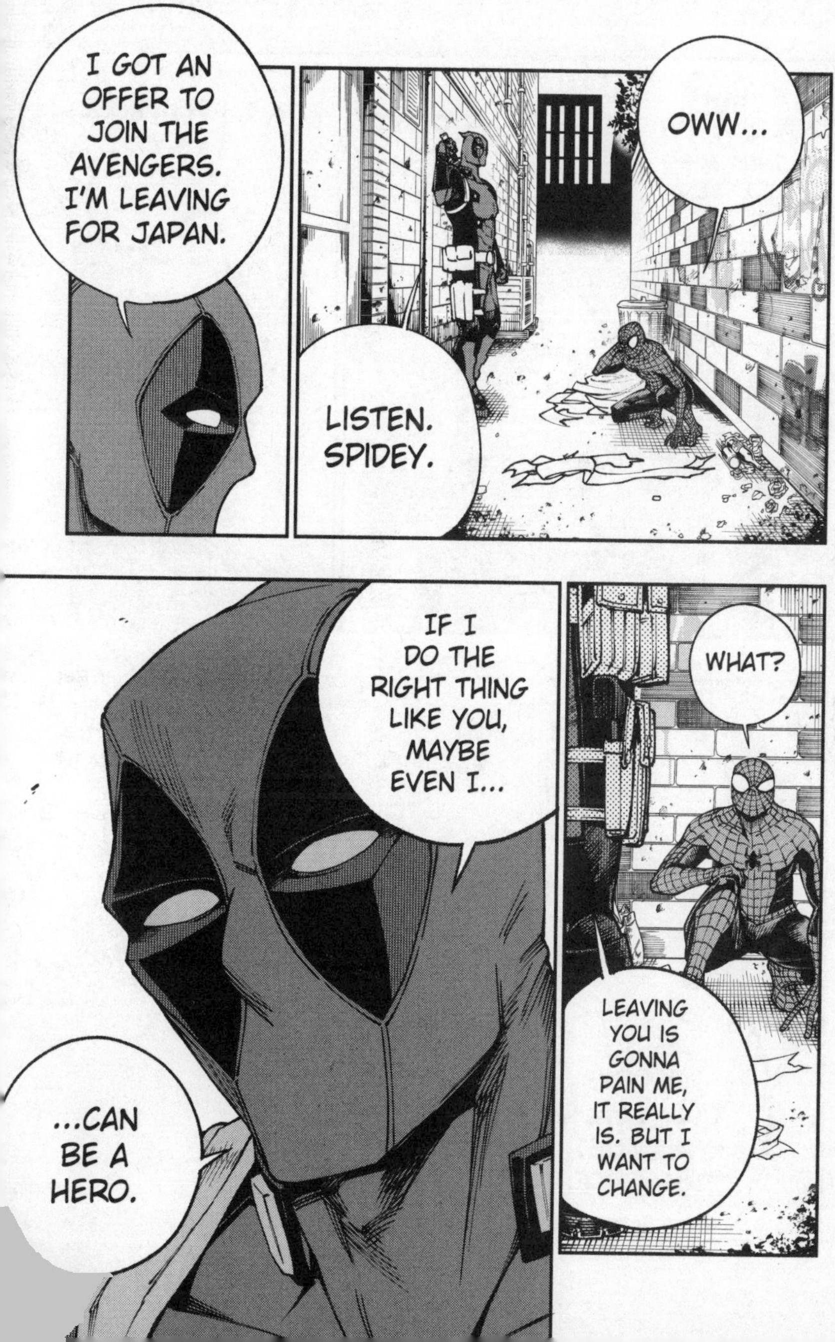
OWW...
LISTEN. SPIDEY.
I GOT AN OFFER TO JOIN THE AVENGERS. I'M LEAVING FOR JAPAN.
WHAT?
LEAVING YOU IS GONNA PAIN ME, IT REALLY IS. BUT I WANT TO CHANGE.
IF I DO THE RIGHT THING LIKE YOU, MAYBE EVEN I...
...CAN BE A HERO.

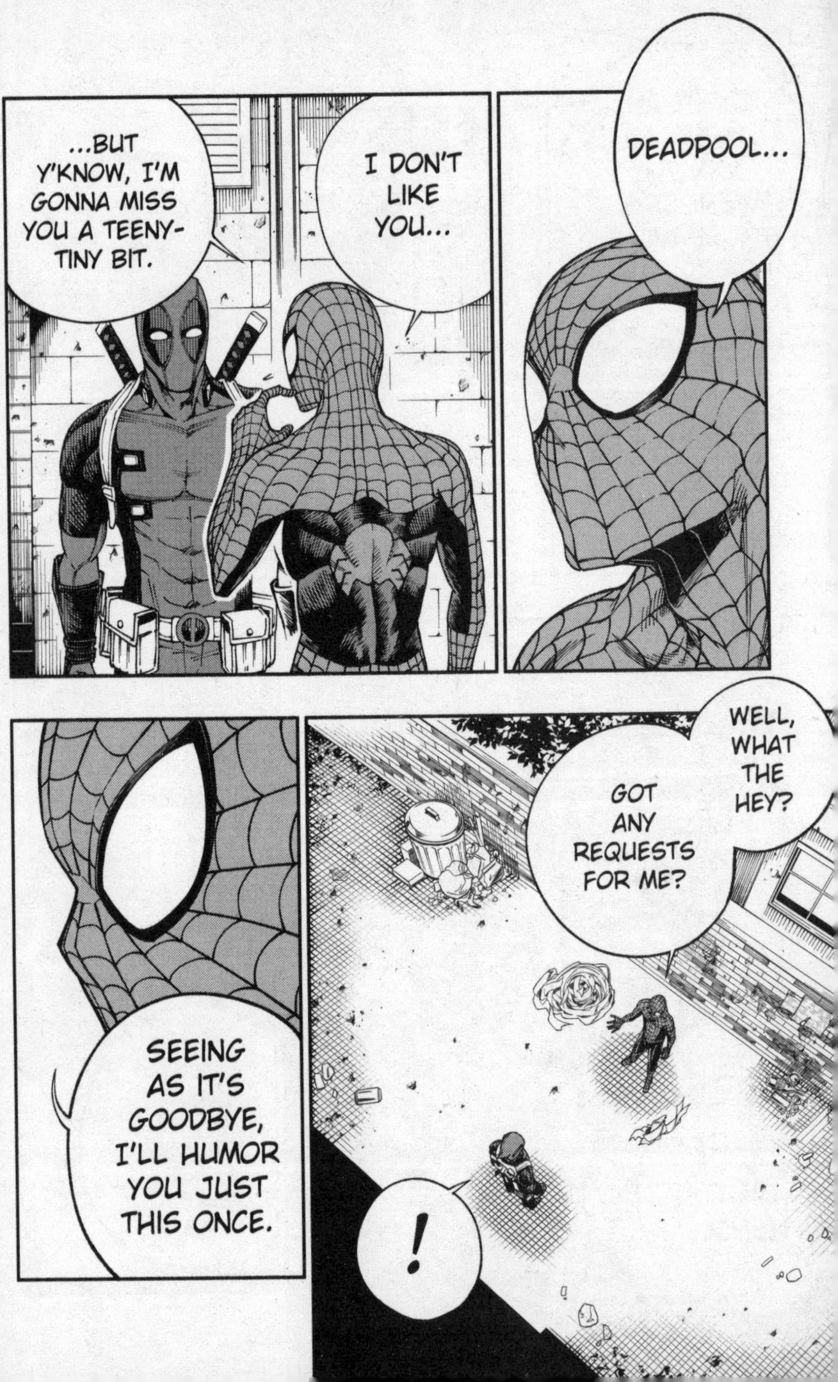
DEADPOOL...
I DON'T LIKE YOU...
...BUT Y'KNOW, I'M GONNA MISS YOU A TEENY-TINY BIT.
WELL, WHAT THE HEY?
GOT ANY REQUESTS FOR ME?
!
SEEING AS IT'S GOODBYE, I'LL HUMOR YOU JUST THIS ONCE.

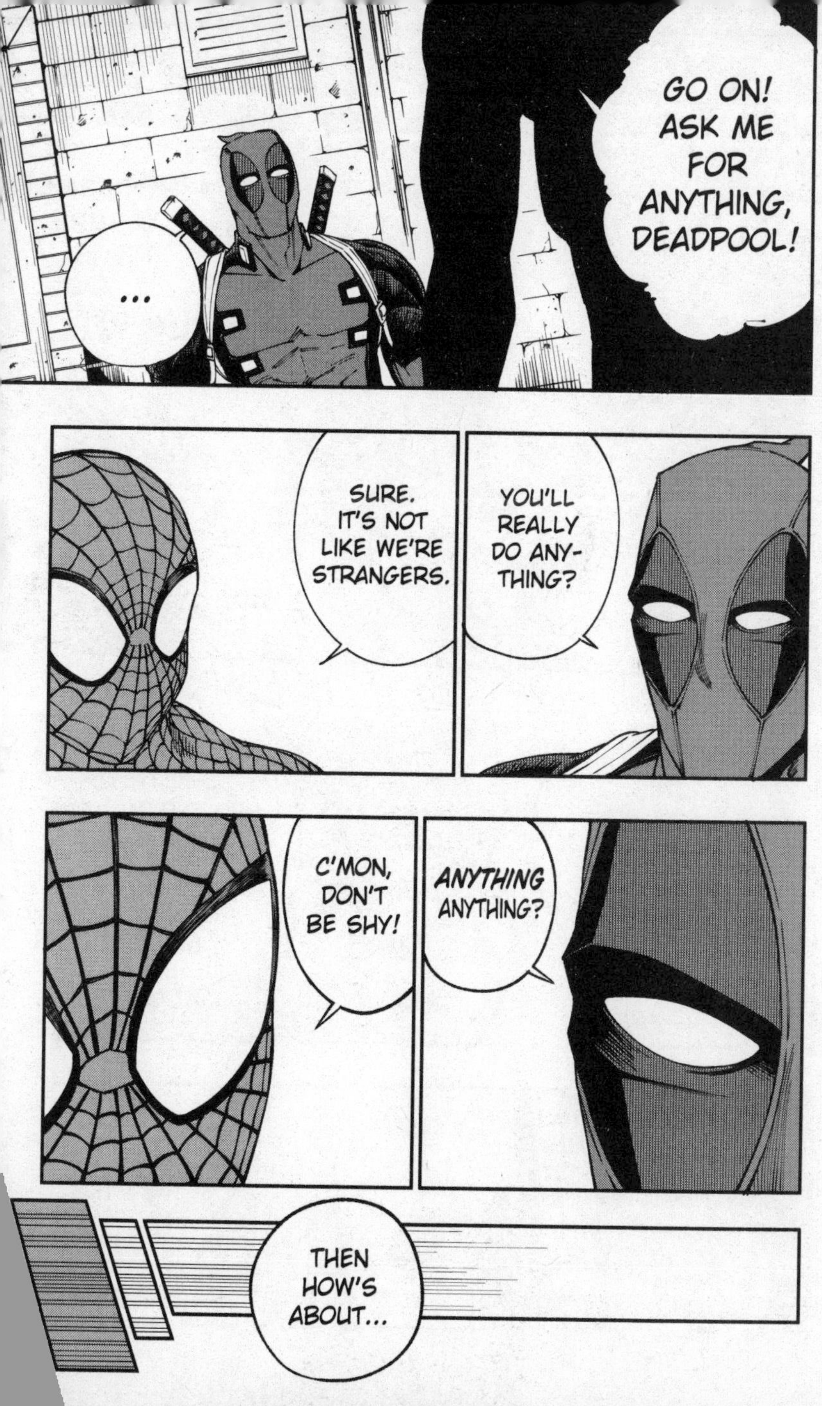
GO ON! ASK ME FOR ANYTHING, DEADPOOL!
...
YOU'LL REALLY DO ANY-THING?
SURE. IT'S NOT LIKE WE'RE STRANGERS.
ANYTHING ANYTHING?
C'MON, DON'T BE SHY!
THEN HOW'S ABOUT...

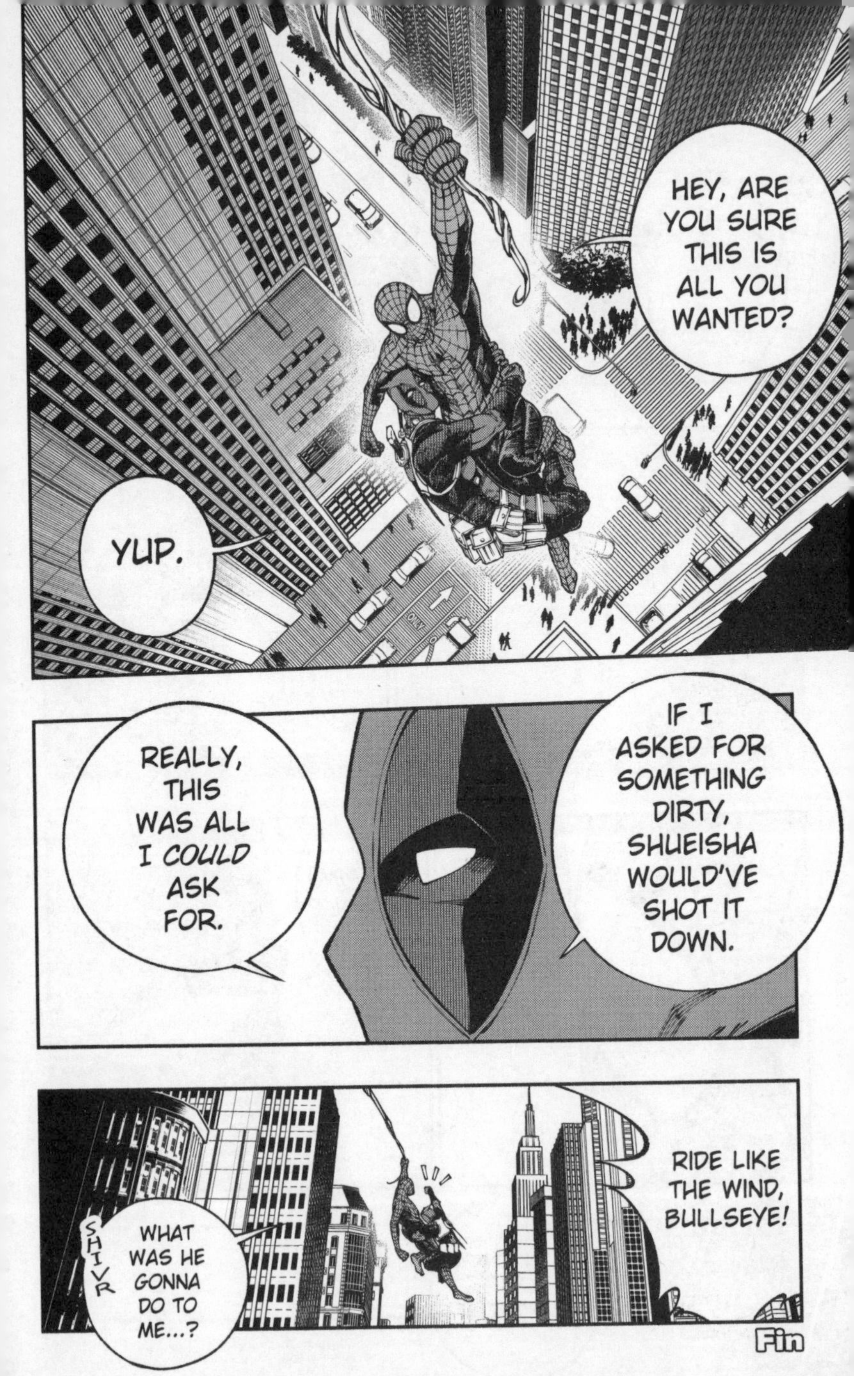
HEY, ARE YOU SURE THIS IS ALL YOU WANTED?
YUP.
IF I ASKED FOR SOMETHING DIRTY, SHUEISHA WOULD'VE SHOT IT DOWN.
REALLY, THIS WAS ALL I *COULD* ASK FOR.
RIDE LIKE THE WIND, BULLSEYE!
SHIVR
WHAT WAS HE GONNA DO TO ME...?
Fin

DEADPOOL

SAMURAI

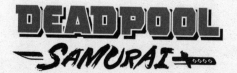

Special Thanks

C. B. Cebulski (Marvel)   Jake Thomas (Marvel)
Kusano-san (Disney)   Fukasaku-san (Disney)
Sakakibara-san (editor)   Kamei-san (design)
A bunch of bigwigs   All our readers

Staff

Yuto Sano-san   Ryo Sugiura-san   Chiaki Nagaoka-san
Kenta Yoshizumi-san   Arata Momose-san   Rei Sugita-san
                       Miyuki Tonogaya-san

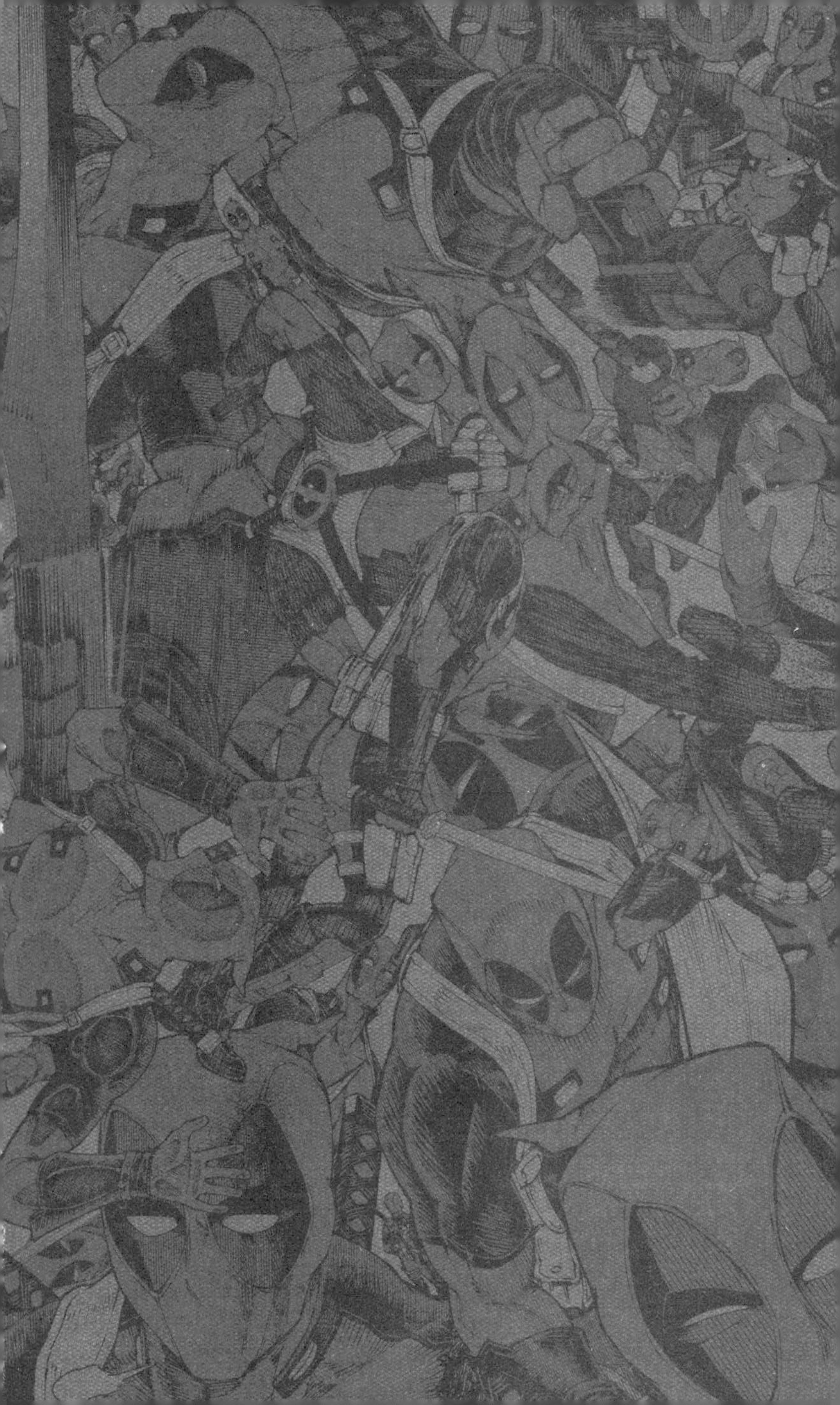

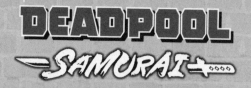

DEADPOOL SAMURAI

Volume 1
VIZ MEDIA Edition

STORY BY SANSHIRO KASAMA
ART BY HIKARU UESUGI

Translation: Amanda Haley
Touch-Up Art & Lettering: Walden Wong
Design: Francesca Truman
Editor: David Brothers

Marvel Publishing
VP Production & Special Projects: Jeff Youngquist
Associate Editor, Special Projects: Sarah Singer
Manager, Licensed Publishing: Jeremy West
VP, Licensed Publishing: Sven Larsen
SVP Print, Sales & Marketing: David Gabriel
Editor in Chief: C.B. Cebulski
Special thanks to Jacque Porte & Jordan D. White

First published in Japan in 2018 by SHUEISHA Inc., Tokyo.
English translation rights arranged by SHUEISHA Inc.

Printed in the U.S.A.

Published by VIZ Media, LLC
P.O. Box 77010 | San Francisco, CA 94107

10 9 8 7 6 5 4 3 2
First Printing, February 2022
Second Printing, March 2022

MARVEL

VIZ MEDIA
viz.com

ratings.viz.com
RATED T+ OLDER TEEN

PARENTAL ADVISORY
DEADPOOL: SAMURAI is rated T+ for Older Teen and is recommended for ages 16 and up. This volume contains violence and gore.

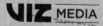

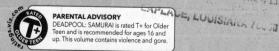

Deadpool: Samurai **reads from right to left, starting in the upper-right corner. Japanese is read from right to left, meaning that action, sound effects, and word-balloon order are completely reversed from English order.**

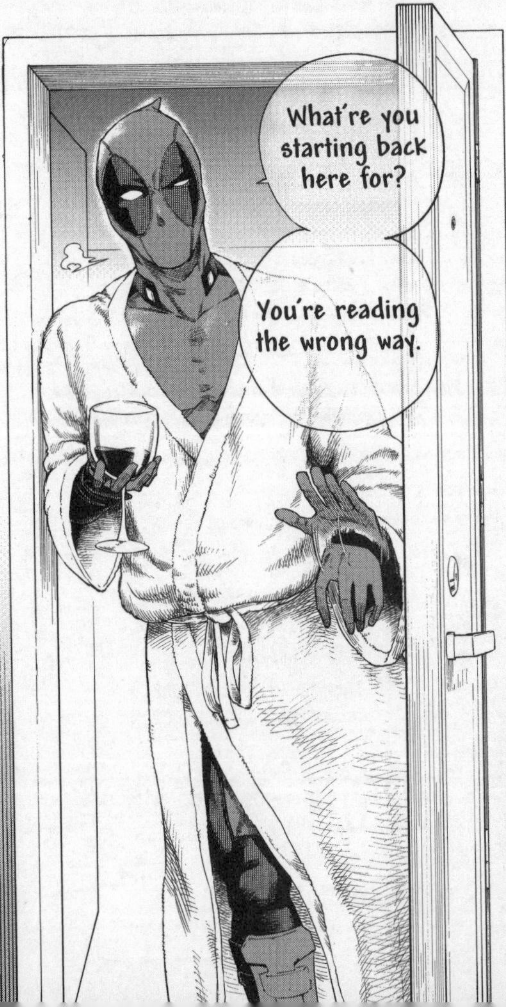
What're you starting back here for?
You're reading the wrong way.